Palgrave Studies in the History of Economic Thought

Palgrave Studies in the History of Economic Thought publishes contributions by leading scholars, illuminating key events, theories and individuals that have had a lasting impact on the development of modern-day economics. The topics covered include the development of economies, institutions and theories.

More information about this series at
http://www.palgrave.com/gp/series/14585

Manuela Mosca
Editor

Power in Economic Thought

palgrave
macmillan

Editor
Manuela Mosca
University of Salento
Lecce, Italy

Palgrave Studies in the History of Economic Thought
ISBN 978-3-030-06780-9 ISBN 978-3-319-94039-7 (eBook)
https://doi.org/10.1007/978-3-319-94039-7

Cover illustration: Chris Hellier / Alamy Stock Photo

This Palgrave Macmillan imprint is published by the registered company Springer Nature Switzerland AG
The registered company address is: Gewerbestrasse 11, 6330 Cham, Switzerland

Contents

Notes on Contributors

Piero Bini is Full Professor of History of Economic Thought in the School of Economics and Management of the University of Florence. He is the general editor of the review *History of Economic Thought and Policy*.

Emmanuel Blanc is Assistant Professor of Economics at the University of Lyon, France. He is a member of the team of editors of the complete works of Jean-Baptiste Say.

Francesca Dal Degan teaches Ethics of economics at the Department of Civilisation and forms of knowledge and collaborates with the Department of economics at the University of Pisa. She is the co-editor of the complete economic works of Jean-Charles Léonard Sismondi.

Joachim De Paoli holds a PhD in Economics, his main topics are the French liberal school, especially economist engineers, the reaction of liberals against the rise of socialism, and the pricing of railways.

Marion Dieudonné holds a PhD in History of Economic Thought. Her research topics focus on the financial theory of business at the turn of the twentieth century, American institutionalists, financial valuation, and governance.

Raphaël Fèvre is research assistant at the Walras-Pareto Centre of the University of Lausanne (Switzerland). His main research interest is in German ordoliberalism related to the early twentieth-century debates about economic and political systems.

Bruna Ingrao is Full Professor of Economics and a historian of economic thought. She has contributed considerably to the history of general economic equilibrium and to interdisciplinary research on economics and literature.

Heinz D. Kurz is Emeritus Professor of Economics, University of Graz, Austria, and Fellow of the Graz Schumpeter Centre. He has published widely in economic theory and the history of economic analysis.

Stephen Martin is Full Professor of Economics at Purdue University (USA). His research concerns all areas of industrial economics, the economics of antitrust, and competition policy.

Manuela Mosca is Full Professor of History of Economic Thought in the University of Salento (Italy). Her main research interests are the Italian marginalists and the theory of monopoly power in a historical perspective.

Cosma Orsi holds a PhD in Political Philosophy and History of Economic Thought and has taught History of economic ideas in Italy, Switzerland, and Denmark. His main research interest is the relationship between economic theory and social legislation.

Mario Pomini is Associate Professor of Economics in the University of Padua, Italy. He has published many articles on the history of Italian economic thought, with particular reference to the Paretian tradition.

Eugenio Somaini is Full Professor of Economic Policy. His recent books focus on egalitarianism, on the spread of democracy, and on the foundations of liberalism.

André Tiran is Emeritus Professor at the University of Lyon, France. He is the chief editor of the complete works of Jean-Baptiste Say.

List of Figures

1

Introduction

Manuela Mosca

1. In an article published in 1898 in the *Economic Journal*, the Italian marginalist Maffeo Pantaleoni claimed that the perspective of economic theory was "singularly narrow" (Pantaleoni 1898, p. 184). For him, the only phenomena studied by economists were those of a contractual, voluntary and peaceful nature, excluding the possibility of considering the strengths and weaknesses of the parties. He identified three political settlements resulting from the division of the world into weak and strong: the *predatory* settlement where the strong eliminates the weak, the *parasitic* one where the strong exploits the weak, and the *mutualistic* one in which there are no opportunities for conflict (and which he considered merely utopistic).[1] This work by Pantaleoni was

[1] De Cecco (1997, p. 192) called this work "a masterpiece".

I would like to thank Piero Bini, Bruna Ingrao, Heinz D. Kurz and Stephen Martin who helped me a lot in the preparation of this volume. I am particularly indebted to Bruna Ingrao for her precious suggestions, especially on the structure of the book.

M. Mosca (✉)
University of Salento, Lecce, Italy
e-mail: manuela.mosca@unisalento.it

M. Mosca (ed.), *Power in Economic Thought*, Palgrave Studies in the History of Economic Thought, https://doi.org/10.1007/978-3-319-94039-7_1

perhaps the first in which an economist had pointed out that the economic theory springing from the marginalist revolution excludes the treatment of power.[2]

Since Pantaleoni's time, in every decade, various voices from economists belonging to different schools of thought have lamented the lack of the concept of power within economic science and have suggested various ways of introducing it. In the 1940s, Yasuma Takata stated that the "effects of power upon an economy are conspicuous, but for the most part ignored" (Takata 1995, p. 3). Building on the assumption that "if rents and wages are distorted by the wielding of power, then their displacement would extend to the price of other commodities and general equilibrium values would be influenced across the board" (Morishima 1995, p. xxiv), he developed a power-based theory of economics. Other attempts made in the 1940s, 1950s and 1960s are collected in a book edited by K.W. Rothschild (1971), who attributed the lack of power considerations in the hundred years after the marginal revolution both to the "complete victory of 'perfect competition' as the basic model for economic theorizing" (p. 8) and to the specialization of disciplines inside the realm of the social sciences (p. 11). However, Rothschild mentioned the "important exception" of "monopoly and trade union questions" (p. 9), and the "big exception" of the Marxist, institutionalist and historical schools (pp. 13–14). The essays included in his book[3] dealt with power in the realms of game theory and bargaining theory; some of them focused on the influence of economic power in the political sphere, others analyzed the power of managers and experts, or expressed doubts on the effectiveness of the countervailing powers, and inquired into the causes and consequence of the uneven distribution of wealth and power at the national and international level. In the 1970s, we find very different approaches to the issue of the relation between power and economics. For the

[2] According to Groenewegen (1998, p. 58) Pantaleoni's "essay is … an insightful attempt at defining what economics can, and what cannot, offer on issues of power, relative strength and weakness".

[3] The book includes essays written by H. Albert, E. Ronald Walker, F. Perroux, J. Harsanyi, J. Pen, E. Preiser, M.D. Reagan, D. Lynch, R.A. Brady, J.K. Galbraith, C.S. Wilson, T. Lupton, M.J. Ulmer, A. Hunter, P.A. Baran, P.M. Sweezy, T. Balogh, G. Adler-Karlsson.

libertarian anarchist M.N. Rothbard (1970), the two elements in the title of his book, *Power and the Market*, cannot co-exist: he stated that where there is the market (the place of voluntary exchanges), there is no power (present in the coercive and "unnecessary" institution of the state). From an opposite perspective, F. Perroux (1973), after stating that the neglect of power in economic theory does not occur by chance (p. 5), proposed an ambitious plan to construct a general theory of power in economic relations (p. 13) incorporating this concept in micro- and macroeconomics.[4] Then, A.O. Hirschmann (1977) investigated "the salutary political consequences of economic expansion" (p. 117) seen as a victory for the disciplinary effect of interests over passions, including those of the powerful. Finally, Foucault (1978–79) has shown how, after the collapse of a state (as in the case of post-Nazi Germany), political reconstruction can take place starting from economic institutions, especially the market. We also mention his notion of "biopower",[5] and his analysis of the intimate relationship between knowledge and power, also considered in its economic dimension.[6] The 1980s opened with the institutionalist book *The Economy as a System of Power* (Tool and Samuels 1980, second edition completely revised 1989) the subject of which was the "locus and use of the power to determine economic institutions and their operation and outcomes" (p. viii).[7] Then, in 1983, another author associated with the institutional school, J.K. Galbraith, wrote a book intended to be a "general theory of power",[8] but "not especially concerned with economics or economic power" (Galbraith and Bartel 1983, p. 26). At the end of the decade, there was a systematic attempt to develop an economic theory of power by R. Bartlett (1989, p. 198), who considered the "possibility of social influences on human utility functions" (p. 170)

[4] Notice that Perroux (1973, p. 5) cites Pantaleoni, and uses his categories in some of his other works.

[5] The term "biopower" refers to the power exercised over the lives of individuals.

[6] The theme of power is central in Foucault's philosophy. These are only a few examples of his contribution on the subject of power and economics.

[7] The book contains articles published in *Journal of Economic Issues*. Most of the articles in the second edition were written in the 1980s.

[8] This was the title Galbraith initially intended to give his book *The Anatomy of Power* (1983). See the interview with the author (Galbraith and Bartel 1983).

and focused on decision-making processes in order to pinpoint how an "external human intervention into the constrained maximizing behavior of individuals" could affect their final utility (p. 37).[9] Bartlett identified power relations in cases of asymmetric information and uncertainty, underlined the role of power as the rationale behind the existence of organizations, its centrality in employment relation and in the creation of rights. He showed that, in many examples taken from microeconomics, power was indeed present, but it was not recognized as such. In the 1990s, S. Bowles and H. Gintis introduced power into the theory of competitive markets by relaxing the "exogenous enforcement axiom"[10]: basing power on the possibility of imposing "sanctions to further one's interests" (1993, p. 325), they show how it is exercised by owners over managers and workers, by employers over employees and by creditors over debtors. At the end of the decade, the volume edited by S. Bowles et al. (1999) analyzed the power relations deriving from transaction costs, incomplete contracts, bargaining costs and opportunistic behavior. The papers therein included[11] showed, for example, the counterintuitive idea that "[t]he exercise of power is a characteristic of voluntary exchange under quite general conditions" (p. 14). They also built on Hirschman's exit/voice categories, proposing a sanctioning/recontracting response to opportunistic practices (Chap. 3), and, following in the footsteps of Hirsch, considered power as a positional good (Chap. 5). Despite these contributions, the dissatisfaction with the absence of power in economic theory continued in the new century. Rothschild (2002) complained again that "the treatment of power problems … [was] almost completely restricted to … monopoly power and bargaining power in goods and labor markets" (p. 433) and identified "*deliberate* strategies to remove power questions to a subordinate position" (p. 437). In 2014, a conference

[9] He considered his theory "suited to an examination of strategic decisions made by identifiable individuals seeking explicitly and intentionally to change the behavior of other identifiable individuals" (1989, p. 68).

[10] It "holds that exchanges between agents in the economy can be enforced by a third party (for example, the judicial system) at no cost to the exchanging parties" (1993, p. 328).

[11] The book includes essays written by S. Bowles, M. Franzini, P. Milgrom, J. Roberts, U. Pagano, J. Dunn, A. Breton, G. Galeotti, V. Vanberg, E. Gellner, R. Hardin, R. Wintrobe, U. Witt.

was organized in France, on the subject of "The Economists and Power",[12] mainly devoted to the role of the economists as experts and policymakers. In the same year, M. Perelman (2014) again denounced "the systematic absence of power in economic analysis … except for what it considers to be abuse of power by government and labor unions" (p. 284). However, in the recent book *Economics and Power*, its author G. Palermo (2016) does not claim that economic theory neglects the role of power but denounces the fact that power is commonly linked to some imperfection in the competitive process. His Marxist critique is addressed to all the approaches which dealt with the concept of power on the basis of the hypothesis of rational individuals. The author develops "an explicit ontology of coercion and power in the capitalist mode of production" (p. 112), surprisingly showing that this "coercive mechanism" is due to the presence (not the absence) of competition. In 2016, the conference "Economics and Power: An Historical Perspective" was organized,[13] which was at the origin of the present book.

2. In order to directly verify whether or not the category of power is present in contemporary economic theory, I made a search in three mainstream economic journals[14] for articles that in the last twenty years used the word "power" in a title.[15] My criterion of selection is therefore far more restrictive than that of Bartlett, who looked for power even where it was not recognized.[16] Despite the limited size of my sample, I found a large number of articles, and their treatment of power falls into four broad areas, in each of which power emerges prevalently from situations of asymmetric information or from bargaining problems, and is mainly dealt with using the formal approach

[12] *Les économistes at le pouvoir*, XVe Colloque international de l'Association Charles Gide pour l'étude de la pensée économique, Lyon (France), 2–4 June 2014.

[13] *Economics and Power: An Historical Perspective*, XIV Conference of the Italian Association for the History of Economic Thought (AISPE), Lecce (Italy), 28–30 April 2016.

[14] The journals are *American Economic Review*, *Journal of Political Economy*, and *Economic Journal*. I thank Raimondello Orsini for his suggestions.

[15] In the case of *American Economic Review*, also in the abstract. I obviously excluded articles in which the word power had a meaning that was irrelevant for this research.

[16] In the *Journal of Economic Perspective*, I also considered both a longer time span (1987–2018) and the articles containing the word power *in the whole text*. This expanded form confirmed the results.

of game theory. The first area is *political power*. It includes economic models of the political process, the analysis of legal power, rent-seeking, lobbying, elections, voting behavior and all the aspects related to the decision-making process in the political sphere. The second concerns *asymmetric positions in private organizations*, that is, the analysis of collective decision-making in private institutions, the power of leaders, elites and private authorities. It also includes the analysis of labor markets, the economics of gender and of minorities. The third area, *market power*, is related to the study of market structures (monopoly, oligopoly, imperfect competition), market performances, firm strategies and firm behaviors. The fourth area is *economic policy*, which deals with the policies decided by the Central Bank and by the government (monetary, fiscal, regulatory, trade policies).The articles I have identified testify to the interest in the subject of power by recent economic theory, an interest also confirmed by the inclusion of the entry "power" into *The new Palgrave dictionary of economics* for the first time since its first publication in the 1890s (Bowles and Gintis 2008).

3. Scholars who complain of the exclusion of power from economic theory seem to be nostalgic for the era when it was an integral part of the discipline. However, their references to economists of the past are brief and infrequent, or not particularly focused on the link between economics and power. Rothschild (2002) sometimes cited Smith and Marx; Perroux (1973) mentioned Ricardo and Böhm-Bawerk, too. Foucault investigated the role played by the economists in the emergence of "biopolitics", that is the form of power exercised over biological elements of human beings (see Guizzo 2015). Hirschmann (1977) reconstructed seventeenth- and eighteenth-century social thought focusing on the rise of the spirit of capitalism. However, a systematic reconstruction of the notion of power in the history of economic thought has never been made, and neither will it be in the present volume. In fact, this book is not intended to be a history of economic thought on the issue of power itself, that is, an examination of the theories of the scholars who dedicated their studies to the specific relation between power and economics, as was the case with the names we reviewed above. Its aim is rather to consider some significant examples of the way economists of the past have used the concept of power in

its different meanings, considering it as pertaining to their realm of inquiry. It is an overview of how this concept has been employed in the various domains in which it was found helpful, and how it was brought into economic theorizing by economists of different orientations. This last point is very important in characterizing the present research: in fact, while it does not attempt to cover all the authors, the book draws on a multiplicity of traditions of thought, offering a plural vision of the many ways in which the concept of power has been employed by economists. A transversal reconstruction of a theme like power is not frequently found in historiography.

4. This book is structured around the four broad areas identified earlier with reference to the articles from recent years. To allow for reflection on the possible parallel between the past and the present, let us focus on the themes it includes, without specifying a time reference for the moment. The first part considers the way economists have handled the issue of *political power*, ranging from authoritarian to democratic forms; it analyzes the theories they elaborated to place limits both on the arbitrary power of the sovereign and on that of political institutions in democratic regimes. The second part examines the way economists have tackled the *asymmetries of economic power* associated with inequality of income and wealth and their position concerning social legislation. The third part focuses on the *market power* of large firms from the standpoint of the institutions, theories and policies; as examples it takes a war of power between educational institutions, such as business schools and the university; it also considers the mathematical treatment of non-competitive markets, and the goals of antitrust policies. The fourth and last part concerns the *power of economists* in the role of both policymakers and experts,[17] and compares their different visions of how to manage a market economy. As can be seen, there is a certain overlapping between these four areas as dealt with in the more distant past and those linked to the articles of the last twenty years that we have examined before. But there are also remarkable differences. A serious comparison between past and present on the issue of power as analyzed by economists would deserve a deeper analysis that we shall put off to another occasion.

[17] A discussion on the role of experts, also in historical perspective, can be found in Levy and Peart (2017).

5. As we said, these chapters are merely examples of how the concept of power has been used in economic thought. However, we can try to link them together, showing the pathways and derivations of ideas so as to draw up a possible history of the four aspects of power mentioned above.

   5.1 As for the first aspect, *political power*, our history begins in the second half of the eighteenth century in France, when the Physiocrats "expressed the utopia of a rationally governed society, where arbitrary power was tamed". This ideal of enlightened despotism was then criticized by Adam Smith, who had a more realistic vision of the state; for him "the deviation of government towards oppression and tyranny is intrinsic to the very goal of controlling the natural course of things" (Chap. 2). At the turn of the century, the complexity of the relation between state power and individual self-determination was fully recognized by the Swiss "scholar of liberty" Sismondi who, under the influence of both Smith and Rousseau, proposed a "slow, repeated and articulated process of plural and inclusive deliberation" in order to "integrate different interests in the expression of a common will" (Chap. 3). The nineteenth century was an age in which different visions of government power co-existed. On the one hand, economists like Cournot and Walras embraced the utopia of a "growing expansion of the rule of rationality with the effect of reducing the turbulence of political life", while also recognizing in the state a "benevolent role, complementary to private activity" (Chap. 2). On the other hand, Marx and the socialists saw the state as an instrument in the hands of the bourgeoisie for pursuing its own interests. The great effort to respond to the Marxist theory of the state, and to its immense political impact, in particular through the development of the workers' movement and the progressive extension of the suffrage, pushed many economists of the following generation to fight a battle of ideas in defense of liberalism and the market economy. It is in this context that the very influential group of

Italian marginalists (Vilfredo Pareto, Maffeo Pantaleoni, Antonio de Viti de Marco and Enrico Barone) tackled "the question of the distribution and the exercise of the political power in a democratic system". In the years between 1882 and 1924, they proposed a new theory of the state based on the circulation of elites, defended social selection against the growing egalitarianism, and denounced the degeneration of parliamentary democracies (Chap. 4). Then, in the 1940s, after the emergence of the totalitarian regimes in Europe, two outstanding economists (Schumpeter and Hayek) reacted to "the cultural atmosphere of hostility to capitalism ... from [two] radically different perspectives", in particular, they had divergent ideas on the relation between centralized economic power and democracy (Chap. 2).

5.2 The second aspect, the *asymmetries of economic power*, is associated with inequality of income and wealth. At the origin, the economists' view was influenced by Hobbes's *Leviathan*, seen as the creature who "brings about a condition of social equilibrium". Hobbes's idea that "wealth is an important source of power" was taken up by Adam Smith, for whom the "persistence of social classes [reflects the] persistence of power asymmetries" due to "differences in property, political power and access to information and knowledge". Smith suggested a measure for the asymmetry of "economic power of capitalists relative to that of workers"; he also thought that the way to remedy these asymmetries could only be through the action of a "good government" (Chap. 5). It was the trust in an active government that in the eighteenth century prompted the call for public policies aimed at improving "the social conditions of the poor". The reforms of the English system of social legislation in the 1780s and 1790s reflected Adam Smith's suggestions to adopt "policies fostering income redistribution", as well as the criticisms he made to the previous systems of assistance for the poor based on workhouses (Chap. 6). At the beginning of the nineteenth century, David Ricardo, greatly influenced by

Adam Smith, gave his well-known explanation of income distribution. For him rents were "tied to the legal institution of private property of land", which gave "power to landlords", whose interests are always opposed to those of the other classes. He also showed that "certain forms of technical change … affected the balance of power between capitalists and workers in favor of the former". The classical approach was then developed by Karl Marx and followed both by the Marxian current, which included scholars such as Hilderfing and Kalecki, and by the neo-Ricardian tradition, among which Dimitriev, Bortkiewicz and Sraffa: the latter's concept of the standard commodity echoed the measure of power suggested by Smith (Chap. 5). At the end of the classical period, the need to help those in a weak position was also felt inside the French liberal school, with the non-secondary aim of limiting the rise of socialism. The question they faced was: "how to help the workers, without giving too much power to the government"? The answer—debated by Guyot, Leroy-Beaulieu, Colson and Cheysson—was that a system of social insurance was needed, but not to be managed by the state (Chap. 7). With the last two engineer-economists (Colson and Chysson), we enter the marginalist period, in which the concern with the asymmetries of power due to income distribution was put aside, following the argument set forth in 1914 by the Austrian marginalist Eugen von Böhm-Bawerk that power can never change economic laws (Chap. 5).

5.3 At the beginning of the twentieth century, the diffusion of new phenomena like trusts and big corporations brought the question of power back to center-stage, this time in the form of *market power*, the third aspect we consider. In a context in which "the distribution of corporate ownership … became the central concern", Thorstein Veblen and the institutionalist economists (like Wesley C. Mitchell) were particularly well equipped to analyze the influence of industrial and financial power on all kinds of institutions, including education. One of the problems they tackled was whether business training should take place inside the university or in private business schools and, in both cases, how to deal with the interference of the big companies in the content of the teaching (Chap. 8). Another consequence of the diffusion of phenomena like cartels, mergers and vertical integrations was that the economists tried to improve their understanding of the functioning of markets characterized by few firms endowed with market power. After the first mathematical treatments of non-competitive markets by Cournot, Edgeworth and the other pioneers, in the interwar period this study became a very active research field. The intense debate that took place on how to deal with the interdependence of firm behaviors saw the effective participation of economists belonging to the Paretian tradition. As always, the "contrast … between the rigor of mathematical models and interpretative realism was very strong" and, despite their undoubted mathematical skill, "in the interwar period, the pendulum swung in favor of the request for greater realism" (Chap. 9). Market power was examined not only from a theoretical point of view but also in its policy dimension. One of the goals attributed to the US antitrust was "the dispersion of economic and other kinds of power", which was initially pursued by promoting competition. The objectives ascribed to US antitrust policy from its formative period through the early 1970s were very hotly debated. In particular in the 1960s, the Chicago economist Robert Bork criticized the received antitrust policy, holding that it "should concern itself with and only with practices that reduce welfare". Although his analysis "has been rejected by the Academy …, the Academy has failed to persuade the judiciary" and today US courts still adhere to this "indefensibly narrow" policy prescription (Chap. 10).

5.4 The fourth aspect we consider is the *power of economists* as managers and advisors of economic policies. We start with an economist whose liberalism marked the history of economic thought: Jean-Baptiste Say, the "staunch republican" belonging to the "second generation of the Enlightenment". He conducted his political struggle directly as a member of the finance commission in the Tribunat, and indirectly through his teaching and his works. In criticizing the 1793 French Constitution, he claimed that "there was no such thing as general will …, only individual wills existed and those that could express themselves were those with a fortune or an education". The fundamental role he attributed to the state in disseminating education was due to his conviction that the "passage from the individual to the collective was … achieved through the voluntary adherence to a morality of duty". At the end of his life, "Say sought to define the rules that should govern [the] state action in society", insisting above all on the importance of "responsible individualism" (Chap. 11). As we know, Say's law was accepted for almost 150 years,[18] it was such an essential element in the "classical"[19] analytical scheme that its rejection overthrew that paradigm. The rejection of *laissez faire* and the problem of how to manage a market economy gave rise to two very influential non-socialist policy orientations, among others: demand management and rule-oriented ordoliberalism. The different visions of the two economists who elaborated them, John M. Keynes and Walter Eucken, were strictly linked to their conceptions of power: "if Keynes put his faith in the complementary nature of private and public bodies as a way to reach a balance of interests, Eucken favored the existence of an independent office in charge of monitoring competitive market structures, disempowering private agents" (Chap. 12). The calls for an active government from the interwar period produced their major effects in the 1970s, when most of the economists advocated a "greater intervention by the government in the economy, also supporting some forms of planning". In the Italian case, Sraffian, post-Keynesian and Marxist scholars suggested economic policies in favor of the workers. After the 1980s, an ineffective disinflationary policy, the use of "public resources to maintain electoral consensus" and a contractionary monetary policy were described as "a schizophrenia

[18] In the words of Keynes (1936, pp. 32–33), "Not only was his theory accepted by the city, by statesmen and by the academic world. But controversy ceased; the other point of view completely disappeared; it ceased to be discussed".

[19] I am using the word "classical" as used by J.M. Keynes, meaning all the economists of the past who accepted Say's law.

in ruling powers". Then, with the measures adopted for convergence toward the Maastricht parameters in the 1990s, accompanied by very unsatisfactory productivity and growth rates, and *a fortiori* with "the Great Recession in 2008, various criticisms towards the EMU began to emerge", mostly addressed against the policies imposed by Brussels (Chap. 13).

6. This book provides an historical overview of how economists have employed the concept of power in western economic thought. In spite of its inevitably sketchy character, it provides a broad survey of the development of economic ideas on four different aspects of power by economists with different theoretical approaches and political positions, coming from different countries, such as Austria, France, Germany, Great Britain, Italy, Switzerland and the US, and stretching from the age of the Physiocrats to the current debates over the policies of the European Union. Of course, there are lacunas, even significant lacunas. However, the history that emerges shows us in a sufficiently convincing way that power plays an important part in the economic discourse. The economists' different perspectives on the four aspects of power we have identified have since been clarified and criticized, they have disappeared and resurfaced, some have influenced the following generations, others are still lost to history.

References

Bartlett, R. (1989). *Economics and Power. An Inquiry into Human Relations and Markets*. Cambridge: Cambridge University Press.

Bowles, S., Franzini, M., & Pagano, U. (1999). *The Politics and Economics of Power*. London: Routledge.

Bowles, S., & Gintis, H. (1993). Power and Wealth in a Competitive Capitalist Economy. *Philosophy and Public Affairs, 21*(4), 324–353.

Bowles, S., & Gintis, H. (2008). Power. In S. N. Durlauf & L. E. Blume (Eds.), *The New Palgrave Dictionary of Economics* (2nd ed., 8 vols, Vol. 6, pp. 565–570). Houndmills: Macmillan.

De Cecco, M. (1997). The Role of the Institutions in Pantaleoni's Thought. In M. Baldassarri (Ed.), *Maffeo Pantaleoni. At the Origin of the Italian School of Economics and Finance* (pp. 187–195). Rome: SIPI.
Foucault, M. (1978–79]). *The Birth of Biopolitics.* New York: Palgrave Macmillan, 2004.
Galbraith, J. K. (1983). *The Anatomy of Power.* Boston: Houghton, Miffin.
Galbraith, J. K., & Bartel, R. D. (1983). The Anatomy of Power. *Challenge, 26*(3), 26–33.
Groenewegen, P. D. (1998). Maffeo Pantaleoni. In F. Meacci (Ed.), *Italian Economists of the 20th Century* (pp. 44–68). Cheltenham: Elgar.
Guizzo, D. (2015). Foucault's Contributions for Understanding Power Relations in British Classical Political Economy. *Economia, 16*(2), 194–205.
Hirschmann, A. O. (1977). *The Passion and the Interests.* Princeton: Princeton University Press.
Keynes, J. M. (1936). *The General Theory of Employment, Interest and Money* (pp. 32–33). New York: Harcourt Brace.
Levy, D. M., & Peart, S. J. (2017). *Escape from Democracy. The Role of Experts and the Public in Economic Policy.* Cambridge: Cambridge University Press.
Morishima, M. (1995). Foreword: Yasuma Takata (1883–1971). In Y. Takata (Ed.), *Power Theory of Economics* (pp. xi–xxv). New York: St. Martin's Press.
Palermo, G. (2016). *Economics and Power. A Marxist Critique.* London/New York: Routledge.
Pantaleoni, M. (1898). An Attempt to Analyze the Concepts of "Strong" and "Weak" in Their Economic Connexion. *The Economic Journal, 8*(30), 183–205.
Perelman, M. (2014). The Power of Economics vs the Economics of Power: Introduction. *World Review of Political Economy, 5*(3), 284–296.
Perroux, F. (1973). *Pouvoir et économie.* Paris: Dunod.
Rothbard, M. N. (1970). *Power and the Market.* Menlo Park: Institute for Humane Studies.
Rothschild, K. W. (Ed.). (1971). *Power in Economics.* Harmondsworth: Penguin.
Rothschild, K. W. (2002). The Absence of Power in Contemporary Economic Theory. *Journal of Socio-Economics, 31*, 433–442.
Takata, Y. (1995). *Power Theory of Economics.* New York: St. Martin's Press.
Tool, M. R., & Samuels, W. J. (Eds.). (1980). *The Economy as a System of Power.* Oxford: Transaction Books.

Part I

The Republic and the Sovereign: Economists on Political Power

2

The Dream to Tame the Leviathan: Authoritarian Power and the Market

Bruna Ingrao

2.1 Ideas and Definitions of Power

Ideas of power form a large semantic field in political philosophy and in economic thought. What is power is controversial, and the word 'power' admits alternative interpretations in social science. As the political philosopher R. Dahl suggests, its open semantics with the broad range of meanings it involves might be an insidious trap more than a sound scientific conception (Dahl 1957: 201). In popular imagination, power is often identified with the extraordinary capacity some elite circles are endowed with, whose members complot in secrecy with formidable underground resources to change the course of events. These may be banks, multinational corporations, financial speculators or the media, which are deemed to globally regulate the state of markets or world events. In social science, the range of meanings involves disparate notions such as the institutional state authority on subjects or citizens, the unstable equilibrium of States on the international scenery, the hierarchical

B. Ingrao (✉)
University of Rome La Sapienza, Rome, Italy

M. Mosca (ed.), *Power in Economic Thought*, Palgrave Studies in the History of Economic Thought, https://doi.org/10.1007/978-3-319-94039-7_2

order among social groups, the conflicts on income distribution and the norms that regulate status by gender or age. Philosopher Foucault tried to decipher the underground, reticular web of power built in by the shaping of personal identities and the control over bodies in repressive social institutions. The Panopticon, the 'ideal' prison born out of Bentham's imagination, becomes the theoretical model to portray the impersonal, pervasive nature of power through the dominance on bodies and minds.[1]

In 1789, Bentham defined power in terms of the pleasures experienced in exercising it:

> The pleasures of power are the pleasures that accompany the persuasion of a man's being in a condition to dispose people, by means of their hopes and fears, to give him the benefit of their services: that is, by the hope of some service, or by the fear of some disservice, that he may be in the way to render them. (Bentham 1789 [1909], Cap.V, VIII, 6)

Dahl, echoing Bentham's definition, looks at power as a relationship between two 'actors': on the power basis including all the resources that actor A has the capacity to mobilize, A forces the choices or influences the behaviour by actor B, against or beyond B's will. Power works by threat, promise or persuasion; it may be evaluated in terms of its amount or the range of scopes to which it extends (Dahl 1957: 203):

> My intuitive idea of power, then, is something like this: A has power over B to the extent that he can get B to do something that B would not otherwise do. (Dahl 1957: 202)

This open definition covers a large range of social interactions. In political science, authoritative scholars such as J. March, H. Simon, L.S. Shapley or J. Harsany advanced alternative ideas of power, some of which formalized within game theory (Harsanyi 1971). Controversies on definitions dealt with their overall consistency or compatibility, or with the residual ambiguities in the underlying ideas of causality and the core scope of power relationships (Riker 1964; Wittman 1976). In political

[1] Digiser signals the distance of Foucault's idea of power from both the 'liberal' and the 'radical' vision (Digiser 1992).

science, concepts of power aim at explaining and measuring the capacity various political actors have to influence political choices, government and the voting process in general elections (Parsons 1963a, b). Controversial is the idea of power in international relations, in the theoretical constructions that address the issue; in historical interpretation, the label 'power' may be too easily applied as a shortcut, in lieu of appropriate reconstruction of the context to deal with (Guzzini 1993: 478).

In this chapter, we deal with the controversial notion of power as related to State authority within societies with established and more or less stable, fragile, contested, political institutions; notably, we deal with arbitrary power as built up in authoritarian or totalitarian States, looking both at the tragic experiences of totalitarianism in the twentieth century and at the return of authoritarianism in the contemporary global world. The focus is on arbitrary power as the capacity to force choice or behaviour on individual persons or communities through threat, promise, or persuasion not explicitly sanctioned by the rule of law, or extending well beyond what the law dictates. The instruments include discretionary, hierarchical command, acts of violence and physical coercion, acts of cruelty, abuse of legal power, but also the building up of political charisma, the apparatus for organized persuasion, the systematic abuse of asymmetric information, spying activities with the intrusion in private life, the imposition of personal stigma and social exclusion. In the twentieth century, authoritarian power was a devastating force that left deep marks on economic life. How should scholars in economics deal with the arbitrary exercise of power that shapes the workings of the markets and affects the economic aspects of social life?

In the first half of the twentieth century, totalitarian rule forced vast communities in the territories under the control of totalitarian States to face arbitrary power in the most cruel and brutal aspects that contemporary history witnessed, in peace and war. Let the numbers speak. More than one million[2] people died in the Armenian genocide during World War I. The victims under Nazi rule were 17 million or up to 21 million or even more, including 6 million Jews who died in concentration camps. Around three million or more civilians died in the 'Holodomor', the terrible famine in Soviet Ukraine between 1932 and 1933; in the estimates including

[2] According to other estimates up to 1.5 or 2 million lives were lost.

persecuted people or people forced to escape from Soviet Ukraine, the victims go up to four or five million. In the two years 1937–1938 of Stalin's Terror, the victims were around 1.6 million, counting casualties and arrests; in the 1930s almost 25% of the adult population was hit by repression under Stalin's rule. Historians calculate that more than 20 million people were affected (Graziosi 2007: 426). Beyond such tragic figures, in the first half of the twentieth century, totalitarian States destroyed human capital by killing intellectual elites. Totalitarian rule caused the massive, irreversible destruction of skills and knowledge, including technical training, administrative capacities, political and managerial abilities. Millions of children were deported or taken away from their families; the survivors suffered devastating trauma in their psychical growth to adulthood.[3] In the second half of the century, in communist China during the 1958–1962 period, famine killed 23 million people, cautious estimates say; recent calculations have raised the losses to up to 36 or 38 million people, if not 47 million (Dikötter 2011: 324). Military rule in authoritarian regimes in South America, notably in Brazil, Chile and Argentina extolled high number of losses. In the years 1975–1979, in Cambodia the Khmers Rouge genocide murdered 1.5 to 2 million people.[4] To these figures should be added the victims of African conflicts during the Cold war; the Tutsi genocide in Rwanda in 1994; the civilian deaths in Congo between 1998 and 2003, which might reach more than five million people, and the massacres still are ongoing. It is a long, tragic list.

After the fall of the Soviet bloc and the end of Maoist China, authoritarian rule with aspects of brutal arbitrariness and patrimonialism is still widespread in the world; it affects the lives of millions. In the milder experience of partially authoritarian States, with an apparent democratic base, political power and economic interests mingle; a legitimate question arises on where the dividing line runs separating private interests and the State apparatus. A complex picture emerges of how the State and the market interact in parliamentary democracies set up in postcolonial States or after the disintegration of the Soviet bloc, where in the market space the commixture prevails of public influence and private activity,

[3] On the hardship and trauma children suffered under Soviet repression till Stalin's death, see Frierson and Vilensky (2010).

[4] According to some estimates, the victims were two million or more.

affecting the opportunities for growth. In tragic circumstances, the commixture nurtures vicious paths, capturing in poverty traps the countries involved in political conflicts or civil wars. How to draw a line between the State and the market, political power and economic activity, individual and collective choice, if political elites arbitrarily restrict personal freedom, appropriate both private and collective resources, and systematically use threat and promises to force choices? Does the demarcation line that is supposed to distinguish private interests in the market from public choices disappear? Research on contemporary authoritarian regimes calls into question the disciplinary borders separating economics, political science and historical studies.

In economic thought, authoritarian power was examined in specific research niches, such as the studies on imperialism in the first half of the twentieth century. Since the late eighteenth century, the damages and distortions created by the excess of public control over economic life have been a major theme in economic literature, from the elementary visions of laissez-faire to the sophisticated contributions in the *public choice* approach, which refuse to deal with the decisions by public bodies as if they were the enlightened dictates of a benevolent dictator. In the theory of markets at the core of economics, the image prevailed of exchanges regulated by the rule of law protecting property rights, under the benevolent State. Even the Marxist approach proposing the polemical image of the State as the managing committee of the bourgeoisie accepts the inner legality regulating markets in capitalism, though in a dialectic evolution. The State is the instrument of class interests, not of individual whimsical wills. The idea of competitive markets is built on the dream to tame the Leviathan, erasing the disturbing influences of discretionary authoritarian power or totalitarian terror.

2.2 History and Reason: The Dreams to Tame the Leviathan in Economic Thought

In the second half of the eighteenth century in Europe, at the fluid frontier between economics and political science, so rich in ideas within the unifying framework of moral philosophy, illustrious intellectuals came face to face with the task of fighting to free civil society from the stranglehold of the powerful. This stranglehold could distribute favours or ruin, and it was feared because it was capricious, subject neither to transparent rules nor to adequate checks, perceived as threatening because it dissipated human lives in war or burnt them with unjust sentencing. It was felt to smother positive energy that could bring about the transformation to achieve goals of wellbeing and safety. The holders of capricious power over life and death are the sovereigns, the courts, the great landowners, but also the magistrates who make laws and administer justice, the financiers who collect taxes, the coalitions of rich shopkeepers or the extremely powerful trading companies. This theme traverses the whole of Enlightenment culture and there is no need here to mention Montesquieu, Beccaria or Kant.

In France, the Physiocrats expressed the utopia of a rationally governed society, where arbitrary power was tamed and the exercise of power took the form of enlightened despotism, with a monarchic government legitimized by subordination to the natural law, that is, by a system of principles and rules dictated by reason, spread by education to all social classes and learned by the sovereign himself, who was supposed to be its greatest guarantor. The lack of transparency, the ambiguity and uncertainty of fiscal and juridical norms, as well as their arbitrary interpretation by courts or officials in charge of their enforcement, with very high costs for the security and wellbeing of citizens, are central themes in the writings of Turgot. They are recurrent in the *Eloge de Vincent de Gournay*, in *Mémoire sur les prêts d'argent*, in the letter about *La Marque des fers*, in the *Lettres au Contrôleur Général sur le commerce des grains*, just to mention the best known texts (Ingrao 2013, cap. I.). A major theme in Turgot's writings is the ill-defined and variable feature of the French judicial system. He repeatedly points to the capricious application of the laws, which puts the subjects of the French kingdom at the mercy of the power of single officials and magistrates. In the *Eloge*, he critically refers to how crucial issues such as succession rights could be determined by custom and courts could arbitrarily pronounce death sentences for some crimes. He credited de Gournay with constant attention for the reform of the 'abuses' due to the excessive, arbitrary intervention of public authority in economic activities and also due to the powerful influence of coalitions of vested interests in trade corporations.

It would be wrong to see in these political projects, in which there is a clear central role of the state represented in the power of the absolute monarch, projects of extreme economic liberalism in the (controversial) sense of the contemporary debate. Both the Physiocrats and Turgot felt the central state should have an active yet enlightened role in education, taxation, public works, transport and in the promotion of technical progress. In his role as intendant and then minister, Turgot, more pragmatic and flexible in his conception of the art of governing than the Physiocratic circle around Quesnay, managed during his brief periods in government to promote immediate interventions and wide-ranging reforms, with a rationalizing activism that was only partly successful and, as we know, accelerated his fall.

In *The Wealth of Nations* Smith's disenchanted dream of taming the authoritarian Leviathan appears to be more sober and realistic, with overtones of scepticism on the possibility of mitigating or controlling the follies of the government, explicitly critical of the Physiocratic claim that the perfect government regime could be achieved. He wrote in *The Wealth of Nations*: 'The violence and injustice of the rulers of mankind is an ancient evil, for which, I am afraid, the nature of human affairs can scarce admit of a remedy' (Smith 1776 [1976], IV.iii.: 493). The arbitrary nature, the abuse and the rapacity of power are among the great themes of Smith's historical discourse not only in *The Wealth of Nations*, but also in *Lectures on Jurisprudence* and *The Theory of Moral Sentiments*. They recur in his interpretation of the ancient world and its historical catastrophes, in his analysis of slavery and colonization, in his denunciation of the imbalance among peoples on the international scene, in his vision of the conflict between monarchs, feudal lords and free cities in medieval Europe, in the denunciation of the power of life and death applied arbitrarily in commercial legislation, in the critique of trading companies and destructive experiences such as the dispossessions and impoverishment produced by the colonial government in Bengal. Many scholars have pointed out Smith's lack of faith in the rationality of politics and in the correct behaviour of the government and the public administration. As Viner has acutely observed, Smith was dealing with cynical and corrupt state powers (Viner 1927: 221–223). At the time of the first colonization of the Americas, the international scene had been a theatre of terrible violence and abuse against indigenous populations, a tragic experience recalled by Smith in *The Wealth of Nations*. Wars for the control of the seaways and commercial traffic, the expansion of the British empire, the conflict with the colonies in North America offered ample first-hand material on the abuses of authoritarian state power unmitigated by the law or the control exercised, though to a limited extent, by elected assemblies.

Smith's ideal of natural liberty is among the fertile utopias that fuel the dream of taming the Leviathan. It would be reductive to interpret it from the viewpoint of the contemporary debate, forgetting the historical context and Smith's emphasis in all his works on justice as the foundation of the social order and specifically of the institutional order, which has to regulate and moderate the interplay of private interests (Rosenberg 1960; Hollander 1977). In its first formulation, which we know only indirectly, the deviation of government towards oppression and tyranny is intrinsic to the very goal of controlling the natural course of things, deforming it.[5]

In Smith's work, history is central, as a reasoned narration of events, a reconstruction of paths of development, an evolutionary anthropology of human societies. The image of the markets is contaminated by history even in the vision of the natural course of the 'commercial society'. In the nineteenth century, the mathematization that progressively conquered economic theory expurgated market theory from history, and with it the impure interweaving of markets and authoritarian state power in historical experience. The idea of the market—the theoretical space of human interaction established by the contract of exchange—is represented in the mathematical model as a place of interpersonal relations dominated by legality, that is, governed by its own laws. This theoretical vision, formulated in different ways by different authors, explores the space of social interaction based on the voluntary contract, conceived as the

[5] 'Little else is requisite to carry a state to the highest degree of opulence from the lowest barbarism, but peace, easy taxes, and a tolerable administration of justice; all the rest being brought about by the natural course of things. All governments which thwart this natural course, which force things into another channel, or which endeavour to arrest the progress of society at a particular point are unnatural, and to support themselves are obliged to be oppressive and tyrannical' (quoted in Stewart 1795 [1980]: 322).

product of agents' far-sighted rationality; it excludes the individual's arbitrary power over the choices of another person and, a priori, the arbitrary use of power by the political elite of the authoritarian state. The market is a system of social relations governed by internal laws: in the conflict of desires and in the allocation of resources, what prevails is the objectivity of social relations, never the arbitrary will of one individual against the other.

History is still a large presence in the work of A.A. Cournot, a central figure in the mathematization project, but also the author of hundreds of pages of epistemological, philosophical and anthropological reflections in an ambitious attempt to systematize and classify knowledge ranging from probability theory to the theory of evolution, from biology to linguistics and anthropology. The uneasy balance between materialism, vitalism and rationalism or, in human affairs, between history and rationality, are aspects of his thought of controversial interpretation. As argued by F. Vatin, a careful scholar of Cournot, as civilization evolves the 'historical' phase follows the prehistoric one and precedes the one at the end of history, dominated by rational behaviour (Vatin 2006: 119). In 1838, in the *Recherches*, Cournot foresaw the drive towards rational order that dominates the development of the market economy. In the rationalized, global society towards which human experience is moving, market relationships, purified of any crude form of power, are made fluid by moderation and by far-sighted rationality (Cournot 1838 [1971]: 10). In the *Traité* published in 1861, he repeated the prediction of the growing expansion of the rule of rationality with the effect of reducing the turbulence of political life (Cournot 1861 [1982]: 482, 484, 552). However, the political sphere is deeply rooted in the collective imagination based on emotions and identity, and it remains elusive, extraneous to full rationalization and open to fresh turmoil. Cournot conceives it from the viewpoint of the 'social body' rather than from that of mechanical equilibrium. In 1875, in *Matérialisme, vitalisme, rationalisme* the risk of 'shocks' heralding disaster in the political sphere is announced in almost pessimistic tones. Governing men requires 'an organism that has the flexibility and spontaneity of life' (Cournot 1875 [1987]: 130). The hope of stabilization for the political sphere emerges from the distinction between the 'regime' of government and politics, in the strict sense. By 'regime', Cournot means the institutional and normative system (e.g. the monetary or judicial regime) that is established in a sovereign state and can be governed with intelligence and honesty by the administration, competently carrying out functions that are distinct and separate from political action, which nevertheless remains its driving force (Cournot 1875 [1987]: 131–132). Cournot has some faith in this moderate utopia of successful, competent management of public functions, free from political interference, despite underlying its ideal character. If the ideal were to prevail the disturbances caused by the repeated turbulence of politics would remain confined to the surface level (Cournot 1875 [1987]: 132). Whatever the faith in this form of taming the Leviathan, Cournot's theory of the market still remains firmly anchored to the foundations laid in 1838, although in the *Principes*, in 1863, the emphasis on the possibility of mathematizing the economic discourse is toned down and caution is explicitly expressed (Cournot 1863 [1981]: 329–330).

The dream of markets without power and of the benevolent Leviathan is clearly embodied in the Walrasian construct of the general economic equilibrium. The definition of the market given by Walras in *Éléments d'économie politique pure*, which lies at the heart of the vast construction of the model of general economic equilibrium, is a market of perfect competition where the price is formed as a 'natural fact' depending on the objective nature of scarcity, beyond the will and arbitrary power of any individual trader (Walras 1900 [1952]: 26–27). While Walras admits the possibility of voluntary actions to alter the price established according to scarcity, for instance by destroying part of the stocks of some good, in his epistemology, the science of pure political economy deals with the determination of relative prices in perfectly competitive markets, where such prices are formed transparently without arbitrary interference (Walras 1900 [1952]: 45). The long-standing dispute about the normative or descriptive nature of the Walrasian model cannot disregard the importance Walras attributes to the pure theoretical model in scientific explanation, side by side with its role as the normative ideal. The theoretical model of the system of markets, the key to interpret reality, must be an abstract, ideal representation of exchange in perfect competition precisely because it is pure science; it is a normative ideal, because it responds to the criterion of commutative justice: markets not subject to arbitrary power in relations between private parties. The equilibrium relative prices depend neither on discretion nor on the ability to exercise pressure by this or that trader or by institutions outside the trading process. In the market interaction, individual free will, which underlies the individual traders' optimizing decision-making, is subject to the law of price regulation operationalized by the auctioneer. The desire for power and subjugation does not disappear, but is curbed by the mechanism of competition operating in trade. This ideal model of the perfectly competitive market is totally lacking in elements of power. In the paradise of ideal markets, nobody exercises pressure on others to force them to act by way of threat or promise. Nobody could even imagine doing so, if the premises of the ideal model are upheld. The images of the ideal market in the writings of Walras include, in the 34th lesson in *Éléments d'économie politique pure*, the famous one that compares the majesty of the economic world as governed by the law of supply and demand to the system of the astronomical world governed by universal gravitation (Walras 1900 [1952]: 362).

The legality of the market is grounded on the condition of 'legitimate appropriability' of goods and therefore on the definition of property rights; but in pure market theory, there is no discussion of the fundamental principles that should regulate them, nor precise references to their normative definition in the institutions of a state or a time in history. The capital good of which Walras at length discusses the conditions of legitimate appropriability is land, with evaluations that do not concern pure political economy but the complementary field of the social economy (*économie sociale*). In *Éléments d'économie politique pure*, Walras deals with the question of property in a double register, historical and theoretical, relegating appropriability by force and through conflict to past ages and expressing the faith that human history will evolve towards 'the final order of principles' (Walras 1900 [1952]: 36). The final order has the connotation of a rational ideal corresponding to the epistemological fusion of the normative ideal and the scientific one.[6] According to the perspectives of applied science and

[6] See Walras (1898 [1992]: 434). The constructive standard defined in applied science should be based on the principles of pure science.

social economy, the scientific disciplines constituting the theoretical architecture of social science along with pure political economy, Walras formulates the dream of the state that embodies distributive justice: it is a scientific ideal towards which positive action must be rationally addressed and towards which the course of history moves.[7] In a note written in 1875 about the possible nationalization of the railways, critical of Chevalier and the French free trade school, Walras reaffirmed the importance of the state's effective and benevolent role, complementary to private activity (Walras 1898 [1992]: 211–212). In constructive terms, he conceived the possibility of building the state administration with well trained, dedicated civil servants, honest magistrates and competent engineers, driven by the desire to serve the public good. He reaffirmed his faith in the efficiency and effectiveness in the actions belonging to public responsibility (Walras 1898 [1992]: 212). The theme runs through all the essays collected in *Études d'économie politique appliquée*, as well as being of central importance in *Études d'économie sociale* (Walras 1896 [1992], 1898 [1992]).

In the Lausanne school, Pareto separated pure market theory from his broader conceptual construct, although he was engaged in the analysis of power, to which he devoted a large part of his sociological work. In the *Manuale*, the realm of theoretical economics is confined to the sphere of repeated logical actions alone (Ingrao 2013: 429–430). In his late political writings, Pareto anticipated an explicit interest in the connections between markets and institutional construction, with a very critical attitude towards liberal democracy.

The ideal character of Walras's vision of the market is accentuated in the neo-Walrasian general equilibrium model, which still plays an important role as a reference point among economists, despite the composite nature of the core of economic theory today. Recent literature underlines the normative value of the general equilibrium model between the 1940s and 1960s, and its connection to the literature of 'mechanism design', openly oriented to constructing mechanisms of social engineering for the purposes of planning (Boldyrev and Ushakov 2015). In the vision of

[7] See Walras (1898 [1992]: 413).

centralized planning as overlapping with the Walrasian model, which marked the literature of the 1940s called market socialism,[8] as well as in its later developments in stability theorem research, and more explicitly, in the search for social engineering mechanisms designed for planning, the public authority immediately takes the rational, transparent form devoid of any trace of power that Walras attributed to ideal competitive markets that do not violate commutative justice. The image of the state as the organizer and rationalizer of economic activity is built looking at the ideal image of transparent markets governed by laws that exclude irrationality, abuse, violence, oppression or the individual's arbitrary power over the destiny of his fellow man.

In the current state of economics research, there are no dominant models of markets, which might claim the theoretical primacy attributed to the neo-Walrasian general equilibrium model in the 1950s and 1960s. After having been at the frontier of research till the late 1970s, the neo-Walrasian model was superseded by new families of partial models, many of them in game theory, with applications in different fields. Whole research fields, like behavioural economics, reject the Walrasian premises advancing new epistemological perspectives and behavioural hypotheses. However, difficulties in conceptualization and formalization hinder the emergence of a unified paradigm that coherently incorporates cognitive biases, asymmetric information, transaction costs or disequilibrium dynamics in the market mechanisms, abandoning the transparency of perfect competition. For ideological reasons and a lack of alternative, unifying visions, the neo-Walrasian model remained the reference point until the start of the twenty-first century in New Classical Macroeconomics and, with appropriate variations, in New-Keynesian Macroeconomics. Today it is still the basic image of the market in the economist's tool box, although a new anarchy is advancing in economic theory.[9]

---

[8] 'But market socialists took Walrasian construct not just as a general model of market, but also as a guide to action, a normative ideal one needed to achieve. It turned out that the same mathematical object (equilibrium) could be interpreted both as an outcome of spontaneous decentralized market process and as a result of centralized socialist planning duly organized and implemented' (Boldyrev and Ushakov 2015: 5).

[9] The evolving core of mainstream economics is fragmentary; a single theoretical tool box has vanished (Ingrao 2018).

2.3 The Many Leviathans in Contemporary History

Hobbes's Leviathan is an artificial giant playing a civilizing role; it is built to establish some measure of reciprocal security founded on recognized natural laws.[10] The totalitarian Leviathans in the time of wolves, as the poet Osip Mandel'stam named the epoch being himself a victim of the wolves, were not so reassuring. In Europe, great minds tried to unveil the hidden nature of the authoritarian States that emerged in the 1930s, under the pressure of the dramatic change in the political scene. In 1936, historian Élie Halévy, who underlined the similarities among the power apparatus of Nazi rule, the various forms of fascism, and the new Bolshevik power, connected them as the various faces of the age of tyrannies (*L'ère des tyrannies*). He looked at their common roots in the devastating political experience of World War I. Halévy chose the word 'tyranny' with Greek root in continuity with Aristotle's political thought; he preferred it to 'dictatorship' that in its original Latin meaning indicated the power that established the transitory suppression of freedom in a situation of emergency (Halévy 1938 [1990]: 214). On the contrary, Hannah Arendt emphasized the novelty of twentieth-century totalitarianism, marking its difference from authoritarian forms of government as already classified in political thought (Arendt 1951 [1967]; Arendt 1954a [1994]: 309–310, 313; Arendt 1954b [1994]: 339–340). In her book on *The origins of totalitarianism* and in the essay prepared for *The Partisan Review*, she argued that the emergence of totalitarian regimes was the crucial challenge for the understanding of the contemporary history. She placed totalitarian regimes at the heart of historical change in the twentieth century, comparing the difficult task of deciphering totalitarianism to deciphering the "central event of our world" (Arendt 1954a [1994]: 308). Arendt underlined the terrible novelty of both the Nazi and the Stalinist rule, distinguishing these

[10] 'The final cause, end, or design of men who naturally love liberty, and dominion over others, in the introduction of that restraint upon themselves, in which we see them live in commonwealths, is the foresight of their own preservation, and of a more contented life thereby; that is to say, of getting themselves out from that miserable condition of war which is necessarily consequent, as hath been shown (Chap. 13), to the natural passions of men when there is no visible power to keep them in awe, and tie them by fear of punishment to the performance of their covenants, and observation of those laws of nature set down in the fourteenth and fifteenth chapters' (Hobbes 1651 [2014]: 131).

regimes at their peak from other contemporary dictatorships, such as the fascist one party rule or the early Bolshevik one party dictatorship. At the roots of totalitarian power are ideologies, which believe in the inevitable evolution of history moving towards the purification of the race or the eschatological purification of society. The ideologies on which the totalitarian regime is built deny all rights to life and freedom to entire groups of people, perceived as not belonging to the purifying evolution. Individuals or minority groups, who by stereotype classification or by mere accident are perceived as not belonging to the privileged final destiny, obstruct the revelation of history: they must be destroyed by the power machine. The superior evolution dictated by nature or by society justifies killing them, even in mass massacres. For inferior human beings, the Leviathan is no more a protecting power; on the contrary, the totalitarian Leviathan should accelerate their annihilation in the advance of times. In the terror justified by natural or social transformation, human beings disappear as such; they are just instrumental agents of the immanent, inevitable change according to the final law of evolution. Those who clean the world from inferior races or individuals, or from decadent classes and peoples, may tomorrow be the ones who will be sacrificed in the march towards the inevitable, eschatological future (Arendt 1954b [1994]: 349). According to Arendt, in Nazi Germany and Stalinist Russia these are the tragic marks of totalitarian rule at its peak. Power is the kingdom of terror (Arendt 1953 [1994]).

In *Crowds and Power,* Elias Canetti identified another aspect of power relations.[11] The 'crowd' is a psychic phenomenon, in which individuals lose the separateness of their individual identity that is usually accompanied by a repugnance at being touched: 'the dense crowd, in which body is pressed to body; a crowd, too, whose psychical constitution is also dense, is compact' (Canetti 1962 [1981]: 15). Canetti's 'crowd' is a powerful psychic experience in the mass rituals of authoritarian regimes. As regards German historical experience, Canetti argued that in the unification of Germany the army became the founding symbol of the nation in the collective experience of German citizens. After the Versailles treaty, in Hitler's speeches against the 'Diktat' of Versailles, the claims against

[11] In the book, Canetti explores the crowd in the most varied and diverse historical circumstances.

the disbanding of the German army acted, by inversion, as a powerful appeal to national cohesion, with immediate hold over his listeners (Canetti 1962 [1981]: 181 ff). Canetti evoked the 'crowd' in German hyperinflation as a collective experience of devaluation of both the currency and personal identities. He looked at the paroxysm of anti-Semitism as rooted in the same psychic experience (Canetti 1962 [1981]: 186 ff.).

In her works, Arendt carefully distinguished the various authoritarian governments with reference to the analysis of power in Montesquieu's and Kant's political thought; but in some paragraphs on totalitarian regimes, she placed the focus on liquid institutions, pointing out at the ruthless power of the secret police or of elite paramilitary corps, whose members could in turn be crushed by the terror machinery (Arendt 1951 [1967]: Part 3, chap. XII).[12] Although her lesson cannot be forgotten, her interpretation of totalitarianism does not account for all authoritarian regimes.[13] Historical studies on the evolution of the Soviet State after Stalin's death, or of communist States in Eastern European countries before 1989, show how these regimes developed a complex institutional architecture to legitimate government and capture the consensus of civilians. The capture of consensus is built by building collective values and aspirations through the machinery of active propaganda; these may be anchored in deep cultural roots in national history. On a parallel path, consensus is built by building welfare systems or networks of cronyism relationships, which provide to individuals or groups better incomes, status advancement and social visibility, in strict connection to economic life. Violence and consensus are the two poles for the longer-term stability of authoritarian rule.[14]

---

[12] Arendt's book offers an articulate analysis of the institutions in the terror machinery in the later phases of totalitarian regimes, after their first stage as revolutionary movements (see Arendt 1951 [1967], chaps. XI and XII).

[13] For the same reason her interpretation of totalitarianism is controversial, even if some scholars, and notably R. Aron, recognize its dramatic relevance (Martinelli 2009; Forti 2009). On the cultural roots of totalitarianism see also Shorten (2012).

[14] D. Augustine effectively underlined this balance in his history of the German Democratic Republic (GDR). 'GDR history stands between the opposing, yet connected poles of coercion and consent, neither of which can be ignored. In fact, this is true of all regimes known to historians. It is even true of the most ruthless, dictatorial and violent phases of Stalinist and Nazi rule' (Augustine 2011: 633–652).

2.4 Hayek and Schumpeter on Totalitarianism

During the 1940s, two outstanding economics scholars, J.A. Schumpeter and F. Hayek, dealt with totalitarian institutions and the emerging new totalitarian States. In 1942, Schumpeter examined political institutions and the idea of socialist planning in *Capitalism, Socialism and Democracy*; in 1944, Hayek argued the irreversible drift towards totalitarianism in centrally planned economies in *The Road to Serfdom*. Both scholars reacted to the anti-market climate prevailing in Europe in the 1930s and early 1940s even within democratic countries.[15] They were both concerned with the cultural atmosphere of hostility towards capitalism they perceived in intellectual circles, but reacted from radically different perspectives and with divergent interpretations.[16]

In Schumpeter's thought, power is an important subject. In his theoretical construction, markets are still conceived in isolation from the political sphere, but Schumpeter deeply eroded the Walrasian core in economics dealing with innovation, historical change and the evolution of institutions. In 1912, in *The Theory of Economic Development*, the abstract view of the market economy ('the circular flow') brings the mark of the Walrasian idea of equilibrium, though with adaptations and missing something of Walras's refined theoretical purity (Schumpeter 1934 [2012]: 41). For 'the purpose of theory', the system of competitive markets is static and stable, as Schumpeter remarked in his essay on the instability of capitalism in 1928:

> The economic system in the sense of conditions and processes reduces itself for the purpose of Theory to a system in the scientific sense of the word – a system, that is, of interdependent quantities – variables and parameters – consisting of quantities of commodities, rates of commodities and prices,

[15] See Furet (1995: 180).

[16] Schumpeter wrote in chapter XIII in *Capitalism, Socialism and Democracy*: 'From the analysis of the two preceding chapters, it should not be difficult to understand how the capitalist process produced that atmosphere of almost universal hostility to its own social order to which I have referred at the threshold of this part' (Schumpeter 1942: 143).

mutually determining each other. This system has been found to be stable, and its stability amenable to rational proof, under static conditions. (Schumpeter 1928: 364)

In his essay, Schumpeter drew a clear line of demarcation to cut out issues of political or social instability from the discourse on economic instability to be focused on the endogenous volatility in economic processes, notably endogenous business cycles[17] (Schumpeter 1928: 361–363). He defined 'capitalism' as the combination of private property, the market economy and the credit system, the latter being its distinguishing characteristic. The long-term evolution of capitalism as a social and institutional order of society was neatly distinguished from the instability of the market economy in consequence of endogenous economic fluctuations. Obviously, Schumpeter did not deny that events outside the economic sphere, as properly defined, influence economic trends; he explicitly reminded 'the breakdown of Russia' (Schumpeter 1928: 364). Political shocks belong to the exogenous environment; they are out of the core of properly defined economic discourse.

If absent from the circular flow, power is at the heart of Schumpeter's conception of competitive capitalism, being at the core of the idea of entrepreneurship. Innovative entrepreneurs win thanks to the leadership they exercise on other people, though such leadership is not akin to the political charisma acting by confidence, glamour and persuasion. The entrepreneurial *leadership* requires the capability to stand resistance, and get things done, influencing other peoples' behaviour. Leadership in innovative change, as distinguished by the entrepreneur's role according to Walras or Marshall, requires the ability to convince the bankers, who will provide the funds for the innovative projects. The successful entrepreneur raises the motivations of technicians and workers, who collaborate in innovative projects; he forces new products on consumers; he drags imitators. The illusion of power is moving him to action. Such non-romantic leadership creates economic change, though it has nothing

[17] 'In short, the economic stability we mean, although it *contributes* to stability in other senses, is not *synonymous* with them, nor does it *implies* them' (Schumpeter 1928: 362). In 1927, Schumpeter had underlined how economic cycles had to be explained by endogenous economic phenomena, excluding shocks from political events (Schumpeter 1927).

to do with the affective charisma of politicians, or the State Leviathan as guarantor of the social order. In markets, it spreads disorder by 'destructive creation'.

Seemingly to Cournot, Schumpeter looks at economic phenomena within social, institutional and political evolution in history; the dynamics in the political sphere has its own degree of liberty, with disquieting effects of turbulence or autonomous change. In 1942, in *Capitalism, Socialism and Democracy*, Schumpeter eventually argued the prophecy of the dissolution of the capitalist order. In his analysis, as in Cournot's theorizing, political power gains legitimacy and stands only when grounded on deep emotions. If the entrepreneur builds endogenous economic change, the bourgeoisie as a social group is incapable to sustain the charismatic foundations of power that rule societies, because of its individualistic values, its training and the myopic concentration on profits. Markets and the creative destruction process stand on State institutions in continuity with the feudal order. The innovative entrepreneur is not the charismatic leader of the political community; capitalism survives thanks to its temporary symbiosis with public powers of feudal roots. Government, as the force to impose order and establish orderly, collective conditions of life (Hobbes's Leviathan fundamental role) rests on institutional pillars from the feudal age. The symbiosis works thanks to the metamorphoses of class and status roles; governing elites enclose both people from the new classes and representatives from the old dominant groups (Schumpeter 1942: 136–137):

> With the utmost ease and grace the lords and knights metamorphosed themselves into courtiers, administrators, diplomats, politicians and into military officers of a type that had nothing whatever to do with that of the medieval knight. And -most astonishing phenomenon when we come to think of it- a remnant of that old prestige[18] survives even to these day, and not only with our ladies. (Schumpeter 1942: 137)

This symbiosis is unstable, and Schumpeter reads the growing hostility towards capitalism in contemporary society as the visible signal of a

[18] The reference is to 'the mystic glamour and lordly attitude' of ancient feudal lords.

self-destruction process by capitalism itself. Capitalism as a social order is mined by the disgregating nature of its values, by the failing legitimacy of its leading characters, by the progressive decomposition of 'protective' social groups, that is the stable strata of small proprietors, craftsmen, farmers, whom technical progress and great enterprises destroy (Schumpeter 1942: 139–142). Schumpeter wrote in the Preface:

> In the second part – Can Capitalism Survive – I have tried to show that a socialist form of society will inevitably emerge from an equally inevitable decomposition of capitalist society. Many readers will wonder why I thought so laborious and complex an analysis necessary in order to establish what is rapidly becoming the general opinion, even among conservatives. (Schumpeter 1942 [1992]: 409–410)

The political arena is portrayed in a dismal way. Schumpeter looks at politics as dominated by the perverse competition operating through the manipulation of opinion and the deception of constituencies, which are easily cheated because the common voters have myopic views. After the progressive disintegration of the capitalist order, he forecasts the combination of democratic institutions deprived of real power with centralized market socialism leaded by a number of great trusts. Paradoxically, the adumbrated system represents a return to the Walrasian dream to tame the Leviathan. Market socialism, whether fully or partially centralized, even if dominated by monopolies, is managed according to inner rational laws of effective administration; it is autonomous from the inflammable world of politics, and only apparently in the grips of democratic institutions. In the hypothetical socialist society thus constituted, the equilibrium between democracy and socialism, in the meaning Schumpeter attributes to these concepts, may be unstable; it requires a certain degree of welfare and economic growth to smooth social tensions. To maintain the balance between centralized economic power and democracy, people should be highly civilized, and the political elites fairly stable; citizens should freely legitimate the institutional structures (Schumpeter 1942 [1992]: 301–302). If the balance breaks down, the centralized socialist structure attributes to political elites a tremendous amount of power over common people. Socialist democracy, then, becomes a terrible imposture, much more than it is in any mature democracy in capitalism (Schumpeter 1942 [1992]: 302). A subtle poison comes to light in cynical tones: Schumpeter was conscious of the imposture in Soviet Russia as regards the brutality of the socialist discipline. In some pages, he highlights the 'sinister connotations' of Soviet rule, arguing that they are the effects of the historical context and the underdeveloped economy (Schumpeter 1942 [1992]: 212 ff.). The brutality of the totalitarian Leviathan, although remarked, looks as far apart from the inner laws of socialist markets.

On the contrary, in 1944, in *The Road to Serfdom* Hayek argued that the planned economy centralizing resources under government control escalates towards the centralization of political power leading to totalitarian rule. Totalitarian rule drives society towards both ethical and economic disasters. The centralization of control on resources in socialist planning blocks the creative impulse that nurtures discovery and innovation, and severely undermines the efficient use of dispersed knowledge. The main thesis of the book is that central planning, far from being a neutral frame for the collective organization of production and distribution, forces political institutions to degenerate into totalitarian rule. Liberal democracies cannot survive under the hierarchical frame of command that central planning requires; such command erodes the responsible initiative, the values and the shared norms of trust on which open, free market societies stand. In his vision of totalitarianism, Hayek echoes themes similar to those Halévy, and later Arendt, refer to. Nazi and Bolshevik ideologies share the dream of returning to a compact society, whose members have no value as independent persons; they are grains of the whole governed by the common end. Under totalitarian rule, the very idea of ethics disappears. The attribute of humanity pertains to the individual person only as far as he or she is recognized as belonging to the community, in conformity to totalitarian ideology (Hayek 1944 [2008]: 162). To continue with the metaphor above, according to Hayek, the totalitarian Leviathan has no limit in ethical principles, all being admitted by the collective end cementing society. Cruelty becomes the effective tool of historical logic. This gloomy vision of totalitarianism and planning was neatly opposed to Schumpeter's arguing, although Schumpeter was not openly attacked in the book. Two chapters notably dealt with how totalitarian rule progressively undermines habits and norms of civil ethics by harassment and propaganda, the diffusion of official lies, the reward of ferocity and intrigue, the promotion of ruthless individuals to top positions. Totalitarian rule destroys moral identity, and the inner texture of values which frame social intercourse in liberal societies. In *The Road to Serfdom,* two sets of arguments are strictly linked: the impossibility to democratically manage the political institutions in societies with centralized planning; the consequent totalitarian drift in State power, with the ethical decay of political elites, and the loss of moral values in society at large. Hayek will develop these subjects in some of his writings soon after the war, concerned for the fragile rebuilding of liberal constitutions in European countries.

In their opposed prophecies on the Leviathan and the market in dynamic interaction in socialist societies both Schumpeter and Hayek dealt with the complex evolution linking changes in institutions, the building up of individual identities and social values, and economic activities. Both dealt with ideologies, and the ways in which people subjectively perceive their links to the political community, or how moral feelings influence economic life. There is no doubt that Hayek captured effectively the bias towards totalitarianism inherent in the illiberal ideologies extolling collective governance. In the contemporary world, most authoritarian Leviathans take milder forms with respect to the totalitarian regimes of the 1930s and 1940s; in a number of countries, the borders between autocracy, democracy and the market economy seem blurred. They are also highly unstable, just as Schumpeter and Hayek guessed.

2.5 Institutions and Authoritarian Power in Development Economics

After the end of the cold war and the fall of the Soviet Empire, political changes towards democratic transformation took place in various areas of the world. Many of these processes get stuck, and the emerging democratic States remain hybrid. Formally liberalized, they are dominated by political elites, which in various ways violate human rights, block the access to power to opposition forces according to alternation rules, use and abuse public resources to support their leaders or their cronies. The contemporary world sees authoritarian Leviathans, whose political elites manage discretionary power in the use and abuse of State functions, even when they rule within the legal frame of constitutional law, under competitive elections for the nomination of State authorities, legislative assemblies or local municipalities. Scholars in political science propose alternative classifications of such hybrid regimes, debating their persistence and stability versus their evolution towards full democracy or totalitarianism.

In a recent study, Levitsky and Way explore the political experience in 35 States classified as 'competitive authoritarian regimes' (Levitsky and Way 2010). These scholars refuse the label 'transitional' democracies, as if these States were in sure transition towards democracy; the evolution of unfinished democracies admits a variety of outcomes: the progressive transformation in stable democracies, the stabilization of hybrid structures or the reversal to authoritarian rule. To the procedural definition of democracy on the criterion of competitive elections, with Schumpeterian roots, they add the requirement that both the ruling elite and the opponents share fair access and opportunities in the elections' competition.[19] In fully authoritarian regimes, which still exist in the global world, the political opponents have no access to power by legal means in competitive elections. Authoritarian regimes are classified as closed regimes, where no democratic institutions exist at the national level, and hegemonic regimes, where the political opponents are persecuted or forced to exile, and elections are divested by human rights violations, obstacles in accessing them, or frauds.

> We define full authoritarianism as a regime in which no viable channels exists for opposition to contest legally for executive power.(…) Competitive authoritarian regimes are distinguished from full authoritarianism in that

[19] 'Competitive authoritarian regimes are civilian regimes in which formal democratic institutions exist and are widely viewed as the primary means of gaining power, but in which incumbents' abuse of the state places them at a significant advantage vis-à-vis their opponents. Such regimes are competitive in that opposition parties use democratic institutions to contest seriously for power, but they are not democratic because the playing field is heavily skewed in favour of incumbents. Competition is thus real but unfair' (Levitsky and Way 2010: 5–7).

> constitutional channels exist through which opposition groups compete in a meaningful way for executive power. Elections are held regularly and opposition parties are not legally barred from contesting them.(…) What distinguishes competitive authoritarianism from democracy, however, is the fact that incumbent abuse of the state violates at least one of three defining attributes of democracy: (1) free elections, (2) broad protection of civil liberty, and (3) a reasonably level playing field. (Levitsky and Way 2010: 6–7)

In regimes of competitive authoritarianism, the ruling elites try to manage elections by committing local frauds, intimidating political activists, committing legal abuses, appropriating public resources, silencing the press on charges of defamation or other spurious charges, or imprisoning political opponents on false allegations under formally legal procedures. Public funds are systematically used to support the campaign of members of the elite running for office; electoral promises or cronyism capture the votes of individuals and communities in the constituencies.[20]

In political science, the classification of 'illiberal democracies' is controversial (Zacharias 1997). Alternative definitions of hybrid regimes are adopted, all relevant to the contemporary international scenario: constitutional autocracies, with limited access to vote; regimes whose elected assemblies are under the superior guard of religious, military or dynastic authorities; restricted democracies, where some political forces are excluded from the competition (Diamond 2002). The dynamics of these regimes is complex.[21] Various interpretations contest the idea of 'modernization', that is the assertion that the evolutionary processes of democratization basically depend on the trend of per capita income. Levitsky and Way underline that effective political apparatuses play an important role in the middle-term evolution of political institutions. They influence the capacity of elites to stay in power, much as the stability and the cohesion of the State administration on which elites depend. International relations in terms of alliances, agreements, sanctions, aid have a primary role; the amount of trade flows, tourism, foreign investment, participation in international networks for training or education also play a relevant role

[20] See the summary table in Levitsky and Way (2010: 13).

[21] On divergent paths of evolution, see for example, Pepinsky (2009) or Slater (2010). On the evolution of political regimes see also Huntington (1968 [2006]).

(Levitsky and Way 2010: 13). The plurality of actors involved in patterns of economic development, in international geopolitics, and in domestic political governance affect the evolution of political regimes: the stabilization of the authoritarian regime versus the stabilization of democracy; the regime change, new political forces emerging within the old institutional structure; the dissolution of the State, if the political competition opens dramatic crises that end into civil war in contested States.

The contemporary hybrid regimes manage market economies; their elites intrude into market activities. There is a wide literature dealing with neo-patrimonialism in postcolonial African States, many of which are competitive authoritarian regimes, or authoritarian hybrid regimes according to other definitions.[22] Patrimonialism is associated to foreign aid and the complex bargaining on aid and debt with international organizations and foreign governments. International or local NGOs work within the market economy, supplying services which should be provided by public institutions. Military commercialism, that is the systematic presence of the military in economic activities, is a worldwide phenomenon. Moyo, who studied the case of Zimbabwe, lists a number of countries where it is prominent in economic life.[23] In hybrid authoritarian States, the political dynamics calls into question the ambiguous relations of the incumbents in power with the market space, and the way markets work at the junction of private interests and public power. Which new questions does this commixture present to the old core or the new disorder of economic theory?

The literature of public choice and the 'new political economy' explores the dynamics of political choice starting from optimizing decision-making according to optimal decision theory, assuming rational choice and the intelligent forecasting of costs and benefits also by actors in the public sector (Lazear 2000; Waterman 2002; Besley 2007). Economic modelling of

[22] See Englebert and Dunn (2014) for a survey on neo-patrimonialism in African States.

[23] 'The contemporary phenomenon of military intrusion into the political economy is not unique to Zimbabwe. It appears in a number of countries around the world, including Angola, Bangladesh, China, Cuba, the Democratic Republic of Congo (DRC), Egypt, El Salvador, Guatemala, Honduras, Indonesia, Pakistan, Rwanda, Thailand, Turkey, and Vietnam. These countries were a mix of communist-oriented regimes or post-communist societies and military dictatorships, authoritarian and semi-authoritarian regimes' (Moyo 2016: 352).

political behaviour is applied to issues of public finance, administrative decisions, electoral systems, regulation and incentives. This ample research field (with disputable results) does not lead to the radical rethinking of the neo-Walrasian paradigm, or to the investigation of market dynamics in the shady mixture of public decision-making and private choice in countries where government invasiveness is that of hybrid or fully authoritarian regimes. Meanwhile, in contemporary theory, the breakdown of the paradigm of Olympian rationality, to put in Simon's terms, is a theme of growing relevance. Bowles and Gintis coined the term contested exchanges to account for the capacity to impose a contractual obligation in exchange: such capacity is assumed a priori in the neo-Walrasian model, including a built-in enforcement clause; in real markets it operates thanks to disciplinary mechanisms regulated by power relations (Bowles and Gintis 1993). Bowles and Gintis refer to various scholars who studied the interaction between internalized social norms, sanctioning mechanisms for contractual violations and power hierarchies. The capacity for power relations to impose sanctions is relevant in long-term contracts, or in contracts with personal and trust aspects.

These issues arise in the studies on advanced market economies, within the frame of reasonably functioning institutions protecting property rights and democratic rights. They are of primary importance for markets in societies ruled by authoritarian regimes, where access to resources is subject to political whim, sanctions can be set arbitrarily, public decisions are tied to influence peddling, and likewise. Agency problems, transaction costs, contested or uncertain property rights, the unequal distribution of income and wealth, the entanglement between political hierarchy and market transactions, affect how markets work, their roles depending on political change and the stability or instability of State power. There is an urgent need to recognize the gap between the ideal model of the rational economic agent and behaviour under authoritarian rule. The ideological machine that fuels authoritarian power, silencing free choice in repression, captures support thanks to cognitive, emotional and identity-based pressures aimed at promoting mimetic behaviour. The agent is not an isolated individual, whose preferences are independent of the dynamics of social interaction. In the totalitarian society, even when individuals fight to defend their private space and resist, they are affected in their decisions by promise, persuasion, threat and brutal violence exerted by the State. The control over the body, the techniques of mass repression, the fabrication of opinion and information by propaganda, spying and the wiping of historical memory, all impose heavy pressure; it weights on the youth, vulnerable in education or in family uprooting. The elimination of the opposition destroys the heritage of political, ethical and spiritual experience; it weakens the capacity for criticism and intellectual dialogue. Carnage cancels social groups, which are the bearers of technical, moral or cultural knowledge. The rational foresight paradigm is meaningless for totalitarian experiences like the massacre of a quarter (or a third) of the population in Cambodia, the Stalinist purges in the 1930s, Hitler's plan to exterminate the Jews and Romani or the mass deportation of Slavs, the famines caused by crazy policies in Ukraine and China. In milder authoritarian regimes, the invasive manipulation of opinion hardly justifies ideas of consumer sovereignty within given preferences. Without denying the ugly presence of opportunism, identity-based dynamics make it difficult to explain political allegiance as the optimal solution to a cost-benefit computation.

In such broader perspective, economists need new theoretical tools, as much as studies on specific historical experiences. In development economics, interpretations based on the dynamics of institutions have long remained in the background compared to the neoclassic growth model, the various endogenous growth models, or the econometrics of growth differentials, where supposedly exogenous long-term factors (ethnic fragmentation, tropicality, closed boundaries, etc.) play a crucial role. These attempts confine the understanding of development to methods of applied econometrics, without deep knowledge of context and events. Even if the models include several variables, they signal again the elimination of authoritarian rule from the market picture, not only in atemporal equilibrium but in reading long-term evolution. In recent literature, the many Leviathan's avatars return to the forefront in historical-developmental narrations, presenting dynamic change in the economies in a discursive style (North et al. 2012; Acemoglu and Robinson 2012; Fukuyama 2014). In the course of history, the forms of state power, property rights and other social institutions, the extent and the types of markets create stories of successful economic development, or cases of stagnation or decline. Among these narratives, let us recall the scenarios Acemoglu and Robinson outlined in *Why Nations Fail*, and the alternative vision Fukuyama proposed in *Political Order and Political Decay*.

In *Why Nations Fail* Acemoglu and Robinson collect historical episodes to explain, within a unified theoretical framework, the foundations of power, institutional evolution and the wealth or poverty of nations. They range over diverse ages and places to argue that institutional arrangements, not geography or culture, promote paths leading to prosperity or to vicious circles trapping communities into stagnation and poverty. They focus primarily on property rights and freedom of initiative, but they acknowledge the importance of the contingencies of history, with the accumulation of differences. 'Inclusive' institutions promote growth in contrast to 'exclusive' ones, which defend constituted social powers aimed at extracting rents, in a *conventio ad excludendum* (Acemoglu and Robinson 2012: 73 ff.). Freedom in economic activity fuels technological innovation and creative destruction; the supply of public services and infrastructure, and the defence of justice play their part. In development, there are no dynamic 'laws' of capitalism but different frames of society and many kinds of equilibrium (Acemoglu and Robinson 2012: 462, 2015: 4). Their extensive picture is oversimplified; but the book emphasizes the temporality of history. In theoretical explanation, complex transition processes play the crucial role, beyond the formal dynamics of growth models; historical experience is acknowledged, and historical narration is the language of investigation. The authoritarian state and its methods of exclusion are at the centre of the discourse, although the authors deal only in passing with the political dynamics of authoritarian regimes. The authors bluntly reject the paradigm of modernization, forecasting a difficult transition towards democracy in hybrid authoritarian regimes such as China or Russia, which promoted growth and enjoyed its benefits to support their patrimonial elites under authoritarian rule. The symbiosis between markets and hybrid authoritarian regimes cannot produce sustainable prosperity in the long run (Acemoglu and Robinson 2012: 441 ff., 446).

In *Political Order and Political Decay*, Fukuyama reflects on the ways political institutions change, claiming that their evolution cannot be reduced to the economic discourse, and affirming the specificity of their dynamics, even within the theoretical schematization of what he calls political universals. In his picture, a great deal of space is devoted to the weakness of the state in its inability to provide adequate public services, perform the function of guaranteeing security, assuring justice and respect for the law. States that are strong in the 'despotic' power of repression can be weak in the infrastructural power of making laws and making people obey them, providing quality public services in the fields of security, education and health[24] (Fukuyama 2014: 38). According to Fukuyama, today the construction or consolidation of the state according to these broader parameters is the disturbing theme in many of the world's nations, apart from the processes of democratization, which may leave patrimonialism intact in the management of public authority, or even consolidate it.

> Modern political systems are built on a tripod consisting of a modern State, rule of Law, and democratic accountability. States are about accumulating and using power, while law and accountability seek to constrain and channel power. If the tripod becomes unbalanced in either direction, it falls over into either dictatorship or weak – or at an extreme, failed – government. Patrimonial or neo-patrimonial governments – political systems in which the rulers regard the state as a species of private property from which they can privately profit – are universally present throughout the developing world and are in fact one of the primary cause of underdevelopment and poverty. Getting from such a patrimonial state to 'Denmark' – that is, an impersonal state that treats citizens equally, protects their rights, and observes a clear line between public and private interest- is a much more difficult transition for most societies than moving from authoritarian government to democracy. (Fukuyama 2014: 550)

A broad area of research is open from the historical and theoretical point of view on the economy of the authoritarian state, on the ways the state and the market intermingle in different institutional models and paths of development. It is a crucial theme for the prospects of the world economy. This is the spectrum of issues we should be looking at, rather than focusing solely, as is too often the case today, on the conventional opposition between the State and the market as regards the macroeconomic and welfare policies of advanced economies.

---

[24] Fukuyama adopts the terminology introduced by the sociologist Michael Mann (Fukuyama 2014: 38).

References

Acemoglu, D., & Robinson, J. A. (2012). *Why Nations Fail. The Origins of Power, Prosperity, and Poverty*. New York: Crown Publishers.

Acemoglu, D., & Robinson, J. A. (2015). The Rise and Decline of General Laws of Capitalism. *The Journal of Economic Perspectives, 29*(1), 3–28.

Arendt, H. (1930–1954 [1994]). *Essays in Understanding. 1930–1954. Formation, Exile and Totalitarianism* (J. Kohn, Ed.). New York: Schocken Books, 1994.

Arendt, H. (1951 [1967]). *The Origins of Totalitarianism* (3rd ed.), 1966. London: George Allen & Unwin.

Arendt, H. (1953 [1994]). Mankind and Terror. In J. Kohn (Ed.), *Essays in Understanding, 1930–1954. Formation, Exile and Totalitarianism* (pp. 297–306). New York: Schocken Books.

Arendt, H. (1954a [1994]). Understanding and Politics (The Difficulties of Understanding). In J. Kohn (Ed.), *Essays in Understanding. 1930–1954. Formation, Exile and Totalitarianism* (pp. 307–327). New York: Schocken Books.

Arendt, H. (1954b [1994]). On the Nature of Totalitarianism. An Essay in Understanding. In J. Kohn (Ed.), *Essays in Understanding. 1930–1954. Formation, Exile and Totalitarianism* (pp. 328–362). New York: Schocken Books.

Augustine, D. L. (2011). The Power Question in GDR History. *German Studies Review, 34*(3), 633–652.

Bentham, J. (1789 [1909]). *An Introduction to the Principles of Morals and Legislation*. Oxford: Clarendon Press.

Besley, T. (2007). The New Political Economy. *The Economic Journal, 117*(November), F570–F587.

Boldyrev, I., & Ushakov, A. (2015). Adjusting the Model to Adjust the World: Constructive Mechanisms in Postwar General Equilibrium Theory. *Journal of Economic Methodology*. https://doi.org/10.1080/1350178X.2014.1003581.

Bowles, S., & Gintis, H. (1993). The Revenge of Homo Economicus: Contested Exchange and the Revival of Political Economy. *The Journal of Economic Perspectives, 7*(1), 83–102.

Canetti, E. (1962 [1981]). *Crowds and Power*. New York: Continuum.

Cournot, A. A. (1838 [1980]). *Recherches sur les principes mathématiques de la théorie des richesses*. Paris: Hachette (Reprint in Cournot, A. A. (1980).

Oeuvres complètes (G. Jorland, Ed., VIII). Paris: Librairie philosophique J. Vrin).

Cournot, A. A. (1861 [1982]). *Traité de l'enchaînement des idées fondamentales dans les sciences et dans l'histoire*. Paris: Hachette (Reprint in Cournot, A. A. (1982). *Oeuvres complètes* (N. Bruyère, Ed., III). Paris: Librairie philosophique J. Vrin).

Cournot, A. A. (1863 [1981]). *Principes de la théorie des richesses*. Paris: Hachette (Reprint in Cournot, A. A. (1981). *Oeuvres complètes* (G. Jorland, Ed., IX). Paris: Librairie philosophique J.Vrin).

Cournot, A. A. (1875 [1987]). *Matérialisme, vitalisme, rationalisme*. Paris: Hachette (Reprint in Cournot, A. A. (1987). *Oeuvres complètes* (V. C. Salomon-Bayet, Ed.). Paris: Librairie philosophique J.Vrin).

Dahl, R. (1957). The Concept of Power. *Behavioral Science, 2*, 201–215.

Diamond, L. (2002). Thinking About Hybrid Regimes. *Journal of Democracy, 13*(2), 21–35.

Digiser, P. (1992). The Fourth Face of Power. *The Journal of Politics, 54*(4), 977–1007.

Dikötter, F. (2011). *Mao's Great Famine*. London: Bloomsbury.

Englebert, P., & Dunn, K. C. (2014). *Inside African Politics*. Cape Town: UCT Press.

Forti, S. (1951 [2009]). Le figure del male. In H. Arendt (Ed.), *Le origini del totalitarismo* (pp. xxvii–Liv). Torino: Einaudi.

Frierson, C. A., & Vilensky, S. S. (2010). *Children of the Gulag*. Yale: Yale University Press.

Fukuyama, F. (2014). *Political Order and Political Decay. From the Industrial Revolution to the Globalization of Democracy*. New York: Farrar, Straus and Giroux.

Furet, F. (1995). *Le passé d'une illusion. Essai sur l'idée comuniste au XXe siècle*. Paris: Calmann-Lévy.

Graziosi, A. (2007). *L'URSS di Lenin e Stalin. Storia dell'Unione Sovietica. 1914–1945*. Bologna: Il Mulino.

Guzzini, S. (1993). Structural Power: The Limits of Neorealist Power Analysis. *International Organization, 47*(3), 443–478.

Halévy, E. (1938 [1990]). *L'ère des Tyrannies. Etudes sur le socialisme at la guerre*. Paris: Gallimard.

Harsanyi, J. C. (1971). The Dimension and Measurement of Social Power. In K. W. Rothschild (Ed.), *Power in Economics* (pp. 77–96). Harmondsworth: Penguin Books.

Hayek, F. (1944 [2008]). *The Road to Serfdom*. London: Routledge (reprint Caldwell, B. (Ed.). *The Road to Serfdom. Texts and Documents: The Definitive Edition*, Vol. 2, *The Collected Works of F.A. Hayek*. New York: Routledge 2008).
Hobbes, T. (1651 [2014]). *Leviathan, or the Matter, Form and Power of a Commonwealth Ecclesiastical and Civil*. Ware, Hertfordshire: Wordsworth Editions Limited.
Hollander, S. (1977). Adam Smith and the Self-Interest Axiom. *Journal of Law and Economics, 20*(1), 133–152.
Huntington, S. P. (1968 [2006]). *Political Order in Changing Societies*. New Haven/London: Yale University Press.
Ingrao, B. (2013). *Portraits of European Economists* (pp. 1–673). Rome: Aracne editrice.
Ingrao, B. (2018, June). Models in Economics. Fables, Fictions and Stories. *Annals of the Fondazione Luigi Einaudi, LII*(1), 109–131.
Lazear, E. P. (2000). Economic Imperialism. *Quarterly Journal of Economics, 115*, 99–146.
Levitsky, S., & Way, L. (2010). *Competitive Authoritarianism: Hybrid Regimes After the Cold War*. New York: Cambridge University Press.
Martinelli, A. (1951 [2009]). Introduzione. In H. Arendt (Ed.), *Le origini del totalitarismo* (pp. vii–xxv). Torino: Einaudi.
Moyo, G. (2016). The Curse of Military Commercialism in State Enterprises and Parastatals in Zimbabwe. *Journal of Southern African Studies, 42*(2), 351–364.
North, D. C., Wallis, J. J., & Webb, S. B. (2012). *In the Shadow of Violence. Politics, Economics and the Problems of Development*. Cambridge: Cambridge University Press.
Parsons, T. (1963a). On the Concept of Political Power. *Proceedings of the American Philosophical Society, 107*(3), 232–262.
Parsons, T. (1963b). On the Concept of Influence. *The Public Opinion Quarterly, 27*(1), 37–62.
Pepinsky, T. B. (2009). *Economic Crises and the Breakdown of Authoritarian Regimes*. New York: Cambridge University Press.
Riker, W. H. (1964). Some Ambiguities in the Notion of Power. *American Political Science Review, 58*(2), 341–349.
Rosenberg, N. (1960). Some Institutional Aspects of *The Wealth of Nations*. *Journal of Political Economy, 18*(6), 557–570.
Schumpeter, J. A. (1927). The Explanation of the Business Cycle. *Economica, 21*(December), 286–311.
Schumpeter, J. A. (1928). The Instability of Capitalism. *Economic Journal, 38*(151), 361–386.

Schumpeter, J. A. (1934 [2012]). *The Theory of Economic Development: An Inquiry into Profits, Capital, Credit, Interest, and the Business Cycle* (Translated from the German by Redvers Opie). Reprint New Brunswick/London: Transaction Publishers.

Schumpeter, J. A. (1942 [1994]). *Capitalism, Socialism and Democracy.* London: Routledge.

Shorten, R. (2012). *Modernism and Totalitarianism: Rethinking the Intellectual Sources of Nazism and Stalinism, 1945 to the Present.* Houndsmills: Palgrave Macmillan.

Slater, D. (2010). *Ordering Power: Contentions Politics and Authoritarian Leviathans in Southeast Asia.* New York: Cambridge University Press.

Smith, A. (1776 [1976]). *An Inquiry into the Nature and Causes of the Wealth of Nations* (1st ed.). W. Strahame & T. Cadell, London 1776, Critical Edition *An Inquiry into the Nature and Causes of the Wealth of Nations,* W. B. Todd Ed., The Glasgow Edition of the Works and Correspondence of Adam Smith, Vol. II, 1976.

Stewart, D. (1795 [1980]). *Account of the Life and Writings of Adam Smith, LL. D.* (Reprint in *The Glasgow Edition of the Works and Correspondence of A. Smith*, Vol. III, 1980).

Vatin, F. (2006). Influences on the Economic Theory of A. A. Cournot. Mechanics, Physics and Biology. In V. Mosini (Ed.), *Equilibrium in Economics* (pp. 114–129). London: Routledge.

Viner, J. (1927). Adam Smith and Laissez Faire. *Journal of Political Economy, 35*(2), 198–232.

Walras, L. (1896 [1990]). *Études d'Économie Sociale.* (*Théorie de la Répartition de la Richesse Sociale).* In A. Walras & L. Walras (Eds.), *Œeuvres Économiques Complètes* (Vol. IX) Paris: Economica

Walras, L. (1898 [1992]). *Études d'économie politique appliquée: Théorie de la Production de la Richesse Sociale.* In A. Walras & L. Walras (Eds.), *Œeuvres Économiques Complètes* (Vol. X). Paris: Economica.

Walras, L. (1900 [1952]). *Éléments d'économie politique pure ou théorie de la richesse sociale* (Definitive 1926, Ed., Reprint 1952). Lausanne: F.Rouge.

Waterman, A. M. C. (2002). 'New Political Economies' Then and Now: Economic Theory and the Mutation of Political Doctrine. *The American Journal of Economics and Sociology, 61*(1), 13–51.

Wittman, D. (1976). Various Concepts of Power: Equivalence Among Ostensibly Unrelated Approaches. *British Journal of Political Sciences, 6*(4), 449–462.

Zacharias, F. (1997). The Rise of Illiberal Democracy. *Foreign Policy, 76*, 22–43.

3

Sismondi's Political Economy: Translating Power into Sociability

Francesca Dal Degan

3.1 Introduction

The question of the relationship between the State and individual self-determination becomes crucial when economic activity is consolidated as an area of civil action, thus taking on a specific organizational form. Such an organizational form provides an opportunity to emancipate from, on one hand, some pressing needs by distributing the surplus produced, and, on the other, from the "tight embrace of the powerful" by improving the human lot through the exercise of citizens' capabilities. Therefore, it is not surprising that throughout the eighteenth century when a particular organization of the economy based on the division of labour and the market became widespread, and a scientific reflection on the ongoing economic phenomena developed almost simultaneously in different cultural contexts (civil economists in Italy, physiocrats in France, Scottish philosopher-economists), the need to identify the limit between the sovereign's spectrum of action and that of the single citizens stood out. This

F. Dal Degan (✉)
Department of Economics, University of Pisa, Pisa, Italy

M. Mosca (ed.), *Power in Economic Thought*, Palgrave Studies in the History of Economic Thought, https://doi.org/10.1007/978-3-319-94039-7_3

identification was made possible by asking the following questions: to what extent the enlightened sovereign's will or the various wills of the single citizens influence economic choices and determine the shaping of reality? Do economic actions reflect a set of natural laws or they are rather the historical by-product of social evolution? Are they the causal result of interactions taking place in a complex reality or rather the result of some exogenous coordination mechanisms? Asking such questions does not only mean addressing the limits of State intervention or the regulation of individual action, but more significantly, it redefines the "reason" which is no longer considered to be the privilege of a single central authority, no matter how enlightened it is, but rather the fruit of a wider set of social interactions.

Whereas during the eighteenth century, François Quesnay laid the foundations of his analysis of economic action on the idea of a rationally governed society based on enlightened despotism able to interpret and execute natural laws, Adam Smith conceived a reasonable action to be the result of an exercise of judgement embedded in the relationship between individuals. In this sense, he recognized as rational those actions capable of triggering socializing processes and those objectives that could be empathically shared. In the nineteenth century, Sismondi reverted to Smith's position and, by interpreting it in the light of the contract theory categories formulated by Rousseau, managed to grasp even more profitably the political dimension of rationality of human action, especially understood as citizens' plural activity within society. In this sense, the concept of sociability—a bridge concept that reveals its nodal nature between moral and anthropological theory, politics and political economy—serves to penetrate Sismondi's concept of "reason" and to thoroughly evaluate the hermeneutical power of his institutional analysis.

The author's exceptional personal experience "between revolution and reaction" and his immersion in different cultural traditions (mainly Swiss, English and Italian), helped him elaborate an original or "heterodox" view of the political and economic relationships. Jean Charles Léonard Sismondi was born in Geneva in 1773 in an upper class, Calvinist family of Italian origins. Similarly to several Swiss intellectuals, he had to emigrate to England during the Swiss Revolutionary period (1792–94) and, finally, to take refuge in Italy in the final years of the eighteenth century, before going back to Geneva (albeit continuing to frequently visit Italy afterwards).

During the historical period starting with the process of annexation to France (1798) until its adherence to the Swiss confederation, Geneva was transformed from a city-state into a Swiss canton. From a centre of commerce, in contact with both European and Mediterranean countries, it turned into a "lieu" where the consequences of a widespread system based on the industrial production threatened the economic organization based on both "trade" and high-quality products, and the distribution of properties fostering processes of reciprocal recognition and access of citizens to wealth.

During this crucial period, the political and economic debates adopting different preferences for different forms of governments or systems of production and exchange of goods were imbued with a particular sensitivity towards the possible ways "to be together while remaining ourselves". In a nutshell, they reveal a particular idea of sociability, which constitutes the "invisible" but effective "cement" of the social context. In the circle of Coppet liberty, it was considered as individual capacity for judgement, choice and creativity but fully flourishing only in a plural context and through a complex and fragile system of positive interactions with others. This idea of liberty was at the basis of social evolution and of economic well-being. In the Genevan debates, the deep aspiration to contribute to both independence, and human happiness, are often associated through the process of reconciliation of different social interests, and not simply yield to those of the majority but establishing concrete conditions for an effective experience of "unity". As a consequence, Sismondi's institutional research often overlaps with a search for structures and dynamics of aggregation of the various individual interests able to bring about a social order that reflects the underlying intrinsic and vital diversity, and avoids the risk of absolutism or centralization of power.

During his stay in England, Sismondi thoroughly read from the English tradition of historical and constitutional thought, namely Delolme, Blackstone and Woodeson, whose writing had an important formative influence on his view of the necessity for institutional guarantees to establish political and civil liberty and promote a well-functioning economy. In England, he also appreciated Adam Smith's views of economic activities seen as a space open to the expressions of individual and collective decisions concerning the production of wealth (a term encompassing here both well-being and goods). In Italy, he discovered the historical and economic tradition of civic humanism which, with its main focus on the importance of the plural dimension of civil life, became a pivotal reference for the author who devoted one of the most articulated and extended studies of the period to "social science".[1]

According to Sismondi, by exercising their individual capacity and collaborative actions citizens become more aware of their own "social power", especially as a means of attaining wealth and *bonheur*. As a co-author of collective well-being, each citizen could be considered the agent of reason and, thus, aspire to obtain some degree of recognized sovereignty rights. Sismondi's political and economic reflection is right at the heart of this interaction between the need to redefine the areas of civic action in order to rethink the substance of being reasonable, and therefore, to readjust the idea of wealth to a different notion of sovereignty. As far as his political reflection is concerned, Sismondi examines the difficult relationship between state power and individual self-determination by drawing on the republican tradition, especially identified with the experience of Medieval Italian republics, in order to delineate the modalities of a wider participation in the exercise of sovereignty. At the economic level, the author developed a historical, contextual and causal analysis of the different forms of production and their effects on the production of real wealth and happiness. Thus, in *Essais sur les constitutions des peuples libres* (1796–97) and in *Tableau de l'agriculture toscane* (1801), he began pointing out how the distribution of properties among citizens produces positive effects on the creation of wealth and well-being, due to the fact that a surplus share could be owned by workers.

Furthermore, the analysis of the specific property distributional structure serves to penetrate the crucial relationship between wealth and power within society thus distinguishing "real" wealth (effectively appropriated and enjoyed by every citizen) from "artificial" wealth (appropriated only by a social class or a group). This becomes clear in the course of Sismondi's

[1] *Etudes sur les sciences sociales*, published in 1836–38.

economic reflection constantly crossing the political one and starting from *Essais sur les constitutions des peuples libres* (1796) and *Tableau de l'agriculture toscane* (1801), until *Etudes sur l'économie politique* (1836). The size and the specific property structure of a social organization was, in Sismondi's opinion, the "political" element that needed to be taken into account in an economic analysis aimed at establishing the correct causal relationships between different kinds of social revenues, as well as between wealth and happiness. Farms or manufactures are not only considered by the author to be neutral spaces of production; their political dimension is also important. Thus, within the economic discourse, frameworks derived from political studies can become powerful tools that serve to detect the non-neutral value of the form of social institutions and to establish the wide and multi-stratified bases of economic analysis, as we can see in the *Tableau* developed in the text.

At the same time, in *De la richesse commerciale ou Principes d'économie politique appliqués à la législation du commerce* (1803), Sismondi was particularly interested in showing that an institutional organization articulated around manufactures based on specialized work and decentralized markets as the ones present in Geneva in that time, could produce the most of income for each single citizen, fostering not only her spending capacity but also her access and enjoyment of goods. Finally, in *Nouveaux principes d'économie politique ou de la richesse dans ses rapports avec la population* (1819, 1827) and *Etudes sur les sciences sociales* (1836–38), he sought to distinguish the industrial structures better at generating real growth, that is, not consisting simply of transfer of wealth from one social class to the other, thus making the "few" increasingly richer to the detriment and impoverishment of the "great part of a nation".

3.2 A Narrative of Liberty

It is difficult to adequately qualify Sismondi's scientific work using rigid disciplinary distinctions. Yet this cannot be avoided if our aim is to encapsulate his intellectual and human perspective within the image of a vague eclecticism rather than to enhance his intellectual need to narrate "liberty" through the lens of historical, political and economic discourse.

This statement is not based merely on an abstract observation of Sismondi's multidimensional approach evident in thousands of pages of economic, political and historical (and literary, philosophical and sociological) inquiry. It stems from the "ex ante" basis of all of Sismondi's science, that is, it was born as a "narrative" of the experience of liberty and because of this, it maintains all the features of its complexity as well as necessary nuances. This becomes clearer when Sismondi entrusts his vision of freedom to correspondence, diary pages or popular texts. But it remains true even when we refer to his scientific texts where the need to narrate and describe the experience of being free with different languages is repeatedly stressed:

> Political economy is not based solely on calculation since a host of moral observations cannot be subjected to it as they constantly alter the facts. Constantly leaning towards abstraction is tantamount for the mathematician to randomly removing essential figures from each of his equations.[2]

Or when the author stresses the importance of adopting history as the basis of social sciences because "it presents a collection of all the lessons given by experience".[3]

Furthermore, in the author's opinion, it is through history that the objects of economics, politics and social sciences, in general, have acquired a structure that can be studied from a scientific point of view.

Beginning with Medieval cities and republics,[4] a modern idea of liberty emerged from a political experience characterized by associations and mutual relationships. This new idea of liberty was understood primarily as non-domination, as a non-dependence on a single figure, as well as an expression of virtuous attitudes achieved thanks to experience of unity within society:

> The Italians [...] shared all that life, all that activity that their neighbours missed. In the middle of the chaos of the Middle Ages, their souls heated

[2] J. C. L. Sismondi (2012a [1803]) p. 80.

[3] J. C. L. Sismondi (1821), I, p. iv.

[4] Analysed by the author in the 16 volumes of *Histoire des republiques italiennes* published in 1809–18.

> up; it is the right motto incaluere animi, of the learned Muratori, who himself contributed so much through his work to unravel this chaos. Indeed a powerful and universal fermentation led to a new existence a dead and inert matter [...] The Italians, convinced that they had nothing to hope for from the empire, sought support in themselves; they associated, they promised each other mutual help, and even before coming together for defence and engaging in this noble league, they were learning devotion, patriotism, love of freedom, and that with these generous sentiments came the seeds of all virtues.[5]

But also modern economy[6] emerged as a fruit of a process of liberation of work that began with the abolition of slavery, the emancipation of feudal servitude, and the organization of work based on the division of labour and market exchange. Once the bonds that had subjugated individuals to the authority and control of the feudal dominus that guaranteed subsistence were broken, the citizens could produce surplus through their industrious activities, and discovered the value of individuality in being able to depend on one's own economic decisions. On different occasions, Sismondi stated that the complexity of actions resulting from the cooperation with others, required by the modern system of production and exchange, opened the field to experiencing a greater liberty.

This new and modern form of liberty, as well as the connected system of creation of wealth, required a "narrative" to be expressed in scientific terms.

As Sismondi wrote in *Nouveaux Principes,*[7] at first it was the "advisers" of the king (Sully, Colbert are among those he recalls) and the mercantilists who tried to thoroughly investigate the causes of the wealth of the nations, then the physiocrats who, even though they first recognized the production of surplus within the economic system, erroneously attributed its origin to a gift of nature, that is to the productivity of the earth and not to the work of man. It was the historical reflection on "the nature and causes of the wealth of nations" inaugurated by Adam Smith that

[5] J. C. L. Sismondi (1835), II, pp. 406–407 but also Idem (1809–18), I, p. 352.

[6] As Sismondi specifies in the first chapter of *Richesse commerciale* and further upholds in the second book of *Nouveaux principes*.

[7] Book I, Ch. 5.

proved decisive for the affirmation of political economy as a modern science. The latter was, thus, born with the reflections and historical narrative of the Scottish philosopher, of whom Sismondi several times declared to be a "disciple", and was then fully admitted to the social sciences by Sismondi's own writings:

> We have given the name social sciences to this whole division of the human sciences which relates to the formation and maintenance of societies, to all the speculations of theory, to all the layers of experience which can enlighten men and make them better attain the goal for which they unite and associate, namely their common good.[8]

3.3 "I Am a Liberal or, Rather, a Republican"[9]

In order to tackle the issue of "modern liberty" and its link to the notion of power, it is useful to refer to a tradition initiated in the context of the intellectual debates in the Coppet's circle, where classical liberalism was integrated with a republican perspective.[10]

The beginning of the intellectual, relational and cosmopolitan adventure of the Coppet group dates back to the Enlightenment. In fact, the founder of the Movement was Germaine de Stael who grew up in her mother's Paris "salon", a place where intellectuals of her time gathered to defend the ideas of her father M. Necker. In 1786, Germaine de Stael opened her own "salon", debating on and exchanging ideas with a new generation of intellectuals such as Benjamin Constant, Charles Victor de Bonstetten, August Wilhelm Schlegel, Wilhelm von Humboldt and, from 1804, Sismondi himself.

---

[8] Sismondi (2018a [1836–38], I, p. 5).

[9] As Sismondi states in 1835 in a letter to Eulalia de Saint-Aulaire: "I'm liberal and, better yet, Republican, but never Democratic. I have nothing in common with the part that frightens you by its violence, by wild theories, any more than with the one who is drunk with order and furious with tranquility". Sismondi (1933–54), III, p. 284.

[10] On "liberty of the moderns" in Constant's terms, see Constant (1820), pp. 238–374 and more generally on Sismondi and Coppet republican tradition of thought see Jaume (2000), Sofia (2000, 2007), Romani (2005), Urbinati (2012) and Dal Degan and Sofia (2014).

In particular, in the "light" of the Coppet culture, Sismondi sought to reinterpret the main "object" of liberalism, the difficult, dangerous and fragile relationship between individuals and social community, within a context signed by the profound reflection on tangible liberties and social relationships. In such an environment Sismondi developed a set of political ideas which, as he himself admits, would later change only slightly with respect to his first political writings.[11] Sismondi endeavours to give the outlines of Swiss liberalism:

> true liberalism as opposed to democracy, which dominates among practical men. With the former, I recognize rights to sovereignty only in the nation itself; but it is the sovereignty of intelligence that I invoke, not that of material force or number. It is the sovereignty of the constant as well as enlightened will; and I have endeavoured to establish how all should compete, how some should resist; how all rights, all feelings, should have their organs, so that the national reason matures, is purified, calmed down, before pronouncing its judgments.[12]

The doctrine of liberties had to be revised in the light of the need for participation in the new framework of modernity. As Constant wrote in his 1819 lecture at the Athenée Royale, while the ancient notion of liberty was based on the direct participation of citizens in political life, the modern one involved the protection of the rights of the individual to the pursuit of her own goals and, thus, required a more complex system of expression and transmission of individual to collective decisions:

> Far, then, gentlemen, from giving up either of the two kinds of freedom I have mentioned to you, we must, as I have demonstrated, learn to combine them with each other. By respecting their individual rights, by preserving their independence, by not disturbing their occupations, they must nevertheless consecrate their influence on public affairs, call upon them to compete, by their determinations and by their votes, in the exercise of power, guarantee them a right of control and supervision by the manifestation of

---

[11] In particular the *Essais sur les constitutions des peuples libres* (published in 1998 but written in 1798) which constitute a first draft of *Recherches sur les constitutions des peuples libres* and *Recherches*.
[12] Sismondi (1836–38), I, p. VI.

their opinions, and thus train them by the practice to these high functions, give them both the desire and the faculty to fulfil them.[13]

And one year earlier, in the first volume of *Histoire des républiques italiennes* published in 1818, Sismondi stated: "The liberty of the ancients, like their philosophy had virtue as its goal. The liberty of the moderns, like their philosophy, proposes no more than wellbeing". The problem was to find the way to combine the two, thus, "the legislator should no longer lose sight of the security of the citizens and the guarantees that the modern have into a system. But he should also remember that it is important to find ways to promote citizens' greater moral development". And the moral education of citizens was to be attained: "by multiplying their rights, by inviting them to share sovereignty and to redouble their interest in public affairs, they would come to know their duties and acquire a desire and an ability to fulfil them".[14]

In a nutshell, Sismondi's main problem becomes understanding the process that makes it possible to express the identity of the single individuals involved in modern social organizations which complexity could hamper their direct participation in political life.[15] More precisely, according to Sismondi, in modern societies political liberties are inseparable from civil ones and, therefore, strictly connected to the participation of citizens in social life with its multiple activities. The main issue here is, as in ancient societies, neither the direct expression of will within the context of the polis, nor untrusting citizens' preferences with regard to the voting mechanisms. What is needed is rather an effective presence of citizens in concrete activities where they can meet each other, activating in this way processes of dialogue, mutual relationships and association. Therefore, at a first level, the political space is rooted in civil life which, with its plural dimensions fosters the creation of "common values" and agreement among citizens.[16] Sismondi's pragmatic idea of the social

---

[13] Constant (1820) pp. 373–374.

[14] Sismondi (1809–18), I, pp. 405–406.

[15] If the purpose of reconciling the individual and social dimension of human experience fails, the ambiguity of modern age goals becomes blatant. Rousseau expressed this tragic characteristic of modern times with words of rare incisiveness as Starobinski (1971) demonstrates.

[16] Bruni and Zamagni (2007).

contract is conceived in order to identify and defend the integrity of these civil spaces from political interference. His idea belongs to the social contract tradition going back to Rousseau[17] in which the social pact consists of "thinking about what could be justified to others on grounds that they, if appropriately motivated, could not reasonably reject". The social contract is therefore considered a form of shared will that, through performative acts of words, manages to mediate our private demands and find a basis of justification that others also have reason to accept. Moreover, following his predecessor Rousseau,[18] Sismondi recognizes that "sovereignty belongs to the whole nation",[19] but he rejects the idea that the social pact implies the transfer of all individual rights to the Government and the political sphere. It rather serves to ensure the existence of the civil sphere where liberty is perceived as an infinity of renewable ways of being free and serves as the basis of the perception and experience of personal development and concrete *bonheur*.[20] It is easy to imagine that for Sismondi liberty was strictly linked to the possibility of activating human capabilities contained in the acknowledgement of human rights. Government is called to operate in a way to recognize and distribute equal rights among all citizens so as to allow for the free expression of capabilities. This perspective makes Sismondi's approach similar to the contemporary reflection of Amartya Sen. In fact, liberty becomes effective only when it is shared by all social parties; it is attained only if all citizens can enjoy equal conditions of well-being.[21] Finally, within modern societies, liberty does not exclude the existence of moral and civil values but is rather based on them. As a matter of fact, no actual contract

[17] Scanlon (1998), p. 5.

[18] Rousseau was read daily in Sismondi home as can be seen from the report that Sismondi's mother entrusts to her diaries, see Dal Degan (2006). More generally, on the influence of Rousseau on Sismondi's political thought, see Minerbi (1965), Sofia (1981, 1997, 2000), Paulet-Grandguillot (2010).

[19] Sismondi (1965), p. 86.

[20] In relation to the concept of liberty understood as the outcome of the historical process of civilization after the rupture of feudal bonds which transforms individual differences (les intérêts divers) into common values and ideas (*opinion publique*), see Pappe (1979), while for the Scottish historical school which has many affinities with Sismondi's idea of liberty see Meinecke (1954), pp. 155–196 and Cantimori (1959), pp. 557–563.

[21] As he precises in his *Ressources de la Toscane* (1799) now published in Sismondi (2012b), p. 26.

between citizens would be possible without the presence of reciprocity and mutual recognition which, as in the classical republican tradition, are recognized to lay the basis for any experience of unity and association within society. In a nutshell, the difficult relationship between diversity and unity, between plurality and singularity, translating the age-old question of the relationship among the many, the few and the individual, could not be solved immediately by choosing a democratic or an absolutist model. In these cases, minorities or individuals would be excluded from political processes. It rather had to be submitted to a new ideal of "participation" according to which the "ratio" of modernity, linked to the perception of individual identity, would be embedded in the "relationship" per se[22] as in the republican tradition.

Through this complex conception of social contract and liberties, Sismondi combines, on one hand, the eighteenth-century heritage of a civil life concept based on the concrete experiences of citizens who, by meeting, talking and exchanging produce the substance of the social dimension of life, and, on the other, the acquisitions of modernity in terms of individual interests. The output of this scientific operation was one of the last attempts undertaken in Europe to save the existence and integrity of civil life from its submission to political conduct, in an attempt to oppose State Government (Hobbes) and idealistic liberalism, to the generative power of the concrete experience of human beings. This clarifies why it would be simplistic to ascribe the author either to the liberal tradition due to the simple fact that he acted without compulsion and external impositions (*Richesse Commerciale*) or, alternatively, to the interventionist positions (*Nouveaux Principes*).[23] This clarification is important in order to understand better that the juvenile and, later, more mature phase of his thought and production did not reflect different kinds of inspiration. Sismondi attempted to solve the issue of reconciling

[22] Jaume brilliantly describes the drift of the reflection on liberty at Coppet which is deeply different from the doctrine which will affirm based on an abstract idea of reason, cfr. Jaume (2000), pp. 226–227. About the idea of participation see Dupuigrenet-Desroussilles (1972).

[23] The question of conversion has caused much discussion in our discipline over the years partially compromising an adequate comprehension of some important aspects of Sismondi's approach to the study of social phenomena. On the idea of Sismondi's "conversion" from Smithian to Interventionist positions see Babel (1967), Nuccio (1974), Batignani Bartolozzi (1978), Roggi (1979), Gislain (2013).

different points of view by marrying the Smithian vision on the role played by interests in supporting the processes of economic and social development, with the ideas established in the Coppet circle, where Rousseau's social contract theory was interpreted in favour of the concrete participation in civil life.[24] The need to think of new ways of defining the difficult relationship between individuals and plurality, mainly perceived in its economic dimension, becomes here imperative. In a nutshell, the quality of the processes of integration of different individuals in a social group determines the conditions of liberty and allows avoiding the distinct risks of absolutism (triumph of one) and slavery ("separation").[25] "Reciprocal independence" is one of the pivotal concepts coined by Sismondi in his economic writings. It brings together ideas of sociability and liberty and it is useful to describe human interactions at the basis of modern experience of "unitiy" within society.

3.4 The Cement of Society

The topic of the theory of relationships recurs throughout the whole intellectual production of Sismondi. It constitutes the field where Hume's gnoseological question on what did the "cement of the universe" consist in,[26] was transposed. The problem of organizing human experience into a rational and unified account was transformed into the pragmatic and ethical question on the possibility of establishing an agreement among different human beings. In this perspective, economic science assumes a particular role. As a matter fact, as a science of "measure", "commerce", of human competition to create wealth and of distribution, it is immediately concerned with the following challenge: to offer a pragmatic solution

[24] In relation Sismondi's critical reading of Rousseau, see Sismondi (1965) and Sofia (1981).

[25] In line with the Aristotelian tradition, Sismondi sees separation as the first precondition of slavery.

[26] Hume wrote: "It will be easy to conceive of what vast consequences these principles must be in the science of human nature, if we consider that so far as regards the mind. These are the only links that bind the parts of the universe together, or connect us with any person or object exterior to ourselves. For as it is by means of thought only that any thing operates upon our passions, and as these are the only that any thing operates upon passions, and as these are the only ties of our thoughts, they are really *to us* the cement of the universe", Hume (2007 [1740]), p. 417.

to the question of the possibility of establishing social bonds and common evaluations within societies. A problem that Sismondi faced at the political level in *Essais* and *Recherches sur les constitutions des peuples libres,* and that, thanks to the economic processes, seems to find more effective solutions.

In this perspective, it would be useful to underline that drawing a distinction line between two separate phases in Sismondi's intellectual production (the Smithian one associated with *Richesse commerciale* and the critical one with *Nouveaux principes*) does not help us to grasp the theoretical message of the economist who describes himself as a Smithian disciple in *Richesse commerciale* as well as in *Nouveaux principes.*[27] It would be rather more helpful taking into account Sismondi's schemas of analysis referring to specific structural *trama* and adopted with reference to different productive contexts: agricultural, commercial or industrial. In particular, the two crucial elements to be focused on in order to describe the economic functioning within these contexts, are property rights distribution implemented and the access to collective spaces such as markets. While in economic systems like the one in the United States analysed in *Essais,* or the one in Tuscany described in *Tableau* and *Etudes*, or the one in Leman region focused in *Richesse commerciale*, a new form of independence could be experienced thanks to a better distribution of property rights and a more flexible access to the productive spaces and markets, the same experience was not possible in industrial systems based on the division of social classes and property rights concentration (of capitals and means of production). In the latter case, establishing more equal conditions for accessing civil spaces was of crucial importance in order to guarantee to every citizen a position within society and the possibility to strive for well-being.[28] More precisely, the possibility of moral and civil education derives both "from another cause, a more distant cause, the nature of properties[29]", and wealth: "The less the rent of the land is, all things equal, and the greater the part of its product to be distributed between the farmer and the labourer, the greater will be the profit of the former, and

[27] On this topic, see editors' Introduction to Sismondi (2015b).

[28] In fact, Sismondi conceived property rights as "positional rights".

[29] Sismondi (1998), pp. 568–569.

the wage of the latter, but the rent of the land will be all the less as there will be more good land to establish, and fewer farmers to take it".

3.5 Reciprocal Independence

In his historical writings, drawing on Adam Smith's view, Sismondi states[30] that by combining the perception of one's personal independence and being an important part of a whole, the modern sentiment of reciprocal independence becomes the reflection of the "reason". Such a reciprocal independence is mainly experienced in the realm of commercial activities which are based on a set of civil virtues, as if an "invisible hand" had infused a sentiment of dignity and personal independence in the human spirit:

> An invisible hand, a liberal hand seemed to have sowed in all hearts at the same time the feeling of man's dignity and natural independence.[31]

At a first stage, the feeling of independence overlaps with the perception of one's personal identity and intangibility. According to Sismondi, however, it has a plural, more complex value: it is the outcome of the division of labour and market exchange which set the preconditions for the production of surplus gains as well as the consequent emancipation of human beings from feudal dependence:

> It was then that the human race spread over the face of the earth, and that in mutual independence, in the midst of abundance and virtues, the nations whose fate would later be played by politics and war grew up.[32]

In Adam Smith's perspective, reciprocal independence represents the most important achievement of modernity. In a famous paragraph of the *Wealth of Nations* he writes:

---

[30] The concept of independence is largely reiterated in *Etudes sur les sciences sociales*. More precisely, it is defined like "reciprocal independence" and described in relation to economic development in the essay devoted to *Richesse territoriale*, see Sismondi (2018b [1836–38]), p. 355.

[31] Sismondi (1809–1818), I, p. 401.

[32] Sismondi (1836–1838), vol. II, p. 117.

> It is not from the benevolence of the butcher, the brewer, or the baker that we expect our dinner, but from their regard to their own interest. We address ourselves not to their humanity but to their self-love, and never talk to them of our own necessities, but of their advantages.[33]

Smith underlines two possible perspectives to citizens' choices: on the one hand, it is possible to live like a dog or beggar depending on the benevolence of the butcher for survival; on the other hand, one can exchange with others. From Smith's point of view, independence from others is the result of multiplying human relationships. Since the single individual is involved in a series of relationships with different actors, he/she does not finally depend on anyone and has, therefore, greater freedom. Any tradesman or craftsman derives her income from hundreds or thousands of customers. Although, to a certain extent, she is related to each one of them, in reality she does not depend on anyone in an exclusive way. In this sense, the "dispersion" or multiplication of relationships with others as a consequence of the breakdown of the vertical and hierarchical bonds within society, reduce the risk of submission of one's destiny to the power of another person's single will.

According to Smith, plural and market relationships make citizens mutually independent. However, in order to gain such independence, the stability of individual existence must be protected similarly to social plurality. In this sense, the Smithian concept of "reciprocal independence" had to be combined with a more accurate reflection on the underlying institutional structures and forms that interpersonal relationships took in a given social context. Following this perspective, the ideas established in the Coppet circle,[34] helped Sismondi analyse the institutional and relational structure of societies in an attempt to identify which organizations would be more appropriate for making citizen's participation to civil life more effective.

In *History,* Sismondi emphasizes that the energy or life principle of individuals and human organizations is related to the bringing about of unity among the different elements of society. Such unity has to be built

[33] Smith (1976 [1776]), p. 17.

[34] In relation to the critical reading of Rousseau by Sismondi, see Minerbi (1965), Sofia (1981) and Raffaelli (1999).

upon mutual independence so as not to turn into dependence or despotism,[35] and that constitutes the fundamental energy of a social group as he stated in a beautiful page of *Chute de l'empire romain*:

> this force resembles, by its effects, the vital principle found in man and in all organized beings; but it is not like him a mystery of nature.[36]

This force is neither a mystery of nature, nor the product of an invisible hand, but rather the final product of a complex process of establishing relationships within which reciprocity can be attained together with liberty and equality.

In order to identify such elements, we may refer to one of the last works of Sismondi which can, in a way, be considered a summary of his thoughts on social organization and civil life: *The colonies of the ancients compared to those of moderns*. This article published in "Bibliothèque Universelle" in 1837 opens with the following note: if we want to know the causes that contributed to spreading all the advantages connected to social life and civilization, we have to observe colonies and their history. Regarding ancient colonies we can observe the elements that make their political, social, cultural and economic organization "civil" because the model of the ancient colonies was the *cité,* while the model of the modern ones is the empire.

Because the foundation act of a colony is destructive in itself of all social links, the sentiment of social life is the most important to re-establish:

> for mutual need to bring them together, for fraternity to be established between adventurers, often resembled only by chance, they must begin by being small, they must feel weak between strangers.[37]

Moreover, the distance between citizens should not be such as to cause the decline of their direct relationships:

---

[35] J. C. L. Sismondi (1837), p. 378 and p. 104.

[36] Idem, p. 247.

[37] Sismondi (2015a), p. 712.

> We must be careful not to allow them to disperse in the deserts, for if they can establish their dwelling at a great distance from all their brothers, soon they will no longer recognize any laws other than their own whims.

Without frequent and direct relationships with others, the human being "foreign at his equals", cannot exercise "the art of persuasion" and enjoy the "art of conversation". Moreover, away from the gaze of his fellows, the single will be deprived of the experience of recognition, emulation and limits. To see and to be seen is a sort of basic capability, a "positional right", in Sismondi's terms, directly involved in the creation of goods. According to Smith, the partially positive[38] role of sight is highlighted by the metaphor of the "impartial spectator", who makes individual behaviour, ideas and values uniform and socially acceptable, while order is a consequence of the unintentional action of an invisible hand. Bentham conceptualizes the existence of a central eye, exercising invisible control on the thoughts and desires of individuals, leading to their re-civilization, while from Sismondi's point of view, it is thanks to the very activity of meeting gazes that a fellow feeling is established among human beings.

In a society where everyone, in her own social position, can meet the gaze of others, recognizing their identity, the formation of the motivational bases of the single individual can be influenced by plurality. As Sismondi recognized, there is a "power of attraction" of sight which enables experiencing the feelings and perspectives of others.[39] Meeting someone else's gaze, sharing their opinions and sentiments, in a frequent exercise of putting oneself in the shoes of others, is a precondition of the formation of the invisible "capital" consisting of civic virtues, confidence, trust, social credit (in contemporary terms, social capital) on which good economic functioning is grounded. When distance between agents increases and results into an actual separation, this invisible but powerful substance elapses. In *Nouveaux principes,* Sismondi further enriches his

---

[38] "Positive" in the sense of "constructive" and having the effect of reinforcement on the agent's motivations. The opposite of exercising control and having a limiting effect on the individual agent.

[39] During Sismondi's lifetime, many studies on the eye, vision and mind's power of attraction were undertaken. Goethe wrote *Elective Affinities* in 1809 which was translated into French in 1810; Cabanis wrote about "elective attraction", see Delon (1988), pp. 174–175.

view of this ability "to see" and gives it an additional informative value[40] as a crucial element of "economic" imagination. More precisely, in times of economic crisis, the ability to see into the future becomes vital in order to determine the right direction and measure of various investment decisions, thus, foresee the potential levels of demand, wages and, subsequently, decide whether to diminish or increase production. As a matter of fact, in a society in which workers are in a condition of submission to capitalists, investment decisions are shaped by the "blind" and "narcissistic" desire for profit without connection neither with the real conditions of markets, nor with effective demand.

In a nutshell, a society where everyone, from her own social position, has the possibility to meet each other's eyes, in a basic social interaction in which their identity is reflected, the formation of individual motivation is inclined to consider the presence of others.

3.6 "Positional" Power

Conscious of the political value of the spatial and temporal structure of economic systems, Sismondi uses theoretical and analytical instruments that can help reveal the contextual and historical nature of power. The integration within his economic analysis of historical, political and even psychological dimensions, responds to the need to detect the tacit or implicit influence of the institutional context and moral attitudes of society on economic functioning. As the author clarifies in 1837, he refers to economic institutions in order to detect the architecture of human and social relations, just as a naturalist or an antiquarian would:

> Moreover, I am convinced that we have fallen into serious errors, for having always wanted to generalize everything that has to do with the social sciences. On the contrary, it is in the details that it is essential to study the human condition. It is necessary to be attached sometimes to time, sometimes to a country, sometimes to a profession, to see well what is the man, and how the institutions act on him.[41]

[40] For an interesting comment on the topic, see Stiglitz (2000).

[41] Sismondi J. C. L. (1836–38), II, p. IV.

In particular, Sismondi's analytical progress highlights the existence of some conditions that cannot be established ceteris paribus. This is clearly stated in his article "Balance des consommations avec les productions"[42] in which Sismondi criticizes the Ricardian perspective to the natural economic mechanism of adjustment between supply and demand, observing that such adjustment appears spontaneous only if we take away considerations of space and time, that is, the structural dimensions of our social experience and life:

> To study this social mechanism, we will choose agriculture, as an example, and we will see in agriculture only ploughing, ignoring its other products… but at the same time, we will take society in its current organization, with workers without property, whose salary is fixed by competition, and that their master can dismiss, as soon as he no longer needs their work, because it is precisely on this social organization that our objection bears.[43]

In particular, taking into account the specific structure of property rights distribution in a certain context serves to analyse the relationship between the increasing wealth at disposal of every citizen and the centralization of power within society, as I have already underlined taking into account Sismondi's reflection on United States and Leman region. Here I shall focus on Sismondi's first economic publication, *Tableau de l'agriculture toscane* for the part dedicated to the size of farms.[44] In paragraph XXIII "Grandeur des fermes", Sismondi admits that he focused on one of the questions "the most thorny and complicated". The size and specific structure of properties present in a social organization was, in fact, the "political" element that needed to be taken into account in an economic analysis aimed at establishing the correct causal relationships among different kinds of social revenues, and between wealth and happiness. Farms are not only considered by the author to be neutral spaces of production; their political dimension is also important. Therefore, frameworks derived

[42] Published in 1824 in *Revue Encyclopédique* and later reprinted in the second edition of *Nouveaux Principes*.

[43] Sismondi (2015b [1827]) p. 573.

[44] Which was imported from his political writing, *Essais sur les constitutions des peuples libres*. See Dal Degan (2002).

from political studies can be used as powerful tools also in the economic analysis. More precisely, they can serve to detect the potentially non-neutral value of the kind of social institutions adopted and to set wider and multi-stratified bases for the economic analysis.

All this becomes more clear if we take into account an "episode" described by Sismondi in his personal correspondence. A "short debate" with his philosophy teacher at the Academy of Geneva, Pierre Prevost,[45] led Sismondi to clarify that an important element had to be taken into account in economic analysis in order to explain the dynamic of production of social wealth: property rights distribution. In the *Tableau of agriculture toscane*, Sismondi writes that the production of "produit brut" (gross product),[46] the real indicator of wealth, also depends on the size of farms, because only through a decentralized spread of *petites fermes*, the surplus produced could be transformed into real wealth for people and not just into profit for a few landowners: "The net product may be higher in the vast domains but the gross product is more considerable in the small ones; they feed a larger population".[47]

However, in interpreting Adam Smith's view on this topic, Pierre Prévost states that Sismondi could not make the increase in profit and the progressive decrease of land revenues dependent on the farms' size. There was another crucial element: "wages increase in direct proportion to the progress".[48] The automatic increase of workers' income as a due to progress was precisely the core of the reasoning criticized by Sismondi. The direction of changes in revenue levels depended, in his view, on the particular property right structure present in a specific context, that is, on the institutional structure of society.

In particular, Sismondi invokes a decentralized property right structure, on the one hand, as a means to a greater efficiency in the distribution of wealth among citizens. On the other hand, the specific distribution of

[45] Pierre Prévost translated the *Philosophical Essays* of Adam Smith and the *Account of the life and writings of Adam Smith* of Dugald Stewart.

[46] In Sismondi's economic analysis the distinction between "produit brut" and "produit net" has a central value for identifying a real increasing of wealth for all participants to economic activity. On these concepts, see Dal Degan (2014).

[47] About this aspect, cfr. Gislain (2001), pp. 335–421.

[48] Letter to Sismondi, March 3, 1802, in Sismondi's Archive of Pescia (Florence), AS A 16 n. 182.

property rights in a social context determines the direction of causal links between economic factors such as profits and salaries.[49] Moreover, property enables the exercise of personal powers in the social production of values and images, the participation in the organization of the *polis,* as well as the control of the means of production to respond to the emerging needs of society. A social position from which it is possible to directly participate in the civic life, is a necessary condition to the attainment of knowledge and contribution to the production of social values—the *opinion publique* in Sismondi's terms—through the individual intellectual activity, and, simultaneously, the control over the economic process. If one has no opinion or perspective, he/she is excluded from social functions, access to surplus and investment decisions. On the contrary, sharing opinions is a precondition for the formation of the invisible "capital" consisting of civil virtues, confidence, trust, social credit (in contemporary terms, social capital) on which good economic functioning is grounded.

3.7 Managing Time as a Key for Non-domination

In subsequent phases of his intellectual activity, Sismondi focused on the mechanisms of concentration of capital and power characterizing industrial societies. *Nouveaux principes,*[50] constitute the masterpiece of the critical economist. In this work, Sismondi conducted an analysis of the economic system based on salaried work, concentration of capitals and division of classes with reference to the concrete experience of England which he knew from the writings of J. B. Say (*De l'Angleterre*), Lord Brougham, and also thanks to his personal relationships with Carlyle and Mackintosh. Sismondi focused, in particular, on time as an element inherent to the structure of the social organization. Taking into account the temporal dimension of our industrial organizations, he grasped the entrenched and invisible powers linked to the capitalistic mechanism of production and distribution of wealth, and denounced the negative

[49] Letter from Sismondi to Pièrre Prevost, March 2, 1801, in Sismondi (1933–1954), pp. 14–16.

[50] Which first edition was published in 1819, and a second one – in 1827.

influence of this "historical" mechanism on the conditions of life in industrial societies. It is as a consequence of this temporal structure that workers depend on capitalists for their subsistence and are obliged to accept bad work conditions. However, as Rousseau observed, it is not possible to establish a contract in which one party is forced to accept the conditions imposed by the other. Sismondi enhanced:

> civil duties are destroyed, the social contract is nothing more than a cruel fiction, for the individual who dies of misery.[51]

Sismondi criticized the fact that the income of workers depended on decisions taken by capitalists at the initial stage of production (*ex ante*), and not on the basis of the effective surplus obtained through the market exchange (*ex post*).[52] Such decisions are determined by capital and not on the basis of a social process of recognition of the value of the final product on the market. Thus:

> work which forms the poor's income only acquires commercial value when exchanged with circulating capital; it devotes itself entirely against this capital and its price decreases when this capital decreases.[53]

Therefore, capitalist motivations are moulded by individual interests to reduce the workers' share of wealth and do not reflect the social interests which can be formed only in a system where capital and work are somehow associated:

> The attention of the manufacturer is therefore constantly directed to finding ways to make savings in labour or the use of materials which would enable him to sell at a better price than his competitors…these savings are constantly reduced, in the end, to employing less work for the same product.[54]

---

[51] Sismondi (2012b), p. 26.

[52] As Schumpeter wrote about Sismondi's analytical model: "(it) is a system of periodicities and lags, the money income in the period 't' responds to decisions taken in the same period but they are spent for the product that is the outcome of the previous period 't-1' so that the imbalances between two quantities can be frequent", see Schumpeter (1954), p. 494.

[53] Sismondi (2015b [1827]), p. 215.

[54] *Idem.*

The economic dynamics based on such motivations and behaviours become cumulative and contribute to producing a social structure characterized by the concentration of wealth and a locked market. This structure can reproduce and reinforce itself by further enlarging exchanges:

> In this way the concentration of fortunes among a small number of owners means the interior market is increasingly squeezed and industry is increasingly reduced to seeking outlets in foreign markets.[55]

Furthermore, shedding light on the intrinsic limits of the capitalist system due to its temporary nature, enables recognizing the information weakness of a system of production in which investment decisions and demand for consumption are taken in two separate periods.[56]

In Sismondi's words:

> The knowledge that isolated man had of his own means and needs had to be replaced by knowledge of the market, including its demand and extent, for which social man works.[57]

and

> The number of consumers, their tastes, the extent of their consumption and income, constitute the market for which each producer works. Each of these four elements is variable independently of the other three and each of these variations delay or accelerate sale…These market revolutions are difficult to understand in exact terms and are difficult to calculate.[58]

According to Sismondi, attitudes towards sharing both losses and surplus become the key factor to re-establish the system of production on more reactive and efficient bases, taking into account the real distribution of resources and the role of "demand".

---

[55] *Idem*, p. 336.

[56] Sowell (1972) revealed: "Sismondi was concerned with production for the following year, with reproduction. He was concerned with whether expectations *ex ante* were realized *ex post*".

[57] Sismondi (2015b) p. 214.

[58] *Idem*, p. 214.

In order to underline in what way shared-oriented relations can help facing critical situations between production and consumption whenever they occur in his 1824 article "Sur la balance des consommations avec les productions", published in *Revue Encyclopedique*, he wrote:

> The exchange of each year must cause a small loss, at the same time as it improves the future condition. If this loss is small and well distributed, everyone bears it without complaining about his income, that is what the national economy is all about, and the series of these small sacrifices increases capital and public wealth.[59]

According to Sismondi, following what can be seen as a paradoxical logic, there is a value inherent the experienced "losses" that the economic sphere needs to learn to appreciate. Losses, understood as small sacrifices, are the necessary adjustments that each economic actor has to be ready to incur so that everyone's income can be proportionate to the surplus achieved throughout the previous economic cycle (even when it has decreased because the demand has not been adjusted yet).

Moreover, sharing the economic losses also means dividing the weight of difficulties among all responsible individuals, and giving value even to downturns in the economic cycle by fostering the use of time for human training, socialization and innovation in the management of firms.

Following an even more interesting perspective, the element of sharing losses means that "savings" necessary for investments, have to be sustained by every participant of the production process. In fact, in Sismondi's vision of the economic dynamics, the extension of the market (and then of production) should not be obtained through the reduction neither of prices, nor of the levels of the main factor directly controlled by capitalists —wages. On the contrary, market expansion has to be attained thanks to the real increase of wealth, that is, thanks to the increased purchasing power resulting from a better surplus distribution. It is, in fact, the expansion of demand that induces a real process of economic growth and not the simple reduction of production costs.

As a matter of fact, focusing on enterprise organization and particularly on the ways of distributing surplus gains, Sismondi displays a way to

[59] Sismondi (2015b), p. 91.

share profits among all participants that can be considered as the outcome of a sort of incomplete contract according to which the share due to each party is decided ex post on the basis of the effective gain obtained on the market.[60]

In relation to this aspect, Demaria observes:

> The very important Sismondi, the one that will last for centuries is not so much the literary Sismondi, the historical and passionate political correspondent …so much as another Sismondi…the theoretical economist", in his role as critic of the law of markets and advocate of the law of effective demand. He was able to develop these two positions because he "formulated economic analysis on the division of economic time in 'theoretical' periods of time, each inevitably distinctive and insisted on the technical necessity of this division".[61]

In a similar perspective, scholars such as A. Aftalion, G. Demaria, J.A. Schumpeter, T. Sowell, A. Parguez and J. Gislain highlighted the importance of the Sismondian operation which, through the construction of a dynamic model of the economic cycle, introduces time as a fundamental dimension to explain the possibilities of economic growth for the benefit of all.[62]

3.8 Conclusion

Pointing out the importance that Sismondi recognized to structural elements such as distribution of properties, participative institutions, different systems of production and organization of time, as well as to non-material factors concerning the form of interpersonal relationships, my objective was to emphasize the critical role of Sismondi's economic analysis. Sismondi would turn, through history, to politics and economics

[60] See Hart (1995) and Hart and Moore (1999). For a reflexion about incomplete contracts in relation to Sismondi, see Dal Degan (2013).

[61] Demaria (1973), pp. 263 e ss.

[62] As their writings confirm, the relevance of the Sismondian economic reflexion was obtained by integrating the temporal dimension in analytical reconstruction.

to find the traits of a social asset demonstrably effective in dissolving the oxymoronic condition of man called on to challenge the paradox of a bond that does not bond or liberty that constrains to a relationship. The outcome of these inquiries, in thousands of pages, makes up the material of his social science. In particular, the social scientist taking into account spatial and temporal dimensions of reality and maintaining the dynamical nature of phenomena into rational reconstruction, could bring the concept of sociability back to the hearth of economic theory.

References

Babel, A. (1967). Sismondi. Sa 'conversion' et son apport aux sciences économiques et sociales. *Cahiers d'histoire publiés par les Universités de Clermont-Lyon-Grenoble, XII*(1–2), 143–152.

Batignani Bartolozzi, S. (1978). *Si può parlare di una seconda conversione di Sismondi economista? Ricerche Storiche*, mag-ago, *8*, 437–473.

Bruni, L., & Zamagni, S. (2007). *Civil Economy: Efficiency, Equity, Public Happiness*. Oxford: Peter Lang.

Cantimori, D. (1959). *Studi di storia*. Torino: Einaudi.

Constant, B. (1820). *De la liberté des anciens comparée à celle des modernes, in Id., Cours de politique constitutionnelle* (Vol. IV, pp. 238–374). Paris/Rouen: Béchet.

Dal Degan, F. (2002). La permanenza della natura e la "scoperta" della forma istituzionale nell'analisi economico-sociale di Sismondi: racconto di un inizio. *Storia del pensiero economico, 43*, 153–182.

Dal Degan, F. (2006). *Sismondi nei diari della madre. 1792–794 e 1809*. Bologna: Pàtron.

Dal Degan, F. (2013). L'économie comme espace de participation : le regard de Sismondi. In B. Kapossy & P. Bridel (Eds.), *Modern Republicanism and Critical Liberalism*. Genève: Slatkine.

Dal Degan, F. (2014). *Sismondi – Che cos'è l'economia*. Roma: Donzelli.

Dal Degan, F., & Sofia, F. (2014). Constant as a Reader of Sismondi. In F. Allisson & R. Baranzini (Eds.), *Economics and Other Branches in the Shade of the Oak Tree: Essays in Honour of Pascal Bridel* (pp. 135–147). London: Pickering & Chatto.

Delon, M. (1988). *L'idée d'énergie au tournant des Lumières (1770–1820)*. Paris: Presses Universitaires de France.

Demaria, G. (1973). Il Sismondi veramente importante. In *Atti del Colloquio internazionale sul Sismondi*, Pescia, 8–10 settembre 1970. Roma: Accademia dei Lincei.

Dupuigrenet-Desroussilles, G. (1972). Sismondi et la participation. *Economies et sociétés*, Paris, *VI*, 9–10.

Gislain, J.-J. (2001). Le modèle économique et social toscan de Sismondi et la pensée économique francaise au dix-neuvième siècle. In F. Sofia (Ed.), *Sismondi e la civiltà toscana* (pp. 395–421). Firenze: Olschki.

Gislain, J.-J. (2013). La conversion de Sismondi. *Cahiers d'économie Politique/ Papers in Political Economy*, *64*(1), 111–134.

Hart, O. (1995). *Firms, Contracts and Financial Structure*. Oxford: Oxford University Press.

Hart, O., & Moore, J. (1999). Foundations of Incomplete Contracts. *Review of Economic Studies*, *66*, 115–138.

Hume, D. (1740). *An Abstract of a Book Lately Published Entituled a Treatise of Human Nature & c: Wherein the Chief Argument of That Book Is Farther Illustrated and Explained*. London: Borbet.

Hume, D. (2007 [1740]). *A Treatise of Human Nature*. Oxford: Oxford University Press.

Jaume, L. (Ed.). (2000). *Coppet, creuset de l'esprit libéral. Les idées politiques et constitutionnelles du groupe de Madame de Staël* (pp. 75–98). Paris: Economica.

Meinecke, F. (1954). *Le origini dello storicismo*. Firenze: Sansoni.

Minerbi, M. (1965). Introduction. In J. C. L. Sismondi (Ed.), *Recherches sur les constitutions des peuples libres*. Genève: Droz.

Nuccio, O. (1974). La presunta conversione di Simonde de Sismondi. *Rivista di Politica Economica*, agosto, 383–419.

Pappe, H. O. (1979). Sismondi's System of Liberty. *Journal of the History of Ideas*, *40*(2), 251–266.

Paulet-Grandguillot, E. (2010). *Libéralisme et Démocratie. De Sismondi à Constant, à partir du Contrat social (1801–1806)*. Genève: Slatkine.

Raffaelli, T. (1999). Citizenship and the Market. Roussevian and Smithian Themes in the Evolution of Sismondi's Thought. In G. F. Davanzati & V. Gioia (Eds.), *Reflections on Economic Development. From the Enlightenment to the Classical School* (pp. 63–64). Lecce: Milella.

Roggi, P. (1979). La 'effettiva conversione' di Simonde de Sismondi. *Bollettino degli Interessi Sardi*, pp. 111–26.

Romani, R. (2005). The Republican Foundations of Sismondi's Nouveaux Principes d'économie politique. *History of European Ideas*, *XXXI*, 17–33.

Salis de, J.-R. (1932). *Sismondi, 1773–1842. La Vie et l'Œuvre d'un cosmopolite philosophe*. Paris: Champion.

Scanlon, T. M. (1998). *What We Owe to Each Other*. Cambridge, MA/London: Harvard University Press.

Schumpeter, J. A. (1954 [1983]). *Histoire de l'analyse économique*. Tome II. L'Âge Classique (1790 à 1870). Paris: Gallimard, coll. " nrf".

Sismondi, J. C. L. (1809–18). *Histoire des Républiques italiennes du Moyen-Age*, I–XVI. Paris: Nicolle; Treuttel et Würtz.

Sismondi, J. C. L. (1821). *Histoire des Français* (Vol. I). Paris: Treuttel et Wurtz.

Sismondi, J. C. L. (1824). Sur la balance des consommations avec les productions. *Revue Encyclopédique, XXII*, 264–298.

Sismondi, J. C. L. (1835). *Histoire de la chute de l'empire romain*. Paris: Treuttel et Wurtz.

Sismondi, J. C. L. (1836–38). *Etudes sur les sciences sociales.* 3 voll. Paris: Treuttel et Wurtz.

Sismondi, J. C. L. (1837). *Histoire de la chute de l'Empire Romain et du declin de la civilisation*. Bruxelles: Wahlen.

Sismondi, J. C. L. (1933–54). *Epistolario*. Firenze: La Nuova Italia.

Sismondi, J. C. L. (1965). *Recherches sur les constitutions des peuples libres*. Genève: Droz.

Sismondi, J. C. L. (1998). *Essais sur les constitutions des peuples libres*, a cura di Di Reda R. Roma: Jouvence.

Sismondi, J. C. L. (Bridel, P., Dal Degan, F., & Eyguesier, N., Eds.). (2012a [1803]). *De la richesse commerciale ou principes d'économie politique appliqués à la Législation du Commerce*, vol. II, Œuvres Economiques Complètes. Paris: Economica.

Sismondi, J. C. L. (Bridel, P., Dal Degan, F., & Eyguesier, N., Eds.). (2012b). *Ecrits d'économie politique 1799–1815*, vol. III, Œuvres Economiques Complètes. Paris: Economica.

Sismondi, J. C. L. (Bridel P., Dal Degan F., & Eyguesier N., Eds.). (2015a). *Ecrits d'économie politique 1816–1842*, Œuvres Economiques Complètes, vol. IV. Paris: Economica.

Sismondi, J. C. L. (Bridel P., Dal Degan F., Eyguesier N., Eds.). (2015b). *Nouveaux principes d'économie politique*, Œuvres Economiques Complètes, vol. V. Paris: Economica.

Sismondi, J. C. L. (Bridel P., Dal Degan F., & Eyguesier N., Eds.). (2018a). *Tableau de l'agriculture toscane*, Œuvres Economiques Complètes, vol. I. Paris: Economica.

Sismondi, J. C. L. (Bridel P., Dal Degan F., & Eyguesier N., Eds.). (2018b). *Etudes sur les sciences sociales*, Œuvres Economiques Complètes, vol. VI. Paris: Economica.

Smith, A. (1976 [1776]). *An Inquiry into the Nature and Causes of the Wealth of Nations*. 2 volumes. Oxford: Clarendon Press.

Sofia, F. (1981). Sul pensiero politico-costituzionale del giovane Sismondi. *Rassegna Storica del Risorgimento, LXVIII*, 131–147.

Sofia, F. (1997). Sismondi tra rivoluzione e reazione. In *Sismondi esule a Pescia: i tempi e i luoghi, Atti della giornata di studi – Pescia*, 4 novembre, 1995. Pescia: Benedetti.

Sofia, F. (2000). Formes constitutionnelles et organisations de la société. In L. Jaume (Ed.), *Coppet, creuset de l'esprit libéral. Les Idées politiques et constitutionnelles du groupe de Madame de Staël*. Paris: Economica.

Sofia, F. (Ed.). (2001). *Sismondi e la civiltà toscana*. Firenze: Olschki.

Sofia, F. (2007). La république mixte de Sismondi face à la rupture révolutionnaire. *Cahiers Staeliens, LVIII*, 137–149.

Sowell, T. (1972). Sismondi, a Neglected Pionee. *History of Political Economy, IV*(1), 62–88.

Starobinski, J. (1971). *La transparence et l'obstacle*. Paris: Gallimard.

Stiglitz, J. E. (2000). The Contributions of the Economics of Information to Twentieth Century Economics. *The Quarterly Journal of Economics, 115*(November), 1441–1478.

Urbinati, N. (2012). Republicanism After French Revolution: The Case of Simonde de Sismondi. *Journal of the History of Ideas, 73*(1), 95–109.

4

The Question of Democracy for the Italian Marginalists (1882–1924)

Manuela Mosca and Eugenio Somaini

4.1 Introduction

In the forty years between the early 1880s and the first quarter of the twentieth century, an influential close-knit group of four Italian economists combined the commitment to theoretical and applied economics with a deep and passionate interest for political problems and especially for the nature of power relations in a democratic regime. The group which we will call "Italian marginalists"[1] was formed by Vilfredo Pareto (1848–1923), Maffeo Pantaleoni (1857–1924), Antonio de Viti de Marco (1858–1943), and Enrico Barone (1859–1924). They were all endowed with a cosmopolitan culture and in consonance with the main intellectual developments

[1] On the idea that the Italian marginalists constitute a specific cultural tradition, see Mosca (2018).

M. Mosca (✉)
University of Salento, Lecce, Italy
e-mail: manuela.mosca@unisalento.it

E. Somaini (✉)
University of Parma, Parma, Italy

M. Mosca (ed.), *Power in Economic Thought*, Palgrave Studies in the History of Economic Thought, https://doi.org/10.1007/978-3-319-94039-7_4

of the time. In addition to their personal links, they shared the adoption of the marginalist theory, to which each of them made fundamental and original contributions. At that time in Italy, the historicist approach inspired by the German historical school was still dominant, and their works marked a clear turning point in the history of economic thought.

Their attitude towards economic theory stands out for the ability to associate a high level of abstraction and formalization with a realistic vision that emphasized the dynamic and institutional aspects of economic phenomena. This attitude, reflected in their political thought, bears the imprint of a typically Italian tradition of political realism, which dates back to Machiavelli[2] and also characterized the contribution they made to the origins of Public Choice.[3] Along with their scientific work, they showed a lively, lasting interest in politics, which led to a considerable amount of publicist writings as well as to active militancy. De Viti de Marco was an MP for almost twenty years (from 1901 to 1921 with a few brief interruptions); Pantaleoni was elected to Parliament in 1900 but stayed only four years; Pareto unsuccessfully attempted a political career twice (in 1880 and in 1882),[4] and Barone too stood in vain for election in 1904. They also carried out their commitment through the pages of a prestigious journal, which they took over in 1890[5]: the *Giornale degli Economisti*, which they thought should "deal with the *economic issues of the day* in a *scientific spirit*", without ruling out "questions of pure and theoretical economics".[6]

Their political involvement covered a crucial, dramatic period of Italian history, which saw the gradual transition from a combination of constitutional monarchy and parliamentary regime to a full parliamentary

[2] References to Machiavelli are explicit, for instance, in Pareto who, as we see, frequently refers to the Machiavellian figures of the fox and the lion.

[3] This applies to all of them, but especially to the Italian school of Public Finance, of which De Viti de Marco was the founder. See Giuranno and Mosca (2018).

[4] He would later say that nothing was further from his mind than the desire to get into politics because "whoever is a liberal must now *necessarily* stay out of active politics" (Letter from Pareto to Pantaleoni of 11 February 1898, Pareto 1960, vol. II, p. 171). Pareto often repeated that he wanted to stay *au dessus de la mêlée*. The translations of quotations are ours, except where indicated otherwise.

[5] It was purchased by De Viti de Marco and Pantaleoni (with Mazzola and Zorli); later Pareto was a regular contributor (from 1891 to 1897), writing *Cronache*, a column of harsh political commentary. It also published numerous articles by Barone.

[6] Letter from Pantaleoni to Loria of 11 April 1890, in Fiorot (1976, p. 481).

democracy. It also saw the development of the workers' movement and the appearance both of socialist forces and of movements inspired by democratic Catholicism. The period prior to the First World War (which for Italy began in 1915) witnessed the alternation of governments of conservative and nationalist orientations with governments aiming at the integration of the working classes into the system through an alliance with moderate factions of socialism. These years were marked by the phenomenon of "transformism", a system of political patronage, of shifting political alliances, and frequent crossing of party lines by parliamentarians. It was condemned in unison, despite their differences, by the authors we are examining. The war marked the end of this phase and highlighted in rapid succession the culmination of the process of democratization and its dramatic conclusion. The first was achieved at the 1919 elections with the introduction of universal male suffrage (extended also to the illiterate) and of the proportional system and the party list vote. The second was due to the inability of the political forces to form stable and effective governments in the troubled aftermath of the war and to cope with the social tensions triggered by the government's failure to keep the promises made during the war in order to convince the lower classes to bear the immense sacrifices asked of them. These tensions were exacerbated by the widespread public belief that, in the post-war treaties, the allies had not upheld the pledges they had made to bring Italy into the war on their side. These years culminated in Mussolini's seizure of power in 1922. Similar phenomena occurred in these same years in other European countries, where the attainment of democracy was rapidly followed by its overthrow, signalling the dramatic conclusion of what Huntington (1991) has called the "first wave of democratisation".

These events were strongly felt and acutely debated by the authors we are dealing with and had a deep impact on their writings. They started out from radical-liberal positions, an initial faith in the development of democracy, and an alliance with the socialist reformists in support of the free market and free trade, as part of a general process of moral regeneration of Italian politics. This prospect, however, turned out to be short lived. Pantaleoni became a nationalist but remained essentially loyal to the ideal of an intensely socially selective political system. His concept of democracy as competition open to all classes of society had strong anti-socialist connotations and, as we shall see, made it easy for him to support the early stages of fascism, confident that it would be able to retain the "Manchesterian" features of its initial programme. At the end of the century, Pareto became profoundly sceptical. He regarded democratic regimes as highly dynamic systems, profoundly unstable, and, in general—particularly in the case of Italy—destined to be short lived. Especially in his *Treatise on General Sociology* (1916), he tried to maintain the attitude of a purely detached, objective scholar, though clearly not a sympathizer with democracy. Barone was aware of the fact that none of his models of the state was realizable in practice, neither the planned economy (Barone 1908b) nor the private-property market economy with a minimum role for an enlightened government.[7] De Viti alone preserved his original faith in democracy: parallel to the idealized view of democracy as cooperation expressed in his *First Principles of Public Finance* (1928), he presented in his political works (De Viti de Marco 1929) a lucidly realistic vision of the political processes. Pessimism gradually gained the upper hand, but it never made him give up his early vision, at least as a theoretical construction.

In the following sections, we will examine issue by issue the most significant and original aspects of the political thought of the four economists, comparing their opinions about the distribution and the exercise of the political power in a democratic system.

4.2 The Circulation of Elites and Its Implications

According to the theory of the circulation of elites, populations are always ruled by a minority holding power; in turn, the ruling class is subject to a perpetual turnover. The distinction between a ruling class and a class of

---

[7] The following quote sums up his position very well: "There is not any general principle that says when it is appropriate for the state to intervene and when it is not: both the Spencerian thesis and that of the socialists are aprioristic" ([1911–12] 1937, p. 7). Barone also writes: "the limit of the functions that one must and can assign to the state is a question of opportunity [...]. It is not a question that can be solved with a priori criteria" (Barone [1914–15] 2002, p. 141). Similar statements are also found in Barone ([1911–12] 1937, p. 119).

ruled was first expounded in 1884 by the political scientist G. Mosca[8] and was espoused, albeit in different terms, by all the economists we are considering.[9]

Pantaleoni identified the ruling elite with the small, educated, industrious, innovative, and civilized class, which had emerged in the Western world. He saw it as the only class interested in reproducing the conditions for selection, the only one capable of recognizing and pursuing the general interest, as he thought that the interest of this class coincided with the collective hedonistic maximum.[10] Pantaleoni (1892 1925, pp. 31–32) claimed that—as in nature, selection saves the species—in society, collective interests have to prevail over individual interests; therefore, the elite had to recourse, if necessary, to coercion. For Pantaleoni inequality was both the premise and the inevitable effect of the struggle for existence. He distinguished a kind of social mobility, that we might call natural, which originated in competition under shared rules, and another brought about by the intervention of an external authority. He believed that the socialist version of equality was simply unnatural, and it would cause the rebellion of the skilled who, deprived of a reward, ceased to work, causing the return to primitive, violent systems of conflict through which selection continued to operate, since it could never be suppressed, and finally the end of collectivism itself ([1900] 2001, p. 279). Society had neither to violate nor to hinder natural selection by protecting the incapable.

Pareto's reply to Pantaleoni's was sceptical; he asked: "how to entrust power to the best people, without them abusing it? ... it seems a less evil

[8] Without referring to the word "class", the phenomenon had already been pointed out by H.S. Maine in essays published from 1882 onwards in the *Quarterly Review* and collected in 1885 in *Popular Government* (Maine 1886), where the author clearly refers to the circulation of elites, which he calls aristocracies.

[9] The idea that political power was by its nature elitist was also shared by eminent exponents of the left like Antonio Gramsci and Piero Gobetti, who linked the revolutionary perspectives to the formation of workers' aristocracies.

[10] In 1892, Pantaleoni referred to Sidgwick's idea of the collective hedonistic maximum, then, in 1897, he regarded the question of the general interest as questionable, while, in 1907, he stated that the concept had still not been clarified by economic theory. He complained about the absence of theoretical tools to calculate it, and later he concluded that only history could reveal a country's *true* interests ([1916b] 1917, p. 197).

that power should be in the hands of those who … do not pursue the interests of too small a group of people".[11] Some years later, he (Pareto 1896–97) statistically demonstrated his "law" of the invariability of income distribution over time, which was at the base of his version of the theory of the circulation of elites. For him, the inevitable mobility between the classes never changes the shape of the income distribution curve: he thought that no aristocracy lasts, but that there is no society without an aristocratic class. Finally, in 1900, Pareto formulated for the first time his theory of the circulation of the elites: the aristocracy[12] is always made up of those most capable of conquering and remaining in power. At the same time, it is doomed to decline: the inner energy and force needed for ruling are inevitably waning, while some select elements of the lower classes are naturally endowed with such qualities.[13] The circulation of elites can occur both at individual level, with gifted members from the ruled classes replacing the less capable members of the old ruling class, or in a collective revolutionary form with the replacement of an entire ruling class by a new one, usually including defectors from the old class. The fact that the members of the ruling class combine power and wealth[14] led Pareto to refer to them as a "plutocracy". Unlike Marx, to explain the class nature of society, Pareto referred above all to psychological traits and not to structural features. For him, power and wealth coincide because the gifts needed to procure and make use of power coincide with those required to procure and make use of wealth. The difference between the two approaches is that, while Marx's classes tend to maintain indefinitely the same characteristics until the system finally collapses, those of Pareto tend to alternate or to change their character due

[11] Pareto (1960, vol. I, pp. 99–100, Letter to Pantaleoni of 6th December 1891).

[12] Up until *The Mind and Society. A Treatise on General Sociology* (1916), the elite and aristocracy were synonymous for Pareto. See Barbieri (2003, p. 55).

[13] For instance, when he mentions "the movement which enables part of the working class to earn high wages; which group therefore constitutes a first nucleus of the new elite" (Pareto [1900] 1991, p. 74). The theory of the circulation of the elites was then developed in Pareto (1902–03) and finally in Pareto (1916).

[14] Although usually with the specialization of one component (made up of politicians and/or the military) focused mainly on power and of another (made up of businessmen) focused above all on wealth.

to the effects of circulation.[15] In his *Treatise on General Sociology*, Pareto (1916) further clarified the theory, linking it to the presence of two basic elements (which he called residues[16]) common to everyone but developed to different extents in single individuals. The first, which he linked to the Machiavellian metaphor of the fox, is the "instinct of combinations" (residues of the first type), especially developed among members of the ruling class, and expressed in adroitness and the ability to take advantage of the opportunities that are presented. The second, linked to the metaphor of the lion, is the "persistence of the aggregates" (residues of the second type), predominant in the ruled classes, manifested in loyalty to traditions, ability to resist, and in the propensity to believe in and to be inspired by myths, which can sometimes give rise to violent outcomes in times of crisis. According to Pareto, every political regime, especially the one he analysed and experienced, which he called "demagogic plutocracy",[17] goes through a cycle, which follows the trajectory of a parabola through three different stages. The first is the stage of its affirmation, usually marked by expansion on the economic, social, and cultural planes but within which there gradually emerge the signs of the involution to come. The second is the intermediate stage, in which the negative potential already present in the first stage develops, and there is an abnormal growth of residues of the first type in the ruling class, a more and more intensive pursuit of immediate advantages, and an unscrupulous exploitation of opportunities. This is accompanied by the emergence of tensions and conflicts which the rulers try to overcome through concessions which, instead of settling the tension and conflict, perpetuates and increases it. The third stage is the actual crisis, in which the ruling class intensifies its use of its typical weapons, while in the ruled classes the residues of the second type intensify and radicalize, giving rise to violent

[15] If one compares the dichotomy of ruling class and ruled classes, based on power and the ability to use it, with the Marxian one of proletarians and capitalists, based on the control of the means of production, it must be acknowledged that the first has decidedly more power to explain political phenomena than the second. Buchanan (1960) too pointed out that the conception of the state according to the theory of the ruling class is broader than that of Marx.

[16] Pareto calls "residues" all the permanent drives of human action.

[17] The notion of plutocracy, and more specifically that of demagogic plutocracy, refers to the combination of wealth and power, represented, respectively, by speculators and demagogic politicians and to their interaction, that is, the use of wealth to acquire power and power to acquire wealth.

reactions that can lead to the emergence of a new potential ruling class, at least temporarily immune from the vices of the old one. This class may be helped by defectors from the old ruling class who see in the emergence of the new class the opportunity to gain a power from which the leaders of their original class had excluded them.[18]

The theory of the ruling class elaborated by G. Mosca certainly inspired De Viti de Marco[19] who, in 1886, contrasted two ideal types of state organization based on the "participation of the ruled in the government" (1888, p. 92). For him, the general interest coincided with the interests of the majority: "the politics that I work for is a democratic politics, and it must benefit the greatest number" (De Viti de Marco [1919] 1929, p. 379). In order to defend the interests of the majority of citizens, he opposed class legislation, defined as laws that grant benefits to small groups in collusion with political power, at the expense of the most numerous class. In his view, the links between "the executive power and other organs of economic and judicial and administrative life" aimed "to monopolise the legislation … to the detriment of the great number" ([1897] 2008, pp. 86–87 e p. 98). As a Public Finance Scholar, De Viti de Marco was particularly focused on the problem of redistribution of wealth. He proposed a system of fiscal levy, which he called "degressive", combining features of proportionality and progressivity. This system excludes taxation for lower-income brackets, applying gradually increasing tax rates to higher ones up until a ceiling, reached in correspondence with the intermediate tax brackets, beyond which the marginal rate becomes constant. The logic underlying this approach may be summed up as follows: (1) the coverage of the production costs of public goods with a tax proportional to income[20] corresponds to a large extent to the application of a single price for the utilization of the services of these goods; (2) the rule of the single price is not, however, constraining for the state, which enjoys a monopoly position; (3) the state may use this position to carry out functions additional to the production of public goods;

---

[18] For a reconstruction of these aspects of Pareto's thought, see Somaini (2017).

[19] Cardini (1985, p. 366) recalls the friendship between Mosca and De Viti, as well as their affinity.

[20] De Viti looks upon income level as a plausible proxy of the extent to which individuals utilize public goods.

(4) among the latter, there should be the guarantee of special benefits for the less advantaged social categories[21]; (5) the guarantee of these services would probably turn out to be convenient for the members of the latter and may, therefore, enjoy their consensus, satisfying feelings of solidarity they share, encouraging a reduction in conflict in society, and the renunciation by the lower classes of subversive and revolutionary attitude. Progressivity, however, for De Viti, should be limited to these functions; he decidedly rejected its employment to achieve a general and egalitarian redistribution because it would represent a form of exploitation, analogous to that of absolutist regimes, simply through an inversion of the role of exploiter, and exploited.

As for Barone, he explicitly stated that "the classes that hold the economic power also hold the political power" ([1898] 1928, p. 34), and he thought that the rise "of chosen individuals from the lower classes" ([1914–15] 2002, p. 96) had to occur only on the basis of skill and in a context of dynamic changes in income distribution.[22]

4.3 Democracy and the Masses

At that time, the term "democracy" implied the involvement of the popular masses in politics, through the extension of the right to vote for all. In Pantaleoni's view, the fundamental principle of the real democracy was that of "selection and competition" as opposed to the "crystallization of positions achieved selectively" (1918, p. 179). This is a feature of strong continuity in his thought, which characterized his vision from the beginning until the end (Mosca 2015). Pantaleoni claimed that selection was needed to eliminate the "social slag" of losers, overcoming the protection they were offered by the state (Pantaleoni [1900] 2001, p. 359). For him, the extension of the suffrage induced parliamentarians to protect the mass of losers, who represented the most numerous class of voters, and transformed authentic

[21] An anticipation of the *welfare state* may be glimpsed here.

[22] On these dynamics, see Michelini (2007, pp. 404–405).

democracy into a pseudo-democracy.[23] He saw real democracy as equivalent to the recognition of the social conditions that emerged from the selection after a battle on equal terms (Pantaleoni 1902, p. 68). Otherwise, there was the return "to the old domination by an upper-class oligarchy, or [a degeneration] into a caricature of a democratic regime which will be the reign of little oligarchies, formed amongst the masses, that is, the reign of the new privileged, worse than the old class" (1902, p. 68). Authentic democracy for him occurred when no individual or group enjoyed privileges from which others were unjustifiably excluded and in which each might freely enjoy the fruits of what he had obtained in the competitive contest with others. The task of a democratic state of this kind, according to him, therefore, consisted in simply guaranteeing these conditions. For Pantaleoni, with the development of democracy, economic policy decisions ended up "in the hands of the masses that are less and less educated and intelligent" (1907, p. 196). He thought that the masses were terrified of change, and that they asked for protection from the state, as in the case of public employees ([1913] 1925, pp. 151–152). He shared Pareto's belief that the masses were guided by myths (Pantaleoni [1916a] 1917, p. 167).[24]

Barone is commonly considered a non-democratic thinker, due to his clear opposition to the form of parliamentary democracy that he witnessed. However, he shared an ideal of an impartially selective democracy with Pantaleoni and came to regard the idea of the circulation of elites as a democratic doctrine, but democratic in the real sense, insofar as it requires that the rise of individuals coming from the lower classes be based "not on metaphysical premises or on the hypothetical rights of

[23] Pantaleoni's writings provide what could be called a scathing version of political economics. In his words: "the distribution of sovereignty among all citizens via universal suffrage, pulverizes this sovereignty into such small quotas that they end up by not having any value at all, even in the eyes of the innumerable little sovereigns themselves. This can be seen through the fact that they abstain from taking part in the elections, unless induced to either by money distributed by the candidates, by the parties or by the government itself transformed for the occasion into a party, or by sporadic attacks of political or religious fervour, or by iron discipline and organization, in other words by serious damage inflicted on them by party leaders" (Pantaleoni 1918, p. 160).

[24] According to Pareto (1916), the strength of myths was due to the fact that individuals tended to rationalize their behaviour and motivations using constructions that were seemingly logical but actually arbitrary and based on mere abstractions and common beliefs, which he called "derivations".

man, but … on the social organism's own need for preservation" ([1914–15] 2002, p. 96). To preserve this character, he thought it would be indispensable to limit the power of parliamentary democracies. Barone opposed universal franchise and the participation of the masses in running the country. He considered as irrational the behaviour of the masses, moved by instinct, and he was severely critical of mass democracy which he considered part of a trend towards statocracy (Barone [1914–15] 2002, p. 140).

As for Pareto, there is certainly a discontinuity in his initial positive vision of democracy which characterized his thought at the end of the nineteenth century. In 1916, in his *Treatise* he stated that:

> Evolution towards "democracy" seems to stand in strict correlation with the increased use of that instrument of governing which involves resort to artifice and to the "machine", as against the instrument of force … A political system in which "the people" expresses its "will" – given but not granted that it has one – without cliques, intrigues, "combines", "gangs", exists only as a pious wish of theorists. It is not to be observed in reality, either in the past or in the present, either in our Western countries on in any others. … Such phenomena … are usually described as aberrations, or "degenerations", of "democracy"; but when and where one may be introduced to the perfect, or even the merely decent, state from which said aberration or "degeneration" has occurred, no one ever manages to tell (1916, pp. 1589–1591).

According to him, universal suffrage would, in the expectations of its supporters, strengthen the democratic mechanisms and, if not facilitate the achievement of a consensus, at least expand its scope. In fact, he thought it would produce the opposite effects, that is, an increase in conflict, a tendency to seek solutions outside formal democratic channels, and finally the generalized use of force by all those involved. As we said, the 1919 elections with universal suffrage were followed by a rapid radicalization of political debate, with the occupation of factories by workers and of landholdings by farm labourers, which triggered, especially in the countryside, the reaction of fascist squads supported and financed by the landowners. Pareto felt that, in theory, the extension of the suffrage could favour the working class who, thanks to the nature of the industrial processes in which they were involved, had acquired a level of concentration and organization that made of it the potential embryo of a new ruling class. In reality, Pareto observed that universal suffrage worked at the same time as a unifying and as a divisive factor between the various components of the socialist movement. Unifying, because it created favourable conditions for the development of class consciousness, and provided a useful training ground for the emergence of leaders coming from the working class.[25] Divisive, since the various socialist factions had different or even incompatible ideas of the best use of parliamentary action and of its relation with other forms of struggle.

De Viti de Marco's attitude towards democracy was totally different. In 1897, his position aroused criticism from Pareto (1960, vol. II, p. 102) who called him: "an *optimist* ... who believes that with fine words one may change a country's system for the better". De Viti's definition of the democratic state as cooperative was a direct result of the idea that public finance relations boil down to paying taxes and using public services and of the fact that with the advent of democracy, there were no longer tax-exempt classes that had the exclusive power to decide how the state's tax revenues were spent. Once it was clear that in the democratic state everyone was at the same time producer and consumer, De Viti believed that conflicts of interest would gradually lessen and finally disappear, thanks to the alternation in government that he thought democracy would not only allow but guarantee. He was aware of the purely ideal (and, in reality, utopian) character of this model but thought that in the long run there would be a tendency to move in that direction.[26] De Viti de Marco continued to believe in the necessity of maintaining the consensus of the masses, especially of the workers of the agricultural sector who were paying the price of the protectionist policies of most governments of the

[25] Or also only for the formation, within and around it, of the core of a ruling class. He wrote: "It is an illusion to believe that it is the people who stand at the head of the dominant class today. Those who stand there – and this is a very different matter – are part of a new and future elite which leans upon the people. Already there are some slight signs of contrast between the new elite and the rest of the people" (Pareto [1900] 1991, p. 72).

[26] During the Great War, De Viti credited Wilson's America with the actual achievement of this democratic ideal (see Martelloni and Mosca 2018).

period.[27] For him, universal suffrage would give all classes access to political representation and, sooner or later, leverage on government. He thought that the main beneficiaries would be the peasant masses, the weaker sectors of the northern working class, and the consumers in general. The electoral reform of 1913 was welcomed by De Viti as a magnificent event:

> with the extension of the suffrage we have [...] broken the electoral monopoly, by which the few trampled on the masses [...] but it is only now that [...] we can break the administrative and bureaucratic, tax and customs, financial and banking monopolies that made up the real content of the electoral monopoly just destroyed (1913, p. 318).

He was not, however, unaware of the risk it entailed: organized groups, especially new parasitic groups, including sections of the working class, could turn universal suffrage to their own advantage. They could exert electoral pressure on the leaders of the people's parties and encourage them to join forces with the old parasitic groups of the bourgeoisie, exchanging protectionism and privileges for those groups with social legislation favouring the section of the working class of the industrial north they represented (De Viti de Marco 1929).

4.4 The State in Parliamentary Democracies

As regards the nature of the state and the role of political parties, the positions of the four economists were very far apart.

Following Spencer and social Darwinism, Pantaleoni thought that competitive selection operates not only among individuals but also at the level of institutions.[28] According to both of them, in the course of history, institutional selection had witnessed a shift from forms of competition based on submission or expropriation, brute force or military

[27] As an agricultural entrepreneur, he was an opponent of the kind of protectionism demanded by a large section of the industrialists of the north and continued to hope in a stable alliance between the farmers of the south and at least a part of the working class of the north.

[28] This aspect of Pantaleoni's thought has been explored in detail in Mosca (2015).

capability, towards more peaceful, consensual forms, based on spontaneous adherence, contracts, stable forms of cooperation, and shared rules.[29] The strong normative connotation of Pantaleoni's idea of selection, soon noticed by Fisher (1898), had the important political implication that the government had to be at the same time very small, and very strong.[30] As for the role of political parties, Pantaleoni made an interesting distinction between parties vertically and horizontally structured.[31] He thought that in political systems like those of the United States, the parties were of a vertical type, embracing various classes, or even the entire spectrum of significant social classes. The parties of the horizontal kind were the expression of just one numerous and potentially majority class and promoted "class privileges *in the name of democracy*"! (1918, p. 177).

The analysis made by Pareto in his *Treatise* of what he called "demagogic plutocracies" revolves around the interaction of three pairs of dichotomies or poles: (1) ruling class and ruled classes, (2) residues of the first and of the second type, and (3) consensus and force as the basis of power. We have already dealt with the first and the second poles. As for the third, according to Pareto, the preservation of power was based on the combination of the consent of those who are subject to it and the readiness to make use of force by those who hold it. According to him, the crisis of the plutocratic-demagogic regimes was due to an exasperated search for the former and the inability to resort to the latter. In fact, he thought that the plutocratic ruling class was extremely reluctant to using force or signalling willingness to use it. He always scorned the parties that had dominated the Italian political scene and was largely sceptical about the role of Parliament, even though he considered it an indispensable institution that could not be eliminated. The clearest expression of his ideas on this point is found in a work known as his "political last will and testament"

---

[29] This approach also reflects the influence of H.S. Maine, in particular, of his fundamental work *Ancient Law* (1861), which Pantaleoni had discussed early on.

[30] This vision of government of Pantaleoni's was highlighted by Sraffa (1924, p. 650).

[31] Pantaleoni writes: "When there is a *vertical* division of the parties, the government party includes a considerable part of every social class, and every sector of the population has direct participation in government. By contrast, if the division is *horizontal*, the party is essentially made up of one class and the others do not take part in governing" (1918, p. 161).

(Pareto 1923)[32] in which he proposed a constitutionalization of the fascist regime. He saw Parliament as the place where the different groups and classes could freely manifest their aspirations but suggested that it should not have the right to constitute the government through the vote of confidence, or power over ordinary legislation and the budget, and that its task should be limited to matters of general relevance: "The Chamber should retain the higher part of politics", he wrote, "in which it can do well. It can express feelings, interests, even prejudices, as long as they are general, of many people, therefore of the State" (1923, p. 797).

Barone's approach was more pragmatic. He shared the idea that every government is a class apparatus that always represents specific interests (Barone [1914–15] 2002, p. 140) and, in general, is not enlightened.[33] The lesser evil according to him was a capitalism regulated by a government in the hands of a class endowed with economic power, which "limits itself ... to its essential functions and carries them out with the maximum effectiveness" (p. 141). For him, the members of the ruling class had to be always subject to competition from new comers (p. 141),[34] but their replacement had to take place without destroying constituted power (p. 176). This could only occur if the state was strong enough to stand up to the attacks of the old and new elites, both of which wanted to alter political organization to their own advantage (p. 183). He also thought that a government expressed by Parliament would put "the delicate apparatus into the hands of the audacious and irresponsible, of shameless improvisers, of ignorant empiricists" (Barone [1908a ed. 1919–20] 1936, p. 699) and recommended limiting as far as possible the power of parliamentary governments.

De Viti de Marco identified two ideal types of state, respectively, designated as absolute (monopolist) and democratic (cooperative),[35] both of

---

[32] The piece opens with the statement that "the following is like an index of propositions deduced from historical experience, and of possible applications to present-day cases. The model is *The Prince* by Machiavelli" (1923, p. 795).

[33] Barone writes, "the individuals brought to power [do not become] more enlightened than they were before, only because they exercise power" (Barone [1914–15] 2002, p. 139).

[34] See also Gentilucci (2002, p. 50, fn. 2) and Michelini (2005, pp. 772–773).

[35] A similar contrast between the state "of conquerors" and the "modern state" is found in Pantaleoni ([1908] 1925, p. 364).

which he interpreted in terms of a dichotomy between producers and consumers of public services. In the *Ancien Regime* "the ruling class was distinguished from the ruled class" (1912–13, p. 15), and the interests of the two classes were in conflict: the aristocratic ruling class was a class of pure consumers who performed no productive activity, paid no taxes, had full (monopolistic) control of the state, and were the main beneficiaries of state action; by contrast, the ruled classes only played the role of taxpayers or producers, without gaining any benefit. He thought that, starting with the French Revolution, a diametrically opposed concept of the state was established, from which grew the modern state, democratic or cooperative, in which, in principle, there is no "conflict of interests between the ruling class and the ruled class: in strictly legal terms we are all rulers and ruled" (1912–13, p. 16). He was a supporter of proportional representation and the list vote, seen as a remedy to the degenerations of parliamentarianism.[36]

4.5 Socialism

At the end of the nineteenth century, the newborn Italian Socialist Party included revolutionary maximalists, trade unionists, and reformers. Thanks to moderate policy of the latter, in these years, the socialists obtained reforms in the field of social policies, trade unions, and the right to strike. The extension of male suffrage in 1913, and then in 1919, resulted in a strong representation, but short of a majority, for the socialist and catholic parties. After the war, the so-called *biennio rosso* or "two red years" (1919–1920), witnessed attempts by the more radical socialist forces to repeat the experience of the Bolshevik revolution. The socialists were divided between those who felt that seemingly revolutionary actions could be part of a successful negotiating strategy for further reforms and those who, taking the teachings of historical materialism literally, believed that since control of the means of production was the foundation of bourgeois power, the occupation of the factories by workers and of the landholdings by farmhands represented the first and necessary step

[36] As said, Italy passed from the majoritarian to the proportional system in 1919.

towards the conquest of power. Even those revolutionaries inspired by the Soviet model ignored Lenin's lesson on the priority of the armed conquest of power and its subsequent ruthless use to eliminate the adversary. This tumultuous period was followed by the victorious counter-mobilization of fascist squads and nationalist forces.

Until the 1910s, the Italian radical-liberals envisaged, and then realized, an alliance with the moderate socialists on an anti-statist and anti-protectionist programme.[37] This idea having soon proven to be a delusion, hope gave way to anguish at the growing threat of a socialist success.

Pantaleoni thought that the socialist version of democracy consisted in the use of the coercive powers of the state to alter the results of free and fair competitive processes to the advantage of certain groups. To him, socialist democracy was the extreme form of pseudo-democracy or demagoguery. Socialism, basically, would have merely been a new version of those forms of exploitation and abuse of power that, in the past, the dominant and ruling classes made use of. The only difference was that the role of exploiters was now performed by the losers in the competitive process. Pantaleoni contemptuously defined the Socialist Party as "the syndicate of all those who appeal to the state or local council so that it realises in their favour that which their activity and spontaneous discipline cannot produce".[38] He proceeded by arguing that "the political syndicate, that of the inept, does not suppress competition, but transforms it, reinstating types of competition which historical selection has already suppressed, as the least fecund of progress" (Pantaleoni [1900] 2001, p. 362).

In 1897, Pareto discussed the problem in private with Pantaleoni. They came to different conclusions, which found expression in two articles published in 1900—the first by Pantaleoni denying that socialism

[37] On 31 December 1891, Pareto wrote to the socialist MP Napoleone Colajanni: "it seems to me that a stretch of road should be travelled together by socialists and economists, to oppose the bad arts of those who govern us" (Pareto 1973, p. 175). It should be remembered that the authors we are examining did not believe that Marxism, especially in its Leninist version, was the only authentic expression of socialism but rather one lacking in ethical appeal.

[38] Pantaleoni ([1900] 2001, p. 359). Considering the Socialist Party as a particular case of league or union is a parody and does not imply a condemnation of the actions of socialist trade unions. Pantaleoni, like the others, in fact, was in favour of trade unions.

could ever prevail and the second by Pareto affirming instead that "its victory is highly probable and almost inevitable".[39] The reasons for this prediction seem to have been based on the fact that, for Pareto, socialism: (1) like every religion had the merit of instilling strength and morally elevating the lower classes, (2) gave a noble guise to their feeling of greed and envy, (3) appealed to the universal feeling of benevolence towards our fellow men, a feeling that was taking root in the ranks of a decadent bourgeoisie, and (4) was used by the dissident members of the older elite to gain the support of the lower classes.[40] Pareto devoted a whole important book to the analysis of socialism (1902–03). Moreover, he tried to evaluate a socialist system in terms of welfare with the theoretical tools of economics, but his result was that "pure economics provides us with no truly decisive criterion with which to choose between a system of organization based on private ownership ... and a socialist system" (Pareto [1906] 2014, p. 184). However, when put to the test, he said he was sure that no other political regime could offer a "system more favourable to the utility of the people" than the system then in force (Pareto 1919b, p. 272). During the crisis that preceded the victory of fascism, Pareto considered even more seriously the possibility of a socialist victory. He saw it in the moral energy expressed by socialism and in the signs of the emergence of a new aristocracy within the working class. Soon, to his unstated but evident relief, this prospect was undermined by the hesitant, contradictory conduct of the socialist forces. In spite of this, and maintaining his (presumed) detachment, Pareto predicted that a possible socialist victory would inevitably be followed in a short time by its failure (Pareto 1919a).

Barone, too, in different terms from both Pantaleoni and Pareto, targeted socialism. He developed Pareto's idea to analyse socialism with economic tools, and the outcome was his famous essay on the "Ministry of

[39] Pareto ([1900] 1991, p. 36) wrote: "Professor Pantaleoni, in a recent treatise denies that socialism will win; I have maintained that this victory is most probable and almost inevitable". See Pantaleoni (1900).

[40] Busino ([1979] 1980, p. 348) rightly thinks Pareto highlighted "the logical inconsistency of all the socialist doctrines and at the same time their extraordinary success, being catalysts of passions, instinct, feelings, will-power".

production in the collectivist state" (1908b). There he showed that, theoretically, both a perfectly competitive equilibrium and a collectivist equilibrium were characterized by optimality, but he thought that, in practice, socialism was "actually harmful to the maximum collective utility" (Barone [1914–15] 2002, p. 140), as it inevitably destroyed wealth and lowered social welfare. In fact, he affirmed that the planned economy could *theoretically* be achieved, while demonstrating that it did not correspond at all to the Marxist idea of collectivism, since it would have included the same economic categories found in the market economy. However, he reiterated its *real* impossibility, unless there were "higher beings, capable of achieving outcomes that are obtained with free competition" (Barone [1908a] 1936, p. 63). For mere mortals, reaching the collective optimum would have required a process of trial and error and large-scale economic "experiments".[41] All the same, he claimed that, in practice, this wouldn't have happened in the collectivist regime, because even the omniscient Ministry would have been under political pressure to let "firms survive that it would be in the interests of society if they disappeared" ([1908a ed. 1909] 1936, p. 340). He, therefore, stated the impossibility of economically efficient collectivism in practice. The difference in the assessments made by Pareto, on the one hand, and Pantaleoni and Barone, on the other, must not be overstated: while for a certain time Pareto did believe in a possible victory by socialism, his opinion on the economic unsustainability of a regime of collectivization was in full agreement with that of his friends.

After the breaking of the agreement between socialists and free traders, De Viti de Marco did not miss a chance to denounce the collusion of the socialists with other forces favourable to government intervention in the economy. Like Pantaleoni, he saw the Italian socialists as a pressure group demanding social laws for the benefit of the industrial workers, offering their electoral support in exchange.

[41] Barone argued that "having to proceed by trial and error and experiments [...] the collectivist ministry of production could not in any way avoid for higher cost firms [...] those destructions that one thinks are an exclusive effect of the present economic regime" (Barone [1908a ed. 1909] 1936, p. 645). Michelini (2005) has gone very thoroughly into this subject.

4.6 Fascism

To complete the picture, let's see briefly their attitudes towards fascism, or more precisely to early fascism, since three of them died before the establishment of Mussolini's fully authoritarian regime in 1925, while the fourth retired to private life.

During the war and in the subsequent years, Pantaleoni's vision had taken on markedly nationalistic tones, and it had led him to welcome the role played by fascism, in which he saw a sort of muscular version of liberalism. In it he thought to recognize a pro market orientation and a model of selective democracy. He saw clear signs of this approach in the "Manchesterian" speech Mussolini delivered in Parliament on 21 June 1921.[42] Pantaleoni was advisor to Alberto de' Stefani, the free-market-oriented Minister of Finance in Mussolini's first government (1922–24),[43] and in 1923, he was appointed Senator.[44] For him, the elitist liberalism of the previous century had been swept away by the "great tide of demagogic democracy that swept over our country and to which no resistance could be made until … fascism's 'march on Rome'" ([1924] 1938, p. 345). Barone too was in favour of Mussolini's rise and of his first government's economic policy with de' Stefani and expressed the hope that Mussolini would succeed in strengthening the Italian economy by

[42] It is worth noticing that Mussolini calls this speech "reactionary", "anti-democratic", and "anti-socialist", while Pantaleoni sees in it the core of what he considered to be authentic democracy. Pantaleoni ([1921] 1922, p. 212) summed up his model in the following passage: "The functions of the state should be reduced to those that create the general conditions for the carrying out of individual activities in economic life … the state should not give privileges to any class, and hence subjugation to others; it should not be the industrialist, the farmer, the trader, the mariner, the railway-man, the banker, the co-operator, the journalist, the monopolist and censor of thought through the postal service, the school, the maintainer of do-nothings with unemployment pay paid for by those who work, the monopolist of migration flows, nor should it provide profits for some and losses for others through protectionism and through state procurements awarded to the most costly producer for him to employ the least efficient workers. Only in this way will the bureaucracy be reduced. Only in this way will the state avoid bankruptcy. Only in this way will there be economic and intellectual development. Only in this way will there be equality before the law for citizens. It should guarantee safety and security to people and their property. It should provide rapid justice. It should guarantee security of contract and not provide examples of dishonesty".

[43] This government was a coalition of liberals, Catholics, and members of the Fascist Party.

[44] For a contemporary comment on Pantaleoni's positions in these years, see Dalton (1923).

fostering nationalist feeling (Barone 1923, p. 139). Both of them saw in fascism the final defeat of the socialist threat and the victory of a new energetic and strong elite.

Pareto, giving up the detachment and scepticism that he had long shown, rediscovered after decades his youthful political enthusiasm.[45] He looked with relief at the crumbling of the weak bourgeois government (Pareto 1921, p. 120) and saw the declining elites finally challenged by "forceful men of the new elite" (1921, p. 79). We have already mentioned his proposal of a constitutionalization of the fascist regime (Pareto 1923). His enthusiasm was also due to the fact that, for him, the crisis of democracy and the rise of fascism represented a striking confirmation of his theory and proof of his own remarkable forecasting ability.

Only De Viti survived the initial stage of fascism; he was, therefore, the only witness of its transformation into a real dictatorship. He described the years preceding the victory of fascism as a "fearful period of total anarchy", "typical of civil war" culminating in the disappearance of the state (1929, pp. v–ix). In 1922, before the fascist regime decreed the end of democracy, he withdrew from Parliament, from every corner of the political scene (in the twenties), and from university (in the thirties),[46] devoting himself almost exclusively to the revision of his lecture notes, which he would transform into a proper textbook.

4.7 Were They Liberals?

The Italian marginalists shared the opposition to an active government, although in different shapes and degrees. Pantaleoni's authentic democracy, represented by the individualistic and selectionist regime, may undoubtedly be described as liberal. Witness the following passage, a mark of the true Pantaleoni that may be considered the expression of a classical liberalism, with the explicit accentuation of its non-egalitarian character:

[45] There is a historiographical debate concerning Pareto's support to the fascist regime. We think that Pareto was a fascist, but, as said, his support was directed only to the initial stage of fascism, as he died in 1923.

[46] In 1931 De Viti de Marco applied for retirement so as not to have to swear the oath of allegiance to the fascist regime imposed on university professors.

> Fundamental principles of a democratic regime are that no class, no citizen, may be above the law; that the laws do not allow the formation of privileged classes; that there must be equality of the citizens only in the use of the laws, but freedom of action in their area, this would entail inequality in their social and economic situation as a result of selection and competition, of activity, intellect, good sense, foresight, skilful management, boldness, courage and luck.[47]

De Viti de Marco was a liberal democrat to the core: he saw in every country a conflict between liberal forces and authoritarian ones and fought all his life against the latter.[48] Pareto's position was different. He always stated that freedom of thought and speech were indispensable, and he even urged Mussolini to respect them after he came to power (1923, p. 798). Equally clear was his rejection of any state interference in religious questions.[49] However, the limitation of the role of legislation (and, therefore, ultimately of the state) that Pareto had in mind at the end of his life was not of the sort typical of the liberal tradition. He did not assign the power taken from the state to markets, entrepreneurs, and individual initiatives[50] but instead to a hierarchical organization ultimately based on force. His position was similar to that of Barone, whose military background predisposed him to favour some type of centralized control and planning; in one of his works (Barone 1923), one can, however, find that his faith in the theory of elites corresponded to opposition to open dictatorship.

---

[47] Pantaleoni (1918, p. 161). This text, occasional and not scientific, but crammed with theoretical content, was published in March 1918 in *La Vita Italiana*, the review of militant nationalism destined to merge with fascism. In this text, Pantaleoni's anti-socialism is clearly outlined, as well as his persisting liberalism and a great open-mindedness, shown in his scrupulously demonstrating the conditions where the validity of his these would not apply, or at any rate be open to question. On Pantaleoni's liberalism, see also Ricossa (1976).

[48] The Anglo-Saxon source of De Viti de Marco's liberalism is dealt with in Martelloni and Mosca (2018).

[49] "There are great currents of feeling that never disappear … such as the current of faith and that of scepticism, of materialism or idealism, of positive religions and free thought. He who thinks they can be suppressed is deceiving himself" (1923, p. 799).

[50] Unlike Pantaleoni, Pareto had really turned his back on the free market. In a letter of 1 October 1921, he wrote, "Allow me to laugh, thinking of our campaigns for free trade, economic freedom, and so many other wonderful things. Aren't you content with the disillusionments?" (Pareto 1960, vol. III, p. 293).

All the economists we have examined, while differing in their opinions, took the question of the distribution and the exercise of the political power in a democratic system very seriously. They saw the advent of democracy as a phenomenon of extraordinary importance and bearer of profound changes. In their analysis, they made use of all the theoretical and conceptual weapons they had elaborated: their particular interpretation of the nature of the state, their notion of classes, and of the psychology of both the masses and the elites. This was all done by drawing heavily not only on economic theory but also on a deep knowledge of ancient and modern history of which it is hard to find an equal today.

References

Barbieri, G. (2003). *Pareto e il Fascismo*. Milano: Angeli.

Barone, E. ([1898] 1928). Le istituzioni militari e le condizioni politico sociali. In *Studi sulla Condotta della Guerra* (Vol. I, pp. 13–52). Torino: Schioppo.

Barone, E. ([1908a] 1936). *Principi di Economia Politica* (Vol. II). In *Le Opere Economiche*. Bologna: Zanichelli.

Barone, E. ([1908b] 1935). The Ministry of Production in the Collectivist State. In F. A. Hayek (Ed.), *Collectivist Economic Planning* (pp. 245–290). London: Routledge & Kegan Paul.

Barone, E. ([1911–12] 1937). *Principii di Economia Finanziaria*. Bologna: Zanichelli.

Barone, E. ([1914–15] 2002). La rivoluzione francese. In C. E. Gentilucci (Ed.), *La Rivoluzione Francese in Enrico Barone* (pp. 53–187). Camerino: Affinità elettive.

Barone, E. (1923). Italia e Stati Uniti. *Per la Nostra Ricostruzione Economica, I*(5), 131–142.

Buchanan, J. M. (1960). "La scienza delle finanze": The Italian Tradition in Fiscal Theory. In *Fiscal Theory and Political Economy. Selected Essays* (pp. 24–74). Chapel Hill: The University of North Carolina Press.

Busino, G. ([1979] 1980). Pareto Vilfredo. In M. Finoia (Ed.), *Il Pensiero Economico Italiano 1850–1950* (pp. 345–351). Bologna: Cappelli.

Cardini, A. (1985). Antonio de Viti de Marco. In *La Democrazia Incompiuta 1858–1943*. Roma: Laterza.

Dalton, H. (1923). Pantaleoni Fascist. *The Economic Journal, 33*(129), 66–69.

De Viti de Marco, A. ([1888] 2001). *Il Carattere Teorico dell'Economia Finanziaria*, Roma: Pasqualucci, trans. of the first charter *The "Theory" and "Application" of Economic Doctrines.* In M. Baldassarri & P. Ciocca (Ed.), *Roots of the Italian School of Economics and Finance: From Ferrara (1857) to Einaudi (1944)* (Vol. III, pp. 505–529). New York: Palgrave Macmillan.
De Viti de Marco, A. ([1897] 2008). Discorso politico agli elettori liberali del collegio di Gallipoli. In A. L. Denitto (Ed.), *Mezzogiorno e Democrazia Liberale* (pp. 81–98). Bari: Palomar.
De Viti de Marco, A. (1912–13). *Lezioni di Scienza delle Finanze, raccolte per cura di I. Foschi.* Roma: F.lli Ferri, lithography, n.d.
De Viti de Marco, A. ([1913] 1929). Per un programma d'azione democratica. In *Un Trentennio di Lotte Politiche* (pp. 315–342). Roma: Collezione meridionale editrice.
De Viti de Marco, A. ([1919] 1929). Discorso agli elettori. In *Un Trentennio di Lotte Politiche* (pp. 371–392). Roma: Collezione meridionale.
De Viti de Marco, A. ([1928] 1936). *First Principles of Public Finance.* London: Cape.
De Viti de Marco, A. (1929). *Un Trentennio di Lotte Politiche.* Roma: Collezione meridionale.
Fiorot, D. (1976). Lettere di Maffeo Pantaleoni ad Achille Loria. *Storia e Politica, 15*(3), 439–495 and *15*(4), 553–604.
Fisher, I. (1898). Review of M. Pantaleoni "Pure Economics". *Annals of the American Academy of Political and Social Science, 12*, 122–125.
Gentilucci, C. E. (2002). Introduzione. La rivoluzione francese di Enrico Barone tra storia e sociologia economica. In C. E. Gentilucci (Ed.), *La Rivoluzione Francese in Enrico Barone.* Camerino: Affinità elettive.
Giuranno, M., & Mosca, M. (2018). Political Realism and Models of the State: Antonio de Viti de Marco and the Origins of Public Choice. *Public Choice, 175*(3–4), 325–345.
Huntington, S. P. (1991). *The Third Wave: Democratization in the Late 20th Century.* Norman: University of Oklahoma Press.
Maine, H. J. S. (1861). *Ancient Law.* London: Murray.
Maine, H. J. S. ([1886] 1976). *Popular Government.* Indianapolis: Liberty Fund.
Martelloni, F., & Mosca, M. (2018). De Viti de Marco, the "European War" and President Wilson. *Journal of the History of Economic Thought, 40*(2), 179–199.
Michelini, L. (2005). Innovazione e sistemi economici comparati: il contributo di Enrico Barone e il pensiero economico italiano (1894–1924). *Società e Storia, 28*(110), 741–797.

Michelini, L. (2007). Equilibrio generale e storia: I *Principi di economia politica* di Enrico Barone. In M. M. Augello & M. E. L. Guidi (Eds.), *L'economia Divulgata, Manuali e Trattati* (Vol. I, pp. 383–411). Milano: Angeli.
Mosca, M. (2015). "Io che sono un darwinista": la visione di Maffeo Pantaleoni. *Il Pensiero Economico Italiano, 23*(1), 23–45.
Mosca, M. (2018). *Monopoly Power and Competition. The Italian Marginalists' Perspective.* Cheltenham: Elgar.
Pantaleoni, M. ([1892] 1925). Cenni sul concetto di massimi edonistici individuali e collettivi. In *Erotemi di Economia* (Vol. II, pp. 1–47). Bari: Laterza.
Pantaleoni, M. ([1900] 2001). The Twentieth Century Viewed by an Individualist. In M. Baldassarri and P. Ciocca (Ed.), *Roots of the Italian School of Economics and Finance: From Ferrara (1857) to Einaudi (1944)* (Vol. I, pp. 347–368). New York: Palgrave Macmillan.
Pantaleoni, M. (1902). La legislazione di classe e la democrazia. *Giornale degli Economisti, s. 2, 25*(13), 67–83.
Pantaleoni, M. ([1907] 1925). Una visione cinematografica del progresso della scienza economica. In *Erotemi di Economia* (Vol. I, pp. 189–221). Bari: Laterza.
Pantaleoni, M. ([1908] 1925). Della divisione del lavoro in attribuzioni maschili e femminili. In *Erotemi di Economia* (Vol. I, pp. 362–375). Bari: Laterza.
Pantaleoni, M. ([1913] 1925). L'atto economico. In *Erotemi di Economia* (Vol. I, pp. 67–155). Bari: Laterza.
Pantaleoni, M. ([1916a] 1917). Tre categorie di problemi post-bellici. In *Tra le Incognite* (pp. 161–174). Bari: Laterza.
Pantaleoni, M. ([1916b] 1917). Aspetti post-bellici della politica estera degli Stati Uniti. In *Tra le Incognite* (pp. 197–212). Bari: Laterza.
Pantaleoni, M. (1918). Demagogia e democrazia. In *Politica. Criteri ed Eventi* (pp. 157–189). Bari: Laterza.
Pantaleoni, M. ([1921] 1922). *Plutocrazia e bolscevismo giudaico sgretolano il fascismo, in Bolscevismo italiano* (pp. 206–215). Bari: Laterza.
Pantaleoni, M. ([1924] 1938). In occasione della morte di Pareto: riflessioni. In *Studi di Finanza e di Statistica* (pp. 327–358). Bologna: Zanichelli.
Pareto, V. ([1894] 2008). The Maximum of Utility Given by Free Competition. *Giornale degli Economisti e Annali di Economia, 67*(3), 387–403.
Pareto, V. ([1896–97] 1971). *Cours d'Economie Politique.* Lausanne: Librairie de L'Université, Italian trans. *Corso di Economia Politica.* Torino: Utet.
Pareto, V. ([1900] 1991). *The Rise and Fall of Elites: An Application of Theoretical Sociology.* New Brunswick: Transaction Publisher.
Pareto, V. (1902–03). *Les Systèmes Socialistes.* Paris: Giard & Brière.

Pareto, V. ([1906] 2014). *Manual of Political Economy. A Critical and Variorum Edition* (A. Montesano, A. Zanni, L. Bruni, J. S. Chipman, & M. McLure, Eds.). Oxford: Oxford University Press.

Pareto, V. ([1916] 1935). *The Mind and Society. A Treatise on General Sociology*. London: Cape.

Pareto, V. ([1919a] 1920). Il fenomeno del bolscevismo. In *Fatti e Teorie* (pp. 251–268). Firenze: Vallecchi.

Pareto, V. ([1919b] 1920). Cose vecchie sempre nuove. In *Fatti e Teorie* (pp. 269–275). Firenze: Vallecchi.

Pareto, V. (1921). *Trasformazioni della Democrazia*. Bologna: Cappelli.

Pareto, V. (1923). Pochi punti di un futuro ordinamento costituzionale. In G. Busino (Ed.), *Scritti Politici* (Vol. II, pp. 795–800). Torino: Utet.

Pareto, V. (1960). *Lettere a Maffeo Pantaleoni 1890–1923* (G. De Rosa, Ed., 3 Vols). Rome: BNL.

Pareto, V. (1973). *Epistolario 1890–1923*, (G. Busino, Ed., 2 Vols). Roma: Accademia Nazionale dei Lincei.

Ricossa, S. (1976). Prefazione. In S. Ricossa (Ed.), *M. Pantaleoni, Il manicomio del mondo e altre pagine scelte*. Roma: Volpe.

Somaini, E. (2017). Il Trattato di Sociologia di Pareto e il passaggio dal regime plutocratico-demagogico al fascismo. In P. P. Portinato (Ed.), *Vilfredo Pareto. A 100 anni dal Trattato di Sociologia Generale* (pp. 57–90). Torino: Accademia delle Scienze.

Sraffa, P. (1924). Obituary. Maffeo Pantaleoni. *The Economic Journal, 24*(136), 648–655.

Part II

The Asymmetries of Power: Income, Wealth and Social Control

5

Elements of a Science of Power: Hobbes, Smith and Ricardo

Heinz D. Kurz

5.1 Introduction

According to Bertrand Russell (1938), economics ought to be a "science of power". Alas, in large parts of contemporary economics, power is not even mentioned as a factor, let alone an important factor, shaping the results of economic life.[1] There are, however, notable exceptions to the rule. In non-mainstream economics, in the classical, the Marxian, the Kaleckian and the Postkeynesian currents of thought, power is often a

[1] The situation is quite different in sociology and political science.

This is a substantially revised and considerably shortened version of a keynote lecture given at the 14th conference of the Italian Association for the History of Economic Thought (AISPE) at the University of Salento, Lecce, 28–30 April 2016. I am grateful to the participants for useful discussions and to Manuela Mosca also for her hospitality. Tony Aspromourgos, Amit Bhaduri, Christian Fleck, Christian Gehrke, Geoff Harcourt, Peter Kalmbach, John King, Ulrich Krause, Fabio Petri and Richard Sturn kindly sent me valuable comments and suggestions on earlier drafts of the chapter. Any remaining misconceptions are, of course, entirely my responsibility.

H. D. Kurz (✉)
University of Graz, Graz, Austria
e-mail: heinz.kurz@uni-graz.at

M. Mosca (ed.), *Power in Economic Thought*, Palgrave Studies in the History of Economic Thought, https://doi.org/10.1007/978-3-319-94039-7_5

central analytical category. It also assumes an important role in Industrial Organization and Game Theory. Yet in the main parts of mainstream economics, especially in much of conventional micro- and macroeconomics, power is largely absent. And when it is dealt with at all, it is typically done in a partial equilibrium framework, focusing attention on single markets or agents, leaving out the importance of power relationships in the economy and society as a whole, that is, *systemic* power.

Power is often difficult to see: it is hidden and works secretly. There are two common responses to this. Its low visibility is mistaken to mean that it is unimportant or even inexistent. Its secret character gives rise to conspiracy theories of various sorts. And the powerful are often keen to camouflage their self-seeking activities as being in the public interest. How to separate the wheat from the chaff in all this? How to find out the power that effectively pulls the strings?

The classical economists deserve to be praised for their deep analyses of power relationships. Alas, their respective contributions have largely fallen into oblivion after the advent of the marginalist approach to the theory of value and distribution in the latter part of the nineteenth century. This should be enough to justify recalling their ideas and their view of socio-economic affairs and outcomes as driven by, and reflecting, power relationships. The view that economic matters are best studied by assuming people living in a "powerless" vacuum, these authors would probably have received with disbelief and qualified as utterly unrealistic and contrived. If with the sung hero of our subject, Adam Smith, economics is an *Inquiry into the Nature and Causes of the Wealth of Nations* (Smith 1976 [1776]), and if according to Thomas Hobbes (1651) "wealth is power", a judgement Smith expressly shared, then the study of power relationships should be a major concern of economists.

The composition of the chapter is the following. Section 5.2 deals briefly with different meanings of power. Section 5.3 turns to Thomas Hobbes' treatment of power in *Leviathan* and the social theory he erected thereupon. Hobbes' advocacy of the absolutist state involved a major challenge to scholars opting in favour of a social order based on the principles of "equality, liberty and justice", as Adam Smith famously put it. Section 5.4, therefore, provides an account of the Scotsman's sophisticated approach to the problem of power, the reasons for his rejection of

Hobbes' social theory and his concern with "good government". Section 5.5 turns to David Ricardo, who corrected and deepened Smith's analysis in important aspects. Section 5.6 concludes by drawing the attention first to authors who elaborated on the classical economists' analysis and then to some marginalists who advocated its abandonment in favour of the assumption of "perfect competition" according to which no agent has any market power whatsoever.

5.2 Concepts of Power

Different Meanings of Power Power can have several meanings in economics, yet all of these meanings boil down to an asymmetry or disproportion in human relations, whether the reference is to pairs of individuals, to different groups and social classes or to entire populations or nations. Max Weber (1972: 28, 1947) defined power as "the opportunity that one actor within a social relationship will be in a position to carry out his own will despite resistance, regardless of the basis on which this opportunity rests".[2] In a similar vein, Herbert A. Simon wrote: "influence, power and authority are all intended as asymmetric relations" (Simon 1957: 4). With Robert Dahl (1957), we can express the asymmetry under consideration as regards people in a causal way as follows: to say that person *i* has power over person *j* is equivalent to saying that *i*'s behaviour causes *j*'s behaviour, not the other way round.

While these definitions are useful, they are somewhat narrow, because they do not connect power relationships and socio-economic institutions, the legal, political and cultural systems that support given power structures, and the mechanisms by means of which these structures are reproduced.[3] These institutions and mechanisms have an influence on

[2] In Weber's writings, especially in *Wirtschaft und Gesellschaft* ([1922] 1972), the concepts of power and domination played a significant role in numerous contexts. He discussed, for example, the distribution of power amongst the different ranks of people in Italian towns in the middle ages, the power of guilds at the time, the power assumed by bureaucracies in modern times, the power of the Roman Catholic Church and the "power of capital".

[3] Jessop (2012: 3) speaks of power relations in the Marxist tradition "as manifestations of a specific mode or configuration of class domination rather than as a purely interpersonal phenomenon lacking deeper foundations in the social structure".

the perceptions, aspirations and mind-sets of people and typically cause the dominated strata of society to acquiesce to the situation. Power typically allows some people to affect some other people's needs and wants, or preferences, and the financial and other constraints subject to which they act. Closer inspection shows that power blurs the neat distinction between preferences, on the one hand, and constraints, on the other, entertained in mainstream economics. The impact of power may also limit the kind of technical and organizational knowledge that can be employed by certain groups.[4]

As regards the origins or sources of power, numerous have been identified. They go from physical strength and various means and devices to enforce one's will upon others to the capability of capturing other people's minds.

Forms of Power At each step of a hierarchy (and not just that of a dictatorship), what matters are the means of the various ranks of people to exercise their power and enforce their will. Power, the German sociologist Heinrich Popitz ([1986] 1992: 22) maintained in accordance with Max Weber, "is the capability to prevail over other forces [Kräfte]". He distinguished between various fundamental forms of the exercise of power, the most important of which are the following three: (1) "Power of action" is rooted in the fact that people can hurt others and can also be hurt. It often involves the use of violence in seeking to change other people's behaviour (e.g., in the case of acts of revenge). Power of action is typically short lived and disappears in the moment in which it is being used. (2) "Instrumental power" is employed to influence the behaviour of other people by means of promises or threats and generally positive or negative sanctions. Instrumental power is more durable than the power of action because it is applied with regard to a longer time horizon. (3) "Authoritative power" relies on the need of people to be respected by their peers (or at least not give them the impression of being disobedient). Such respect,

[4] The set of data typically invoked by general equilibrium theory thus loses much of its appeal as providing a solid platform to start from. We may already here renounce the widespread view that general equilibrium theory managed to formalize Adam Smith's social theory. This view cannot be sustained vis-à-vis, inter alia, Smith's insistence on the shaping of the needs and wants of agents by the social milieu from which they come and the social strata to which they belong.

whether real or imagined, may increase a person's self-esteem and tie it to its peers. This kind of power can be used to affect not only the observable behaviour of people but also their unobservable attitudes and mind-sets and the norms they follow. It typically does not employ force or violence but suasion and professional excellence.

Each agent is typically in contact with several other agents. What we may call "basic agents" (adopting a concept Sraffa (1960) coined with regard to commodities in the theory of production) are bound to deal with each other, being exposed to reciprocal influences. At the same time, they exert some influence, directly or indirectly, via other agents, on all "non-basic" agents, without being influenced by them. Agents belonging to distinct groups of non-basic agents are exposed to reciprocal influences by all other agents in the group and exert some influence, directly or indirectly, on all non-basic agents of lower orders, and so on. The basicness or non-basicness of some agents may be more or less closely related to whether, for example, the firms they control produce basic or non-basic products. A business leader in the energy sector, for example, can be expected to be possessed of greater economic power than a business leader in the industry producing napkins. The degree of concentration and monopolization within an industry also matters a great deal and affects the weight to be attributed to the business leader. This weight may differ as between agents he does business with.[5]

For a given power structure, the location of a particular agent, that is, whether he or she is a basic or a non-basic agent, and if the latter, whether he or she is a non-basic agent of the first, second and so on order, is obviously a factor co-determining his or her power. Another factor is the kind of means at the agent's disposal relative to those at the disposal of his or her counterparts or opponents. A third factor is the institutional setting, the channels of communication, the rule of law and the rules of the game, the opportunities to build coalitions or monopolies, the social security system and so on that have an impact on the outcome of the socio-economic process.

[5] With multiproduct firms, which are the normal case, the power or influence of a business leader could be conceptualized as some weighted average of these product-specific powers.

Reproduction and Transformation of Power Structures A specification of the power structure in terms of a hierarchy can be the starting point of an inquiry both into the reproduction of this structure and into its erosion and eventual abandonment in favour of some new structure. As in the theory of innovations, technical change and economic growth, important movers and shakers of a given power structure are breakthroughs in technical and organizational knowledge. These may have various effects. First, they may affect the magnitudes of what we may call the "coefficients of power" to be attributed to agents in the hierarchy, retaining the dimension of it. Second, they may elevate a non-basic agent of a given order to some higher order or even to the position of a basic one, or, conversely, downgrade the agent in a variety of ways. Third, disruptive changes may affect the dimension of the matrix: some rows may disappear and others enter the picture. The increase in variety (new positions of power) need not be exactly matched by a parallel decrease in it (the elimination of certain positions). Hence, the dimension of the matrix will change in all probability.

5.3 Thomas Hobbes and the Absolutist State[6]

In Chap. X, "Of Power, Worth, Dignity, Honour and Worthiness", of Part I, "Of Man", of his *Leviathan*, published in 1651, Hobbes defined "the power of man, to take it universally, as his present means to obtain some future apparent good". This power, he added, "is either original or instrumental" (Hobbes 1651: 53). He distinguished between "Natural Power" possessed by people with extraordinary qualities, such as intellectual eloquence, physical strength, prudence and so on and "Instrumental Power", which refers to means or devices used to increase one's personal power; these include especially wealth but also reputation, influential friends and networks. The quest for power, Hobbes was convinced, is ultimately *a quest for command over the power of other people*. If a person

[6] Another influential and much earlier author was Niccolò Machiavelli (1469–1527), whose book *Il Principe* was published posthumously in 1534. It was read and commented upon by many economists, including Adam Smith.

can get another person to use his or her power on behalf of the first person's interests, then the latter can add this power to his or her "arsenal". Hobbes observed: "The greatest of human powers is that which is compounded of the powers of most men, united by consent, in one person, natural or civil, that has the use of all their powers depending on his will; … Therefore to have servants is power; to have friends is power; for they are strengths united" (Hobbes 1651: 53–4).

Hobbes then enumerated the following sources of instrumental power: riches, reputation, popularity, to be loved or feared, good success, affability if already in power, reputation of prudence, nobility, eloquence, form and appearance (ibid.: 54). Instruments of war, fortifications and so on contribute to a sovereign's power. Wealth and riches are seen as an important source of power (see ibid.: 57). One form of increasing one's power is to buy the compliance of others. Hobbes stressed: "The value or worth of a man is, as of all other things, his *price*; that is to say, so much as would be given for the use of his power" (ibid.: 54; emphasis added).

Hobbes insisted that power is a *relative* concept—relating the powers of several people. If one person has less power than another one, then the former person is effectively powerless in the presence of the latter. In his opinion, this was the origin of a perpetual struggle for power amongst men, initiated by "puer robustus", a troublemaker, vying for greater and greater power and seeking to acquire the power of others. The condition of men, Hobbes insisted, "is a condition of war of every one against every one, in which case every one is governed by his own reason, and there is nothing he can make use of that may not be a help unto him in preserving his life against his enemies." He concluded:

> it followeth that in such a condition every man has a right to every thing, even to one another's body. And therefore, as long as this natural right of every man to every thing endureth, there can be no security to any man, how strong or wise soever he be, of living out the time which nature ordinarily alloweth man to live. (1651: 80)

According to Hobbes, there is only one possibility to escape the state of nature and perpetual war, the *bellum omnium contra omnes*: in the interest of peace, man is to cede all power to a central authority. This

Fig. 5.1 Leviathan

leads to a monarch or absolutist state endowed with absolute power—Hobbes' "Leviathan" (see Fig. 5.1), the monstrous and fearsome sea creature in the book of Job that ends the state of nature and brings about a condition of social equilibrium by keeping the "children of pride" in check.

Numerous authors after Hobbes took up his view that wealth is an important source of power. For example, Sir James Steuart (1713–1780) in his *Inquiry into the Principles of Political Oeconomy*, published in 1767, ten years before Adam Smith's *Wealth of Nations*, supported Hobbes' conviction by stating: "wealth will give power" (Steuart 1966 [1767]: 213). With the rise of nation-states in Europe, the discovery of new worlds, the expansion of long-distance trade and the growing tensions amongst nations over their overseas dominions, a major concern of mercantilist authors was with a nation's performance in foreign markets and its capability to prevail in the case of war. This directed the attention to a nation's economic and military power. In addition, these authors were often concerned with the relative power of the monarch and the great lords of the country. The dispersion of power within a nation and struggles over it could weaken the position of a nation relative to that of its competitors in the dispute over spheres of influence abroad.

We now turn to Adam Smith, who took issue with Hobbes' doctrine. The richness of his argument and the influence he had on Ricardo and Marx justify a detailed treatment of his ideas.

5.4 Adam Smith and the Well-Governed Society

The Systemic Aspect of Power The problem of power—economic, political, institutional—permeates Adam Smith's *The Wealth of Nations*.[7] The characteristic features of his perspective on the problem are the following: Smith saw power rooted in various kinds of asymmetries, especially regarding wealth, education, information and the ease or difficulty

[7] For the following, see also Samuels (1973, 1979), Elliot (2000), Kurz and Sturn (2013) and Kurz (2016a).

with which groups of people can organize and defend their interests. He was perfectly aware of the problem of collective decision and action large groups (e.g., workers) face vis-à-vis smaller ones (e.g., employers). His attention focused on the systemic aspect of the problem—*the working of the socio-economic system as a whole*. The power relationships in any such system are typically expressed in the existence and continual reproduction of social classes. These are defined in terms of the roles of their members in the process of the production, appropriation and use of the social product; their different degrees of information about and understanding of what is going on in the economy and their very uneven participation in public life. The persistence of social classes and the low rate of circulation of elites reflect a remarkable persistence of power asymmetries, which often erode only slowly, if at all. At the root of such asymmetries, Smith saw essentially differences in property, political power and access to information and knowledge. Society moulds people, and while people also mould society, the latter is hardly noticeable in the short run. The social backgrounds of people and how they have been brought up shape their motives, mind-sets and economic opportunities. Needs for achievement, attitudes and behaviours, consumption patterns and so on are shaped in no small degree by the social milieu from which a person comes. Treating tastes and preferences as givens that deserve no further examination, as in marginalist theory, mistakes the effects of the social fabric for its ultimate cause. The widespread idea that marginalist economics is deeply rooted in the Smithian tradition is difficult to sustain.[8]

Smith on Hobbes Smith advocated a socio-economic order in which large parts of economic life are coordinated via interdependent markets in conditions of free competition. Such an order, he was convinced, was not only economically highly successful, by favouring "equality, liberty and justice" (WN IV.ix.3) in society, it was also to be welcomed from an

---

[8] We only mention in passing that Smith, the moral philosopher, was convinced that the acquisition of power and riches does not keep the promises man associates with them. He insisted: "Power and riches ... keep off the summer shower, not the winter storm, but leave [man] always as much, and sometimes more, exposed than before to anxiety, to fear, and to sorrow; to diseases, to danger, and to death" (TMS: 302). He added: "And it is well that nature imposes upon us in this manner. It is this deception which arouses and keeps in continual motion the industry of mankind" (TMS: 303).

ethical point of view. He was convinced that pursuing one's interests did not necessarily lead to chaos and anarchy—at least not in a well-governed society. *The Wealth of Nations* was explicitly designed to elaborate a "science of the legislator" that showed the way towards good government. Smith was decidedly not of the opinion that is frequently, but wrongly, ascribed to him, that nothing but selfishness was needed to yield socially beneficial outcomes (see the discussion in Kurz 2016a, c). This view was exactly the opposite of the one Hobbes had advocated. To Smith both were fundamentally flawed: the former shut its eyes before the dark sides of man, whereas Hobbes ignored the bright sides.

In *The Theory of Moral Sentiments* (1969 [1759]), Smith attacked Hobbes' doctrine head-on by calling it "odious" and "offensive to all sound moralists, as it supposed that there was no natural distinction between right and wrong; that these were mutable and changeable, and depended upon the mere arbitrary will of the civil magistrate" (TMS: 504). In order to refute Hobbes' doctrine, Smith stressed, "it was necessary to prove that, antecedent to all law or positive institution, the mind was naturally endowed with a faculty, by which it distinguished, in certain actions and affections, the qualities of right, laudable, and virtuous, and in others those of wrong, blameable, and vicious" (TMS: 504). Peace and an agreeable state of social affairs, Smith was convinced, could not be attained by means of a Leviathan, who would spell trouble for most of his subjects but rather by good government that did not unduly limit the freedom of action of agents.

While Smith rejected Hobbes' overall construction, there is an element in it, which in *The Wealth of Nations*, he firmly endorsed:

> *Wealth, as Mr. Hobbes says, is power*. But the person who either acquires, or succeeds to a great fortune, does not necessarily acquire or succeed to any political power, either civil or military. … The power which that possession immediately and directly conveys to him, is the *power of purchasing*; a certain *command over all the labour*, or over all the produce of labour, which is then in the market.

This echoes Hobbes' concept of the price that would have to be given for the use of someone else's power. Smith went on:

> His fortune is greater or less, *precisely in proportion to the extent of this power*; or to the quantity either of other men's labour, or, what is the same thing, of the produce of other men's labour, which it enables him to purchase or command. *The exchangeable value of everything must always be precisely equal to the extent of this power which it conveys to its owner.* (WN I.v.3; emphases added)

Labour Commanded Versus Labour Embodied: Smith's Measure of Power The difference between the amount of labour embodied in a commodity and the amount of labour that can be commanded by the owner of a unit of it is Smith's measure of the owner's power. His idea can be explained with the help of some simple formal analysis. Assume a classical Smithian system of "natural prices" in the simple case of circulating capital only (and abstracting from scarce natural resources),

$$\mathbf{p} = (1+r)(\mathbf{A}\mathbf{p} + w\mathbf{l}),$$

with $\mathbf{p}$ as the n-dimensional price vector, $\mathbf{A}$ as the n x n material input matrix, $\mathbf{l}$ as the n-dimensional vector of (homogeneous) labour inputs, r as the general rate of profits and w as the wage rate (see Kurz and Salvadori 1995: Chap. 4). All value magnitudes are expressed in terms of some standard of value, a single commodity or a bundle of commodities $\mathbf{d}$, that is,

$$\mathbf{d}^T\mathbf{p} = 1.$$

Labour commanded prices, $\mathbf{p}^{\circ}$, equal natural prices or prices of production divided by the wage rate, $\mathbf{p}^{\circ} = \mathbf{p}/w$, and thus:

$$\mathbf{p}^{\circ} = (1+r)(\mathbf{A}\mathbf{p}^{\circ} + \mathbf{l}).$$

Solving for $\mathbf{p}^{\circ}$, gives.

$$\mathbf{p}^{\circ} = (1+r)\left[\mathbf{I} - (1+r)\mathbf{A}\right]^{-1}\mathbf{l},$$

with $\mathbf{I}$ as the $n \times n$ identity matrix.

The vector of quantities of labour embodied in the different commodities, **v**, is instead given by:

$$\mathbf{v} = \mathbf{A}\mathbf{v} + \mathbf{l} \text{ or } \mathbf{v} = (\mathbf{I} - \mathbf{A})^{-1}\mathbf{l}.$$

Comparing the last two systems of equations, one can see at a glance that when the rate of profits happens to be equal to zero, labour commanded and labour embodied magnitudes coincide:

$$\mathbf{p}^{\circ} = \mathbf{v} \text{ iff } r = 0.$$

Yet when the rate of profits is positive, labour commanded prices exceed labour embodied values:

$$\mathbf{p}^{\circ} > \mathbf{v} \text{ iff } r > 0,$$

where $0 \leq r \leq R$, with R as the maximum rate of profits for the given system of production corresponding to zero wages. Since, as can be shown (see, e.g., Kurz and Salvadori 1995: Chap. 4, especially 116), labour commanded prices are positive functions of the rate of profits, that is,

$$\frac{d\mathbf{p}^{\circ}}{dr} > 0,$$

the higher is r, the larger is the difference between labour commanded and labour embodied.

This corresponds to Smith's conviction that all property incomes indiscriminately imply a "deduction from the produce of labour" (WN I. viii.7). Here, this "deduction" is caused by the existing asymmetry with regard to the economic power of capitalists relative to that of workers. The size of the deduction reflects the magnitude of the asymmetry.

Sraffa's Standard Commodity The measure of power Smith suggested found an echo in Piero Sraffa's concept of the Standard commodity.[9]

[9] See also the related concepts of the integrated wage-commodity sector and the profit function in Garegnani (1984).

While the latter evolved from a reformulation of David Ricardo's concept of an invariable measure of value (i.e., invariable with regard to changes in income distribution), Sraffa (1960: 94) pointed out that it "should be found to be equivalent to something very close to the standard suggested by Adam Smith, namely 'labour commanded'". With the Standard commodity employed as the measure of value and wages taken to be paid post factum (i.e., at the end of the production period), the constraint binding changes in the rate of profits, *r*, and the share of wages in national income, Ω, or wage frontier, is given by

$$r = R(1 - \Omega),$$

with *R* as the maximum rate of profits. Solved for Ω, we get

$$\Omega = \frac{R - r}{R}.$$

The inverse gives the labour commanded value of the net social product,

$$\Omega^{-1} = \frac{R}{R - r}.$$

Obviously,

$$\mathrm{d}\frac{(\Omega^{-1})}{\mathrm{d}r} > 0.$$

With *r* approaching its finite maximum value *R* (and, correspondingly, the share of wages vanishing), the labour commanded value of the net social product tends to infinity. In Fig. 5.2, the abscissa gives the rate of profits and the ordinate the labour commanded value of the net social product. At $r = 0$ the share of wages equals unity, $\Omega = 1$, and so does the labour commanded value of the net social product, $\Omega^{-1} = 1$, which for *r*

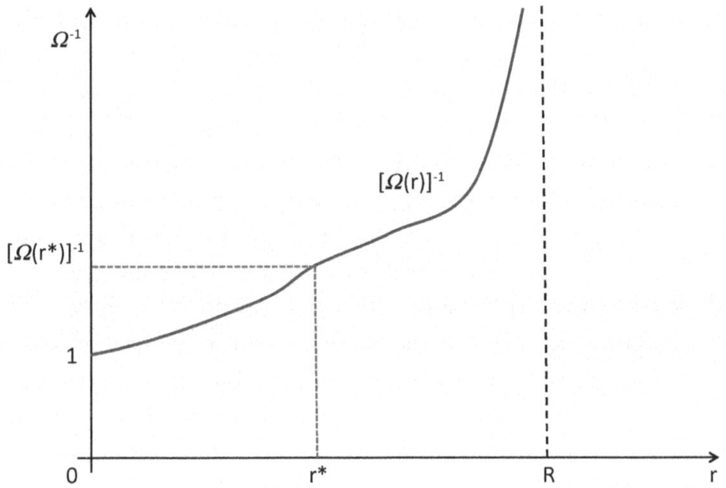

Fig. 5.2 A measure of the power of capital

= 0 equals also its labour embodied value.[10] If r approaches its upper limit R, the labour commanded value rises without limit. The upward bending curve $[\Omega\ (r)]^{-1}$ illustrates the relationship. Following Smith's suggestion, for any given value of r, such as, for example, $r = r^*$, the difference between $[\Omega\ (r^*)]^{-1}$ and unity is a measure of the power of capital relative to labour.[11]

Different Stages of Society Smith distinguished between three stages of society with regard to the distribution of the product amongst the various claimants. The stages are defined in terms of whether or not the objects and instruments of labour are in private ownership and are unevenly distributed amongst people. In the "original state of things", there are no significant means of production employed by men, and land is not yet privately appropriated. In this case, "the whole produce of labour belongs to the labourer. He has neither landlord nor master to share with him" (WN I.viii.2). All economic power is in the hands of producers.

[10] Sraffa normalizes the system by taking total employment as equal to unity.

[11] A measure of power alternative to Smith's and Sraffa's is, of course, Karl Marx's concept of the rate of surplus value or "exploitation"; see Garegnani (1984).

As soon as land becomes private property in the hands of only a few members of society, a two-class society with workers and landlords emerges, the latter demanding, and obtaining, a rent for the use of land, which "makes the first deduction from the produce of the labour which is employed upon land" (WN I.viii.6). Smith called rent explicitly a "monopoly price" (WN I.xi.a.5) to be paid to the feudal aristocracy. It has to be paid because landlords could otherwise withdraw their lands from productive use by others and thus threaten their survival.

With regard to the third stage, in which produced means of production play a significant role and are in private and concentrated ownership, Smith provided a first reason why the workers' bargaining position in the conflict over the distribution of the product is weak: "It seldom happens that the person who tills the ground has wherewithal to maintain himself till he reaps the harvest" (WN I.viii.7). The same applies essentially also to "all arts and manufactures", to which masters, that is, the proprietors of "stock" (plant and equipment and all kinds of means of production and subsistence), "advance the materials of their work, and their wages and maintenance till it be compleated" (WN I.viii.8). This leads to a "second deduction" from the produce of labour, which constitutes profits.

The "Dispute" over Income Distribution Smith then asked what determines the "common wages of labour". These depend, he observed, "every where upon the contract usually made between those two parties, *whose interests are by no means the same*", which is shown by the fact that "The workmen desire to get as much, the masters to give as little as possible. The former are disposed to combine in order to raise, the latter in order to lower the wages of labour" (WN I.viii.11; emphasis added). Smith insisted that:

> It is not, however, difficult to foresee which of the two parties must, upon all ordinary occasions, have the advantage in the *dispute, and force the other into compliance with their terms.* [1] The masters, being fewer in number, can combine much more easily; and [2] the law, besides, authorises, or at least does not prohibit their combinations, while it prohibits those of the workmen. … [3] In all such disputes the masters can hold out much longer.

> A landlord, a farmer, a master manufacturer, or merchant, though they did not employ a single workman, could generally live a year or two upon the stocks which they have already acquired. Many workmen could not subsist a week, few could subsist a month, and scarce any a year without employment. (WN I.viii.12; emphasis added)

Because of reasons [1]–[3], the bargaining position of the "labouring poor" is weak, which compels them to succumb to the conditions dictated by employers in the "dispute" over wages. "Masters", Smith added, "are always and every where in a sort of *tacit*, but constant and uniform combination, not to raise the wages of labour above their actual rate. To violate this combination is every where a most unpopular action, and a sort of reproach to a master among his neighbours and equals". He went on: "*We seldom, indeed, hear of this combination, because it is the usual, and one may say, the natural state of things which nobody ever hears of*" (WN I. viii.13, emphases added). We might say: *power walks on silent paws.*

Power Due to Information Asymmetries Workers, Smith observed, are typically little educated, they often do not know what their interests really are and how these can most effectively be pursued, and they hardly understand the working of the socio-economic system in which they live. They are thus easily the victims of others who deliberately mislead them in favour of their own interests.

Information asymmetries permeate *The Wealth of Nations*. Interestingly, Smith's classification of people as landlords, workers and capitalists corresponds not only to whether or not they possess some property but also to their access to information and knowledge. Landlords, as we have already heard, "love to reap where they never sowed": they receive revenue (rent) that "costs them neither labour nor care, but comes to them … independent of any plan or project of their own". This makes them indolent and "renders them too often, not only ignorant, but incapable of that application of mind which is necessary in order to foresee and understand the consequences of any publick regulation" (WN I.xi.p.8).

The situation is a great deal worse with respect to the great majority of people, its second order: the worker's "condition leaves him no time to receive the necessary information, and his education and habits are commonly such as to render him unfit to judge even though he was fully informed". The worker, Smith stressed, is most in danger of being manipulated: "In the publick deliberation, therefore, his voice is little heard and less regarded, except upon some particular occasions, when his clamour is animated, set on, and supported by his employers, *not for his, but their own particular purposes*" (WN I.xi.p.9, emphasis added). The idea entertained in much of modern economics that all people are well (and often even perfectly) informed and capable of sound judgement is entirely alien to Smith's view.

According to Smith, the people who are best informed about economic and political matters are merchants and master manufacturers, who "during their whole lives … are engaged in plans and projects" and who therefore "have frequently more acuteness of understanding than the greater part of country gentlemen" (WN I.xi.p.10). These men, possessed of a "superior knowledge of their own interest", are, on the one hand, the source of economic development. Their selfishness may, on the other hand, harm the interests of the other classes and society at large. Smith emphasized with special reference to the "dealers" or market intermediaries that their interest "is always in some respects different from, and even opposite to, that of the publick. To … narrow the competition, is always the interest of the dealers" because it allows them to raise their profits and thus "levy, for their own benefit, an absurd tax upon the rest of their fellow-citizens." Smith inferred from this:

> The proposal of any new law or regulation of commerce which comes from this order, ought always to be listened to with great precaution, and ought never to be adopted till after having been long and carefully examined, not only with the most scrupulous, but with the most suspicious attention. *It comes from an order of men, whose interest is never exactly the same with that of the publick, who have generally an interest to deceive and even to oppress the publick, and who accordingly have, upon many occasions, both deceived and oppressed it.* (WN I.xi.p.10, emphases added)

Those who are better informed and able to assess the facts—businesspeople of all kinds—can be expected to use their superior knowledge to the disadvantage of others, whether in discussions of political or commercial matters. Their counterparts—consumers and workers—are exposed to what nowadays is called "moral hazard". Smith did not use the notion, but he was perfectly familiar with the concept and illustrated it in terms of numerous examples. He also stressed variously that asymmetric information in combination with moral hazard may lead to what is now called "adverse selection". An important case in point is the banking sector, as was evidenced by then recent events in Scotland and France: bankers are willing to take risks, knowing that in case of failure the potential costs of their decisions will be borne by others (see Kurz 2016a: Sect. 6).

Smith left no doubt that the banking trade ought to be regulated. The question was, which regulations would look after "the security of the whole society" and at the same time leave enough room for the pursuit of self-interest and allow banks to provide the needed credit for doing so. He was clear that a regulatory framework installed at one time could not settle the matter once for all but had to be adjusted in response to innovations carried out in the banking trade, many of which were designed to circumvent the regulations. Success or failure in this area tended to diminish or strengthen existing power asymmetries.

Free Versus Perfect Competition The importance of power in the classical economists can be put in sharp relief by contrasting the classical concept of "free competition", on the basis of which Smith, Ricardo and many others developed the main parts of their analyses, with the marginalist concept of "perfect competition" (see also Salvadori and Signorino 2013). In the literature, the two are frequently confounded, although they ought to be strictly kept apart. The system of equations giving natural prices mentioned earlier reflects a situation of free competition but not a state of affairs in which none of the agents is possessed of economic power. Free competition means that there are no significant barriers to entry into or exit from any market. In such a state of things, there will be a tendency towards a uniform rate of profits throughout the economic system and hence across all industries and towards a uniform wage rate for each kind of labour (and a uniform rent per acre for each quality of land). It does *not* mean that there will be a tendency for profits (and rents) to vanish: the resulting prices exceed costs of production and include a positive rate of profits as an expression of capital's power.[12]

Whether the rate of profits is high, and the real wage rate correspondingly low, depends on a number of factors, including those mentioned earlier in the context of a discussion of the dispute over wages. Two important factors are now added. They concern, firstly, the pace at which capital accumulates in the economy and, secondly, the rate at which population grows. Smith stressed that it is only in conditions of rapid economic expansion, when the growth rate of the "demand for hands" exceeds that of supply, that masters tend to violate their combination: "The scarcity of hands occasions a competition among masters, who bid against one another, in order to get workmen, and thus voluntarily break through the natural combination of masters not to raise wages" (WN I.viii.17). Concerned predominantly with the causes that improve the living conditions of the "labouring poor", it comes as no surprise that Smith would focus attention first and foremost on factors affecting capital accumulation and economic growth.

The "Wretched Spirit of Monopoly" The concern mentioned also explains Smith's repeated attacks on what he called the "wretched spirit of monopoly" that was constantly seeking to restrict competition and establish monopolistic conditions. The monopolist does not have to fear competitors, who underbid his price, reduce his market share and curtail his profits. Monopolies are able "to keep up the market price, for a long time together, a good deal above the natural price" (WN I.vii.20). This allows them to pocket the difference as supernormal or extra profits. Restricting competition, Smith was convinced, is another device for single firms or entire sectors of the economy to increase their profitability.[13]

---

[12] For a more general formulation that includes also the use of fixed capital and scarce natural resources, see Sraffa (1960: Chap. XI) and Kurz and Salvadori (1995: Chap. 10).

[13] Because of incessant attempts of firms to restrict competition, Smith would have in all probability received with disbelief Böhm-Bawerk's view that it is legitimate to start from the assumption of perfect competition. Smith was aware that "improvements" of the productive apparatus would give the innovating firms a temporary monopoly, but this case was different from trying to be granted privileges by the Crown as, for example, in the case of the East India Company.

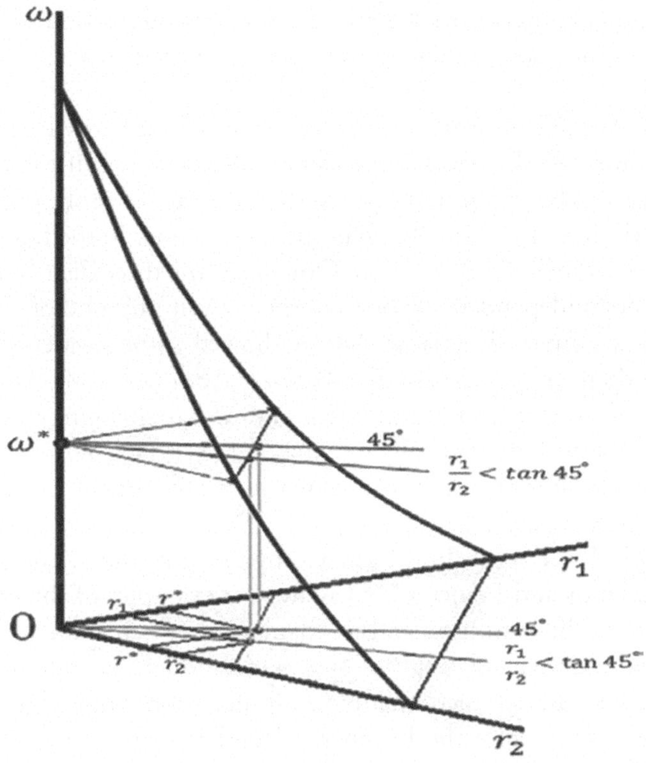

Fig. 5.3 The wage frontier

We may illustrate the argument with the help of the wage frontier (see Kurz and Salvadori 1995: 50–51) in the case in which there are only two industries, one of which manages to reap supernormal profits. The wage frontier in the example under consideration gives the constraint binding changes in the distributive variables, the real wage rate, ω, and the rates of profit in the two industries, r_1 and r_2, where $r_j > 0, j = 1, 2$. Each set of (feasible) rates would typically lead to a different set of relative prices. In Fig. 5.3, the real wage rate (in terms of one of the commodities or a bundle of them) is measured along the vertical axis, whereas the industry-specific profit rates are measured along the two axes on the bottom plane. In conditions of free competition, at a given natural wage rate ω^*, the rate of profits would tend to be uniform, that is, $r^* = r_1 = r_2$. It would be given by the intersection of the 45° line and the intersection of the wage frontier and the plane parallel to the level ω^* of the real wage rate.

Clearly, if in one industry, because of a monopolistic privilege, a higher rate of profit than the natural one can be obtained, and if the real wage rate happens to be unaffected by this, then the rate of profit in the other industry will have to be smaller than the natural one. In the figure, $r_2 > r^* > r_1$ represents such a constellation. Obviously, the three distributive variables are not independent of one another: given any one of them, the other two are inversely related. Smith showed some awareness of this (although there are passages in *The Wealth of Nations* that shed doubts on the depth of his understanding). He also saw that changing income distribution, that is, hypothetically moving on the surface of the wage frontier is typically accompanied by changes in relative prices (see Kurz and Sturn 2013: Sect. 2.6.3).

To Smith, the English East India Company and similar companies in the Netherlands and France were frightening examples of the enormous power monopolies can have and the damage they can cause. And while Smith was a fervent advocate of free trade, he left no doubt that his respective doctrine was incompatible with such monopolies. He deplored "The savage injustice of the Europeans [that] rendered an event, which ought to have been beneficial to all, ruinous and destructive to several of those unfortunate countries" (WN IV.i.32).

Unintended Consequences of Human Actions One of the central doctrines of authors of the Scottish Enlightenment was the doctrine of the unintended consequences of human action. In Smith's works, the reader encounters numerous cases exemplifying this doctrine. He famously discussed the relationship between the Roman Catholic Church, the secular lords and the masses, how the Church was able to defend its position as the monopoly supplier of religious services for centuries and how the monopoly broke down during the Reformation. While the Church had a disadvantage compared to the secular lords as regards military power and violence, it had an advantage as regards appeasing and controlling the masses. This prompted the worldly rulers to cooperate with the Church.

The price to be paid for this was stunted growth because economic development and increasing wealth of the people were understood by the ecclesiastic lords to threaten the authority and power of the Church. Poverty and ignorance kept people dependent and easily manipulable.

The Reformation changed all this. Newly emerging religious sects contested the Church's monopoly and weakened the dependence and subordination of the masses. As a consequence, also the relationship between the secular lords and the Church changed significantly, with the Church gradually losing its political influence and privileges. As Max Weber was to stress later, and much more than Smith had done, the fact that Protestants were supposed to read the Bible by themselves, and thus had to learn how to read and write, contributed greatly to the erosion of the power and influence of the Catholic clergy and, at the same time, paved the way towards a climate of innovation and economic growth.

Certain innovations in religion, the economy and other fields may look small and insignificant when they first make an appearance, but as time goes by, their full potential becomes visible. Some of these innovations affect fundamentally the received distribution of economic and political power. A case in point is Smith's discussion on the rise of towns and manufacturing and the concomitant decline of the power of the feudal lords. Smith argued: "what all the violence of the feudal institutions could never have effected, the silent and insensible operation of foreign commerce and manufactures gradually brought about" (WN III. Iv.10). Foreign trade and industry gave the wealthy access to extravagant "luxuries". While in the past the feudal lords for a lack of alternative uses had to share their surplus with tenants and retainers, now they could follow the "vile maxim of the masters of mankind"—"All for themselves, and nothing for other people … and thus, for the gratification of the most childish, the meanest and the most sordid of all vanities, they gradually bartered their whole power and authority" (WN III. Iv.10). Selfishness may be self-defeating: it may be good for others but bad for oneself.

5.5 David Ricardo on Individual Versus Collective Interests

David Ricardo thought highly of Smith's achievements and saw his own contribution as concerned essentially with correcting what in his, Ricardo's, view was incorrect or based on too narrow a foundation or adding what he felt was missing in Smith's analysis. For the rest, he was in agreement with the doctrine of the Scotsman.[14] Here, we limit the discussion to just four aspects: Ricardo's theory of profits and rents, his criticism of the Corn Laws, his sophisticated analysis of different forms of technical progress and their impact on workers and his criticism of the Bank of England and its monetary manoeuvres.[15]

The Surplus Approach to Property Incomes Prompted by a move before Parliament to restrict the corn trade in early 1813, Ricardo began to study in abstract terms the impact of such a restriction on the rate of profits and the rate of capital accumulation. He saw swiftly that Adam Smith's doctrine was flawed. In February 1815, Ricardo published his *Essay on Profits*, which laid the ground for his theory of value and distribution that was further developed in his magnum opus, *On the Principles of Political Economy, and Taxation*, which came out in April 1817. He insisted that "Profits come out of the surplus produce" (*Works* II: 128), which remains after all necessary costs of production, including the necessary wages of labour, have been deducted from gross outputs. For a given system of production characterized by given outputs and given methods of production used to produce these outputs, different levels of proportional wages would be associated with different levels of the general rate of profits. This is Ricardo's "fundamental law of distribution"—the inverse relationship between the *rate* of profits (r) and the *share* of wages (see *Works* VIII: 194)—arguably one of his most important analytical discoveries. Both real wages and the rate of profits could not rise, given the system of production in use, as some writers had contended.

[14] On Ricardo's political economy, see Sraffa (1951), Kurz (2015, 2016b) and King (2013).

[15] For a more detailed discussion, the reader might wish to consult Kurz (2015, 2016a, b) and Kurz and Salvadori (2015).

The harmonious view of society implicit in this contention was not only naïve—it was wrong.

Smith had explained the rent of land as a "monopoly price" and had argued in a physiocratic manner that rents reflect the "generosity" of nature: in agriculture, he opined, nature collaborates with workers but does so for free. This led him to the peculiar view that productivity in agriculture is higher than anywhere else in the economy, from which he concluded that economic policy should promote first and foremost the development of agriculture and not that of manufacturing and other sectors. Ricardo disagreed. First, rents reflect the "niggardliness" of nature and not its generosity: if land of the best quality was available in an unlimited quantity, there could be no rent. Only because its quantity is limited, also lands of inferior quality will eventually have to be cultivated in case effectual demand for wheat rises. The differences in unit costs between the least fertile quality of land that has to be employed in order to meet effectual social demand, later called "marginal land", and intra-marginal lands give rise to differential rents obtained by the proprietors of these lands. The price of wheat has to rise as the quantity produced of it increases, but since the price is determined on the no-rent-bearing quality of land, rent "cannot enter in the least degree as a component part of its price" (*Works* I: 77), contrary to Smith's view. Rent was not the cause but the effect of a high price of corn.

Ricardo developed his argument on the assumption of free competition and showed that no "monopoly price" concept was needed in order to understand the phenomenon of rent. He confirmed, however, Smith's proposition that the proprietors of (intra-marginal) lands reap where they never sowed and are the lucky beneficiaries of economic growth that tends to increase the scarcity of lands and swell the rents of land. Since according to the formula for a perpetual rent, the price of an acre of a given quality of land (an asset with infinite life) equals the rent divided by the rate of interest, the price of land will also rise (given a constant or even a falling rate of interest) and make landlords richer and richer, although they have done nothing at all for this to happen. Rents are effortless incomes, tied to the legal institution of private property of land; they reflect the dynamism of the economic system as a whole. The institution of property of land gives power to landlords, which tends to increase together with an expansion of the system.

Criticism of the Corn Laws Ricardo developed his theory of value and distribution in a deliberate move to provide a solid foundation for his criticism of the Corn Laws, which, after having been suspended during the late eighteenth century, were reinstated again after the Napoleonic Wars in 1815. Against the background of Ricardo's new theory, the effects of the Corn Laws were straightforward. By reducing imports, the price of corn would rise on the English isle. This would be immediately favourable to landlords, whose money rents would increase, and it would be immediately detrimental to workers, whose real wages would decrease, given money wages, and to consumers at large. Eventually, money wages would have to rise in case population growth happened to be negatively affected by a fall in real wages. This would in turn depress profitability and decelerate the accumulation of capital and economic growth. Because of rising domestic costs of production, the Corn Laws would also negatively affect the international competitiveness of the manufacturing sector. Clearly, the reinstatement of the Corn Laws was not in the interest of society as a whole: the only class that benefited were the landlords, whereas both workers and capitalists suffered from it. The Corn Laws were thus a typical case in which private interests were misleadingly passed off as collective ones. In Parliament, Ricardo belonged to a small minority of advocates of free trade. According to him, the reinstatement of the Corn Laws was just an expression of the fact that "the interest of the landlord is *always* opposed to that of the consumer and manufacturer" (*Works* I: 335; emphasis added).[16] He insisted: "All classes, therefore, except the landlords, will be injured by the increase in the price of corn", and added: "the loss is wholly on one side, and the gain wholly on the other; and if corn could by importation be procured cheaper, the loss in

[16] Vis-à-vis statements like these, it comes as no surprise that the landed gentry was hostile towards Ricardo; see expressions of Ricardo's anticipation in this regard and his expectation to be exposed to "all the charges and vituperation of the landed gentlemen against me" (*Works* IX: 262; see also X: 349). Landlords, he also argued, had a permanent interest in restricting trade in corn and other agricultural products, whereas the manufacturers' interest in protecting their business was only temporary.

consequence of not importing is far greater on one side, than the gain is on the other" (*Works* I: 336).[17]

Redressing the Balance of Power Between Capitalists and Workers: Machinery and Unemployment Ricardo had a much clearer understanding than Smith that technical change was an essential part of the development of modern society. He also saw that different types of technical change ought to be distinguished because they typically entail different effects. The widespread view that Ricardo saw the stationary state lurking around the corner mistakes his method of counterfactual reasoning—what would happen in the absence of technical progress?—for a statement concerning an actual tendency towards the stationary state. While Smith had argued that the manufacturing sector produced essentially only luxuries for the rich, Ricardo glimpsed its key role for economic development as an engine of growth.

Ricardo was also clear that certain forms of technical change were detrimental to the interests of workers. Under the impact of the Luddite movement, he re-considered his position on the question of improved machinery, and in the third edition of the *Principles*, published in 1821, added a new chapter. In "On machinery", he recanted his previous view that "the application of machinery to any branch of production, as should have the effect of saving labour, was a *general good*, accompanied only with that portion of inconvenience which in most cases attends the removal of capital and labour from one employment to another" (*Works*, I: 386; emphasis added). Previously, he had been convinced (in accordance with John R. McCulloch's theory of automatic compensation) that any displacement of workers due to technical change would swiftly be compensated by a growth in effectual demand in either the same or some other sectors. Technical progress, Ricardo now insisted, was not an unam-

[17] It deserves to be mentioned that Nicholas Kaldor, inspired by Ricardo, took the repeal of the Corn Laws in 1846 to exemplify the compensation criterion he suggested as a solution to the problem in welfare theory that policy measures typically have gainers and losers. According to Ricardo's above argument, landlords benefiting from the Corn Laws could not compensate workers and capitalists because their gains in physical terms were smaller than the losses incurred by the other classes of society.

biguous and immediate blessing for all members of society. The system may rather experience prolonged periods of what was later called "technological unemployment". Ricardo stressed: "I am convinced, that the substitution of machinery for human labour, is often very injurious to the interests of the class of labourers" (*Works*, I: 388).

Whereas prior to the third edition Ricardo had maintained that maximizing profits came almost to the same thing as maximizing employment levels, he had now convinced himself that there are cases in which this need not be so. In such cases, technical progress will increase the "net income" (profits), but decrease the "gross income", which equals the amount of productive labour performed during a year and thus employment: "the same cause which may increase the net revenue of the country, may at the same time render the population redundant, and deteriorate the condition of the labourer" (*Works* I: 388).

Ricardo called machines the "mute agents" of production (*Works*, I: 42) because, unlike workers, they do not ask for higher wages or better working conditions. He saw machinery and labour "in constant competition" with one another (*Works* I: 395) and even contemplated the limiting case of a fully automated system of production: "If machinery could do all the work that labour now does, there would be no demand for labour. Nobody would be entitled to consume anything who was not a capitalist, and who could not buy or hire a machine" (*Works* VIII: 399–400). Obviously, the introduction of improved machinery affected the balance of power between capitalists and workers in favour of the former. In the extreme case, when no labour was needed any longer, workers were deprived of any power whatsoever. One is reminded of Adam Smith's statement: "In the long run the workman may be as necessary to his master as his master is to him; but the necessity is not so immediate" (WN I.viii.12).[18] In the hypothetical case of a fully automated system, this necessity would completely vanish.

---

[18] Smith's earlier idea was developed by Anonymous (1821) and recurs in Piero Sraffa's papers and notes drafted in the late 1920s and early 1930s, which eventually led to his 1960 book; see Kurz (2012). In the perspective assumed, the claims of the different parties to the product resided in their power to threaten society by "withdrawing" their productive resources. Workers have to be paid, Smith stressed, at least a real wage that allows their "race" to reproduce itself. In case of a lack of alternatives to the use of their land, landowners, Sraffa surmised, have to be paid a zero rent if their land is not scarce. To capitalists, interest (profits) has to be paid, Sraffa argued at the time—

Criticism of the Bank of England Ricardo was highly critical of the Bank of England (which remained a private institution until 1946) and the governor's and bank directors' policy, which often had a single goal only: self-enrichment. In February 1816, Ricardo published some *Proposals for an Economical and Secure Currency* (see *Works* IV: 43–141), in which he put forward anew his "Ingot Plan". The plan suggested a return to the Gold Standard by making bank notes convertible not into specie (coins) but into bullion (gold ingots), which implied the demonetization of gold in domestic circulation. This would have several desirable effects: it would allow Britain to continue to use paper money as the actual means of payment, which Ricardo endorsed; it would reduce the need for gold reserves held by the Bank of England and thus dampen the upward pressure on the value of gold; and, last but not least, it would curb the huge profits pocketed by the governors and directors of the Bank, who benefited from the appreciation of gold. These profits, Ricardo insisted, belonged to the public. The House of Commons decided on a plan for the gradual return to note convertibility in bullion, starting in early 1820 and ending in May 1821 at the pre-1797 parity. During this period, Ricardo's Ingot Plan was implemented. However, immediately after the old parity had been restored, the Bank of England decided to return to note convertibility in coin. This led to huge profits being reaped by its directors, who in anticipation of the move and reflecting some sort of insider trading *avant la lettre* had amassed large amounts of gold, which they now sold to their bank at very favourable terms—precisely the kind of self-enrichment Ricardo chastized.

In 1823, Ricardo composed a *Plan for the Establishment of a National Bank*, which was published posthumously in February 1824 (see *Works* IV: 271–300). His plan had first taken shape in 1815 while he was composing the pamphlet *Economical and Secure Currency* and was then put forward in the first edition of the *Principles* (*Works* I: 361–3). Of the two operations that the Bank of England performed—issuing paper currency

again in accordance with Smith, in order to prevent capitalists from withdrawing their circulating capital (including the wear and tear of fixed capital), thus thwarting the "self-replacement" of the economy.

and advancing loans to merchants and other investors—the former should be taken away from it and given to independent commissioners, who acted as bankers to the government but were "totally independent of the control of ministers". This would not thwart the provision of the economy with money, but "in a free country, with an enlightened legislature" (*Works* I: 362), it would transfer a part of the profits of the Bank to the national Treasury and thus to the public, where they belonged.

5.6 Concluding Remarks

The classical economists' ideas resound in the writings of many authors. Karl Marx provided a critical account of them and elaborated on important classical doctrines. Scholars such as Vladimir K. Dmitriev, Ladislaus von Bortkiewicz and, in particular, Piero Sraffa reformulated the classical approach to the theory of value and distribution, with Sraffa providing a logically coherent and comprehensive version of it. As regards the Marxist tradition, the work of the Austrian economist Rudolf Hilferding on finance capital (Hilferding 1910) and the Polish economist Michal Kalecki on economic dynamics (Kalecki 1939) deserve to be mentioned, amongst others. The Italian philosopher Antonio Gramsci (1971), inspired by Marx's concept of "commodity fetishism", elaborated the concepts of "hegemony" and "manufacture of consent" designed to capture the pacifying effect of institutions and rules that keep the tensions besetting a socio-economic system that is antagonistic and inherently crises ridden under control.

The abandonment of a concern with power in (what was to become) mainstream economics is to no small degree due to Eugen von Böhm-Bawerk's highly influential essay "Macht oder ökonomisches Gesetz" (Power or economic law) (1914). Böhm-Bawerk argued that while in the short run power may exert some influence on economic outcomes, competitive forces will never sleep and swiftly undermine the foundations of such power. Therefore, economists do not go significantly astray when basing their reasoning on the assumption of perfect competition. This view still dominates important fields in mainstream economics. However, already at the time when Böhm-Bawerk's essay was published, its message looked anachronistic vis-à-vis the trend towards monopolization and trustification, stressed, for example, by American institutionalists from Thorstein Veblen to John Maurice Clark. Some mainstream economists, most notably Arthur Cecil Pigou and Abba Lerner, responded to the challenge by dealing with the impact of power in terms of persistent monopolistic distortions of product and factor markets. In this perspective, power is reflected by deviations of product prices from their marginal costs and of rates of remuneration of factors of production from (the value) of their marginal productivities.

This was not the end of the story. Non-mainstream economists continued to emphasize and analyse the impact of power in the economy, whereas large parts of mainstream economics went on cherishing the utopia of a powerless state of affairs. In 1971, the Austrian economist Kurt Rothschild published a widely circulated Penguin modern economics reader entitled *Power in Economics* (Rothschild 1971), which deplored the neglect of power in much of marginalist analysis and contained a fervent plea to take power seriously in economics. Alas, the book's success was modest, to say the least. Things might, and hopefully will, change. On the one hand, financialization has deeply affected capitalism and had a substantial impact on the distribution of economic and political power in favour of the banking and financial sector of the economy. The liberalization of the sector has caused a major economic crisis, threatening the world economy. On the other hand, what is occasionally called the "Fourth Industrial Revolution" can also be expected to affect profoundly the distribution of power among members of society, away from workers in general and towards capital owners and especially those that control, and are able to manipulate, the most important resource in modern times: information and big data. The old question of how to ward off the dangers involved in the amassment of power in a few hands, discussed since the times of Plato and Aristotle, poses itself forcefully today.

Power is a pervasive phenomenon in the economy and society, associated with inequality of income, wealth, race, gender, information and so on. If wealth is power, as Adam Smith had insisted, and if wealth is getting more and more concentrated, as has been the case in many countries recently, an irreconcilable contradiction obtains between the democratic logic of "one voter, one vote" and the market logic of "one Dollar, one vote". Democracy is in danger of becoming an empty shell. Economic policies have amplified if not precipitated this trend. It is high time for them to reverse it.

References

Böhm-Bawerk, E. v. (1914). Macht oder ökonomisches Gesetz, *Zeitschrift für Volkswirtschaft, Socialpolitik und Verwaltung*, 23, 205–271. American translation by J. R. Metz as *Control or Economic Law*. Auburn: Ludwig von Mises Institute.

Dahl, R. A. (1957). The Concept of Power. *Behavioral Science, 2*(3), 201–215.

Elliot, J. E. (2000). Adam Smith's Conceptualization of Power, Markets, and Politics. *Review of Social Economy, 58*(4), 429–454.

Garegnani, P. (1984). Value and Distribution in the Classical Economists and Marx. *Oxford Economic Papers, 36*(2), 291–325.

Gramsci, A. (1971). *Selections from the Prison Notebooks of Antonio Gramsci*. New York: International Publishers.

Hilferding, R. (1910). *Das Finanzkapital. Eine Studie zur jüngsten Entwicklung des Kapitalismus*. Vienna: Verlag der Wiener Volksbuchhandlung Ignaz Brand & Co.

Hobbes, T. (1651). *Leviathan or the Matter, Forme, & Power of a Common-wealth Ecclesiasticall and Civill*. London: Andrew Crooke. Cited After the Version Prepared by Rod Hay for the McMaster University Archive of the History of Economic Thought.

Jessop, B. (2012). Marxist Approaches to Power. In E. Amenta, K. Nash, & A. Scott (Eds.), *The Wiley-Blackwell Companion to Political Sociology* (pp. 3–14). Oxford: Basil Blackwell.

Kalecki, M. (1939). *Essays in the Theory of Economic Fluctuations*. London: Allen & Unwin.

King, J. (2013). *David Ricardo*. London: Palgrave Macmillan.

Kurz, H. D. (2012). Don't Treat Too Ill My Piero! Interpreting Sraffa's Papers. *Cambridge Journal of Economics, 36*, 1535–1569.

Kurz, H. D. (2015). David Ricardo on the Art of "Elucidating Economic Principles" in the Face of a "Labyrinth of Difficulties". *European Journal of the History of Economic Thought, 22*(5), 818–851.

Kurz, H. D. (2016a). Adam Smith on Markets, Competition and Violations of Natural Liberty. *Cambridge Journal of Economics, 40*(2), 615–638.

Kurz, H. D. (2016b). David Ricardo (1772–1823). In G. Faccarello & H. D. Kurz (Eds.), *Handbook on the History of Economic Thought* (Vol. I, pp. 120–143). Cheltenham/Northampton: Edward Elgar.

Kurz, H. D. (2016c). *Economic Thought: A Brief History*. New York: Columbia University Press.

Kurz, H. D., & Salvadori, N. ([1995] 1997). *Theory of Production: A Long-Period Analysis*. Cambridge: Cambridge University Press. Revised Paperback Edition.

Kurz, H. D., & Salvadori, N. (2015). *Revisiting Classical Economics. Studies in Long-Period Analysis*. London: Routledge.

Kurz, H. D., & Sturn, R. (2013). *Die größten*. Ökonomen: Adam Smith, Konstanz: UVK.

Popitz, H. ([1986] 1992). *Phänomene der Macht* (2nd enlarged ed). Tübingen: Mohr Siebeck.

Ricardo, D. (1951–1973). *The Works and Correspondence of David Ricardo*, 11 vols. Edited by P. Sraffa with the collaboration of M. H. Dobb. Cambridge: Cambridge University Press (cited as *Works*, vol. number, page number).

Rothschild, K. W. (Ed.). (1971). *Power in Economics,* in *Penguin Modern Economics Readings*. Harmondsworth: Penguin Books Ltd.

Russell, B. (1938). *Power: A New Social Analysis*. London: Allen & Unwin.

Salvadori, N., & Signorino, R. (2013). The Classical Notion of Competition Revisited. *History of Political Economy, 45*(1), 149–175.

Samuels, W. J. (1973). Adam Smith and the Economy as a System of Power. *Review of Social Economy, 31*(2), 123–137.

Samuels, W. J. (Ed.). (1979). *The Economy as a System of Power*. New Brunswick: Transaction Books.

Simon, H. A. (1957). *Models of Man*. New York: Wiley.

Smith, A. (1969 [1759]). *The Theory of Moral Sentiments*, 1st edn 1759, 6th edn 1790, with an introduction by E. G. West. Indianapolis: Liberty Classics.

Smith, A. (1976). *An Inquiry into the Nature and Causes of the Wealth of Nations*, 2 vols. In R. H. Campbell & A. S. Skinner (Eds.), *The Glasgow Edition of the Works and Correspondence of Adam Smith*. Oxford: Oxford University Press.

Sraffa, P. (1951). Introduction. In *Ricardo* (1951) (Vol. I).

Sraffa, P. (1960). *Production of Commodities by Means of Commodities*. Cambridge: Cambridge University Press.

Steuart, S. J. (1966 [1767]). *An Inquiry into the Principles of Political Oeconomy*, in two vols, edited and with an introduction by A. S. Skinner. Edinburgh/London: Oliver & Bond.

Weber, M. (1947). *The Theory of Social and Economic Organization*. New York/ Oxford: Oxford University Press.
Weber, M. (1972). *Wirtschaft und Gesellschaft* (5th ed.). Tübingen: Mohr. (1st ed. 1922 in *Grundriß der Sozialökonomik*, Part III, Tübingen: J.C.B. Mohr (Paul Siebeck).

6

Power and Poverty: Social Legislation in the Years of Adam Smith

Cosma Orsi

6.1 Introduction

The eighteenth century was a fascinating period of gradually changing political, economic, and social structures and institutions. Especially during the last quarter of the century, England was forced to deal with the speed of the Parliamentary enclosure process, the fear induced by the French Revolution, the subsequent Napoleonic wars, and a series of economic crises that, by the 1790s, threatened to slash the social fabric to its core. In a period marked by growing inequality (Kuznets 1966, 217), the call for public policies on behalf of the poor increased markedly.[1]

Until that moment, the assistance to the poor was codified by the *utility of the poor* doctrine (Furniss 1920); its main tenet was the acceptance

[1] During the seventeenth and the eighteenth centuries, the poor were those "without income from property or profession and, therefore, dependent upon their manual labour for living" (Cowherd 1977, 2). Providing relief to the most needy was never an issue. The problem was how to deal with the able bodied—no matter whether they were unemployed or working poor.

C. Orsi (✉)
Catholic University of the Sacred Heart, Milan, Italy

M. Mosca (ed.), *Power in Economic Thought*, Palgrave Studies in the History of Economic Thought, https://doi.org/10.1007/978-3-319-94039-7_6

of labour by the poor as a necessary condition for national prosperity.[2] In order to become operational, the *utility of the poor* doctrine required not only a State that reduced the wage of labourers to the maximum possible extent[3] but also the establishment of a network of workhouses, both public and private, with the express purpose of putting the poor to work. From the mid-seventeenth century to the mid-eighteenth century, the number of workhouses increased exponentially. The zenith of this process was reached in 1723, when the Parliament passed the *Workhouse Test Act*. The system of relief, from then onwards, became even more closely linked to the commercial needs of local economic elites—always eager to avail themselves of the supply of cheap labour (Ashcraft 1996, 48)—than to those of the mass of unemployed and labouring poor—locked in filthy workhouses, and unable to relocate in search of gainful employment.[4] Under the new legislation, not only could parishes deny relief to those who chose not to enter the workhouses, but they were also legitimised to apply "commercial methods to the poverty problem" (Fideler 2006, 154). The legislation put in place one of the most odious practices which enabled parishes to exploit the poor (privately contracting them out—

[2] This mindset rested on a biased understanding of the poor's human nature and their attitude towards work. Excluding any social or economic cause of poverty, the *utility of the poor* advocates endorsed the a priori view that the poor did not work because they were naturally idle and inclined towards licentious behaviour (Mun 1664; Manley 1669; Dunning 1686; Cary 1695; Locke 1697/1997; Pollexfen 1700; Defoe 1704; Mandeville 1725).

[3] Its advocates maintained that wages above bare subsistence would have not only destroyed the poor's productivity, but they would have also encouraged insolent and impertinent behaviour (Furniss 1920, 118). Thus, low wages were seen as a disciplining tool for transforming the poor into subordinate economic agents.

[4] It should be remembered that from the mid-Seventeenth century, Parliament passed *The Poor Relief Act* (1662), designed to establish to which parish a person belonged. Better known as the *Act of Settlement and Removal,* it stood at the very heart of the *Poor Law* until 1795, clarifying—should a poor person be in need—which parish was responsible for his relief. Although the *Act of Settlement and Removal* firmly established the responsibility to provide the poor with a minimum subsistence, it became the cornerstone for the control of the labouring poor's mobility on the part of local government (Landau 1988, 391, 407). Even if the law was often emended and poorly enacted (Marshall 1926; Fideler 2006), it deprived vast sectors of the workforce of its freedom to move. Furthermore, when enacted, it was often accompanied by manifest acts of brutality (*Parliamentary History* 1814, XVII, 844). For these reasons, no other piece of legislation received so much criticism as the *Act of Settlement and Removal.* See Hay (1735, 10, 119), Bentham (1792 [1823], 234), Eden (1797).

better known as *farming*), sustaining that it was the easiest method for reducing the financial burden of parishes (*ibid.*, 154).

However, as time passed, these schemes for employing the poor generated an array of criticism.[5] Even if workhouses were ideally meant to provide the poor with a chance to reinforce their membership within the broader community, they became a reminder of social dissonance. By closely adhering to *the utility of the poor* doctrine, their administrators put into effect the idea that it was necessary to "resist any [...] forces which promised to break up class status and facilitate the social advance of the lower orders" (Furniss 1920, 145). The way in which the entire system was managed shows that the major concern was controlling the poor and not addressing poverty as such. Namely, workhouses were not conceived as means to improve the social conditions of the poor. They were assisted only in case of extreme hardship (to avoid them dying of starvation), but no one expected inmates to cease to be poor (Mandeville 1725, 213; Alcock 1752; Temple 1758; Young 1771; Townsend 1786).

As a result of the round of reforms the Parliament passed between 1780s and 1790s, up to the establishment of the *New Poor Laws* (1834), the English system of social protection ceased to be shaped by the *utility of the poor* doctrine. The poor were no longer considered "as a set of somewhat troublesome tools", they became instead, fully fledged "human beings whose own comfort and happiness were the proper and primary object of concern for statesmen" (Viner 1927, 56–7).

Social and economic historians have provided a variety of explanations for this shift.[6] The array of different, even contrasting, claims expressed

[5] To some authors of the day, it was an established fact that workhouses were lacking in expediency and justice. Earlier in the seventeenth century, John White (1630, 20), Samuel Hartlib (1649, 8), and John Graunt (1662, 351) had already expressed their concerns about the economic and administrative rationale governing the system of indoor relief. From the last quarter of the century, other influential writers like Thomas Firmin (1678, in Eden 1797, I 204), John Bellers (1696, 28), Daniel Defoe (1704), and Lawrence Braddon (1722) expressed concern for the results obtained by indoor relief. In 1715, the anonymous drafter of an official Report stated that out of 12,000 babies born in workhouses, only a quarter survived; it also reported of stolen money, falsified accounts, paupers starving to death, or being killed (anon. 1715). In 1732, an unknown *Overseer* reported that "we have many here who would choose to starve, rather than be maintained in [...] the house of correction, as they call it" (anon. 1732, 127).

[6] See Hammond and Hammond (1911 [1929], 120, 123, 170), Webb and Webb (1927–29, 223, 419), Marshall (1956, 153–4), Coats (1958, 1960), Cowherd (1960, 1977), Poynter (1969, 16), Himmelfarb (1984), Mandler (1987, 134), Boyer (1990, 2).

on this topic calls for further analysis of a period that has been somewhat neglected as a result of the far-reaching shadow cast on the period by the *Poor Law Commissioners Report of 1834*, which led to the *New Poor Laws* (*1834*).

What role, if any, did the British political economists play in this shift? In order to answer this question, we pursue an analysis into the reflections on poverty and its remedies offered by the leading classical economist, Adam Smith. His reasoning represented the culmination of a long train of thought that targeted the *utility of the poor* as an unsound doctrine for national prosperity and, once implemented, as a tool to exercise strict power and control over the poor, thereby accentuating the gap between social classes.[7] While Smith's direct influence on the round of reforms which occurred in the latter quarter of the eighteenth century cannot be proven, if we look at the matter from the perspective of power relationships within the commercial society, the link between his economic theory and social legislation would appear clearer. In elaborating a new understanding of power relations within the economic (and social) spheres, as precondition to the kind of economic development he envisioned, Smith drew a map for the legislator to deal with the plight of poverty. It is suggested here that although Smith never explicitly mentioned the doctrine, his inclination towards the lower ranks of society can be better understood if we consider his reasoning as a stern critic of the *utility of the poor* and the unbalanced power relationship it entailed.[8] We shall devote our attention to Smith's policy suggestions for reducing the imbalance of power that continued to pervade the commercial society looking for possible signs of influence on the shaping of the round of reforms, which took place in the last quarter of the seventeenth century. This, we hope, offers a broader and insightful perspective of the historical and cultural context in which the *Gilbert Act* (1782), the *Rose Act* (1793),

[7] This understanding reflects closely the one put forward by Krishna Bharadwaj when she pointed out that power relationships ought to be framed as relationships where "one side possessed of a superior socio-economic position … may even imply the domination or subjugation of the other side" (Bharadwaj 1989, 1).

[8] As Christopher Martin noted, while not proving that he read them, both "James Bonar's and Hiroshi Mizuta's catalogs show that Smith owned many works that discuss the doctrine of the utility of poverty" (Martin 2015, 568).

and the *Speenhamland system* (1795) were formulated, approved, and eventually implemented.

6.2 Higher Wages, Inequality, and Economic Development: A New Perspective

By the mid-eighteenth century, England was experiencing "a great expansion and an apparent growth of national income" (Marshall 1926 [2007], 79), but simultaneously, vast sectors of the population, which in the meanwhile had dramatically increased, suffered severe poverty due to high food prices, low wages, and the effects of enclosures. At any rate, the convergence of the above factors was balanced by the emergence of a more vibrant and innovative industrial sector of the economy. That passage definitively altered the traditional restraints on economic growth by creating non-landed wealth in unprecedented abundance.[9] Within a few decades, the industrial revolution would render the English pre-industrial socio-economic landscape almost unrecognisable, and its parish-centred poor relief obsolete.

The industrial revolution was accompanied by the rise of a new and dynamic idea of economic development.[10] Challenging the general wisdom that England might become rich thanks to the poverty of its subjects, it endorsed the view that a prosperous economic system called for a healthy population that, by obtaining greater reward for their labour, would play a non-secondary role in enlarging the domestic market. Corollary to this understanding was the acknowledgment that "causation runs from the poor relief and the minimisation of risk and uncertainty that it entailed to economic success" and not the other way round (Smith 1986, 206). From this perspective, the *utility of the poor* doctrine was an ethics of subjection designed for a dominated population of labouring poor. It was saturated with an alleged moral superiority of the wealthy

[9] The idea of the industrial revolution as a divide between the premodern and modern era has been discussed, among others, by Rostow (1960), Landes (1969), and Hobsbawn (1969).

[10] Between 1725 and 1737, a minority strand of writers anticipated the case against the *utility of the poor* doctrine proposing instead a high-wage society (Gouldsmith 1725; Defoe 1728; Vanderlint 1734; Berkeley 1737).

local landowners over the poor, thereby legitimising the former to view the latter as mere instruments for the achievement of their interests—namely the maintenance of their economic privileges and status.

While the advocates of the *utility of the poor* doctrine presented make-work schemes as the soundest guideline for remedying poverty, its opponents pointed out the extent to which the existing system of poor relief was built on self-deception with the tendency to do more harm than good. Thanks to the insights of authors like Joseph Maisse (1757), John Scott (1773, 36), Robert Potter (1775, 52), Henry Zouch (1776, 6, 19–21, 34, 41–3), Edward Jones (1776, 11–5), and William Blackstone (1776 [1803], 439), it became even more apparent to what extent the combination of indoor relief and the *Act of Settlement and Removal* completed the connection between assistance and control/subjection of the poor. It was in this context that Adam Smith offered his influential ideas in the fields of both social philosophy and economics, thus paving the way for a new vision of poverty and the poor. According to Kurt Rothschild, Smith had the ability to "provide the scientific foundations for the creation of a 'civilized society' based on freedom, justice, and material welfare" (Rothschild 2002, 434). In Smith's analytical framework, the issue of power is at the forefront of the analysis (Kurz [in this volume, page to be determined]). Smith was conscious that "power can play a considerable role affecting the economic process in several ways, creating privileges on one side and discrimination on the other" (Rothschild 2002, 436). Moving from this premise, Smith's writings show a true concern with both the plight of severe poverty (Himmelfarb 1984, 31–35 and 46–62; Fleischacker 2005, 66; Kurz, 13–19 [pages in this volume, to be reviewed]) and the imbalances of economic power among social classes (Baum 1992, 144).

In sharp contrast to the advocates of the *utility of the poor*, Smith had a good opinion of the poor and their motivation to work. In his questioning the received wisdom, he upheld a view of human nature that drew attention to the fact that the labouring poor were not mere beasts of burden. Rather, they were decent, prudent, reflective, industrious, and trustworthy persons owning and selling a commodity—their labour—for a wage. Thus, laziness and intemperance were not inherent traits of the poor, but rather the result of adverse institutional or economic circumstances (Smith 1776 [1976], 19). For instance, those who were unemployed due to sickness or disability bore no responsibility for their condition. It was neither deserved nor a fate that they could escape from with the resources at their disposal. Accordingly, Smith saw no faults in the morals of the labouring poor. The poor were so concerned with their social position that "a creditable day-labourer would be ashamed to appear in public without a linen shirt" (*ibid.*, 399). Most significantly, Smith saw the labouring poor as the rightful owners of their own labour (*ibid.*, 128).[11]

By claiming that the main drive governing human action was not necessity but rather the desire to better one's condition, Smith rejected the argument according to which people work harder when they are afraid, or when real wages are low (*ibid.*, 85 and 92). Such a desire "comes with us from the womb, and never leaves us till we go to the grave" (*ibid.*, 362–63). A poor labourer like any other citizen, was motivated by the prospect of "ending his days perhaps in ease and plenty" (*ibid.*, 91).

6.3 Smith's Understanding of Poverty and Power

For Smith, the unequal distribution of economic power between the social classes, which still pervaded the commercial society,[12] was among the most relevant causes of poverty.

Smith's conviction that economic freedom led to economic growth was coupled with his concern for social and economic inequality.[13]

[11] On these premises, he upheld the *natural liberty* of all British subjects "of exercising what species of industry they please". To deny such a liberty would have been an "evident violation of natural liberty, and therefore unjust" (*ibid.*, 530).

[12] Fiore and Pesciarelli (1999, 95).

[13] Smith shared with Hume the concern for unbalanced power relationship. Hume was well aware that in the real world, power relationships did exist. In 1740, he wrote that "... when a person acquires such an authority over me, that not only there is no external obstacle to his actions; but also that he may punish or reward me as he pleases, without any dread of punishment in his turn, I then attribute a full power to him, and consider myself as a subject or vassal". About ten years later, he still believed that "where the riches are in few hands, these must enjoy all the power, and will readily conspire to lay the whole burthen on the poor, and oppress them still farther, to the discouragement of all industry", concluding that a "too great disproportion among the citizens

Though the *Wealth of Nations'* primary focus was economic growth,[14] he did not fail to emphasise inequality intrinsic to the commercial society: "Wherever there is great property, there is great inequality. For one very rich man, there must be at least five hundred poor, and the affluence of the few suppose the indigence of the many" (*ibid.*, 232). At any rate, Smith was aware of the fact that wealth entails power.[15] And economic power among different classes tends to establish a social order based on social relations geared around two pillars, authority and subordination.[16] According to his stadial theory, the birth of such relations should be placed in the period of pasturage.

> The second period of society, that of shepherds, admits of very great inequalities of fortune, and there is no period in which the superiority of fortune gives so great authority to those who possess it. There is no period, accordingly, in which authority and subordination are more perfectly established. (*ibid.*, 713)

To explain the passage from the pasturage age to the agricultural one and the transformation of the latter into the age of commerce, Smith described the historical trajectory of the progressive relaxation of such relations, which eventually led to a decisive increase of incentives to labour. These incentives, in turn, brought about an increase in the productivity of the land.[17]

---

weakens any state" (Hume 1752 [1955], 15). Building upon these premises, he offered a powerful statement anticipating a modern concept of welfare economics: "Every person, if possible, ought to enjoy the fruits of his labour, in a full possession of all necessaries and many of the conveniences of life. No one can doubt, but such equality is most suitable to human nature, and diminishes much less from the happiness of the rich than it adds to the poor" (*ibid.*).

[14] Smith believed that economic growth was the goal to be achieved because in it "the condition of the labouring poor, of the great body of the people, seems to be the happiest and the most comfortable" (Smith 1776 [1976], 43).

[15] (*ibid.*, 35).

[16] As Kurz cogently noted in his introductory essay "power relationships [...] are typically expressed in the existence and continual reproduction of social classes. These are defined in terms of the roles of their members in the process of the production and appropriation of the social product, their different degrees of information about and understanding of what is going on in the economy and their very uneven participation in public life" (Kurz 7).

[17] For an account of these passages, see Fiori and Pesciarelli (1999, 91–95).

By pointing out that a society based on excessive inequality would have been deleterious to economic growth, Smith attacked the landed aristocracy's way of life and interests in favour of small proprietors. Too much inequality fosters a kind of sterile consumption on the part of the rich depresses industry, and consequently weakens the social order. By underlining that within a flourishing society, consumption, productivity, and wages ought to increase hand in hand, he suggested that letting the labouring poor take part in the benefits generated by economic growth would broaden the potential for further economic progress. From this perspective, keeping the vast sectors of the population in poverty hindered the economic development of a country.

Accordingly, Smith upheld the view that while those who occupy the lowest ranks of today's society were significantly better off than those at the top of a primitive society, their position should be even further elevated. Bettering their living conditions was advantageous to all (*ibid.*, 88). In this fashion, Smith argued that "universal opulence" should "extend itself to the lowest ranks of people" (*ibid.*, 15).

It was on these grounds that he championed fair wages for the labouring poor. Smith considered high wages as an indicator of a flourishing and healthy economy as well as an essential feature of a fair society. As the liberal reward of labour would lead to "the greatest publick prosperity", Smith believed that it ought to become a policy goal (Cannan 1926, 127). This was a sound course of action because high wages would not lead to a decrease in labour supply. He acknowledged that "When wages are high [...] we shall always find the working man more active, diligent and expeditious, then when they are low" (Smith 1776 [1976], 85). It is improbable, he added, "that men in general should work better when they are ill fed than when they are well fed, when they are disheartened than when they are in good spirits, when they are frequently sick than when they are generally in good health" (*ibid.*, 92). "The wages of labour are the encouragement of industry, which, like every other human quality, improves in proportion to the encouragement it receives" (*ibid.*, 91).[18]

However, Smith knew that relying on market forces alone would not lead to the achievement of the social welfare he had in mind. Smith's

[18] This idea has been already expressed by Vanderlint (1734), Berkeley (1737), and Hume (1752).

liberal reward of labour seems to represent a normative ideal. For him, the commercial society had inherited some of the subordination relations that had already characterised the agricultural age. In a capitalist society, the "common wages of labour is established by contract, usually between those two parties whose interests are by no means the same". On the one hand, "the workmen desire to get as much" as possible; on the other hand, "the masters to give as little as possible. The former are disposed to combine in order to raise, the latter in order to lower the wages of labour" (*ibid.*, 83). Smith concluded that in the confrontation between the two parties, the economic power of the rich allowed them to better organise their interests against the poor (*ibid.*, 83–84).

6.4 Smith's Policy Suggestions

Even if he was convinced that, in the long run, the economic inequality between labourers and capitalists would be reduced because wages would rise and profits fall, he did "not wish merely to wait for the realization of the society he envisaged" (Niimura 2016, 903). Rather, he believed that poverty redress called for the implementation of policies fostering income redistribution. Because Smith identified in the unbalanced power relations between social classes, one of the main causes for generating and maintaining poverty, he envisaged a society where the State would be responsible for correcting such inequality. It should mobilise resource to the benefit of the poor.

Smith's reasoning rested on the idea that there were shortcomings in economic progress. If, on the one side, the division of labour improved the worker's dexterity, on the other, it corrupted his "intellectual, social, and martial virtues" (*ibid.*, 327). The shortcomings of the division of labour thus brought about a loss of "civic sense, the cement which binds cives and community together". However, a man who has lost his civic sense

> is as much mutilated and deformed in his mind as another is in his body. The same thing may be said of the gross ignorance and stupidity, which, in a civilised society, seem so frequently to benumb the understandings of all

> the inferior ranks of people. A man, without the proper use of the intellectual faculties of a man, is, if possible, more contemptible than even a coward and seems to be mutilated and deformed in a still more essential part of the character of human nature. (*ibid.*, 787–88)

It was for this reason that Smith's idea of social welfare called for a government concerned with the health of both the mind and the body of its subjects. "Even though the martial spirit of the people were of no use towards the defence of society, yet to prevent that sort of mental mutilation, deformity, and wretchedness, which cowardice necessarily involves in it, from spreading themselves through the great body of the people, would still deserve the most serious attention of government" (*ibid.*, 739).

Although Smith was very cautious in expressing a view with regard to government intervention on the behalf of the poor,[19] namely "to *prevent* the almost entire corruption and degeneracy of the great body of the people" (*ibid.*, 734 emphasis added), he praised publicly funded schools for the working class (*ibid.*, 306). In such institutions, the poor children would acquire "the most essential parts of education [...] to read, write and account" (*ibid.*, 785). Smith's policy suggestion, to enforce an educational programme financed by general taxation, not only entailed a transfer of income from taxpayers to the poor, but also it would provide "children with basic technical education to make them skilled labourers who can earn high wages" (Niimura 2016, 903).

Furthermore, in order to mitigate the negative effects of the division of labour, besides public education for the poor, Smith was favourable to modestly progressive taxation (*ibid.*, 368–9).

---

[19] For him, it was a matter of "the greatest delicacy" (Smith 1759 [1976], 734). This said, one cannot but agree with Blaug's statement that Smith's overall opinion on the *Poor Laws* has been either ignored or, worse, misinterpreted (Blaug 1978, 157). Though Smith was uncomfortable with the *Act of Settlement and Removal* (Smith 1776 [1976], 157), his opposition to it was limited to the hindering of the free circulation of labour throughout the country, which interfered with his system of *natural liberty*. "To remove a man who has committed no misdemeanour from the parish where he chooses to reside, is an evident violation of natural liberty and justice ..." (*ibid.*). Nothing in this argument can be taken as a general attack on *Poor Laws* as such. Geoffrey Gilbert's inference seems to be accurate that Smith had no objections to the principle of *Poor Laws*, or he would have expressed them explicitly (Gilbert 1997, 287; see also Viner 1927 [1958], 241).

> The subjects of every State ought to contribute towards the support of the government, as nearly as possible, in proportion to their respective abilities, that is, in proportion to the revenue which they respectively enjoy under the protection of the State (*ibid.*, 825).

He furthermore argued that

> The necessaries of life occasion the great expense of the poor. They find it difficult to get food, and the greater part of their little revenue is spent in getting it. The luxuries and vanities of life occasion the principal expense of the rich .... It is not very unreasonable that the rich should contribute to the public expense, not only in proportion to their revenue, but something more than in that proportion. (*ibid.*, 842)

Above all, Smith underlined that taxes ought to be levied on rent and not on wages and profits. According to Smith, rent is a "species of revenue which the owner, in many cases, enjoys without any care or attention of his own" (*ibid.*, 844). Hence, "a part of this revenue should be taken from him in order to defray the expences of the state". Smith was confident that "no discouragement will thereby be given to any sort of industry" (*ibid.*, 845). A further redistributive tax, Smith suggested, was an excise upon the luxuries and not on the primary goods necessary of life. "It must always be remembered, however, that it is the luxuries, and not the necessary expense of the inferior ranks of people, that ought ever to be taxed". As they were "just and equitable", he also praised State regulation on behalf of workers, for example, establishing that workers' wages be paid in cash rather than in kind (*ibid.*, 159) and welcomed public works—roads and channels (*ibid.*, 165).

Smith's ideas were not to remain confined to intellectual debates, but spread to the political arena, of his and later times. Both social reformers and political leaders during the 1780s and 1790s would take most of Smith's reflections very seriously. *The Wealth of Nations* "became a textbook for statesmen seeking to avoid the twin specters of famine and destitution" (Cowherd 1977, xiii).

In the following section, we evaluate whether the line of defence devised against the plague of poverty during the last quarter of the century was consistent with the social and economic considerations that emerged from the field of political economy.

6.5 The Political Economy of Inclusion in Action

From the mid-eighteenth century, the system of indoor relief began to crack due to its inability to cope with the sudden rise in the overall population and the concentration of poor people in cities and countryside alike. From an economic stance, Defoe's warning, that the conditions of an unstable labour market impeded the workhouse system to become what it was intended for, is correct. On the institutional side, the paternalistic element strictly linked to an economic vision dear to the landed aristocracy and the bourgeois-industrial approach were destined to collide. The ongoing commercialisation of the economy meant that the middle and upper classes grew in size and wealth to the point that their members began questioning the idea that landed aristocrats alone should run the country as they pleased. In their search for political power matching the economic power they had obtained, most of them found Enlightenment philosophy appealing due to its questioning of absolute power. As soon as the industrial revolution gained momentum, the old merchants now wealthy bourgeoisie, controlled rural industry more and more actively, paving the way to the incipient capitalist mode of production. Business magnates and bankers not only rivalled aristocracy in terms of wealth and prestige but also in the number of employed people working for them.[20] Under these circumstances, the political struggle for the

[20] Discussing the period from 1753 to 1797, Eden argued that: "the Poor Laws seems to have attracted very general attention both in and out of Parliament" (Eden 1797, I 317–8). In this same period, it would appear that a conspicuous number of wealthy bourgeoisies made their appearance in the *House of Commons* (Namier and Booke 1963, 103). The issue of who was ruling the country after 1688 has always been a captivating problem for historians. Even if the bourgeoisie took power in 1688, the landed aristocracy continued to control Parliament until the mid-nineteenth century (Pinkham 1963, 85). Engels attempted to provide an explanation to this apparent contradiction, in 1847: "Ever since 1688, separate sections of the bourgeois class have been ruling in England. But, in order to facilitate their seizure of power, the bourgeoisie has allowed the aristocrats, its dependent debtors, to retain their rule in name" (Engels 2010/1848, 520).

control of the State machinery (including poor relief) became even more fundamental.

The first blow to the *Workhouse Test Act* came from Thomas Gilbert (1719–1798), a zealous reformer whose main goal was to raise the poor's standard of living whilst reducing the tax burden.[21] Considering the changed economic conditions, Gilbert believed that a system based upon stern vigilance and refusal for outdoor relief was no longer sustainable. For the sake of both the poor and the *Rates*, Gilbert proposed to repeal the practice of farming out the poor, to extend mobility to the labouring poor, and to provide outdoor relief to the vast possible number of needy persons.[22] In 1783, Parliament passed three *Bills* that substantially amended the *Workhouse Test Act*. Gilbert's *Bills* made provisions for the unemployed, the rogues, vagabonds, sturdy beggars, and the impotent poor. To meet the needs of the first category, he proposed to make it easier for the unemployed to move from rural parishes to industrial towns whilst creating more job opportunities through public works. Parishes had "to provide for the Maintenance and Employment of their Poor at a common Expence, without farming them out" (Gilbert 1781, 6). For the second group, rather than in workhouses, he proposed to lodge them in *Houses of Correction* since they were less severe in handling the poor (Cowherd 1960, 331). Thus, workhouses were transformed into residences for children, the old, and the infirm. The rationale for this

[21] His first attempt to reform the *Poor Law* in 1764 was firmly grounded in the workhouse system. It was Richard Burn's argument that indoor relief was much more expensive than outdoor relief that induced Gilbert's change of attitude (Slack 1990, 35). In 1781, he wrote that workhouses were "generally inhabited by all Sorts of Persons … Hence arise Confusion, Disorder, and Distresses, not easily to be described. I have long thought it a great Defect in the Management of the common Workhouses, that all Descriptions of poor Persons should be sent thither; where, for the most Part, they are very ill accommodated" (Gilbert 1781, 6–8). What is interesting is that Adam Smith not only praised Burn's scholarly approach but also quoted his work in the *Wealth of Nations*. (Smith 1776 [1976], 153). In order to support his preference for allowances rather than indoor relief, Gilbert also pointed out the inadequacy of wages at a time when the changing economic situation pushed entrepreneurs to "rely on the free competitive market to determine the price of labour" (Mencher 1967, 110).

[22] Gilbert believed that, in most cases, it was preferable for the impotent poor "to remain in their own Habitations (if they have any) or to be placed with any Friend or Relation, at weekly Allowances, adapted to their Circumstances and Situation; it being understood, in all these Cases, that the Persons who keep them shall have the benefit of such Labour as they are able to perform; and weekly Pay to be fixed accordingly" (Gilbert 1781, 8).

resolution rested on the twofold idea that workhouses had high running costs compared to their productive capacities, and that inmates were deprived of their freedom.

Within a decade, England was at war with France and foodstuffs were difficult to import from abroad. Life became extremely harsh and the price of bread soared. The already precarious conditions of the poor were further worsened by a series of scarce harvests, which gave rise to food shortages and riots. It was in this context that a second major reform would play a fundamental role in the demise of the system of indoor relief. By the close of the century, *Friendly Societies* began to be increasingly perceived as the solution "for the dependence of the labouring population on the Poor Law" (Ruggles 1793, II 5; see also Richard Price (1771), Francis Maseres (1772), Thomas Gilbert (1786), Joseph Townsend (1786), John Acland (1786), Eden (1797, xvii, 1801, 10–11), and Colquhoun (1806, 137)).

Yet, not ready to consider the possibility of increasing wages by law, in 1793, the Parliament passed the *Act for the Encouragement and Relief of Friendly Societies*, better known as the *Rose Act*. It was designed to protect and encourage *Friendly Societies* "in the raising of funds voluntarily for the mutual relief and maintenance of members in sickness, old age, and infirmity" (Cowherd 1960, 333). On his part, Rose was quite optimistic with regard to the industriousness of the *Friendly Societies'* members. His *Act* unambiguously stated that they were necessarily industrious, as they had worked hard enough to save the money needed to become a member. This demonstrated their willingness to work, which rendered them unlikely to become "chargeable". Rather than asking assistance to the parish during hard times, a member of a *Society* would go to his club to receive assistance. The *Act* rested upon a solid economic rationale. Rose was conscious of the speed at which industry was expanding and produced an increasing demand for labour, especially in wealthy districts and towns (Vernon-Harcourt 1860, 525). In order to help the labouring poor to move where job opportunities were greater, he established that "No member of a *Friendly Society* was to be removed from any parish until he should become actually chargeable" (33 *Geo*. III. c. 54). Furthermore, the increased mobility of the labour force brought about by the *Rose Act*, albeit partially, addressed the problem of the increasing costs of poor relief. The *Act* introduced the idea of voluntary "separate funds for the mutual relief and maintenance of the said member in sickness, old age, and infirmity, is likely to be attended with very beneficial effects, by promoting the happiness of individuals, and at the same time diminishing the public burthens" (33 Geo. III. c. 54).

The combination of mutual aid and fraternity entailed by the *Rose Act* had resulted insufficient to alter the dreadful conditions of the poor. The severity of the situation, however, called for drastic measures. While assessing how best to compensate rural labourers for the decreased standards of living caused by nearly 50 years of Parliamentary enclosures (Thompson 1963, 237; Deane 1965, 52–7; Hobsbawm and Rudè 1970),[23] in February 1795, the authorities considered Samuel Whitbread's (1720–1796) *Minimum Wage Bill.* Whitbread maintained that "in the course of two centuries, the price of labour had not increased more than three or at most four-fold; whereas the price of meat had increased in the proportion of six or seven; and that of clothing, no less than fourteen or fifteen fold in the same time" (*Parliamentary History XXXII 1818*, 703). He believed that the Parliament could effectively protect the labouring poor's living standards by giving them "a right to a part of the produce of [their] labour", and that charity had a negative effect on the labouring poor as it took away his independence. On the contrary, the introduction of a minimum wage would "rescue the labouring poor from a state of slavish dependence; to enable the husbandman, who dedicated his days to incessant toil, to feed, to clothe, and to lodge his family with some degree of comfort" (*ibid.*).[24] Opposed by admirers of Smith (Himmelfarb 1984, 71–2)—Sir William Pitt (*1759–1806*) and his *Tory* government—Whitbread's *Bill* was defeated.

Almost at the same time, the governing elite of Berkshire County, fearing popular upheaval after a poor harvest, decided to pass a resolution based on the premise that "the present state of the poor does require further assistance than has been generally given them" (*Berkshire Session Order of Book 1791–1795*, in Aspinall 1959, 414). The *Justice of the Peace*

[23] The main outcome of this practice was a redistribution of income from small farmers to landowners; see Yelling (1977, 209–13) and Allen (1982, 937–53).

[24] In Whitbread's sentence, we find an echo of the longstanding tradition initiated by Berkeley and reiterated by Smith.

established "that every man has the right to a minimum subsistence, and that if he can earn only part of it then society owes him the difference" (Mantoux 1905, 437). With the blessing of all the parties concerned, it was thus decided that "subsidies in aid of wages should be granted in accordance with a scale dependent on the price of bread, income so that a minimum should be assured to the poor irrespective of their earnings" (Polanyi 1944 [1998], 78). Even if this rule was never formally transposed into law, it radically altered the workings of the *Poor Law* for the 40 years that followed.[25]

The *Speenhamland system* represented a partial, but significant, shift of the cost of production from entrepreneurs to taxpayer. The latter included non-entrepreneurs and often the inhabitants of parishes different from those in which the productive plants were located. A transfer of wealth based on general taxation, from the rich to the poor, was a serious attack to the established social hierarchy since, in due time, it would have obliterated the landed aristocracy's ability to control rural communities.

In 1796, the Prime Minister, Sir William Pitt, presented *The Poor Law Reform Bill*. Reluctant to interfere with the regulation of wages, Pitt preferred to increase the mobility of the labouring poor.[26] He believed that "The poor laws of this country, [...] had contributed to fetter the circulation of labour. [...] They had prevented the workman from going to that market where he could dispose of his industry to the greatest advantage and the capitalist, from enjoying the person who was qualified to procure him the best returns for his advances" (Pitt 1796 [1817], 132). Only when this vicious circle will be broken "the wealth of the nation would be increased, the poor man rendered not only more comfortable but more virtuous, and the weight of the poor rates [...] greatly diminished" (*ibid.*, 133). He further called for the provision of casual outdoor relief to large families and single mothers along with the establishment of *Schools of Industry* in order to offer some kind of education to poor children in the hopes that they would, one day, improve their position in life. The granting of credit to the poor for the "purchase of a cow or other capital which

[25] In 1797, Pitt attempted—and failed—to press the Parliament into passing the *Speenhamland system* into legislation.

[26] Pitt feared "that if once wages were raised to meet the rise in prices it would not be easy to reduce them when the famine was over" (Hammond and Hammond 1911 [1929], 144).

would help them to help themselves" or "for setting up the needy in business where there was a prospect of self-support" (Cowherd 1960, 336) was an integral part of his proposed *Bill*. Pitt's reform was so far reaching that it raised general alarm.[27] He withdrew it realising that an across the board political obstruction would have made it impossible for the *Bill* to pass in any case. His supporters, however, were able to pass the *Bill* piecemeal over the following years.

What is of interest for our discussion is the influence that the *Wealth of Nations* had on both Whitbread and Pitt. Whitbread's plea for high wages and Pitt's call for the elimination of restrictions on the free circulation of the unemployed workforce were both ideas clearly borrowed from Smith (Rothschild 1992, 84; McLean 2006, 90–1). Above all, in his *Bill*, Pitt adopted Smith's idea that poverty should not only be relieved but—possibly more importantly—be prevented. As Pitt put it, "The law which prohibits giving relief where any visible property remains should be withdrawn; no temporary occurrence should force a British subject to part with the last shilling of his little capital, and compel him to descend to a state of wretchedness from which he could never recover, merely that he might be entitled to a casual supply" (Pitt 1796 [1817], 136).

What was the impact of this formidable legislative effort? The *Gilbert Act* signalled the suspension of the workhouse system, unchaining vast sectors of the labouring population from being locked within the boundaries of their parishes. Membership to a *Friendly Society* protected the labouring class from risks to which they were particularly exposed: unemployment, industrial accidents, sickness, and so forth. The *Speenhamland system* helped the labouring population to cope with the inability of the labour market to offer sufficient wages (income) and employment (Smelser 1959, 357). It aided the "victims" of technological change by helping (or preventing) both the labouring poor and the unemployed from becoming dependent on parish relief by providing a wage subsidy on which to subsist (Snell 1985, 104–5). Above all, the system allowed for a considerable amount of resources to be transferred from the landowners, upon which most of the tax burden under the *Poor Law* fell, to

[27] Concern for Pitt's proposal also derived from the fact that it was based on the *Speenhamland System* (Deane 1965).

the manufacturing entrepreneurs, who benefited from the relatively lower wages permitted by the payment of allowances to their workers.

6.6 Conclusion

Between 1780 and the end of the century, political leaders and social reformers took very seriously the idea that an opulent, yet more equal, society was possible. The depth of Smith's analysis showed the legislator that the commercial society, in the process of laying its foundations, required less unbalanced relations among social classes. To run smoothly, the envisaged social order needed to escape from the arbitrary demands of rent-seeking landowners whose understanding of economic prosperity no longer met the needs of the emerging industrial capitalism. Social relations based on stern discipline, control, and subordination of the poor were, in fact, likely to weaken the economic dynamism of the nation. In shifting from a static economy, based on farming, trade, and the cottage industry, to a more dynamic one dominated by industrial production of consumer goods, vast sectors of the population, kept in a perennial state of poverty, were highly incompatible with the need of expanding the domestic market—a precondition for steady economic growth. In addition to economic evolution, the achievement of this tall order involved the gradual loss of political power on the part of the landed aristocracy.

While revolutionary France took the path of the bloody revolt against the *Ancien Régime*, disseminating violent social conflicts across the continent, in England, the emerging bourgeoisie class and the most enlightened aristocracy favoured the establishment of social relations no longer based on the *utility of the poor* doctrine but rather on liberty, flexibility, and inclusion. Thus conceived, the social environment was meant to favour modernisation and economic dynamism, without provoking the misery and resentment of the great mass of the population.

While the rationale for reforming social policy in the last quarter of the eighteenth century basically rested on a wide range of political and social concerns, it certainly gained force from the widespread belief that the introduction of public standards of fairness and support to the labouring poor, was not inconsistent with the requirements of a growing—and rapidly changing—economy.

From 1782, the year Parliament passed the *Gilbert Act*, to the establishment of the *New Poor Laws* in 1834, English social legislation shifted from a safety net scheme devised to deal with emergencies to a social security system implemented to cope with the threat of unemployment and poverty, at any point in time, over a worker's life cycle. Thanks to this legislative effort, in the late seventeenth century, English society ceased to perceive the poor as a collective body of others. By being constantly engaged in capitalist exchange relationships (both as producers and as consumers), wage earners came to be viewed as fully integrated economic agents acting within the broader framework of society.

References

Acland, J. (1786). *A Plan for Rendering the Poor Independent on Public Contribution; Founded on the Basis of the Friendly Societies, Commonly Called Clubs*. London: R. Thorn.

Alcock, T. (1752). *Observations on the Poor Laws*. London.

Allen, R. C. (1982). The Efficiency and Distributional Consequences of Eighteenth Century Enclosures. *The Economic Journal, 92*(368), 937–953.

Anon. (1715). *Report on the Workhouse*. London.

Anon. (1732). *Account of Several Workhouses*. London.

Ashcraft, R. (1996). Lockean Ideas, Poverty, and the Development of Liberal Political Theory. In J. Brewer & S. Staves (Eds.), *Early Modern Conceptions of Property*. London/New York: Routledge.

Baum, S. (1992). Poverty, Inequality and the Role of Government: What Would Adam Smith Say? *Eastern Economic Journal, 18*(2), 143–156.

Bellers, J. (1696). *Proposals for Raising a Colledge of Industry*. London.

Bentham, J. (1792 [1823]). Truth *versus* Ashhurst; or, Law as It Is, Contrasted with What It Is Said to Be. In J. Bowring (Ed.), *The Works of Jeremy Bentham* (Vol. V, pp. 231–237). Edinburgh: Tait.

Berkeley, G. (1735–1737). *The Querist*. London.

Berkshire Session Order Book 1791–95. In A. Aspinall (Ed.), 1959. *English Historical Documents*. London: Routledge.

Bharadwaj, K. (1989). *Themes in Value and Distribution: Classical Theory Reappraised*. London: Unwin Hyman.

Blackstone, W. (1803 [1776]). *Commentaries on the Laws of England.* Philadelphia.
Blaug, M. (1978). *Economic Theory in Retrospect.* Cambridge: Cambridge University Press.
Boyer, G. R. (1990). *An Economic History of the English Poor Law 1750–1850.* Cambridge: Cambridge University Press.
Braddon, L. (1722). *The Miseries of the Poor Are a National Sin, Shame, and Charge.* London.
Cannan, E. (1926). Adam Smith as an Economist, *Economic* Marx and Engels Complete Works *a*, 17, 123–134.
Cary, J. (1695). *An Essay on the State of England in Relation to Its Trade.* Bristol.
Coats, B. (1958). Changing Attitudes to Labour in the Mid-Eighteenth Century. *Economic History Review, 11*(1), 35–51.
Coats, B. (1960). Economic Thought and Poor Law Policy in the Eighteenth Century. *Economic History Review, 13*(1), 39–51.
Colquhoun, P. (1806). *A Treatise on Indigence.* London.
Cornell University Political Theory Workshop, 1–34.
Cowherd, R. (1960). The Humanitarian Reform of the English Poor Laws from 1782 to 1815. *Proceedings of the American Philosophical Society, 104*(3), 328–342.
Cowherd, R. (1977). *Political Economists and the English Poor Laws: A Historical Study of the Influence of Classical Economics on the Formation of Social Welfare Policy.* Athens: Ohio University Press.
Deane, P. (1965). *The First Industrial Revolution.* Cambridge: Cambridge University Press.
Defoe, D. (1704). *Giving Alms No Charity and Employing the Poor a Grievance to the Nation.* London.
Defoe, D. (1728). *A Plan of the English Commerce.* London: Vernon Press.
Dunning, R. (1686). *A Plain and Easie Method.* London.
Eden, F. M. (1797). *The State of the Poor, or an History of the Labouring Classes in England.* London.
Eden, F. M. (1801). *Observation on Friendly Society.* London.
Engels, F. (2010 [1848]). The Movement of 1847. In *Marx and Engels Complete Works* (Vol. 6). London: Lawrence & Wishart.
Fideler, P. (2006). *Social Welfare in Pre-Industrial England.* Houndmills: Palgrave Macmillan.
Fiori, S., & Pesciarelli, E. (1999). Adam Smith on Relations of Subordination, Personal Incentives and the Division of Labour. *Scottish Journal of Political Economy, 46*(1), 91–106.

Fleischacker, S. (2005). *On Adam Smith's Wealth of Nations A Philosophical Companion*. Princeton: Princeton University Press.
Furniss, E. (1920). *The Position of the Laborer in a System of Nationalism*. Boston: Houghton Mifflin Company.
Gilbert, T. (1781). *Plan for the Better Relief and Employment of the Poor*. London.
Gilbert, T. (1786). *A Bill Intended to Be Offered to Parliament, for the Better Relief and Employment of the Poor*. London.
Gilbert, G. (1997). Adam Smith on the Nature and Causes of Poverty. *Review of Social Economy, 55*(3), 273–292.
Gouldsmith, R. (1725). *Some Considerations on Trade*. London.
Graunt, J. (1662). *Natural and Political Observations Made Upon the Bills of Morality*. London.
Hammond, J. L., & Hammond, B. (1929) [1911]). *The Village Labourer 1760–1832: A Study in the Government of England Before the Reform Bill*. London/New York: Longmans/Green and CO.
Hartlib, S. (1649). *London's Charities Stilling the Poore Orphans Cry*. London.
Hay, W. (1735). *Remarks on the Law Relating to the Poor, with Proposals for their Better Relief and Employment*. London.
Himmelfarb, G. (1984). *The Idea of Poverty. England in the Early Industrial Age*. London/Boston: Faber and Faber.
Hobsbawm, E. J. (1969). *Industry and Empire: From 1750 to the Present Day*. Harmondsworth: Penguin.
Hobsbawm, E. J., & Rudè, G. (1970). *Captain Swing*. London: Lawrence and Wishart.
Hume, D. (1752 [1955]). *Writings in Economics*. London/Toronto: Nelson.
Jones, E. (1776). *Observations on the Scheme Before Parliament of the Maintenance of the Poor*. Chester.
Kuznets, S. (1966). *Modern Economic Growth: Rate, Structure, and Spread*. New Haven/London: Yale University Press.
Landau, N. (1988). The Laws of *Settlement* and the Surveillance of Immigration in Eighteenth Century Kent. *Continuity and Change, 3*, 391–420.
Landes, D. S. (1969). *The Unbound Prometheus: Technological Change and Industrial Development in Western Europe from 1750 to the Present*. Cambridge: Cambridge University Press.
Locke, J. (1697 [1997]). An Essay on the Poor Law. In M. Goldie (Ed.), *John Locke Political Essay* (pp. 182–198). Cambridge: Cambridge University Press.
Maisse, J. (1757). *Consideration Relating to the Poor*. London.

Mandeville, B. (1725). *The Fable of the Bees: or, Private Vices and Publick Benefits.* London.

Mandler, P. (1987). The Making of the New Poor Law Redivivus. *Past & Present, 117*, 131–157.

Manley, T. (1669). *Usurie at Six per Cent.* London.

Mantoux, P. (1905). *The Industrial Revolution in the Eighteenth Century: An Outline of the Beginnings of the Modern Factory System in England.* London: Jonathan Cape.

Marshall, D. (1926 [2007]). *The English Poor in the Eighteenth Century.* New York: Augustus Kelly.

Marshall, D. (1956). *English People in the Eighteenth Century.* London/New York: Longmann Green & Co, Ltd.

Martin, C. (2015). Equity Besides: Adam Smith and the Utility of the Poor. *Journal of the History of Economic Thought, 37*(4), 559–581.

Maseres, F. (1772). *A Proposal for Establishing Life-Annuities in Parishes for the Benefit for the Industrious Poor.* London.

McLean, I. (2006). *Adam Smith, Radical and Egalitarian: An Interpretation for the 21st Century.* Edinburgh: Edinburgh University Press.

Mencher, S. (1967). *Poor Law to Poverty Program. Economic Security Policy in Britain and the United State.* Pittsburgh: University of Pittsburgh Press.

Mun, T. (1664). *England's Treasure by Forraign Trade.* London: Thomas Clark.

Namier, L., & Brooke, J. (1963). *The History of Parliament: The House of Commons, 1754–1790.* London: Secker &Warburg.

Niimura, S. (2016). Adam Smith: Egalitarian or Anti-Egalitarian?: His Responses to Hume and Rousseau's Critiques of Inequality. *International Journal of Social Economics, 43*(9), 888–903.

Pinkham, L. (1963). William of Orange: Prime Mover of the Revolution. In G. M. Straka (Ed.), *The Revolution of 1688: Whig Triumph or Palace Revolution?* (pp. 77–85). Boston: Hearth.

Pitt, W. (1796 [1817]). *The Speeches of the Right Honourable William Pitt in the House of Commons.* London: Longman.

Polanyi, K. (1998 [1944]). *The Great Transformation. The Political and Economic Origins of Our Time.* London: Beacon Press.

Pollexfen, J. (1700). *Of Trade.* London.

Potter, R. (1775). *Observation on the Poor Law.* London.

Poynter, R. J. (1969). *Society and Pauperism. English Ideas on Poor Relief, 1795–1834.* London: Routledge & Kegan Paul.

Price, R. (1771). *Observations on Reversionary Payments on Schemes for Providing Annuities for Widows, and for Persons in Old Age; The Method of Calculating the Values of Assurance on Lives; And on the National Debt.* Dublin.
Rostow, W. W. (1960). *The Stages of Economic Growth: A Non-Communist Manifesto*. Cambridge: Cambridge University Press.
Rothschild, E. (1992). Adam Smith and Conservative Economics. *Economic History Review, 45*(1), 74–96.
Rothschild, K. W. (2002). The Absence of Power in Contemporary Economic Theory. *Journal of Socio-Economics, 31*, 433–442.
Ruggles, T. (1793). *The History of the Poor; Their Rights, Duties, and the Laws Respecting Them.* London.
Scott, J. (1773). *Observation on the State of the Parochial and Vagrant Poor.* London.
Slack, P. (1990). *The English Poor Law 1531–1782.* Cambridge: Cambridge University Press.
Smelser, N. (1959). *Social Change in the Industrial Revolution.* New York: Routledge.
Smith, A. (1976 [1759]). *The Theory of Moral Sentiments.* Indianapolis: Liberty Fund.
Smith, A. (1976 [1776]). *An Inquiry into the Nature and the Causes of the Wealth of Nations.* Chicago: University of Chicago Press.
Smith, R. (1986). Transfer Incomes, Risk and Security: The Roles of the Family and the Collectivity in Recent Theories of Fertility Change. In D. Coleman & R. Schofield (Eds.), *The State of Population Theory: Forward from Malthus.* Oxford: Basil Blackwell.
Snell, K. (1985). *Annals of the Labouring Poor: Social Change and Agrarian England, 1660–1900.* Cambridge: Cambridge University Press.
Temple, W. (1758). *A Vindication of Commerce and the Arts.* London.
Thompson, E. P. (1963). *The Making of the Working Class.* London: Penguin Books.
Townsend, J. (1786). *A Dissertation on the Poor Laws, by a Well-Whished to Mankind.* London.
Vanderlint, J. (1734). *Money Answers All Things.* London.
Vernon-Harcourt, L. (1860). *The Diaries and Correspondence of the Right Hon. George Rose*, II. London.
Viner, J. (1927). Adam Smith and Laissez Faire. *Journal of Political Economy, 35*(1), 198–232.

Webb, S., & Webb, B. (1927–29). *English Poor Law History. Part I: The Old Poor Law.* London: London Green.

White, J. (1630). *Planter's Plea.* London.

Yelling, J. A. (1977). *Common Field and Enclosure in England 1450–1850.* London: Macmillan.

Young, A. (1771). *The Farmers' Calendar.* London.

Zouch, H. (1776). *Remarks Upon the Late Resolutions of the House of Commons Respecting the Proposed Change of the Poor Laws.* Leeds.

7

Debates on Social Insurance in the French Liberal School

Joachim De Paoli

7.1 Introduction

From the mid-nineteenth century onwards, the development of industry led to great social inequality between employers and workers. Liberal economists were faced with the dilemma of what policy to adopt with respect to people in a weak position. This gave rise to debates on the problems of social inequality and possible solutions. At the end of the century, governments developed a solution for helping the vulnerable: social insurance.

The first laws are passed in Germany under Bismarck, followed by other European countries, as set out in Table 7.1.

This is a substantially revised and shortened version of a keynote lecture given at the 14th conference of the Italian Association for the History of Economic Thought (AISPE) at the University of Salento, Lecce, 28–30 April 2016. I am grateful to Gérard Klotz, Manuela Mosca, Thibault Guicherd, Alban Mathieu, Patrick Gilormini, Javier San Julian Arrupe and André Tiran for their suggestions on earlier drafts of the chapter.

J. De Paoli (✉)
Université de Lyon, Lyon, France
e-mail: Joachim.De-Paoli@univ-lyon2.fr

M. Mosca (ed.), *Power in Economic Thought*, Palgrave Studies in the History of Economic Thought, https://doi.org/10.1007/978-3-319-94039-7_7

Table 7.1 Social insurance laws in Europe

	Workplace accident insurance	Occupational illness insurance	Pension insurance
Germany	1884	1883	1889
France	1898	1930	1910
Great Britain	1897	1911	1906
Belgium	1903	1894	1900
Spain	1900	1942	1919
Italy	1898	1898	1919

Brasseul (2004) p. 159

This chapter is to report on the debate among liberal economists when said laws making social insurances compulsory were established. The analysis will allow us to highlight the fact that the liberal economists feared political power. However, they recognised the weakness of the workers' position with respect to the power of employers. This conflict gave rise to an interesting and rich debate on what remedies to adopt: how to help the workers without giving too much power to the government?

To demonstrate this, we will focus on the case of the economists of the French Liberal School. We will analyse the contributions of four authors having links with the men holding political and economic power, active in debates on this issue of the very liberal *Société d'économie politique*[1]—scientific society composed by French liberal authors—and representing the different currents of Liberal School: the ultraliberal Yves Guyot[2] (1843–1928), the moderate liberal Paul Leroy-Beaulieu[3] (1843–1916),

[1] On the liberal aspect of this scientific society, we refer to Le Van-Lemesle (2004), particularly, Chap. 3, and Lutfalla (1972).

[2] According to Marco (1991 p. 158), he was one the most extremist authors. Guyot has close ties with the political world. He became deputy in 1885 and Transport Minister from 1889 to 1892. He influenced too the ideas of the Alliance républicaine démocratique, main political formation of center left, then center right of the 3rd Republic. In his writings, as in his political functions, he argued for free trade and against socialism.

[3] See Baslé (1991) pp. 203–246. Several members of his family, including his father and his brother, had functions of civil servant and were elected deputy. His step-father is Michel Chevalier, one of the authors of the free trade agreement between France and Great Britain in 1860. Leroy-Beaulieu held the Chair of Political Economy at the *Collège de France* and taught at the *Ecole libre des sciences politiques*. He was one of the few liberal economists to defend colonisation. In his political and economic writings, he was interested in labour issues and in the fight against socialism.

the economist engineer[4] Clément Colson[5] (1853–1939), the "leplaysien" economist Emile Cheysson[6] (1836–1910) and one of the most famous students of Colson, namely, Jacques Rueff[7] (1896–1978), for the analysis of unemployment insurance.

In the first section, it will be shown that the different members of the French Liberal School had divergent opinions on insurance as a means of protecting workers against risks they face and on the role the State should play. It will subsequently be demonstrated that depending on the risk entailed, the analysis of the different types of social insurance was not the same.

First of all, a few words about social insurance in France. Social insurance became gradually compulsory by law as from the end of the nineteenth century:

- The law of 9 April 1898 recognises the no fault liability of the employer for workplace accidents. The employee victim of an accident can claim compensation without having to prove the fault of his employer. It encourages the latter to take an insurance to cover such an eventuality. Prior to this law, the regime of civil liability had been in force since 1804. The employee then had to prove the employer's liability to obtain compensation since, according to this regime, the person who harms another person must remedy it;

[4] Economist engineers group together with economists trained in one of the French engineering *grandes écoles* institutes, including *Ecole Polytechnique*, *Ecole Nationale des Ponts et Chaussées* and *Ecole des Mines*.

[5] See De Paoli (2017). Colson was professor at *Ecole Nationale des Ponts et Chaussées*. He is described by Bousquet (1960 p. 1) and Divisia (1951 p. 13) as the greatest French economist of the first quarter of the twentieth century after Walras; he also had a teaching career in French higher education institutes outside the main framework of the university system *Les Grandes Ecoles*, of which *Ecole des Hautes Etudes Commerciales, Ecole Nationale des Ponts et Chaussées, Ecole libre des sciences politiques* or *Ecole Polytechnique*. He was also a civil servant: he was Director of railways in 1894 and 1895 and Vice President of the *Conseil d'Etat*—the highest function—from 1923 to 1928. In these functions, he advised and trained political and economic leaders (Picory 1989 pp. 680, 703).

[6] See Le Van-Lemesle (2005) p. 80, Luciani (1991) p. 584. Cheysson was also an economist engineer (Divisia 1951 p. 444). He was Director of Ponts et Chaussées and Professor of political or social economy at the *Ecole libre des sciences politiques* and at the *Ecole des Mines*. He was associated with works of numerous official commissions. In his researches, this specialist of statistic and monographs was interested in issues regarding population and workers' life conditions.

[7] Rueff advised several governments, in particular on monetary issues, especially the Poincaré government from 1926 to 1928 and the general De Gaulle from 1958.

- The law of 5 April 1910 makes insurance for old age compulsory for trade and industry employees, the professions, farmers, stipendiaries and civil servants. It took more than ten years to adopt the obligation: under the Law of 29 June 1894, a pension scheme can be set up for miners, with compulsory employee and employer contributions, the employers being free to choose the type of insurance they want. In 1895, employers had to deposit the amounts in funds approved by the State. A first bill of compulsory insurance managed by the State is proposed in 1901. It was rejected;
- The laws of 5 April 1928 and 30 April 1930 establish compulsory insurance to cover illness, maternity, disability, old age and death. Insurance funds are funded by State contributions and payments payable in half by the employer and in half by the employee.[8]

7.2 The Intervention of the State and the Question of Social Insurance

The State Should Not Manage Social Insurance: Different Analyses Lead to the Same Conclusion

In accordance with their liberal principles, economists agree that the State should not manage social insurance. However, two different analyses justify this idea: for Guyot, in line with his ultraliberal positions, it would be bad for the country's wealth, for Leroy-Beaulieu, Cheysson[9] and Colson, the State does not have the capacity to do so.

In his books, Guyot spoke little about social insurance. The only chapter he devoted, in particular, to social insurance is about its results in Germany where he criticises the *very characteristic socialism* (Guyot 1914 pp. 211–222). He presents his view of social insurance in the debates of the *Société d'économie politique*. He did not theorise the question, he just argues the State should not intervene taking the argument that one

[8] Pollet and Dumons (1995), Sécurité sociale (online).

[9] This author's thought on this point will be treated at the same time as the system he proposes.

should not modify the natural distribution determined by the law of supply and demand. However, when the State intervenes to manage social insurance, it modifies this natural distribution. According to him, the effect thereof is

- To destroy some of the public wealth (Guyot 1923 pp. 180–183). Indeed, as the price of labour increases with the additional social contributions, the costs of production increase, which increases the price of products, of which demand is then reduced and which thus decreases the country's wealth.
- To lead to communism (SEP February 1909a p. 269).[10] He did not further develop this point, but it illustrates the fear of liberals of the time against the surge of socialist ideas and of protectionism.

Leroy-Beaulieu and Colson had another analysis: the State should not intervene in the management of social insurance, not because this is bad for the country's wealth but because it does not have the capacity to manage it.

Leroy-Beaulieu uses a more political than economical argument. He thinks that the State insurance plans arise from jealousy and illusion:

- Jealousy on account of the financial success of insurance companies. He thinks that this is not why the State should put its hands on the insurance company industry which succeeded after taking risks.
- The illusion is to believe the State could collect the profits of the success. Indeed, according to him, the administration is characterised by passivity and uniformity in that it does not have the organisational flexibility needed to adapt to the variable needs of customers while seeking to make savings. Insurance needs this flexibility, only private companies are able to do this (SEP March 1905 pp. 432–433).

Colson develops the aspect that Leroy-Beaulieu calls "illusion," by writing that State formalities are long (SEP March 1905 p. 434). However, this is not why he is against its intervention. His analysis is based on

[10] In his opinion, the communists disregard the law of supply and demand (Guyot 1893 p. 43).

practice, which illustrates the strong link between theory and practice for this author, as stressed by Zoubloulakis (2000 pp. 582–583). He is against the monopoly of social insurance managed by the State because this system would face an insurmountable difficulty, namely, the recognition of premature disability, without the employer being able to determine it. Indeed:

> Only [...] the boss who directly provides pensions to his own personnel is, at the same time, the proper judge of when the insured can no longer earn a wage higher than the annuity to which he is entitled, and is deemed to be an interested party in not getting things wrong, since he pays the salary, on the one hand, and supplements the reserves of pension funds in case of deficit, on the other hand. Give agents appointed by the State the right to grant or deny annuities, when the allocation thereof would be based on something as difficult to appreciate as the inability to earn a specified fraction of the salary, seems to us to be an absolute impossibility, in a country in which public powers arise from the election.[11] (Colson 1917 pp. 399–400)

On this latter point, he thinks that insurance that has to take disability into account is not compatible with universal suffrage. Indeed, to be elected, politicians can promise to take popular but bad decisions for the State's budget. We conclude that Colson here is wary of what the discretionary policies of politicians will become.[12]

So, our analysis highlights the distrust of liberal economists towards State intervention and political power. Indeed, from this sample, it appears that they agree with the conclusion: the State must not manage social insurance. But this unanimity disappears when we enter into the details of possible State intervention in social insurance to encourage workers to take out insurance and so reduce social inequality, as we are going to explain now.

[11] In this quotation, Colson speaks about pension insurance but his reasoning is the same as for the other types of social insurance.

[12] Friedman insisted on the need not to let economic policy at the discretion of politicians (Friedman 1962, Chap. 3). Politicians, to please voters, would be tempted to implement short-term policies to favour their election to the detriment of long-term economic stability.

Civil Liability, Social Insurance or Savings

We highlight here that liberal economists do not have the same view of the role that the State and social insurance must play, particularly, that concerning workplace accidents. Three different analyses appear: Guyot defends the civil liability, Leroy-Beaulieu insurance without State intervention and Cheysson and Colson social insurance.

Guyot explains that there are two systems to remedy workplace accidents[13]: the first one is the French system of civil liability,[14] the second one the German system of compulsory insurance. In this system, firms are grouped into corporations which manage the insurance; the State and workers do not participate in the insurance. When an accident occurs, the payment is made from the fourteenth week of disability; prior thereto, the health insurance supports the funding.

He criticises the German system by showing that the targets sought by the law are not reached:

- The system was to be less expensive for employers. In fact, charges are high: premiums paid to the corporations increased from 0.49% of wages in 1886 to 1.17% in 1892 (SEP February 1895 pp. 263–264).
- The system was to reduce the number of accidents. However, the number of reported accidents increased by 145% from 1886 to 1892, the allowances by 211%. Fatal accidents or accidents followed by total disability changed little, minor accidents increased. In the same way, healing time for the same accident increased. Guyot speaks of "annuity hysteria" (Guyot 1914 p. 215) which means, according to him, that social insurance develops habits of simulation and fraud.
- The system was to guarantee workers against all risks. Workers must be compensated whether they are responsible for their accident or not. In reality, compensation is not always paid.
- The system was to eliminate disputes. The insurer sets the compensation, the insured may appeal the decision and both parties may go to

[13] Guyot writes prior to the law of 1898 on workplace accidents being passed.

[14] See introduction.

the Imperial Office as a last resort. The cases referred to the courts increased from 14,879 in 1890 to 25,348 in 1893, which is one accident out of six;

- The system was to ensure social peace by *State socialism* (SEP February 1895 p. 267). However, the worker is under the impression that he is an annoying and expensive object on account of how the insurance works. As the indemnity is subject to review and decreases as and when the worker's health improves, the latter feels cared for in the interest of the insurer, not in his own interest; the insurance becomes incentive for him not to heal.

He defends the regime of civil liability, but, however, he claims that he is in favour of the employer proving gross negligence or carelessness by the worker injured while working (Guyot 1893 p. 158).[15]

Leroy-Beaulieu agrees with Guyot on one point: with a compulsory insurance system imposed by the State, the latter would end up invading all areas. But Leroy-Beaulieu does not defend the civil liability system. For him, the solution is savings because it allows one to stimulate private initiative. There are two types of savings, group savings—that is, insurance—and free savings.

To safeguard the workers, Leroy-Beaulieu claims that he is in favour of insurance. In his *Précis d'économie politique,* he makes no distinction between insurance and social insurance. He mentions the different types of insurances: fire, life, accidents, hail, livestock mortality, maritime insurance (Leroy-Beaulieu 1888 p. 322). He writes, speaking about accident insurance, that it "would be desirable that all men [...] be affiliated thereto" (*ibid.* p. 324).

However, he is against any State intervention in insurance, whether to make insurance compulsory or for grants.

As regards the first point, the security that compulsory insurance claims to provide is not complete because it concerns only employees, some people are not covered, for instance, small rural proprietors. Moreover, Leroy-Beaulieu highlights that an increase in contributions to finance the insurance would equate to a high tax for small firms. It is an

[15] According to the law in force up to 1898, the worker has the burden of proving that his employer is responsible for his accident (see introduction).

unequal system in his view. Finally, compulsory insurance discourages contingency planning and effort. If it existed, he says:

> We would substitute an automatic being, who will no longer have to think of anything, to the responsible being of today. (Leroy-Beaulieu *in* SEP February 1895 p. 277)

So, the State and the political power must not intervene. On the contrary, he maintains that insurance must be taken out through private initiatives: mutual insurance and assistance organised by employers. Indeed, employers have set up assistance and insurance funds for workers; State intervention destroys these institutions. All these varied combinations which are beneficial for the public disappear to make room for a uniform organisation of the State (SEP February 1895 p. 277).

As regards the second point, Leroy-Beaulieu also criticises grants because they can become a significant burden for the State's budget.

We can note that thereafter he no longer speaks about insurance in his *Traité théorique et pratique d'économie politique* (Leroy-Beaulieu 1914).

Cheysson and Colson criticise the civil liability and defend social insurance to protect workers against the risks they face.

Both of them also think, like Guyot and Leroy-Beaulieu, that compulsory insurance discourages contingency planning and effort. However, they think that one must encourage employers and workers to take out insurance. Contrary to Guyot and Leroy-Beaulieu, Cheysson and Colson accept that the State may have a role to play by encouraging insurance.

More precisely, Cheysson criticises the civil liability system because it is not enough to meet the needs.[16] Indeed, in Germany, one quarter of the accidents is attributable to the employer, one quarter to the workers and one half is attributable to force majeure. Assuming that the proportion is the same in France, under the French system of civil liability, only one quarter of accidents gives rise to worker compensation, provided that the employer's fault has been proved and that the employer's fund is not empty. The regime has survived because it was not applied: big companies help the injured, without taking account of the law; the courts try to

[16] Cheysson writes prior to the law of 1898 on workplace accidents.

hold the employer liable, even if he should not be held liable. Cheysson thinks compensation for accident must be guaranteed (SEP February 1894 pp. 267–268, February 1895 pp. 269–270). We will develop the solution he proposes in the next paragraph.

Colson also thinks that the employer ought to pay indemnities to workers victims of accidents. For him, it is normal that insurance is payable by the employer because he is responsible for the accidents. However, to ensure the true security of the worker, this insurance must be combined with insurance covering illnesses and death due to other causes. Indeed, most illnesses and accidents are partly attributable to occupational hazards and partly to the victim. He thus thinks that one should combine the two insurance schemes to deal with the reality (Colson 1917 pp. 321–324).

At the end of this debate, it appears that, even though Guyot favours the civil liability system, Leroy-Beaulieu accepts that workers must be protected against risks and then defends the mechanisms set up by private initiative to develop contingency planning. The Colson position, which is close to that of Cheysson, is opposite to that of Guyot and Leroy-Beaulieu who consider that the State and the political power must not intervene. So Colson hesitates, on the one hand, between his liberal positions which are against compulsory insurance and, on the other hand, his recognition of practice which accepts that workers must be protected by an insurance. So he defends State intervention.

The State Can Intervene to Encourage Workers' Protection

As Guyot and Leroy-Beaulieu are against any State intervention in social insurance, only Cheysson and Colson propose State intervention to encourage insurance by employers and workers. Cheysson develops the idea of a private social insurance system with State intervention[17] at the

[17] Cheysson (1894) also presents the system at *Société d'économie politique* (SEP February 1894 pp. 261–271) and in the *Revue politique et parlementaire* (Cheysson 1895).

International Congress of accidents at work in Milan in 1894.[18] Colson says nothing about Cheysson's model; however, we will show that he develops a rather close analysis.

Cheysson thinks that an economist must not, on principle, reject any State intervention but he must try to scientifically determine if some State intervention might have a positive effect (SEP February 1894 p. 262). The State protects children and women; it is its role to defend those who are too weak to defend themselves, all the more so in cases of social inequality. Adults can be concerned by disease,[19] accident[20] and old age. With insurance, one can avoid these crises and so workers must take out insurance. He then defends the State intervention to favour workers' insurance and proposes a system where the State encourages workers to protect themselves by means of social insurance while leaving private initiative to organise the insurance. He calls his system *State liberalism* (SEP February 1894 p. 270). We present its main aspects.

Cheysson too is against compulsory insurance managed by the State but it must act by setting up regulations on employers' responsibility so that workers are protected against the risks they face. To avoid too much State intervention, he thinks that one needs an intermediate between the individual and the State and it is for this reason that he defends an association system: he accepts that the State compels the employers to take out insurance for their workers and regulates the responsibility of employers, providing that they are left the choice of their insurance.

So he defends a system where there is association between the insurance companies and the State. The latter can encourage the insurance societies and make grants to them subject to the related documentary evidence: the insurance companies must publish reports and accept State financial and technical inspections.

> If it is worth it for individuals to manage their own interests, the State, for its part, has the double benefit of relieving its responsibility and of contributing to the country's administrative education. Leaving the association

[18] Luzzati develops a closely-related system at this congress (Luzzatti 1894). For this reason, economists speak about the Cheysson-Luzzatti system.

[19] Cheysson develops the system that he proposes with the example of illness and accidents.

[20] Cheysson develops the question of accident compensation in Société d'économie politique (SEP) (March 1888) pp. 427–440.

> act, the State overcomes the obstacles: it encourages, guides, even inspects the association in consideration of the favours granted. This is a fruitful division of labour, which lets the association and the State operate in their legitimate sphere to prompt these public interest services, such as the investment of regulated savings, the organisation of assistance against disease. (SEP February 1894 p. 267)

According to Cheysson, the State would then intervene only in a public interest which firms would not take into account without its intervention: to allow workers to be protected against risks they face. This intervention underlies the private initiative: the State monitors the services which the associations are free to provide. The State, the association and the individual collaborate in that each is left its legitimate sphere of action. He explains that this system gives control to the State and the interested parties are allowed their action (SEP February 1895 pp. 269–273).

Cheysson argues that in this way it is not insurance that is compulsory but the guarantee, that is, the worker is guaranteed benefits in case of accident or illness. With this system, social inequality is taken into account by the political powers while leaving plenty of scope for private initiative. He adds that, to ensure that the employer takes out a guarantee, the State must intervene if the employer does not do anything. The rates then applied by the State fund must be higher than normal rates so that the employer does not opt for this form.

We must point out that even though he defends a system where insurance is not compulsory, if the employer does not take insurance of his own accord, he must then take out State insurance. In fact, the employer really has to take out insurance.

Colson's analysis is close to that of Cheysson. He is against State monopoly and compulsory social insurance but he is not against State intervention (Colson 1917 pp. 320–353). He explains why workers must take out insurance: the worker, when unable to work, can become poor. With insurance, one can obtain resources to meet needs given that the resources are proportional to the loss incurred and they do not disappear early, since they are only paid when unable to work. Colson is therefore in favour of social insurance because of social inequality. Indeed, he adds that the insurance is not intended only for workers; while it is just a precaution for the well-to-do class, it is necessary for the working classes (*ibid.* pp. 289–291).

He does not present a system to ensure that the employers take out insurance, he just thinks, like Cheysson, that the State can intervene with grants in order to encourage insurance and savings (Colson 1912 pp. 154–158). He gives the reason thereof: to wit, how difficult it is for workers to take out insurance against risks is justification for the public grants. But grants must not account for an important share of the insurance budget so that workers do not think that they make huge dips into State's funds. This would discourage workers from making efforts.

Finally, Colson is in favour of the Law of 1898 on workplace accidents at work although this new law is still imperfect. According to him, the professional risk weighing on the employer makes insurance a necessity; firms can choose the insurance they wish. The interest that employers have to seeing their workers insured justifies their intervention in developing insurance. By encouraging their workers to adopt a provident attitude, the employers are of useful to them (Colson 1912 pp. 158–164, 1917 pp. 353–402).

We conclude that Cheysson and Colson's analyses are complementary. They are aware that social inequality exists. While Cheysson argues for a means of workers' protection without making insurance compulsory, Colson places more emphasis on why the State must intervene in order to protect the workers: how difficult it is to them to make payments and the risk of their falling into poverty. We will see now that their analyses differ for the various types of social insurance.

7.3 The Various Types of Social Insurance

Social insurance is insurance to face temporary inability to work—illness—permanent inability to work—the early disability due to an accident—pension and unemployment.

Since Guyot and Leroy-Beaulieu do not devote passages to various social insurance, only Colson's and Cheysson's positions are analysed; added thereto is the position of Rueff, Colson's student, for unemployment insurance. We show that even though Colson gives the State an important role, as just emphasised, he also leaves an important share of initiative to the employers, in accordance with his liberal positions.

Insurance Against Illness and Workplace Accidents

Cheysson and Colson are in favour of insurance against illness and against workplace accidents. Indeed, Cheysson develops his system, by taking, for example, these two types of risks. Colson, for his part, analyses the reasons which justify this insurance.

Colson speaks about the insurance against inability to work. The inability to work affects the worker by depriving him of his wage and by imposing medical expenses on him. A distinction must be made at insurance level between the work stoppage whose duration is limited—illness—and the permanent inability—disability.

He thinks that insurance against illness and disability are needed to give security to workers who would have not built up a reserve and it must be organised at the expense of the employer and of workers.

Colson explains that the main risk of insurance against illness and disability is the risk of fraud. When the insurance has been properly set up, it is an incentive to rest. Effective oversight is essential or the medical service must be severe. He also gives employers an important role. Indeed, he writes that it is not easy for the State to take early disability into account without letting the employer check it. He thinks that the disability pension must be managed by an employer fund which will arbitrate between continuing to pay the wage with reduced labour or paying an allowance lower than the wage. This reveals once again his mistrust of State intervention.

Pension Insurance

Cheysson and Colson disagree on this type of insurance. Cheysson thinks that it is difficult to provide a pension, but that it must be encouraged. Colson maintains exactly the opposite.

For Cheysson, the pension is the most difficult problem. Indeed, as pension insurance concerns the long term, as the aim is not to remedy very short-term damage, this type of insurance implies that one is able to properly anticipate, which seems difficult. And in the case of errors in anticipation as regards the duration of working life, it will be very difficult to change the system: the damage will have been done. Moreover, as the employer holds back a part of the wage to give back in 30years, precautions must be taken to ensure that the debt is paid, especially if the firm goes bankrupt. However, with social inequalities, Cheysson thinks the State must promote this insurance because worker is destined to misery and to requiring social assistance if he has not funded a pension.

Cheysson is, as we can imagine after having studied the system he proposes, against the law of 1910 which makes the old age insurance compulsory. In his opinion, when the State is provident instead of the worker, the state of mind changes and men take it easy. On account of the obligation, the worker no longer has resources for contingency planning: if the State takes a part of the wage for the pension, worker can no longer save (SEP July 1901 p. 112). Moreover, he assumes that the State does not have the capacity to manage the insurance. For this reason, he thinks that the State should not impose contingency institutions; it must establish, as the other types of insurance, technical and financial security rules. It can encourage and make grants in consideration of inspections.

> Only, a free attitude in the matter has the necessary flexibility and elasticity to adapt the solutions to the infinite variety of particular cases, in the same time as it toughens the moral drive instead of upsetting it, as it spares the country's finances instead of crushing them, and as it saves State interferences in private life, which are an inevitable source of embarrassment, suspicion and unpopularity. (SEP July 1901 pp. 109–110)

Colson argues to the contrary that pension insurance is easy to apply. Pension is calculated on the numbers of years of service and the last salary, as payments are proportional to the wage. He recognises it is impossible to calculate exactly the reserves to provide for the pension because the amount thereof depends on the increase of wages and of the development of the firm, but he does not see this as a problem because charges greater than the reserves can be deducted from profits. Moreover, there cannot be fraud with the pension as one has just to set the retirement age. On the other hand, another difficulty crops up there because the retirement entitlement age is set according to a presumption of incapacity (Colson 1917 pp. 370–381). The quotation below is very clear on this point:

> Setting this age is not an easy matter because the age at which different individuals cease to be fit to work varies a lot and absolute inability is usually preceded by an increasingly accentuated period of partial inability. If the age at which the pension is acquired [...] is set low enough to meet the needs of all, the insurance charges rose in a huge proportion [...]. If, on the contrary, we defer the retirement age, many workers will suffer from total inability to work, before this age and almost all will see their wages decrease significantly in the preceding years. The only solution, which meets all needs without imposing excessive charges is the one that sets a quite remote age for obtaining [...] a full pension, but by broadening, during the preceding years, the eligibility for a disability annuity. (Colson 1917 p. 370)

Although he thinks that pension insurance is easy to apply, Colson is against it because according to him it undermines the family ties, which shows the important role he gives to this theme.[21] He explains that old age insurance is presented by its defenders as a real act of solidarity and of social progress whereas, on the contrary, it tends to destroy the only real solidarity, family solidarity. For Colson, this theme is more important than reducing social inequality. Pension insurance is the most selfish form of savings because it consists in encouraging each individual to look after his future only. He even writes that no aid of any kind whatsoever must be paid to those who have no children even if they have no resources.

Adding this analysis to his objection to the obligation, it is not surprising that Colson, who writes in 1917, states that he is against the law of 1910 which makes old age insurance compulsory.

[21] For Cheysson too, the State imposes a method of contingency planning which is against the family but he pays less attention to it since this does not prevent him from being favourable to pension insurance.

Unemployment Insurance and Colson's Influence on Rueff's Unemployment Theory

Cheysson does not analyse unemployment insurance. We can conclude therefrom that he does not think that unemployment needs to be covered by insurance since he writes that the risks which threaten workers are limited to illness, accident and old age (SEP February 1894 p. 265). It is not the case for Colson and Rueff who develop an analysis of the unemployment insurance. Their analysis shows the hostility of liberal economists towards this type of insurance. For them, social inequality created by unemployment is due to the workers, and the State should not intervene to reduce it. Indeed, Colson argues not only that unemployment cannot be insured[22] but he maintains even with Rueff that unemployment insurance leads to unemployment. We will show that Rueff's analysis is inspired by Colson's analysis.

Colson thinks the solution to deal with unemployment is savings. Indeed, unemployment cannot be insured because the risk is not independent of the insured:

> Undoubtedly, there are general crises that affect all the industry's personnel, good and bad workers. But at these times, unemployment can no longer be characterised as an accident affecting some only of the insured, which is the very basis of all insurance. As regards normal unemployment, it mainly impacts the worker who does not satisfy any employer or else who leaves the workshop at any time and does not find other work as soon as he wants. It always will be difficult to convince the good workers to regularly pay an insurance premium in their favour and it would be unfair to force them to do so, whether in the form of a compulsory insurance or in that of a tax burdening the entire industry in order to subsidise the unemployment insurance, which is particularly beneficial to the mediocre workers. (SEP November 1909b pp. 286–287)

Colson and Rueff claim that the trade unions and unemployment insurance lead to unemployment. Rueff builds a theory of unemploy-

[22] Leroy-Beaulieu also thinks that this insurance does not reduce unemployment but without further developing this point (SEP November 1909b p. 289). As Guyot is against social insurance, he does not mention this insurance.

ment in which he shows that real wage and unemployment vary in the same direction. After presenting his theory and showing that it was applied in England after the war, Rueff criticises the minimum wage and unemployment insurance: according to him, they are the cause of permanent unemployment. Rueff's paper will have a significant impact in England, more particularly after its translation in the *Times* of 11 and 12 June 1931 (Alcouffe 1999 p. 10).[23] We show that not only is this theory supported by Colson but that it is also inspired by him.

Before presenting Rueff's analysis of unemployment, a few words need to be said about unemployment insurance in England. In 1911, the country passed the National Insurance Act. The first section sets up social insurance for illness, second section sets up a social insurance for unemployment. To deal with it, the worker and the employer each pay 2.5 pence a week and the State pays 3 pence. After one week of unemployment, the unemployed can receive up to 7 shillings[24] per week from the State for a period of 15 weeks per year.

Rueff studied the unemployment trend in England where the number of unemployed increased from 120,000 in August 1920 to 2,170,000 in June 1921. He seeks the reasons (SEP December 1925 pp. 515–523, May 1931 pp. 242–247, Rueff 1925, 1931).

He noted that the changes in unemployment are related to the changes in the gap between the level of wages and that of prices. Unemployment increases when the gap increases and decreases when the gap decreases.

> *Based on experience it can be asserted that, during the entire 1919–1925 period, there was a permanent causation in England between the number of unemployed and the ratio of the level of wages to the general level of prices as any change in the value of this ratio immediately brought about a concomitant change in the unemployment index.* (SEP December 1925 p. 519, italics from author)

[23] Alcouffe (1999, 2017) analyses the relation between Keynes and Rueff that will follow from this paper. For Keynes, decreasing wages and removing the insurance is not the only way to face unemployment.

[24] Up to 1971, when the United Kingdom adopted the decimal system: 1 shilling is equal to 12 pence.

The ratio is also observed from 1928 to 1931. It is not observed from 1926 to 1927 because of the general strike: during the strike, the changes in wage had no impact on employment.

The immediate cause of unemployment is thus that nominal wages were not adapted to the general level of prices.

He looked then for the deep cause of unemployment. He thinks that, during the period of a rise in the general level of prices, wages increase more slowly than prices; unemployment is at the minimum level; in the period of a drop in the general level of prices, wages decrease more slowly than prices; unemployment increases. He observes too that before the war, the nominal wage decreased until unemployment disappeared, this is no longer the case with unemployment insurance.[25]

From 1923 to 1925, the wages index and prices index stabilised; the number of unemployed was still high. The wage index was still high even though labour supply was higher than demand. Trade union discipline and assistance to the unemployed prevent wages from decreasing; this is the real reason unemployment continues. Trade unions prevent wages from being adapted to the new conditions; assistance to the unemployed allows workers to maintain trade union discipline. The unemployed prefer to collect the *dole* rather than work for a lower wage. So permanent unemployment appears. The following quotation is clear on this point:

> The consequence of such a regime was to establish a minimum wage level, as from which the worker prefer collect the "dole" rather than work for a wage which would give him only a rather weak surplus over the amount he collects as an unemployed. (SEP May 1931 p. 230)

Rueff presents his theory to the *Société d'économie politique* (SEP December 1925 pp. 515–523) in the presence of Colson and it seems clear that the mentor supports the student.

Indeed, Colson takes the floor just after Rueff to highlight the principal points of the theory:

[25] Note that from 1911 to the beginning of the war, England experienced prosperity, thus there is no unemployment. During the war, men are at combat and not at work.

- The coincidence between the changes in unemployment and in real wages is pointed out. The experience shows that no individual will can prevail against the play of natural laws.
- Unemployment insurance is not possible, it disorganises industry;
- Workers must adapt themselves to production conditions, the wage must not exceed the value of the object produced. Trade unions prevent adaptation by wanting to maintain the standard of living of workers whatever the economic conditions. Before the 1911 unemployment insurance law, trade unions agreed to decrease wages when their funds were empty following a period of limited unemployment; since 1911, the benefits are paid by the State; trade unions maintain their claims and unemployment continues (*ibid.* pp. 523–525).

Moreover, Colson replies to the questions put by *Société d'économie politique* members after Rueff's presentation.

Finally, even though Rueff speaks only of "hypothesis" (*ibid.* p. 518) in the relation between the level of wages, of prices and of unemployment, Colson speaks of "law" (*ibid.* p. 529).

We find too that Rueff's theory is strongly influenced by Colson. Indeed, Colson criticises trade unions and unemployment insurance, using arguments close to those used by Rueff. He writes, in 1909, that England, a country where workers' associations are the most developed and where labour legislation was born, is the country where unemployment is the highest. Associations and regulations increase unemployment. Trade unions standardise working time and do not regulate work needs. When demand for goods increases, the industrialist must employ new workers because he cannot increase work time; when the demand decreases, he must lay off the additional worker; he creates then an unemployment. Labour demand undergoes the oscillations observed by Juglar; the interest of the working class is that this demand be met by changing working time, not the number of workers employed (SEP November 1909b pp. 284–285).

Rueff analyses the effect of a minimum wage and of unemployment insurance. They prevent the wage from spontaneously stabilising; permanent unemployment crops up. In our opinion, these points are already in Colson's analysis.

As regards the English situation, according to Rueff, unemployment insurance corresponds to a minimum wage because the unemployed prefer not to work and collect benefits close to their working wage rather than working for a salary of the same level or lower. Unemployment insurance thus causes permanent unemployment.

We suggest that Rueff only develops these lines of his mentor:

> Suppose, for instance, that workers find a way, following a strike, by union pressure or by the intervention of a law, to be paid a wage higher than the normal rate arising from the market situation [...]. By distorting prices, one brings in this army of unemployed which does not exist in a normal situation, and its presence will allow to entrepreneurs to reduce unduly high salaries. (Colson 1915 p. 367)

Rueff explains that the minimum wage is liable to be higher than the market wage. Labour supply is then higher than demand without the wage being able to decrease to restore the equilibrium. Entrepreneurs then will replace the work by capital to be able to produce the same quantity at a lower cost price. Workers who are not hired on account of the minimum wage then stay without work; the effect of a minimum wage is thus to cause permanent unemployment.

He takes the example of rickshaw men in China. They get a very low remuneration; establishing a minimum wage is not a good solution to improve their situation:

> But what will happen if, in China, one set a minimum wage for rickshaw men somewhat higher than their current remuneration? They will be replaced by more modern means of traction, but they will still be unable to find work elsewhere; they will become unemployed and their suffering will certainly not be decreased. (SEP May 1931 p. 241)

We notice Colson's strong influence here; indeed, we see his theory of the joint setting of wage and of the interest rate.[26] Moreover, Rueff quotes the

[26] We will not go into detail on this theory and its paternity; we will just sum up the result of this theory: the wage rate and interest rate settle at the level where their marginal productivity is equal. If the wage increases, firms will replace the work by capital, if interest increases, firms will replace the capital by work (Colson 1915 pp. 359–372).

latter, by explaining that he was the first to demonstrate this link and he also describes this theory as "an essential discovery for the interpretation of economics facts" (Rueff 1933 p. 314). Rueff explains that by letting the market act, wages and interest rate settle at a level where the entire population finds a work, under Colson's law: for a same level of production, entrepreneurs prefer to replace the work by machines because at this wage level, marginal productivity of the capital is higher than that of the workers. Entrepreneurs then obtain a lower cost price with machines than by keeping on workers, unemployment remains high.

We point out too that Colson is aware of the concept of permanent unemployment as he considers that there are two types of unemployment:

- Permanent unemployment: it is the time that a worker who changes work needs to find new work. It mostly concerns bad workers who often change work.
- Unemployment of exceptional intensity, due to crises. It concerns good workers; it can be decreased by increasing labour flexibility (SEP November 1909b p. 285).

Colson and Rueff explain that the State should not intervene to reduce social inequality caused by unemployment. Indeed, the unemployed are generally bad workers, so it is unfair to force good workers to pay for them. Moreover, unemployment insurance is responsible for unemployment, because workers prefer not to work rather than to work for a lower salary. For these reasons, the political powers should let the market act.

7.4 Conclusion

Based on this analysis, we can emphasise that the liberal economists fear State intervention and political power. Indeed, they are against the State intervening to manage social insurance: the State does not have the capacity to do so and it would be bad for the country's wealth. Moreover, to be elected, politicians can promise popular but bad decisions to the State's budget.

But economists are aware of social inequality and that workers are in a vulnerable situation, which leads some of them to propose limited State intervention. We can emphasise the French Liberal School is not a homogenous school of thought since the defended positions go from no State intervention where accidents must be referred to the civil liability of the employer and where social insurance is viewed as socialism to State intervention to encourage the protection of workers by social insurance. Indeed, while the more liberal authors like Guyot think the State must not intervene because it would modify the natural spread of wealth—this would have a negative effect—others take social inequality into account and think workers must be protected from the risks they face. Some authors, like Leroy-Beaulieu, argue in favour of savings without insurance being compulsory, others, like Cheysson and Colson, social insurance. The practical solutions they propose combine State intervention to encourage the protection of workers and giving employers considerable freedom to take out insurance. We thus see a liberal analysis which does not grant too much latitude to State intervention: the State should allow workers to be insured; the employer should have the power to choose the insurance company and whether it is worth continuing to employ the worker with reduced work or paying him insurance premium.

Likewise, even though the most accepted social insurance is that against workplace accidents and illness and unemployment, insurance is rejected because the risk is not independent from the insured; all authors do not think there should be pension insurance.

We think this attitude is not independent of the political context. Indeed, at the end of the nineteenth century, protectionists were back in the government[27] and socialists were beginning to represent an important political force threatening the established liberal order.[28] Each author

[27] In the 1890s, one sees a revival of protectionism. In France, there is a calling into question of the free trade agreement signed with Great Britain in 1860. The Méline law is voted on 11 January 1892. A double tariff protectionist customs tariff is adopted: there is a minimum rate for the normal tariff and a minimum rate for State that grants customs privileges to France; it is the end of free trade set up by the 1860 treaty.

[28] We can note in France the creation of Confédération Générale du Travail (CGT)—trade union drawing one's inspiration from socialist ideas—in 1895 and of Section Française de l'Internationale Ouvrière (SFIO)—political party bringing together the different socialist currents in a unique party—in 1905.

develops a practical vision that can potentially be applied by politicians they train or advise, if they are not politicians themselves. We think that in this way political leaders were able to take decisions which, while still being decisions guided by a liberal approach without giving too much power to the government, took account of the social inequalities and thus contributed to limiting the rise of socialism and interventionism so feared by liberals of the time. Seeing that their plight was being taken into account, workers did not turn to socialism, one of the targets of which was to reduce social inequality. The existing liberal order was not threatened. Like this, seeing their misery is taken into account, workers don't turn towards socialism, one of the targets of which is to reduce social inequalities. The existing liberal order is not threatened.

References

Alcouffe, A. (1999). Keynes and the French Guardians of the Say's Law. In L. L. Pasinetti & B. Schefold (Eds.), *The Impact of Keynes on Economics in the 20th Century*. Cheltenham: Edward Elgar.

Alcouffe, A. (2017). French Planning: How to Cope with Business Cycles? In A. Alcouffe, M. Poettinger, & S. Bertam (Eds.), *Business Cycles and Economic Thought: A History*. New York: Routledge.

Baslé, M. (1991). Paul Leroy-Beaulieu 1843–1916, un économiste français de la IIIe République commençante. In Breton and Lutfalla (Ed.).

Bousquet, G.-H. (1960). *Clément Colson*. Paris: Dalloz, 354 p.

Brasseul, J. (2004). *Histoire des faits économiques: industrialisation et sociétés dans le monde au XIXe et au début du XXe siècle*. Paris: A. Colin.

Breton, Y., & Lutfalla, M. (1991). *L'économie politique en France au XIXe siècle*. Paris: Economica.

Cheysson, E. (1894). L'obligation de la garantie de l'indemnité et la liberté des divers combinaisons d'assurances contre les accidents. In *Congrès international des accidents du travail et des assurances sociales, troisième session tenue à Milan du 1er au 6 octobre 1894. Tome premier, Rapports*, by Congrès international des accidents du travail et des assurances sociales (pp. 849–864). Milan: Imprimerie H. Reggiani.

Cheysson, E. (1895). *La garantie obligatoire de l'indemnité (Extrait de la Revue Politique et Parlementaire de Février et Mars 1895)*. Paris: Bureaux de la Revue politique et parlementaire.

Colson, C. (1912). *Organisme économique et désordre social. Deuxième édition.* Paris: Ernest Flammarion.
Colson, C. (1915). *Cours d'économie politique, professé à l'École polytechnique et à l'Ecole nationale des Ponts et chaussées, Livre premier, Théorie générale des phénomènes économiques.* Paris: Gauthier-Villars: F. Alcan.
Colson, C. (1917). *Cours d'économie politique: professé à l'école polytechnique et à l'École nationale des ponts et chaussées, Livre deuxième, Le travail et les questions ouvrières.* Paris: Gauthier-Villars: F. Alcan.
De Paoli, J. (2017). *Clément Colson (1853–1939), la science économique de son époque et ses prolongements* (PhD Thesis). Lyon, 377 p.
Divisia, F. (1951). *Exposés d'économique: Tome 1 Introduction générale, L'apport des ingénieurs français aux sciences économiques.* Paris: Dunod.
Friedman, M. (1962). *Capitalism and Freedom.* University of Chicago Press.
Guyot, Y. (1893). *La tyrannie socialiste.* Paris: Ch. Delagrave.
Guyot, Y. (1914). *L'industrie et les industriels.* Paris: Doin.
Guyot, Y. (1923). *La science économique.* Paris: *Ses lois inductives.*
Le Van-Lemesle, L. (2004). *Le Juste ou le Riche: l'enseignement de l'économie politique 1815–1950.* Paris: Ministère de l'économie, des finances et de l'industrie, Comité pour l'histoire économique et financière de la France.
Le Van-Lemesle, L. (2005, September). Cauwès et Colson, le juriste et l'ingénieur: une ou deux conceptions du service public? *Revue d'histoire moderne et contemporaine, 52–3*(3), 75–87.
Leroy-Beaulieu, P. (1888). *Précis d'économie politique.* Paris: C. Delagrave.
Leroy-Beaulieu, P. (1914). *Traité théorique et pratique d'économie politique Tome 2.* Paris: F. Alcan.
Luciani, J. (1991). La question sociale en France. In Y. Breton & M. Lutfalla (Eds.), *L'économie politique en France au XIXe siècle* (pp. 555–587). Paris: Economica.
Lutfalla, M. (1972, January 1). Aux origines du libéralisme économique en France LE 'JOURNAL DES ÉCONOMISTES': Analyse du contenu de la première série 1841–1853. *Revue d'histoire économique et sociale, 50*(4), 494–517.
Luzzatti, L. (1894). Avantage du libre choix de l'assureur en cas d'assurance obligatoire; opportunité d'organiser, mais non d'imposer, des caisses officielles ayant pour mission de servir de type au triple point de vue de la solvabilité, de l'économie et de la rapidité des règlements. – Du rôle réservé dans cet ordre d'idées au Caisses nationales constituées par les Caisses d'épargne. In *Congrès international des accidents du travail et des assurances sociales, troisième session tenue à Milan du 1er au 6 octobre 1894. Tome premier,*

Rapports, by Congrès international des accidents du travail et des assurances sociales (865–881). Milan: Imprimerie H. Reggiani.

Marco, L. (1991). Jean-Gustave Courcelle-Seneuil 1813–1892, l'orthodoxe intransigeant. In Breton and Lutfalla (Ed.).

Pasinetti, L. L., & Schefold, B. (1999). *The Impact of Keynes on Economics in the 20th Century*. Cheltenham: Elgar.

Picory, C. (1989). Orthodoxie Libérale et Hétérodoxie Marginaliste: Clément Colson. *Revue Économique, 40*(4), 679–708.

Pollet, G., & Dumons, B. (1995). Aux Origines Du Système Français de Retraite. La Construction D'une Solution Politique Au Problème de La Vieillesse Ouvrière Au Tournant Des XIXe et XXe Siècles. *Sociétés Contemporaines, 24*(1), 11–39.

Rueff, J. (1925, December). Les variations du chômage en Angleterre. *Revue politique et parlementaire, CXXV*, 425–436.

Rueff, J. (1931, April). [signé xxx]. L'assurance-chômage, cause du chômage permanent. *Revue d'économie politique* 45e année (2), 211–251.

Rueff, J. (1933, November). L'enseignement de M. Colson. *Revue Politique et Parlementaire*, no. Tome CLVII, numéro 2, 312–318.

Sécurité sociale. *Historique Du Système Français de Sécurité Sociale* [online]. Available from: http://www.securite-sociale.fr/Historique-du-systeme-francais-de-Securite-sociale. Accessed 14 June 2017.

Société d'économie politique. (1888, March). Réunion Du 6 Mars 1888. L'assurance Des Ouvriers Contre Les Accidents. *Journal Des Économistes* 4e série, Tome quarante-et-unième(3), 426–446.

Société d'économie politique. (1894, February). Réunion Du 5 Février 1894. Les Lois Ouvrières Au Point de Vue de L'intervention de l'Etat. *Journal Des Économistes* 5e série, Tome XVII(2), 261–282.

Société d'économie politique. (1895, February). Réunion Du 5 Février 1895. L'assurance Obligatoire et La Responsabilité Civile Relativement Aux Accidents Du Travail. *Journal Des Économistes* 5e série, Tome XXI(2), 263–283.

Société d'économie politique. (1901, July). Réunion Du 13 Juin 1901. Des Retraites Ouvrières. *Journal Des Économistes* 5e série, Tome XLVII(1), 101–133.

Société d'économie politique. (1905, March). Réunion Du 6 Mars 1905. L'envahissement de l'Etat Dans Le Domaine de L'assurance et En Particulier de L'assurance-Incendie. *Journal Des Économistes* 6e série, Tome V(3), 419–436.

Société d'économie politique. (1909a, February). Réunion Du 5 Février 1909. Les Lois Sociales et Les Lois Économiques. *Journal Des Économistes* 6e série, Tome XXI(2), 256–273.
Société d'économie politique. (1909b, November). Réunion Du 5 Novembre 1909. Les Remèdes Ou Prétendus Remèdes Contre Le Chômage. *Journal Des Économistes* 6e série, Tome XXIV(2), 278–290.
Société d'économie politique. (1925, December). Séance Du 5 Décembre 1925. Recherches Sur Les Variations Du Chômage En Angleterre. *Journal Des Économistes* 6e série, Tome LXXXII(4), 514–535.
Société d'économie politique. (1931, May). Séance Du 5 Mai 1931. Les Causes Du Chômage. *Journal Des Économistes* 6e série, Tome XCIX(2): 222–253.
Zouboulakis, M. S. (2000). Eclectisme théorique et libéralisme pragmatique dans l'oeuvre de Clément Colson. In P. Dockès, L. Frobert, & G. Klotz (Eds.), *Les traditions économiques françaises: 1848–1939* (pp. 581–593). Paris: CNRS Ed.

Part III

Market Power and Institutions in Theory and Policy

8

Power Wars Between Institutions: Business Training in Higher Education

Marion Dieudonné

8.1 Introduction

The second industrial revolution and its upheaval triggered what is known as the *Progressive Era* (1890–1920). As H.T. Warshow pointed out in 1924, "the distribution of corporate ownership in the United States" became the central concern.[1] Indeed, capitalism at the beginning of the century was a period of commercial struggle between large companies seeking to capture market power, which led to conflicting relations that affected society in all its institutions, including education. The new culture of the firm highlighted the importance of new needs, among which is the need for business training.

This era saw the emergence of new figures in the US higher education, a system of education considered as modern (Goldin and Katz 1998, 6).

[1] There is generally a relative lack of interest in contextualizing these major transformations in the United States and work on the history of corporate finance education, which took place more in Europe from 1819 onwards.

M. Dieudonné (✉)
University of Paris-Dauphine, PSL Research University, Paris, France

M. Mosca (ed.), *Power in Economic Thought*, Palgrave Studies in the History of Economic Thought, https://doi.org/10.1007/978-3-319-94039-7_8

In this respect, various economists of the time, including Thorstein Veblen, debated the consequences on the system of education of these economic and social transformations. The problem they saw was that of the relation between economic structures and business training. The creation of the first business schools also raised the question of their relationship with the university system: was it a question of transmitting academic knowledge? Or just practical? A war of power between institutions erupted when the explosion in the number of business schools came to compete with the university. The confrontation of different market visions (what should be and what is according to different ideologies) was reflected in competing visions of business education, whether this new subject had to be taught by scholars or by businessmen. The task of the teachers had to be that of analysing the reality of the new market power relationships established through the concentration of companies, the capital structure, the exacerbation of credit, the use of new governance operations and financial arrangements to dilute property. Our objective is to underline the market power of the large companies that set up at the turn of the century in an already exacerbated balance of power between the power of universities and the growing one of business schools. Businessmen thus impose their power within all the institutions thanks to their power of capitalization which marks the authority of the industrial-financial environment facing the educational system. New consequences and new stakes arise from this domination of businessmen.

In this chapter we present the American debate around education and in particular about the institutionalization of business training in higher education. Through Veblenian categories, we raise the question of authority in the relationship, the power to decide between industry, finance and education in the United States.

8.2 A Period of Change for Industrial Financial Capitalism

The 1890s marked a real turning point in the United States, with the transition to the major financial markets and the trustification of the American economy. At the end of the nineteenth century, finance and industry joined forces. The result was a concentration of the management and organization powers of companies, and therefore of the market, in the hands of a few captains of finance. Indeed, at the turn of the century, capitalist companies and institutions saw their structures change under pressure from the industrial captains, who became finance captains with growing market power. These oligarchic captains were able to assess the performance of business managers' work and draw a signal to guide the market. In this, they dominated its functioning. During the *Gilded Age*[2] the "robber barons" were the embodiment of charismatic businessmen, for they monopolized market power in their hands.[3] While they acted to increase the company's market value because of imperfect market conditions, they were also responsible for fraud and conflicts of interest (De Long 1991, 206, 208). Then, the era of business enterprise (1904–1910) saw the transition from a savage capitalism to an organized capitalism that turned away from industrial preoccupations to focus on trade.

For Veblen (1904), these captains were distinguished according to whether they held preferred or common shares. The captains of industry were the managers (owners of common shares) of the company, while the capitalists were mere contributors of capital and held the preferred shares. In Veblen's view, from 1910 onwards began the predatory phase, a phase in which the industrial captains became strategic captains of business, assisted by experts, technicians and engineers. The category of absent owners, vested interests, captains of finance, asserted itself. With the corporation finance revolution,[4] from the 1920s onwards, the finance captains took over the market, the industrialists became finance business lieutenants (managers), and a powerful *Soviet* engineer was consolidated. In Veblenian vocabulary, the *Soviet* was an institutional response to historically dated means and modes of production. It is a centralization of the technical knowledge of engineers and technicians that offers an alter-

[2] The period between 1870 and 1900 is known as the *Gilded Age*.

[3] "Growing up as he did during the Age of the Robber Barons, Veblen had good reason to be critical of American business practices" (Cowley and Hefferlin 1957).

[4] We use the world revolution because large companies experienced both a technological revolution during the 1910s and a consequent industrial and technological reorganization, marking the end of the progressive era and opening a period of revolution in practices where the new corporate finance discipline emerged. In particular, American Economic Association theorists such as Taussig, Tullock, Ripley, Gay or Young were at the origin of the movement (Carlson 1968).

native to the absentee owners to counter the financial logic that is imposed against the industrial one. Indeed, it was these captains of industry who gave birth to what Veblen called captains of finance or of solvency (1923, 114) in the industrial-financial sector and, as we shall see, captains of scholarship in the academic sector (Veblen 1923 [1997], 354).[5] The problem that then arises was that of the gains derived from business activity and captured by the hands of capitalists "not by virtue of having produced or earned them … but because they own them." (Veblen 1923 [1997], 51). Thus, the financial practice of the modern company appeared at the time of the transition from trusts to holding companies and was accompanied by new power relations between different captainships. Indeed, this excess of financial power in collusion with industry introduced a power of manipulation, hence Veblen's question on the importance of the institutions' captainships in order to preserve balanced relations between the forces involved. The transformations were such that they brought the economy towards a free-market capitalism regime. Indeed, all these mergers and reorganizations motivated by the financial aims of magnates and shareholders disrupted the common industrial relations. There was of course a contradiction between the necessary handing over of power in the hands of these economic subjects, the industrial and financial magnates, and the search for the general interest (Laughlin 1906, 100–1).

Exciting literature emerged at that time, denouncing these changes in society. William Zebina Ripley, for example, in 1927 portrayed early twentieth century corporate governance and fraudulent practices in his work *Main Street and Wall Street*, "a book severely critical of corporate practices, including the public utility holding company device which allowed a few insiders to exercise enormous power on a very narrow investment base" (Carlson 1968, 103).

[5] Burton J. Hendricks took up the notion again in 1919 without ever mentioning Veblen; and Geoffrey Todd discussed in 1932 the contrast between "*sleeping partners*" and "*active directors*", even though they forgot Veblen's work as a potential source of inspiration. However, Veblen was rooted in the reality around him as a privileged witness. R.T. Ely spoke of managers as *dummy directors* who, thanks to the acquisition of power, became part of the *executive committee* or *finance committee*. Veblen also drew on the work of Ely *Monopolies and Trusts* (1900) for his writings as early as 1904 and shared a similar vision.

8.3 The Need for Business Education

As said, in this changing context for corporate structures, new needs emerged. Among them, the need for business education had an important role. This leads us to deal with business training in higher education. As we know, in the United States, the practice of corporate finance had been very active in the last quarter of the nineteenth century. The new entrepreneurial functions in mergers and acquisitions, the new power relations within the company, as well as the new business practices and their massive imposition on the market required theorization. Thus, these new internal power relations within the company imposed new rules and standards that must be reflected in business training. Corporate finance then exercises a coercive power over educational institutions by guiding all of the country's economic activities. In fact, they raised a real academic interest in a practice that became a scientific discipline. Between the 1880s and the crisis of 1929, a new academic field of study appeared: corporate finance. As simultaneously also the science of education became a discipline, scientific considerations emerged about this new field of training. In this period, business training in America was considered to be "unique in its vigor" but also "in its lack of guidance" (Lyon 1922, ix).

In order to propose structures that could meet the expectations for professional training in business, an adaptation of higher education was required: the university had to adapt both in terms of research and curricula, while at the same time the offer of training courses was completed by private business schools, which questioned the supremacy of the university. This is referred to as the commercialization of universities (Bertrams 2008), leading to internal contradictions in the institution's principles. The transformations in society determined new power relations between academia and the business community.

Competition between educational authorities due to the need for specialization and adaptation did not stop at the level of institutions, it also concerned conflicts between economists and managers who sought to position their influence and impose themselves inside the institutions. The already exacerbated internal conflicts within companies also gave rise to divergent pedagogical orientations, despite the immediate needs of businessmen's practice. The changing financial, entrepreneurial and governance context had strong repercussions in terms of setting up training courses for businessmen.

8.4 The Institutions for Business Education

Between 1880 and 1915, there were three levels of business training structures: first, the universities[6]; then, the private schools, called "commercial colleges", "normal schools" or "technical schools" (Cheit 1985, 44); third, the "University based-business schools", also known as "secondary schools" or "graduate schools", which were of better quality than the aforementioned schools, but which developed later. They depended on the university,[7] which made it possible to obtain a university degree at the end of the training.

As we shall see, the evolution was such that professional studies were fully oriented towards an applied approach, while academic studies took a theoretical turn. This is why this was an era marked both by the necessary dependence between university and business, in order to adapt training courses for future businessmen, but at the same time by a hostility of entrepreneurs, whose vision of the practical needs of the company differed from the pedagogical objective and the knowledge of academics. These secondary schools were then supposed to make a link between academic and applied approaches. They took an important and competing place in the training of American youth.

Initially, business schools appeared as a parallel offer to that of universities, which did not have the capacity and/or willingness to accommodate all students. The first business school, in 1881, was the Wharton School of the University of Pennsylvania,[8] which was founded by a wealthy businessman, Joseph Wharton, who wanted to donate $100,000 to the University of Philadelphia to establish the first American school of

[6] Public or private. It is in a private form that the first universities were created and this system is still widespread in the United States.

[7] Colleges were absorbed by the University at the turn of the century (Ollivier-Mellios 2004, 63).

[8] Redlich pointed out that "Wharton, according to James, had created a model of education for successful business management and efficient public service by businessmen" (1957, 83).

finance and commerce. The answer given by the university was that such a school had no place in it (Cheit 1985, 43–45). That's why the Wharton School remained for a long time the only independent institution dedicated to professional business training for aspiring businessmen.

> It was these considerations, then, that determined Mr. Wharton to establish this school. First: the belief that the business classes of our country need a higher training as much or more than any other classes; second, the view that the Commercial of Business College, however valuable its curriculum, is by its very nature unable to give this higher training; third, the fact that the American college, however real and valuable its higher training, does not in its present form furnish a kind of higher training which appeals to the business sentiment of the community, as is shown by the fact of the small number of youths looking to business careers who enter college (James 1892, 14).

It took 17 years before the practical needs for orientation towards entrepreneurial training were taken into account. Indeed, at the beginning of the century, there was a debate on the diversification of educational pathways, the so-called curriculum. The Chicago Booth School of Business and the Haas School of Business in Berkeley were both founded in 1898. With regard to the Chicago school, the impetus was given by the arrival of J.L. Laughlin in 1892 and in 1898 to the College of Commerce and Politics whose vocation was to seek, according to William Rainey Harper (1895), then president of the University of Chicago, "scientific guidance and investigation of great economic and social matters of everyday importance" because they were "the crying needs".[9] The Haans School was affiliated with the University of California and became the first public business school.

The first graduate business school in the United States appears to be Dartmouth's Amos Tuck School, which was established at the same time

[9] In 1892 before the Convention of the American Bankers' Association, on the theme School of Finance and Economy, Edmund J James "perhaps the best observer of business education of the time" (Lyon 1922, 282) gave a speech entitled "Education for Business" to praise the merits of the Wharton School of which he was director. To this end, it recalls the importance of the needs of institutions in relation to the growing number of students, while the number of vocational schools (Lyon 1922, 3) was not growing fast enough (James 1892, 12–3, 19).

as the School of Commerce, Accounts and Finance in New York in 1900. The Harvard Business School[10] was founded in 1904, but only opened in 1908. Twenty-five schools of this type were established between 1900 and 1913 in the United States, while the country became a "temple of consumption", in which advertising, marketing and management played a prominent role (Butler 2008, 349). Indeed, the manager was built and developed as an agent who had integrated all these new sub-disciplines to manage the company on a large scale. The trust, authority and legitimacy of this business manager were owed to the institution that had formed it, whether it was the controversial business schools or the university in internal conflict with the graduate schools that were progressively affiliated with it.

At the turn of the century, the American university was in a very difficult situation.[11] It was relatively young,[12] alert to society's practices, aware of the changes and adaptation costs it had to face. Its original goal was that of providing all undergraduate students with the most culturally comprehensive education. As it had still a central role in the transformation of societies, it was a flagship institution.[13] But it also had to maintain its place among the diversified and competitive range of training courses for young businessmen. The questions were whether or not education was destined to the elite (economic/managerial or intellectual/academic). Were the various needs being met in a utilitarian perspective? Or should the university have proposed a new cultural model in the face of societal and social changes? Faced with the first schools that did not offer much "useful" (Cheit 1985, 45) to their students the vocational training was not well adapted to the needs. That was why it was necessary to find a way to make higher education more dynamic and attractive. This opened two avenues: on the one hand, the establishment of special schools and, on

[10] It initiated a marked influence in the orientation of business schools at the beginning of the century, whose core curriculum was based on the case study (A.M. Kantrow 1986, 82).

[11] Veblen (1918a, b, 1923), RTEP box 16 folder 10, Redlich (1957), Chandler (1959), Ollivier-Mellios (2004), Huret (2005), Bertrams (2008), Payen-Variéras (2009).

[12] American universities were established between 1636 (Harvard University) and 1890 (Chicago University), particularly during the second half of the nineteenth century.

[13] It is on the university, in particular, that innovation capacities and diversity management were based; it ensured objectivity, access to culture for all and the resolution of a number of challenges facing it after the Civil War.

the other hand, the internal modification of curricula at the university, which made it possible to integrate the need for vocational training. At the time, it was clearly difficult to know what adaptation to choose and Harvard and many universities were no exception. The university tried to defend its principles of autonomy, dissemination of culture and research organization. At the same time, it sought funding from partners with whom it would develop partnerships and a benevolent paternalism and did not want to lose face in front of schools offering professional careers that attracted students, teachers and professionals. The gap between the university's principles and role, and the answers it had to provide to societal issues, was at the centre of a lively debate. But despite the fact that the university was aware of this—particularly with regard to the financial interests at stake—it could only fight against this phenomenon. Indeed, the university was caught up in a contradiction between ethical risks and financial profit-sharing.

8.5 The Corporate Problem and the Business of Training

As already said, the development of large business enterprises between 1880 and 1929 coincided with the emergence of corporate finance as a practical activity and then as an academic discipline. The appearance of business schools as early as the 1880s, and their relationship with university, was a reflection of a change in society. The difficulty facing educational institutions was linked to the fact that entrepreneurial ethos developed and intruded everywhere as a central value and created power relations with other institutions.

At the dawn of the twentieth century, despite a number of experiences in both Europe and the United States, the attempt to set up a high-level business training course was still unsuccessful (Redlich 1957, 35). The place of the university in modern life was a real challenge in an American context where business and entrepreneurial training was becoming increasingly important. This can also be linked to current issues that revolve around the involvement of companies in universities or the "corporate university" (Donoghue 2008, 12) to enrich training and skills development structures in the company. Capitalism opened the door to this "corporate problem"[14] that had spilled over into the training of businessmen. It was a reconfiguration of the university that did not have, a priori, to make the apology of finance that spread throughout society. The company interfered in the finance of the university, in its management, as well as in the organization and in the content of its teaching. As soon as the first school in Pennsylvania was founded, the Wharton School raised the issue of the relationship between schools and universities. This is all the more true as businessmen paid massive amounts of money for training programmes and took an interest in what happened in these courses.

We are therefore confronted with an opposition from both types of institutions that stemmed from a war between the central figures of the "captains" of institutions (the captainships at their head evolving with these institutions) but also from the search for domination between training units and disciplinary methods. This opposition confronts two visions of capitalist society and a repositioning of disciplines. In the last quarter of the nineteenth century, there was a rupture between economics and management, with economic theory appropriating management themes. In addition, the new schools, in search of prestige, sought to link up with the university. At the very beginning of the twentieth century, managers tried to consolidate management discipline through the argument of scientificity. The secondary school system saw the businessman enter the university as a "competitive university" (Veblen 1918a, 129), because the university was now challenged by the entrepreneurial system and business schools. Veblen talked about a change in the ethical codes of universities and the imposition of performance criteria. This is what he calls the subordination of erudition to autocracy (Veblen 1904, 299).

Education is central to a country, both for the diffusion of ideas, economic efficiency and techniques, but also because it is through it that life in society is conceived. This period was the death knell for small businesses and academics in the United States, who defended their institu-

[14] This theme appeared later in the writings of Berle and Means (1932), Lippman (1914), Veblen (1923), Carver (1925), Ripley (1927), Wormser (1931).

tions against big business, forcing an end to democracy and transparency. Finally, little by little, the school and the productive market lost their institutional weight in favour of the company and the financial market. As a result, new production processes, new technologies and financial management methods emerged. Indeed, the priorities of universities under pressure from companies changed. The consequences of the consolidation phase of managerial culture (1900–1920) were also passed on to the university as a legitimate culture.

These educational reforms were a solid foundation for guiding the culture of a country that derived from its industrial culture the principles and values of several generations. When power relations, habits and values changed, the reorganization of work required bursting with educational reforms.

Indeed, it is a matter of raising the problems linked to the modes of regulation of capitalism, since the concentration of power in this business community was nothing more than the emergence of oligarchic capitalism. These new relationships and hierarchies reflected the excesses of the society at the end of the century, with the extreme power of their financiers, which imposed itself on the society as a whole. The result was a new power relationship between education and practical bent. From then on, business education itself became a big business of training.

The institutions—business and market—that directed the economy, drove the institution-school towards a monetary goal, and the question of property rights appeared to be a significant one. The needs were obvious: the engineering profession grew from 7000 engineers in 1880 to 136,000 in 1920.[15] In the same way, just as accounting and managerial practices normalized as a profession, clubs and associations of managers were formed, as the title of Louis Brandéis (1914) book indicates, *Business [is] a profession.*

The power relations were increasingly marked because they broke with the traditional problems of the university elite, namely the issues around currency, fiscal policy and free trade. From 1907 onwards, an impulse was given to the United States to integrate industrial organization concerns into curricula. This impulse stemmed in particular from discus-

[15] US Bureau of the Census, 1943, table 8 p. 11; quoted by E. Layton (1962, 70).

sions, forums and scientific communications on industrial and business education (Taksa 2007, 139). Indeed, the analysis of capitalism was henceforth inseparable from that of management in the dynamics of the rent mechanics, and managerial leverage became central to the corporate culture. This managerial culture was then inculcated in the university among students because the institution adhered to it.

Moreover, this managerial logic was also introduced into the university's governance rules. As said, the university had to adapt its training to the teaching needs of knowledge and business management processes. The management of the education units itself was partly run by businessmen. The managerial corporate culture permeated all areas of economic and social life. In this way it naturally became legitimate in the eyes of all. Donoghue (2008) points out the tendency of universities to function as companies. According to him, this is part of a long tradition of "corporate [...] hostility toward higher education" (2008, xiii), and Veblen was the first to identify it (1918a, b, 15).

8.6 Different Visions of Education

While the period 1855–1895 corresponds to the emergence of education as a field of study, the years 1895–1938 refer to the effervescence of its issues and practical recommendations (Knox 1971, 1). This scientific inclination to think about education led to the reform of the American system that gave rise to the High School Movement (Goldin and Katz 1998, 1) between 1910 and 1940. Thus, in the face of a society that was becoming more complex, knowledge did not escape this phenomenon of complexity and opened up a debate because of the de facto relationship between financial tycoons.[16]

We have seen that during the 1910s business education asserted itself as "elective systems with many school subjects became popular, and consolidated high schools offering vocational as well as academic curricula

[16] John D. Rockefeller, for example, financed the Harvard Business School budget from 1908 to 1913 through the creation of a General Education Board. It was an essential funding channel for that institution.

were established" (Knox 1971, 3). Faced with the many students who were looking for business training, the establishment of these new courses also gave rise to a debate between two visions of business education, competing practical and ideal needs. After the structures of business, it was a matter of teaching to change, in its content and methods.

On the training side, we find the academics. Within the framework of the university, they developed their theories and disseminated their principles through their teaching in a generalist formation consisting of knowledge and culture. However, with the emergence of independent schools, businessmen, who were concerned with the practice of business, showed the need for training and know-how applied to their large companies. They required management training. It was at this moment that appeared indistinctly what is called business training, business education, business studies, vocational training or part of management studies. The vision of higher education disseminated by the university and the needs of vocational training met by specialized schools were opposed, highlighting a strong ethical antagonism with the universal values of scholars.

As a "university is in competition with other corporations [2]of learning" (Chandler 1959, 193), and despite the prosperity of universities and related training schools, there was a climate of hostility between academics and businessmen. Businessmen tended to impose their economic-financial power and principles in university education. Conversely, some of the academics who supported an academic education were opposed to the philosophy diffused in the company. Indeed, the latter—among them Veblen, or L. S. Lyon—intended to retain their symbolic power within the university, which was essentially philanthropic.

Academics struggled to impose their vision of education in the face of a strong entrepreneurial lobby: this was the strength of large American industrial families and financial institutions in the industrial and banking sector. For example, J.P. Morgan, which was both present in the banking market but also had a major influence on the corporate market, allowed for reorganizations and consolidations. These coalitions, vectors of both stability and instability, transformed the market and shook up power relations, games of domination, sometimes leading to lobbying and corruption to gain a privileged position in the market. Moreover, educational authorities raised the question of financial partnership, and fears of potential corruption, which ran counter to the collective interest and quality of education. The fact that these businessmen took part in the governance of universities gave rise to fears of corruption on the part of universities in the orientation of the training and research institution for their benefit.

However, a rapprochement between society and university was necessary. The problem was that society was represented here by the business community, whose values were neither in the collective interest nor in that of a disinterested culture. The newly created business schools reinforced their influence at the turn of the century.

8.7 The Institutionalist View

It is in this context, "destined to affect not only the social and business existence of the every-day American but even his political and legal institutions" (Hendrick 1919 [2005], 25), that the writings of Veblen (1904, 1918a, b, 1923, TVP) were anchored, very much in phase with the changes of his time, when educational institutions were perfectly integrated into the organized capitalism of the time. The reformist authors (like Veblen and Dewey) who examined this question at the beginning of the century, sought to raise awareness of the changing role and incarnation of the "education function" (Knox 1971). In this war between universities and companies or between theory and practice, they contributed to the debate by defending an academic point of view against financial capitalists. The question was: who would have the power in the face of the reorganization of the company? This was reflected in the curriculum because institutions had to adapt.

Institutionalists offered a particularly interesting point of view of analysing the business enterprise and had extremely realistic insights into the evolution of different powers and power relations. In fact, their socio-economic vision provided an interesting and atypical discourse on the understanding of the interactions between business and academia, which were rapidly transforming into a relationship of power between the market on the one hand, and knowledge on the other, which is traditionally understood by education as a universal value. Although little studied, and having had little posterity on these themes, institutionalists had much to say about capitalism and especially about the links between machine process and business enterprise.

8.8 The Importance of Veblen's Voice in Education

As Shute (1974) stated, Veblen's "writings on education, vested interests, absentee ownership, nationalism and so forth merit close attention". In 1918, he published a work with an explicit title, *The Higher Learning in America: A Memorandum on the Conduct of Universities by Business Men*, which was considered as a "highly controversial book on education"[17] (Chandler 1959, 7). His commitment can certainly be explained by his academic positions in Chicago—the nerve centre of social science change where a dynamic, multidisciplinary discussion circle was taking place—and in Wisconsin where he was in contact with R.T. Ely[18] and A.A. Young.

Veblen's voice was particularly important for the study of these educational philosophy pleas that were established in the face of the powers of businessmen. Chandler[19] insisted that Veblen belonged to a broad movement, had a keen interest in the training of American youth, but he complained that "Veblen's *writings have been largely neglected by the professional educator*" (Chandler 1959, 1).

Innis's 1929 biography underscored the importance of Veblen's awareness of the place of business training in a more global social critique (Bertrams 2007, 3). The Veblenian positioning, concerning the role of education and the insertion of businessmen in training, is in line with his well-known theories on the separation between industry and finance,

[17] And visibly inspired by James McKeen Catell 's book University Control (1860).

[18] However, it should be noted that Ely did not share Veblen's view on the generalist training of students (Jones and Monieson 1990, 104). So, Ely considered the feedback of experiences as the best of the trainings while J. R. Commons considered that over-practice did not allow for satisfactory training. Institutionalists therefore did not speak with one voice on these issues either.

[19] In his thesis *Institutionalism and Education: An inquiry into the implications of the philosophy of Thorstein Veblen*, defended in 1959 in Michigan.

manager and owner, the theory of instincts and the problems of governance within the entrepreneurial structure. Dorfman (1934) also presented him as a pedagogue. In a letter from C. Hasek Marx to Dorfman of 10 May 1934,[20] the latter gave an account of Veblen's ambitions:

> On October 19, 1919, Veblen wrote me in part as fellows: 'Now, it is an intimate part of the ambitions of the New School to come into touch with the technical men who have to do with the country's industry and know something about the state of things and the needs of industry. In fact, some of us are beginning to see that 'social research' means, in good part, industrial research of a very objective and even mechanical character, if it is to mean anything substantial'.[21]

However, Veblen was not seen as an "educational reformer" in the literature but almost as a traditionalist in his way of perceiving corporate finance in the educational world. Despite his disciples (W. Hamilton, W.C. Mitchell), his overly pessimistic social philosophy made him one of the most pessimistic educators (Chandler 1959, 219), without any real impact in reality. He had no faith in the efficiency of society's ability to obtain a meaningful result from the education system (ibid., 210, 222).

8.9 Veblen on Businessmen in University

Veblen was a pioneer in defending the university system in higher education against the hostility of the entrepreneurial environment (Donoghue 2008, xiii). He reacted against "the greater bulk, of the printed matter issued" (1918b, 35), conservatism and the superficiality they conveyed. He wished to disseminate teaching based on pure knowledge and know-how and attacked in order against these capitalist principles that interfered in all areas of social life. He argued that the knowledge and development of a certain curiosity without constraint had to be the only

---

[20] WCMP, Box 46.

[21] Marx to Dorfman, 10 May 1934, WCMP.

goals of the university (Veblen 1923 [1997], 43).[22] Applying his pragmatic logic to education, he made it clear that for him learning was as an end in itself (1918a, b, 1943, xxvi). Indeed, Veblen seemed to want to guide society against the domination of vocational training. As he pointed out,

> no gain comes to the community at large from increasing the business proficiency of any number of its young men. There are already much too many of these businessmen, much too astute and proficient in their calling, for the common good. A higher average business efficiency simply raises activity and avidity in business to a higher average pitch of skill and fervor, with very little other material result than a redistribution of ownership; since business is occupied with the competitive acquisition of wealth, not with its production. (Veblen 1918b, 108–9)

The challenge for Veblen is thus to show that the power relations between the main institutions are redefined at the turn of the century and involve the entire integrity of society (Chandle 1959, 242). Thus, he appears as an observer of the rise of business in university boards (Chandler 1959, 43) "under the canons of conspicuous consumption and conspicuous leisure" (Chandler 1959, 185) and he denounces the changes in standards, the progressive separation of academic norms for more practice, which take place at the University and which come to lower the level of schools.

He was particularly convinced by the idea that the "classes" who were interested in the functioning of the business enterprise and its practical problems were in fact unable to implement the necessary learning to ensure its proper functioning and sustainability. Veblen's concern was that this class of rentiers was driven by much more short-term concerns than engineers and academics. For him, the businessman presented the figure of the one in whose hands there was no responsibility, neither entrepreneurial nor academic.

Veblen wanted to provide theoretically developed university courses on core business concepts such as credit or management principles (Mayhew 2007). His conception was that this formation had to be

[22] However, "Presidents, governing boards, administrative staff and faculty are all part of the community that has created modern educational accounting" (Mayhew 2007, 165).

detached from the hands of businessmen, who developed a practical bent, and therefore should not be entrusted with the conduct of universities or the choice of training courses that would only be oriented towards financial concerns (Parish 1973, 149–150).[23] In a letter to Mitchell, Veblen expressed his commitment to teaching about "trusts and corporations" at the time of writing *The Instinct of Workmanship*.[24] Vocational education must be excluded from university because it is not its function. In this Veblen can appear conservative and narrow-minded.[25]

The 1918 book is central to Veblen's study because it concentrated the important values concerning the functioning of companies and the influence of executive boards on education in the broadest sense (Veblen 1918a, b, 59).[26] He felt that business people should not encroach on the prerequisites of the academic community by wanting to interfere in choices and introduce their values to the university. In his fight against the "predatory system", he put forward the idea that "the institutions of the higher learning furnish a good example of what happens to ostensibly non-invidious enterprises under the guidance of pecuniary canons" (Dorfman 1934 [1961], 189). Indeed, the control of businessmen in universities was actually concentrated where power lay, namely in the board of directors. Veblen said:

> A college of commerce is designed to serve an emulation purpose only – individual gain regardless of, or at the cost of, the community at large – and it is, therefore peculiarly incompatible with the collective cultural purpose of the university. It belongs in the corporation of learning no more than a department of athletics (Veblen 1918a, 154).

He appeared to be very critical of the institutions he visited. Optimally, the businessman sought to ensure that the hierarchy was the same in the

[23] "*Doubtless the larger and more serious responsibility in the educational system belongs not to the university but to the lower and professional schools.* Citizenship is a larger and more substantial category than scholarship; and the furtherance of civilized life is a larger and more serious interest than *the pursuit of knowledge for its own sake*" (Veblen 1918b, 50).

[24] JDP Archives, 20 February 1913.

[25] However, this vision will be shared by professional trainers who wish to eliminate the theory and not the practice of training.

[26] See Rosenberg (1956), Cowley and Hefferlin (1957).

company, in the administration and at the university (Veblen 1918a, b, Chap. 3).[27] Veblen rebelled against the "pecuniary welfare of the university corporation" (1918a, 50), because the university system allowed itself to impose a capital of rents on its orders. The class trained in speculation interfered to direct the teaching at the university from the moment when industry and finance leaders positioned themselves in the boards of all the institutions. A reproduction of conservative class thinking was maintained in the academic institution with a rejection of culture and knowledge, facing the proposal of methods of corruption and a utilitarianism of technical functions. Veblen presented vocational training as an assumed utilitarian aim, meeting the commercial requirements of large firms with a view to profitability. The teaching which was necessary sought to promote the for-profit counterpart and it is politics (in the broad sense) which had put this in place, the argument of scientificity no longer being "popular" (1918a, 31). With his 1918 work, he presented the academic institution as having to seek not the reproduction of social classes (as can be done by business) and the permanent dichotomy between industry and finance but to orient the behaviour of businessmen towards other practices, in this golden age of the "capitalistic system" (1904 [1996], 1). Veblen justified the misguided orientation of American higher education in the fact that it copied the European model (Veblen 1918a, 16, 22).

According to Chandler (1959, 243), "Veblen has grossly exaggerated the influence of business in the American culture. He has almost entirely neglected the countervailing power of such groups as organized labor". However, for Veblen, the businessman not necessarily had a future, since he thought that the *Soviet* should have replaced this hierarchy and industrial-financial domination. He believed that a new structure of power, ownership and management of the means of production was bound to prevail, eliminating the role of the businessman. In the long run, the idle business elites were not profitable or productive for society. Businessmen seemed disgusting to him as they corresponded to what he defined as the leisure class. They had to disengage themselves from corpo-

[27] The same idea was expressed by Dorfman: "The training given by the American school of 'commerce' is detrimental to the community's material interests, because the principles which dominate them are the business community's principles of financiering and salesmanship" (Dorfman 1934 [1961], 407).

rate life, as they had an ambiguous positioning relative to technical progress, while only seeking profit. For Veblen, industry had to prevail over business. Thus he was convinced that in the long term, engineers and academics would have regained power. And concerning the boards and the administration of the university, he adopted a radical point of view by proposing to abolish them (Chandler 1959, 195).[28] Veblen was guided by an anthropological approach and an understanding of industry's early developments, as F.W. Taussig pointed out in a letter of 20 November 1911 to George Woodwards.[29] For this, he turned to the Carnegie Institution, but in order to develop a completely different ideology than what was woven into the business schools of the time.

8.10 Other Voices on Education

Veblen was not the only one to reflect on the case of conscience posed to the educational institution by the evolutions of which he was contemporary. A number of theorists interested in corporate finance, management and business training such as E.S. Mead, W.H. Lyon, F.W. Taylor, E.F. Gay, A.W. Shaw, and others, gravitated around Veblen and developed a related analysis of this transition period that disseminated and created new power relations. An intellectual connection took place between these authors. And this was as much in the content of their theory as in their vision of the training and education of businessmen.

In parallel to Veblen's words, also Taylor and his disciplines[30] made known and imposed their theories. Their visions of teaching conflicted, although they shared a common position on the need for the preeminence of engineers and a weak belief in the power of the academic institution to train managers. Thus, although Veblen shared a certain number of views concerning the reality of business with F.W. Taylor, E. F.

[28] This seems impossible, however, as long as academic power is in the hands of businessmen.

[29] JDP, Box 54.

[30] With the creation of the Taylor Society in 1912 to disseminate ideas and practices, Edwin F. Gay and Harlow Pearson, among others, advocated the dissemination of the lessons of professional experience so as not to confine themselves to theoretical and abstract knowledge.

Gay and A. W. Shaw, they did not share the same conclusions about teaching.

This antagonistic relation that gave power to Taylor's ideas underlines the importance of the business dynamic, which was seen as social and economic progress. But the university as an institution was obliged to adapt and in fact the curricula changed in favour of the managerial and professional path. In stating "The rest of my work as instructor has to do with the modern organization of business enterprise" (JDP, December 17, 1904), Veblen encouraged his progressive "followers" and in particular Mitchell to set up (in 1919) the "New School for Social Research",[31] "a triumph of clever business management" (WCMP, Box 7). In February 1922, during a conference on "Sciences in Business" Mitchell still wondered:

> Why is there less science in business than in industry? Of what branches of sciences can business make use? What conditions favor applications of sciences to business? What is the present status of science in business? What are the prospects of progress in the calculable future?" (Mitchell, February 1922, WCMP).

This debate took also place during the handover of power from neoclassical to institutionalist hands in major American academic institutions. But the critics could not withstand the shock of the wave of business school creations, and the young students would become the captains of the much criticized business. Most economists who were interested in clarifying the rules of business enterprise operation during the decade 1910 were important members of the American Economic Association and also heads of educational institutions. They tried to understand what degree of specialization to give to their business training courses, a teaching that had until then been marginalized and which had been taught in social science departments. One might wonder what role these emerging

[31] It was during this period that Veblen met Howard Scott. The latter was one of the supporters of the technocratic movement of the 1920s and 1930s on which Veblen worked—even if this social movement was slightly after Veblen's death; he initiated it in his last works. It was in 1920 according to a letter from Mitchell to Dorfman of 18 May 1934, (JDP, box 7) or between 1918 and 1920 according to R. W. Evans (2007, 127). (see Ardzrooni, L. (1933). Veblen and Technocracy. Living Age, 344, 39–42.)

theorists of corporate finance, particularly institutionalist, played in the "American entrepreneurial revolution" at the turn of the century.

It is also important to underline that Veblen trained or had an influence on many New Deal contributors such as Clarence E. Ayres, Walton Hamilton, John R. Commons and W.C. Mitchell, among others, who guided and contributed to economic policy in the early 1930s (R. Tilman 1988, 155). These institutional economists shared a relatively similar view of how the economy should be approached: for them the centrality of institutions determined economic behaviour. They sought to reorganize economics on a new scientific basis and to make it a progressive and critical science. In particular, it is these progressive economists in an institutionalist tradition who appear as the first theorists of business enterprise and its power relations with other bodies that are essential to the functioning of a society.

8.11 New Directions for Higher Education

Despite these objections, higher education followed new directions, guided by the challenge of standardizing training courses across the country. The syllabuses of courses and curricula proposed by the universities changed, specialized journals appeared, as well as doctoral training, which did not deal with corporate finance until late in the 1930s.

Legislation made vocational education a priority from the end of the nineteenth century onwards, but major changes did not appear until 1917. Although in 1910 a report on *Academic and Industrial Efficiency* was published,[32] it was not until 1917 and *The Smith-Hughes Act* that there was a first federal act on vocational training. It was adopted to isolate this training from the general curricula and allow it to receive federal funding. These segregated curricula were thus created in a response, starting at the end of the 1910s, distinguishing between professional and academic training.

[32] By Morris Cooke, who was a fervent defender of Taylorism. Taylor's thinking spread particularly to the Harvard Business School and the Amos Tuck as early as 1907–1911.

American educational philosophy emerged in 1925, especially with the School of Education at Columbia University. Their dean raised then:

> What does it mean that in the ten leading American universities enrolling 87,000 students, 50,000 are registered in professional schools directly preparing for professional careers? It means, in a few years, 50,000 men and women released for trained leadership, free from the bias of creed, free from the blight of pseudo-science, free from the curse of the mere technician, practitioners imbued to a certain extent, we trust, with university ideals of culture, of service, and of public devotion. From them will arise lawyers and businessmen who are also economists, teachers who are also educators, engineers who are nation builders, physicians who are humanitarians and clergymen who are social leaders (Rosett 1982, 4).

However, despite the clarifications made, the subject of corporate finance and its teaching remained difficult to deal with. This is the reason why firms adopted new internal development strategies, thus changing the company's boundaries with the absorption of training. As a result, between 1900 and 1940 the research community reacted, and many "independent research organizations" appeared to face a lack of research on industry in the academic community (Mowery 1983, 353). In 1905, Henry Pritchett, then President of the Carnegie Foundation for the Advancement of Teaching, ironically asked, "Are universities on the way to becoming industrial enterprises?" (Bertrams 2007, 9). But in 1921, Joseph Willis and Anne Bezanson created the first "business school research centre" with the financial sponsorship of the Carnegie Corporation, hence the symbol against which many academics rose up, namely the disappearance of independent professional institutions, from the moment these schools became part of the university.

At the end of the century (1897–1900) 48% of students in vocational schools were in independent schools, compared to 19% in 1934 (Goldin and Katz 1998, 14). Regardless of the fact that there was a relative inertia of academic research, it was the schools that took over, welcoming more and more students and professors. That being said, the university tried to respond, and all stakeholders benefited. In return, the university regained students, but in this way, knowledge was enslaved to capital (Goldin and

Katz 1998, 37–38). At the same time, the university marginalized those who thought differently, more radically and who opposed administrators and businessmen. Business schools in search of prestige abandoned their independence to become graduate schools. It was therefore these vocational schools that had enabled the university to develop fully and democratize, at the cost of profound changes in its principles. Academic programmes dedicated to business were included in these related university courses. Some professors, including those in business schools, deplored this new trilateral education structure: "We have created a monster", said H. Edward Wrapp, Professor of Business Policy at the University of Chicago (cited after Cheit 1985, 43). Thus, businessmen (J. P. Morgan, Carnegie, Cooke, Piermont and Co.) affirmed their real interest in the curricula that took place during this period in educational institutions, as they had to correspond to the practical efficiency needs of the company. This is also the reason why they financed training programmes on a massive scale, allowing them to orient[33] these curricula and trainings according to their needs.[34] One could almost consider that the corporate finance discipline, emerging from practice, was born through the lack of standardization, manipulations and aberrations.

8.12 Conclusion

As pointed out by Reinhold Niebuhr in *Moral, Man and Immoral Society* (1933), the notion of power is everywhere, including in the educational institution which is confronted with a conflict of interest between the methods of financing higher education and its purpose:

> conflict is inevitable, and in this conflict, power must be challenged by power. That fact is not recognized by most of the educators. (Niebuhr 1933, xiv)

[33] See the report of the Carnegie function on the effectiveness of academic and industrial circles (1910).

[34] Marian V. Sears following the Industrial Commission (Vol. XIX, 1902, 636), 1956, 409).

To conclude, we can state that a real challenge of market power management was raised in the relations between the industrial-financial sector and the education sector. These relations of political power reflected the influence of businessmen in society at the turn of the century and especially the importance of short-term financial aims in the face of the industrial economy and of long-term knowledge. A dual reading of the university's role and the challenge of training students to be thinkers or *money-makers* appeared. In this context, Veblen, "witnessed in American higher education in his time" (Parish 1973, 146), was captivated by the actors of power. He defended a university that disseminated knowledge in order to guarantee scientific objectivity to a discipline that had become academic and theoretical when it was only practical. In order to do so, one could not let allegiance to businessmen become established. This debate inaugurated a new economic thinking, at the frontiers of management in these business concerns, which was shaped by the institutionalist tradition, at a time when the United States was experiencing the first consequences of the shock of industrialization.

References

Ardzrooni, L. (1933). Veblen and Technocracy. *The Living Age, 344*, 39–42.

Berle, A., & Means, G. (1932). *The Modern Corporation and Private Property*. Transaction.

Bertrams, K. (2007). Veblen, critique pionnier des "entreprises académiques". *Revue Interventions économiques. Papers in Political Economy, 36*, 3–14.

Bertrams, K. (2008). Le capitalisme académique avant la lettre: Veblen et la critique de la commercialisation des universités. *Education et sociétés, 1*, 151–162.

Butler, N. M. (2008). *The Invention of Business School*, Review of Rakesh Khurana's *From Higher Aims to Hired Hands: The Social Transformation of American Business Schools and the Unfulfilled Promise of Management as a Profession* (2007). Princeton/Oxford: Princeton University Press. *Ephemora: Theory and Politics in Organization, 8*(3): 348–352.

Carlson, V. (1968). The Education of an Economist Before the Great Depression. *American Journal of Economics and Sociology, 27*(1), 101–112.

Carver, T. N. (1925). The Diffusion of Ownership of Industries in the United States. *Proceedings of the Academy of Political Science in the City of New York, 11*(3), 39–46.

Chandler, C. C. (1959). *Institutionalism and Education: An Inquiry into the Implications of the Philos. of Thorstein Veblen*. University Microfilms.

Cheit, E. F. (1985). Business Schools and their Critics. *California Management Review, 27*(3), 43–62.

Cowley, S. W. H., & Hefferlin, J. B. (1957). Experimental Publication, "Epitome Standard University" Book Review in Higher Education. Issue 1 on Veblen and the Higher learning in America. (1957 May–1958).

DeLong, J. B. (1991). Did JP Morgan's Men Add Value? An Economist's Perspective on Financial Capitalism. In *Inside the Business Enterprise: Historical Perspectives on the Use of Information* (pp. 205–250). Chicago: University of Chicago Press.

Donoghue, F. (2008). *The Last Professors the Corporate University and the Fate of the Humanities*. New York: Fordham University Press.

Dorfman, J. (1934 [1961]). *Thorstein Veblen and His America*. Reprint, A.M. Kelley.

Ely, R. T. (1900 [1906]). *Monopolies and Trusts*. Reprint, New York: The Macmillan Company.

Evans, R. W. (2007). *This Happened in America: Harold Rugg and the Censure of Social Studies*. IAP.

Goldin, C., & Katz, L. F. (1998). *The Shaping of Higher Education: The Formative Years in the United States, 1890 to 1940* (No. w6537). National Bureau of Economic Research.

Harper, W. R. (1895). *Joseph Dorfman Papers* (Rare Books and Manuscript Library). New York: Columbia University.

Hendrick, B. J. (1919 [2002]). *The Age of Big Business, A Chronicle of the Captains of Industry* (Vol. 39). New Haven: Yale University Press.

Huret, R. (2005). Le recrutement des élites aux États-Unis au vingtième siècle. *Revue internationale d'éducation de Sèvres, 39*, 25–36.

Innis, H. A. (1929). A Bibliography of Thorstein Veblen. *The Southwestern Political and Social Science Quarterly, 10*(1), 56–68.

James, E. J. (1892). *Education of Business Men. I and II. An Address Before the Convention of the American Bankers Association (etc.)*. Baird.

JDP: Joseph Dorfman Papers. Rare Books and Manuscript Library. New York: Columbia University.

Jones, B. D. G., & Monieson, D. D. (1990). Early Development of the Philosophy of Marketing Thought. *The Journal of Marketing, 54*(1), 102–113.

Kantrow, A. (1986). Why History Matters to Managers. A Roundtable Discussion with Alfred D. Chandler Jr. *Harvard Business Review, 64*(1), 102–124.

Knoedler, J. T., Prasch, R. E., & Champlin, D. P. (Eds.). (2007). *Thorstein Veblen and the Revival of Free Market Capitalism*. Cheltenham: Edward Elgar Publishing.

Knox, H. (1971). *A History of Educational Research in the United States*.

Laughlin, J. L. (1906). *Industrial America; Berlin Lectures of 1906*. New York: C. Scribner's sons.

Layton, E. (1962). Veblen and the Engineers. *American Quarterly, 14*(1), 64–72.

Lippman, W. (1914). *Drift and Mastery*. New York: Mitchell Kennerly.

Lyon, L. S. (1922). *Education for Business*. Chicago: University of Chicago Press.

Mayhew, A. (2007). Veblen on Higher Education. In *Thorstein Veblen and the Revival of Free Market Capitalism* (p. 155).

Mitchell, W. C. (1922, February). *Conference Sciences in Business, WCMP: Wesley Clair Mitchell Papers* (Rare Books and Manuscript Library). New York: Columbia University.

Mowery, D. C. (1983). The Relationship Between Intrafirm and Contractual forms of Industrial Research in American Manufacturing, 1900–1940. *Explorations in Economic History, 20*(4), 351–374.

Niebuhr, R. (1933 [2013]). *Moral Man and Immoral Society: A Study in Ethics and Politics*. Westminster John Knox Press.

Ollivier-Mellios, A. (2004). L'Université américaine entre 1865 et 1920: un monde à part?. *Revue LISA/LISA e-journal*. Littératures, Histoire des Idées, Images, Sociétés du Monde Anglophone–Literature, History of Ideas, Images and Societies of the English-speaking World, *2*(1), 61–76.

Parish, W. (1973). Thorstein Veblen's Position on Vocational and Professional Education. *Journal of Thought, 8*(2), 146–154.

Payen-Variéras, E. (2009). Sciences économiques et cultures de gestion dans la période progressiste: l'administration des affaires à la Harvard Business School, 1908–1917. *Revue française d'études américaines, 4*, 27–43.

Redlich, F. (1957). Academic Education for Business: Its Development and the Contribution of Ignaz Jastrow (1856–1937): In Commemoration of the Hundredth Anniversary of Jastrow's Birth. *Business History Review, 31*(01), 35–91.

Ripley, W. Z. (1927). *Main Street and Wall Street*. Little Brown & Co.

Rosenberg, B. (1956). *The Values of Veblen: A Critical Appraisal*. Reprint, Washington: Public Affairs Press, 1958.

Rosett, R. N. (1982). *Business Education in the United States*. Graduate School of Business, University of Chicago.

RTEP: Richard Theodore Ely Papers. State Historical Society of Wisconsin Library, Madison.

Sears, M. V. (1956). The American Businessman at the Turn of the Century. *Business History Review, 30*(04), 382–443.

Shute, L. (1974). Institutionalism and Marxism. papier présenté au Allied Social Science Association meeting de San Francisco, JDP.

Taksa, L. (2007). Uniting Management and Education in Pursuit of Efficiency: FW Taylor's Training Reform Legacy. *The Economic and Labour Relations Review, 17*(2), 129–156.

Tilman, R. (1988). Thorstein Veblen and the New Deal: A Reappraisal. *The Historian, 50*(2), 155–172.

Todd, G. (1932). Some Aspects of Joint Stock Companies, 1844–1900. *The Economic History Review, 4*(1), 46–71.

Veblen, T. B. (1904 [1996]). *The Theory of Business Enterprise*. Transaction Publishers. Reprint, New York: Charles Scribner's Sons.

Veblen, T. B. (1918a [1943]). *The Higher Learning in America: A Memorandum on the Conduct of Universities by Business Men*. Reprint, New Brunswick/ London, Transaction Publishers, 1943.

Veblen, T. B. (1918b [2015]). *The Higher Learning in America: The Annotated Edition: A Memorandum on the Conduct of Universities by Business Men* (par Richard F. Teichgraeber III). JHU Press.

Veblen, T. B. (1923 [1997]). *Absentee Ownership: Business Enterprise in Recent Times: the Case of America*. Transaction Publishers.

Warshow, H. T. (1924). The Distribution of Corporate Ownership in the United States. *The Quarterly Journal of Economics:* 15–38.

WCMP: Wesley Clair Mitchell Papers. Rare Books and Manuscript Library. New York: Columbia University.

9

The Early Oligopolistic Models: Market Power in the Paretian Tradition

Mario Pomini

9.1 Introduction

In economics, the idea of market power is often associated with the functioning of non-competitive markets. In such markets, firms can set a price over marginal costs.[1] The study of non-competitive markets was a very active research field in the period between the two World Wars also called the years of high theory, to use George L.S. Shackle's (1967) useful expression. During that period, there was not only theoretical interest in this topic but also the aim to find explorations for great emerging transformations in the economic structure, chief among them the growing concentration of large industrial and financial firms. Heinrich von Stackelberg's book, *Market Structure and Equilibrium* (2011), vividly

[1] This difference can be considered a rough measure of market power as in the case of Lerner Index (Giocoli 2012).

Paper presented at the AISPE Conference – Lecce, 28–30 April 2016.

M. Pomini (✉)
Department of Economics and Management, University of Padua, Padua, Italy
e-mail: mario.pomini@unipd.it

M. Mosca (ed.), *Power in Economic Thought*, Palgrave Studies in the History of Economic Thought, https://doi.org/10.1007/978-3-319-94039-7_9

illustrates the complexity and richness of the debate among mathematical economists of the period.

The mathematical treatment of non-competitive markets was proposed by Francis Edgeworth in the seminal 1897 article, "La teoria pura del monopoli," published in Italian in *Giornale degli Economisti*. Maintaining a critical attitude toward Cournot, Edgeworth concluded that in a duopolistic market, it would be impossible to establish a stable equilibrium in production, and therefore in price, because of the interdependence of firms' behavior. This problem would later be taken up from the mathematical point of view by Pareto in the "Mathematical Appendix" of the French edition of his *Manuale* (1909). In the following decades, the mathematical economics literature grew owing to contributions by eminent scholars, such as Joseph Schumpeter (1908), Pareto (1909), Cecil Pigou (1924), Luigi Amoroso (1921, 1930), Arthur Bowley (1924), Edgeworth (1922, 1925), Knut Wicksell (1926), Harold Hotelling (1929), Edward Chamberlin (1929), and Wassily Leontief (1935). The Italian followers of Pareto participated actively in this debate, and indeed Amoroso played a prominent role. In Europe, the Italian economist had always been considered the most authoritative figure in the field and a fierce defender of Cournot's approach. Other Paretians who made important contributions were Arrigo Bordin (1934, 1936), Felice Vinci (1944), and especially Emilio Zaccagnini (1947), who made novel revisions to Pareto's ideas in the 1940s.

This chapter focuses on a particular strand of literature from the interwar period, that is, the analytical developments developed within the Paretian tradition, starting with the original position of Pareto. This historical retrospective is useful for assessing the main problems that emerged in the theory of non-competitive markets. First, the chapter discusses how economists anticipated important analytical results, whose developments only emerged to their full extent in the postwar period. Second, by considering the theory of non-competitive markets in relation to its historical perspective, rather than in relation to other aspects of economic theory, the chapter sheds light on the internal dialectic of economic reasoning between the search for analytical rigor and the necessity of recognizing its full interpretative value.

The chapter is structured as follows. The next section outlines the Paretian approach, and the third section is dedicated to the change brought about by Amoroso, the most brilliant exponent of the Paretian School. In the fourth section, Edgeworth's controversial response and Amoroso's subsequent reply are considered. The fifth section illustrates the different perspective that Amoroso adopted in the 1930s. The sixth section discusses the new mathematical tool developed by de Finetti, the theory of simultaneous maxima. The seventh section examines the renewal of Paretian theory by Emilio Zaccagnini, a mathematician and exponent of the third Paretian generation. The final section provides the concluding remarks.

9.2 Pareto's Ambiguous Position

This section provides a brief overview of Pareto's position. Pareto's "Mathematical Appendix" of the French edition of his *Manuale* (1909) deals with the issue of non-competitive markets in mathematical terms, focusing on the case of duopoly. Paragraph 69 of the text presents the case of two firms and one good, and the subsequent paragraph 70 deals with the case of two firms and two goods. For our purposes, the relevant case is the former. In the discussion, Pareto confronts Edgeworth, albeit without naming him. In a previous long essay published in *Giornale degli Economisti* (1897), Edgeworth concluded that in the case of duopoly, the solution presented an oscillatory character. The individualistic actions of the two firms had continuous fluctuations in quantities produced, and therefore in price. In mathematical terms, the solutions were indeterminate. Therefore, Pareto contests this conclusion, affirming that the problem is rather impossible, since the number of equations is greater than the number of unknowns.

As regards Pareto's reasoning (Stackelberg would in 1934 speak of Pareto's monopoly), in the duopolistic market, price depends on quantities produced together, $p = f(q_1 + q_2)$. Assuming for simplicity, like Pareto, that the costs are null, the profit will be $\pi_1 = q_1 f(q_1 + q_2)$ for one firm and $\pi_2 = q_2 f(q_1 + q_2)$ for the other. Pareto assumes that each firm behaves like a monopolist. This hypothesis, from a mathematical point of view, requires that we have four partial derivatives to consider in the process of optimization. One of the four conditions can be eliminated using the market demand function, but three equations remain in the two unknowns—that is, the quantities produced by the two firms. At the end of his brief discussion, Pareto (2014 [1909]) observes the following:

> From a mathematical point of view it is inaccurate to say, as is often the case, that in the case of two monopolists and one commodity, the equilibrium is indeterminate. On the contrary it is overdetermined since the conditions are imposed that are incompatible. (p. 348)[2]

Pareto therefore refutes Edgeworth's approach, and it is worth noting that he also completely ignores Cournot's approach. The reason for this unsatisfactory state of oligopoly theory at the beginning of the century is clearly stated by Pareto (2014 [1909]) in the following paragraph:

> § 73 From an economic point of view, [the duopoly] it may be observed in the case of the problem in §69 [the duopoly] that by assuming there to be a position in which one of the monopolists obtain s_1, and the other obtains s_2, it is sufficient for the first one to lower his price to increase his gain and reduce his competitor's share to zero; and vice versa. It is therefore impossible to obtain a solution of the problem we have posed, since no position s_1, s_2 is an equilibrium position. (p. 350)

To find a solution, Pareto proposes abandoning pure economics and viewing this problem from another angle, concluding as follows:

> § 75. It is idle to ask pure economics what will happen when two individuals who have the power to act as monopolists in the sale of one and the same commodity confront each other. Pure economics, by telling us that it is impossible for these two individuals to use their monopoly power in fact, for them both to behave according to type II, has answered as full as it can.
>
> Pure economy cannot even tell us that the two individuals will go back and forth infinitely between two extreme positions of equilibrium. This is no way results from the fact that equilibrium is determined by two incompatible equations. (p. 351)

---

[2] The translation of quotations is mine, except when indicated otherwise.

In the Paretian framework, the interdependence of oligopolistic behavior creates situations that are impossible to model in mathematical terms. In Pareto's view, only factual experience can determine what the final economic equilibrium will be. In this case, pure economics is overtaken by both applied economics and sociology. In general, for Pareto, in the oligopolistic market, the solution will not be unique; depending on the particular circumstances, there would be many solutions to verify on a case-by-case basis. Therefore, for Pareto, the theory of non-competitive markets remains an open theory depending on institutional and historical elements.

9.3 Amoroso's Turn in *Lezioni di Economia Matematica* (1921)

Pareto's view was immediately adopted by the young Amoroso, the main exponent of the Paretian School, whose early articles were devoted to disseminating and clarifying his mentor's ideas (Amoroso 1909). The theory of general economic equilibrium was seen with some suspicion in Italy, as it was judged to be too abstract, both for its unrealistic assumptions and for the wide use of mathematics. Amoroso's 1909 article, "La teoria dell'equilibrio economico del prof. Pareto,"[3] considers the case of duopoly and provides the following observation:

> Edgeworth's solution is incorrect: but Loria's article adds nothing. A rigorous solution is given to the problem in *Manuale*. There are two missing equations in system (C), ϕ_{1y} and ϕ_{1z}. All the unknowns can be expressed in function of two of them. These are determined by the two monopolists, who can impose on each one a single condition. However, it is not possible for both to achieve the maximum profit: these two conditions are incompatible. If they swing from one position to another, if they agree, if one dominates the other, or if there is something else which changes the framework of the problem, it is not a task of pure economics. It is a kind of research belonging to applied economics or rather to sociology. Pure economics tells us that the conditions set out in our problem are incompatible, and that is enough. (Amoroso 1909, p. 364)[4]

[3] English transl. "The theory of general equilibrium by prof. Pareto."

[4] The translation of quotations are mine.

The young Amoroso was in agreement with Pareto. He shared the idea that a mathematical treatment of this kind of markets was not possible for logical reasons and that economic theory should have been supplemented with sociological considerations. However, his initial position changed at the end of the subsequent decade. Before becoming an economist, Amoroso was a mathematician; thus, he could not be satisfied with the solution proposed by Pareto.

The 1921 book *Lezioni di Economia Matematica* constitutes Amoroso's first mature and very innovative contribution to pure theory. The book is a collection of his lectures on mathematical economics at the University of Bari (Italy). These lectures present deep mathematical analyses—the first in Europe—of the theory of oligopoly markets, or the theory of *n* monopolists, to use the term of that period. Seeking a coherent mathematical treatment of this topic, Amoroso chose to adopt Cournot's approach. In *Lezioni*, whose content would be strengthened and further developed in his 1930 article "La curva statica di offerta," Amoroso develops oligopoly theory following Cournot's suggestions. Consequently, he would go on to be considered in the interwar period as the main and most prestigious defender of Cournot's approach internationally (Edgeworth 1925).

Amoroso presents Cournot's approach as the natural extension of the monopolistic scheme in the case of *n* producers of the same good—that is, the oligopolistic market. In analytical terms, the system to be solved consists of $n+1$ equations (*n* profit equations of *n* monopolists and the demand function) that determine $n+1$ unknowns, the quantities produced by each firm, and the price, in the spirit of general equilibrium. The maximization of the profits of *n* firms, under the constraint of a demand curve, determines the necessary equations to obtain equilibrium in the market.

Amoroso's published lectures focus essentially on two problems. The first is the existence of a solution (§ 37) that is easily resolved by considering, similar to Cournot but unlike Pareto, that each oligopolistic firm considers as given the production of all the others. This individualistic behavior of the firm determines a very peculiar equilibrium defined by Amoroso in metaphorical terms as an *equilibrium of war* (*Lezioni*, p. 210), since it arises from the contrast of egoistic interests. Therefore, Amoroso was able to overcome the difficulties encountered by Pareto without ever naming him. Following the strategy proposed by Cournot, according to Amoroso, every firm maximizes its proper level of production, and it makes no sense to assume that one firm takes into consideration the production of other firms inside its profit function. The same criticism was vigorously expressed by Chamberlin in the 1929 article, "Value where sellers are few," containing a detailed review of the literature on oligopolistic models including the Amoroso's model.

In keeping with his usual style of reasoning, Amoroso proffers a numerical example. After making the necessary calculations, he notes that the equilibrium values found have a peculiar feature: neither of the two firms has the convenience of varying the quantity produced, given the production of the other. Thus, it is an equilibrium that is optimal in a very restricted meaning. From the historical perspective, we can say that we are faced with a rudimentary early definition of what would be the equilibrium of optimal response or the Nash equilibrium 30 years later. Amoroso does not capture all the potentialities of this new formulation of economic equilibrium, which would be possible only after the publication of *Theory of Games and Economic Behavior* (1944) by John Von Neumann and Oskar Morgenstern and the birth of game theory.

The second problem considered in *Lezioni* is the optimality of the equilibrium reached not only for the individual firm but also for the society. Amoroso observes that if the firms behave like a single monopolist and try to maximize joint profits, a different position of equilibrium will be achieved, which will be more convenient for each oligopolistic firm. In this case, production is lower and the price is higher. Amoroso demonstrates that whether the production in this collusion will be greater or lower depends on the structure of the marginal costs of the single firm compared with the marginal costs of the entire sector. The subsequent problem of the distribution of total profit among individual firms is considered by Amoroso as an institutionally relevant element, but one that is outside of economic theory. Amoroso's approach, which is based on Cournot's model, was followed in the Paretian tradition by Arrigo Bordin, a second-generation exponent of the Paretian School in Italy. The topic is developed in his book, *Lezioni di Economia Politica* (1936), by introducing a novel formal analysis of the optimal dimension of a cartel in the case of an oligopolistic market.

Owing to these works, Amoroso earned a solid reputation as a mathematical economist. In particular, he was considered to be the main exponent of Cournot's approach to the analysis of non-competitive markets. However, this assessment would prove not to be very rewarding, as the community of mathematical economists viewed Cournot's approach as highly unsatisfactory (Chamberlin 1929). The main criticism concerned Cournot's lack of realism. If the mathematical argument was strong and unquestionable, the relevant issue called into question the interpretative power of the model. It seemed to the small community of mathematical economists, from Edgeworth to Pigou and von Stackelberg, that Cournot's assumptions were erroneous because they were in stark contrast to the facts of the economic reality. The hidden contrast, always present in economics, between the rigor of mathematical models and interpretative realism, was very strong. In the interwar period, the pendulum swung in favor of the request for greater realism.

9.4 Edgeworth's Criticism and Amoroso's Response

The paragraphs on the theory of oligopoly contained in *Lezioni* had great resonance internationally, as they induced Edgeworth's criticism. In the following year, Edgeworth responded in *The Economic Journal* via an extensive review of Amoroso's book, with the main part dedicated to providing a critical interpretation of Amoroso's duopoly theory. Edgeworth was very critical of the Paretian scholar, almost to the point of being harsh. In his review, he observes the following:

> We believe that Professor Amoroso is alone among high authorities in siding with Cournot in this matter. The view that in monopolistic competition "the output is indeterminate" … "Is now commonly accepted," says Professor Pigou; And, he adds, "it seems to me to be the right one" (Wealth and Welfare, p. 193). Altogether our author's teaching about duopoly cannot be considered as part of accepted science. We should recommend the omission of this topic, if it was proposed to translate the work into English

> with the view of supplying the much-felt need of an introduction to mathematical economics. (p. 405)

The critical argument was directed essentially toward Cournot's model, which was considered a misleading representation of the functioning of the oligopolistic market. Edgeworth's reasoning, however, proceeded in a indirect way. Since there were no formal or conceptual errors in Amoroso's analysis, Edgeworth chose to use the same numerical example employed by Amoroso adopting prices as strategic variables, as in Bertrand's model, instead of quantities. He demonstrated numerically that in this case, a position of stable equilibrium was impossible and that the price was ever oscillating. Ultimately, Edgeworth intervened to defend the model that he had advanced in 1897 rather than to contest that of Amoroso with purely external criticism.

Amoroso did not respond to Edgeworth's criticism. He revisited this topic only in the 1930 article, "La curva statica di offerta." This work represents a highly relevant contribution (Keppler 1994) in which Amoroso introduces new concepts for analyzing the construction of the firm supply function, such as the relevance of the minimum average cost or the concept of the monopoly power index, whose discovery would be attributed to Abba Lerner in an article printed in English in 1934 (Giocoli 2012). In the third part of "La curva statica di offerta," Amoroso returns to the problem of the duopolistic market and reaffirms the centrality of the Cournot model, but adopts a different approach, focusing on the problem of the stability of the equilibrium obtained. Through a numerical example, Amoroso shows that it is possible to determine a stable equilibrium position depending on the slope of the reaction curves. Thus, he rejects the cooperative solution and instead develops the case for using a nonlinear demand function.

For our purposes, it is relevant to consider the final part of the article, in which Amoroso distinguished his position from those of Bertrand–Edgeworth and Pareto. According to Amoroso, the Edgeworth–Bertrand approach was insufficient because it assumed that each of *n* monopolists tried to put the other firms out of the market. In his opinion, this way of thinking diverged widely from the methods of mathematical economics. He observed the following:

> It also means that Cournot is right and Bertrand and Edgeworth are wrong. In the mathematical theory of duopoly, it is not about predicting what one or the other will do in a certain factual situation, but it is interesting to look for what the two would find worth doing if either of them were pure homo oeconomicus. (Amoroso 1930, p. 17)

He also rejected Pareto's criticism of Edgeworth, since he thought it was based on a logical mistake; that is, it was not reasonable to assume that both duopolists could behave like monopolists. This strong hypothesis was considered incorrect because "It means that it is not possible for A to force B to do his will and even at the same time B forces A to do his" (Amoroso 1930, p. 19). Cournot's idea was different, according to Amoroso, because it involved the assumption that each duopolist was able to achieve the maximum profit within his sphere of action. At the thresholds of the theoretical revolution provoked by Joan Robinson and Edward Chamberlin with the appearance of the theory of imperfect competition, Amoroso remained one of the few within the community of mathematical economists to support the validity of the Cournot model.

9.5 The Partial Monopoly in *Meccanica Economica* (1942)

In the 1930s, Amoroso's research focused primarily on dynamic analysis, returning to the youth project to dynamize the theory of general economic equilibrium (Pomini and Tusset 2009). However, he also revisited the topic of non-competitive markets from a different perspective. The international debate, above all with Chamberlin's publication in 1933, had taken a very specific direction, and Amoroso was trying to adapt to the new context. His first contribution was "La produzione in regime di concentrazione industriale" (1935), followed by Chapter X of the textbook *I Principi di Economia Corporativa* (1938). He established his definitive position in "Lezione XI. Monopolio totale e parziale" included in a collection of lectures on mathematical economics delivered at Istituto di Alta Matematica in Rome entitled *Meccanica Economica* (1942)

Amoroso's new and different perspective took up the problem of analyzing a specific criterion of price formation in the oligopolistic market or in the context of a concentration of firms (Mistri 1970, Gaeta 1967). Since Cournot's scheme was inadequate in this case, it was necessary to change the research direction. Amoroso resumed the equation of monopolistic pricing put forward in the 1930 article and introduced some modifications to account for the relevance of the market share of each firm. The 1935 essay provides the following price equation:

$$\frac{p-m}{\eta p} = \frac{x}{x+y(1+\sigma)} \tag{9.1}$$

In Eq. (9.1), the term η indicates the elasticity of demand, x represents the production of a single firm, y indicates the production of the other firms, and the parameter σ represents the new element, with respect to the previous article, measuring the variation of the production of other firms when the production of a single firm changes. According to Amoroso (1935), this extension of the previous equation was necessary because "in an industrial concentration scheme, the choice of production of a single firm must take into account three things: its costs, what it does, what the competitors do" (p. 951). The new element that Amoroso tried to formalize using the traditional instruments was the interdependence of choices in the oligopolistic market. Equation (9.1) is generalized in the lectures from 1941 to 1942 and assumes the following definitive form:

$$\frac{p-m}{\eta p} = \frac{u}{D+\sigma E} = S \tag{9.2}$$

In the new Eq. (9.2), the term D represents the total demand, E the residual demand of the market, and parameter u the quantity produced by a single firm. In general terms, this equation can assume a value between zero and one. The case $S = 0$ is perfect competition, where the price coincides with the marginal cost. The case $S = 1$ is when the entire production is concentrated in a single firm and the market becomes monopolistic. As Amoroso (1942) observes, "The quantity *S* can therefore be taken as an index of the power of the firm in the market: the greater its value, the greater the possibility for the firm to influence the price, the more accentuated its monopolistic character" (p. 116). In light of Eq. (9.2), Amoroso can be said to have found the general expression for price determination in different market forms (Giocoli 2012).

In the Paretian tradition, the next step of the theory of the oligopolistic market is represented by the contribution of Zaccagnini, who tried to adopt the approach of Pareto in a different mathematical setting which was advanced by the Italian statistician de Finetti in the second half of the 1930s.

9.6 Some Mathematical Developments: de Finetti's Theory of Simultaneous Maxima

In the second half of the 1930s, the young Bruno de Finetti was passionately engaged in the field of welfare economics. His seminal article, "Il tragico sofisma,"[5] was published in 1935 (de Finetti 1935a, b), and in the following years, he produced several related essays. His final contribution, published in 1943, was "La crisi dei principi e l'economia matematica"[6] (de Finetti 1943). The main target of de Finetti's criticism was, in current terms, the first theorem of welfare economics. De Finetti's criticism of Pareto's general equilibrium theory led him to build the theory of simultaneous maxima, which is probably his most important contribution to the field of economic theory. The starting point was a problem that remained open in Pareto's system. In fact, from a given initial allocation, Pareto's optimum position could not be determined uniquely; however, there could be more than one optimum position, as in the well-known case of the Edgeworth box. Consequently, once again, there was a problem of choosing which allocation was preferable for the society as a whole. This problem had no solution within Pareto's approach, as the utilities of each individual were not comparable like they were in traditional utilitarianism.

---

[5] English translation "The tragic sophism."

[6] English translation "The crisis of principles and the mathematical economics."

In his 1937 article, de Finetti dealt with a very general context, which he defined as simultaneous maximization. This type of optimization differed from traditional constraint optimization, which is the common case considered by economists, because the problem was to obtain the maximum values of many functions at the same time, in a particular way. These maximum results were simultaneous in the sense that it was not possible to increase the value of one function without decreasing that of another. The analogy with the case of the Pareto optimum—whose simultaneous maximization constituted a generalization—is evident. De Finetti offered an in-depth analytical discussion on this very peculiar situation. We consider the simplified case of two functions in two variables, $f(x, y)$, $g(x, y)$.[7]

De Finetti starts with the assumption that to obtain a solution of a simultaneous optimum, it is necessary for the total differentials of the two functions to cancel out; otherwise, it would be possible to increase the value of one of the two without decreasing that of the other. In our simplified case, the following expressions must not be greater than zero:

$$\begin{aligned} df &= f'_x\,dx + f'_y\,dy \\ dg &= g'_x\,dx + g'_y\,dy \end{aligned} \tag{9.3}$$

This was because, if all equations in system (9.3) were positive, no point of coordinates x, y could be the optimal one. Moreover, for both differentials of (9.3) to be null, it was necessary that the determinant of the coefficients dx, dy canceled out. Therefore, the following must occur:

$$\begin{vmatrix} f'_x & f'_y \\ g'_x & g'_y \end{vmatrix} = 0 \tag{9.4}$$

This equation represents the curve that contains the optimum points. De Finetti concludes this first step by showing how, in general, the points of the simultaneous maxima belong to a variety of dimension $n-1$, on

[7] In the article, de Finetti considers the general case with n functions and q variables. In the exposition, we follow Zaccagnini (1947).

which the determinant of the matrix of the partial derivatives of the functions to maximize is zero.

De Finetti then takes an additional original step with the aim of offering an operational version of the condition of simultaneous maxima. If the determinant of (9.4) is zero, it follows that the equations in (9.3) will be represented by a linear relationship. In this case, we can find two coefficients, λ_1, λ_2, connected by the following relationship:

$$\lambda_1 df + \lambda_2 dg = 0 \tag{9.5}$$

Substituting *df*, *dg* in (9.5) with their development given by (9.3), the system obtained is as follows:

$$\begin{aligned} \lambda_1 f'_x + \lambda_2 g'_x &= 0 \\ \lambda_1 f'_y + \lambda_2 g'_y &= 0 \end{aligned} \tag{9.6}$$

System (9.6) establishes parameters λ_1, λ_2. For these two parameters to be consistent with (9.4), it is necessary for them to have the same sign. These parameters are easy to determine because de Finetti shows that they are defined by the cofactors of the initial Jacobian matrix (9.4). In general, de Finetti shows that in order to verify if a specific arbitrary vector represents a position of simultaneous maxima for *n* functions, two conditions must be met: the determinant of the Jacobian matrix must be zero and its cofactors must all be of the same sign. These are necessary conditions that become sufficient to the extent that some restrictions are added, such as the concavity of the functions being considered. De Finetti states the following:

> The optimal point belongs to a variety of $n-1$ dimensions, for which the determinant of the partial derivatives cancels out. Knowing the value of the n cofactors, $\lambda_1, \lambda_2, \ldots, \lambda_n$ we can exclude that it is a point of optimum if two of them have opposite signs (de Finetti 1937a, p. 54).

Lastly, de Finetti identifies the entire set of optimal points, starting from the evident property that each point of the maximum of one of the

n functions, given the value of the others, results in a point of optimum. Since this property is true for all points of optimum related to n functions, the conclusion is the topological hypothesis that the set of points of optimum form a simplex of $n-1$ dimension, whose faces are the points of optimum of a function with $n-1$ components, the $(n/2)$ corners for those of $n-2$ components, and so on, up to n vertexes, with each one representing the maximum of one of the n functions. This topological analysis of the positions of a simultaneous optimum occupies a relevant part of de Finetti's 1937 essay and demonstrates the high level of mathematics involved.

The question is what the implications of simultaneous maxima for economic theory are. They are undoubtedly deep, because the optimization process is at the basis of the economic agents' behavior. The fundamental implication for de Finetti is that, in this way, it is possible to prove formally that the optimal points are infinite, and therefore the identification between the Pareto optimum and free competition is purely arbitrary. For de Finetti, anarchic market forces reach only one of the many positions that have this property. Hence, it was de Finetti's belief that he had revealed the logical weakness of the sophism of economic liberalism. According to de Finetti (1937a),

> We demonstrate that normally in the case of n individuals, the points of optimum are∞^{n-1}. Suppose set the ophelimities $\Theta_1 = a_1$, $\Theta_2 = a_2$, ..., $\Theta_{n-1} = a_{n-1}$ of $n-1$ individuals; on the variety so defined, the $\Theta_n = a_n$ will admit a maximum value, and therefore at least a point of optimum. Of such points there are at least ∞^{n-1}; they actually constitute a variety at $n-1$ dimensions. (p. 62)

Thus, de Finetti formally demonstrated a result that would become well known among Italian economists, especially those aligned with the Paretian School (Bordin 1948). Considering the problem from a different point of view, his result implied that the social optimum in Pareto's sense was always a relative optimum, depending on the initial distribution of resources for him. For him this fact was the essential point of the matter and not just a pessimistic assessment of perfect competition.

9.7 Zaccagnini and the Return to Pareto

The theory of simultaneous maxima was then developed by Emilio Zaccagnini.[8] As a graduate in mathematics, Zaccagnini can be considered as belonging to the third Paretian generation, along with Giuseppe Palomba[9] and Valentino Dominedò.[10] He followed the Paretian approach of his teacher Arrigo Bordin in Torino. His first contributions were wholly orthodox, dealing with barter theory and the problem of obtaining the demand function from the preference relation (Zaccagnini 1942). Subsequently, the main focus of his research was the application of de Finetti's simultaneous maxima theory to some topics of economic theory, in particular to oligopoly theory. In several articles (Zaccagnini 1947, 1953, 1958), he attempted to offer the theory of simultaneous maxima as a general methodology for studying many economic phenomena. The main contribution was the article "Massimi simultanei in economia pura" (1947) that was included in the first edition of the *International Economic Papers* (1951) with the title "Simultaneous Maxima in Pure Economics." For our purposes, we limit our attention to the theories of duopoly and oligopoly. Zaccagnini's project was to return to Pareto via the mathematical lens offered by de Finetti.

The starting point of the 1947 article is the traditional criticism of the lack of realism of Cournot's approach. This criticism, as we have seen, was widespread and had reached its peak in the 1930s. The problematic point was the fundamental assumption that each of the two firms considered as given, in its process of maximizing choice, the production of the other. In the essay, Zaccagnini (1947) observes the following:

---

[8] Emilio Zaccagnini (1903–1979) held the chair of Economics at the Faculty of Law of Turin (Italy) from 1953 to 1974. He was also a Fellow of Econometric Society. Both his scientific training and his research career were centered on the theory of general equilibrium.

[9] Giuseppe Palomba (1908–1986), a second-generation member of the Italian Paretian School, devoted his scientific activity to devise an original axiomatic framework for economic dynamics, primarily designed to address economic change.

[10] Valentino Dominedò (1905–1985) did many contributions in the field of demand theory. He was the first economist at the international level to grasp the relevance of the Slutsky's article on the theory of consumers' choice.

> From this point of view, Cournot's hypothesis clashes with common sense and daily observations. It is evident that without experience it is not possible to conceive of any rational economic operation; how it is possible to admit that this experience teaches nothing to the two single firms in the market and it allows them to assume the Cournot hypothesis about the assumption of each operator regarding the quantity negotiated by the rival? (p. 262)

In addition, in Zaccagnini's view, Bowley's solution of conjectural variations could not be considered as an adequate answer, as it introduced a psychological element that was extraneous to economic reasoning. Zaccagnini recognized the need to return to Pareto's position and revise it in the light of the new mathematical contribution of de Finetti.

> To Cournot's solution and to these criticisms, Pareto opposed an important observation which in our opinion is decisive for the general approach to the problem. In fact, writes the ingenious scientist, the two quantities q_1 and q_2 are both variables and have to be considered in the two total profit functions to be maximized. The solution requires considering four partial derivatives. In this case, the number of variables is greater with respect to the number of equations and the problem is indeterminate. (Zaccagnini 1947, p. 264)

Moreover,

> The second solution originates from Paretian criticism and it is really general, as it excludes any subjective hypothesis of an operator on the behavior of the other, and only considers the hedonistic postulate in its more general expression and the simultaneity of the solutions. But it was the technical means adopted by Pareto that were unsuitable and that led the Author to an erroneous conclusion: it is not possible to resolve the two maxima separately when they behave simultaneously. By applying a proper mathematical technique, the problem does not seem determined, as was the case with Cournot, nor was it impossible, as Pareto stated. (Zaccagnini 1947, p. 266)

In Zaccagnini's view, the tool that could allow for overcoming the analytic impasse in Pareto's theory was the application of de Finetti's simultaneous maxima methodology. With this approach, it was possible, on the one hand, to maintain the Paretian assumptions and, on the other hand, to overcome the problem of the modest interpretative capacity of Cournot's perspective, which had never been quite convincing to economists. Zaccagnini considered numerous examples of applications of the theory of simultaneous maxima to economic theory with the aim of demonstrating the generality of de Finetti's analytical scheme. For our purposes, it is sufficient to consider the theories of duopoly and oligopoly.

In his 1947 article, Zaccagnini extensively treats the classic case of duopoly without cost functions and with a linear demand curve, comparing the solution of the simultaneous maximum with that of Cournot. Directly applying de Finetti's methodology (and hence Eq. (9.5)), Zaccagnini comes to the following expression for the price:

$$p = -p'\left(q_1 + q_2\right) \tag{9.7}$$

Equation (9.7), as Zaccagnini observes, is not new; it corresponds to the case in which the firms maximize their joint profits. The price depends on the derivative of the demand function and the total production, while the level of production of each firm remains indeterminate. Zaccagnini concludes as follows:

> To determine the equilibrium between q_1 and q_2 it is necessary to: (1) abandon the static hypothesis of simultaneity and thus admit a particular sequence of actions and reactions based on specific assumptions of each operator on the behavior of the rival; or (2) impose additional conditions that cancel the indeterminacy of the problem (arbitration, hedonistic strength, etc.). (Zaccagnini 1942, p. 268)

In Eq. (9.7), the old, non-uniqueness of the equilibrium solution reappears, but this fact does not seem to be a problem for Zaccagnini. In the case of n monopolists, Eq. (9.7) can easily be extended, and the following general expression is obtained:

$$p = -p'\left(\sum_{i=1}^{n} q_i\right) \tag{9.8}$$

Zaccagnini concludes his analysis of oligopoly theory with these words:

> We believe that the economic applications of the mathematical process of simultaneous maxima of different functions, show, in our opinion, how it is possible to obtain the equilibrium conditions of a whole class of economic problems quickly and rigorously. Such conditions are based on the economic explanation which is often confirmed by ordinary reasoning in a way that really fulfills our requirements of logical representation of reality. (Zaccagnini 1947, p. 292)

The final result is not a single equilibrium position but an entire path depending on the choice of firms, as in the Bertrand's case. From a geometric point of view, the equilibrium points identified by Eq. (9.7) are found on the tangency of the isoprofit curves of the duopolists. It is an equilibrium different from that of Cournot, with higher prices and less quantity produced. However, the problem of the distribution of production between the two firms remained unresolved, and, as in Pareto, it could not been solved using pure economic theory. In the following years, Zaccagnini attempted to extend his interpretation of the simultaneous maxima in various directions, especially in the case of a socialist economy and the labor market (Zaccagnini 1958).

The attempt to overcome the difficulties posed by Cournot's model with a different alternative derived from de Finetti's mathematical model did not enjoy success in the theory of non-competitive markets. The reasons for this failure can be noted immediately, considering Eqs. (9.7) and (9.8), which show a situation where the price is the same as that in the monopolistic market, while the quantities produced by *n* firms remain indeterminate. From the mathematical point of view, Cournot's model is a more powerful logical scheme, as it allows for determining the quantities produced, and thus the market price. It does not matter that for decades it has been considered an inappropriate framework for studying the market with few firms. The model of simultaneous maxima could certainly be more coherent with the logic of economic maximization, but this left open the economic discourse to sociologically or institutionally external factors. This perspective did not create any discomfort for a Paretian economist such as Zaccagnini. Pareto's scholars were well aware of the limitations of the applications of mathematics to economic theory. On the contrary, the request for mathematical rigor would become, after the Second World War, the main lens through which to judge the validity of economic reasoning. The indeterminacy of the equilibrium solution would be considered as a fatal mistake and the Cournot model would become a fundamental starting point for the study of non-competitive markets, mainly for its analytical virtues.

9.8 Conclusions

The period between the two World Wars was characterized by intense debate over the theory of oligopolistic markets. In 1934, von Stackelberg documented in detail the variety and complexity of the different positions emerging among mathematic economists. It was not a purely theoretical or academic debate. The economic transformations that were taking place, with the increase in the size of firms and industrial concentrations, required the economists to offer a proper theoretical interpretation. In particular, most economists critically considered the Cournot model for not being for a convincing interpretation of the economic reality, and new ways were sought. We saw how, in this context, the Paretian economists participated actively in this debate, openly defending the Cournot model. In particular, Amoroso became an authoritative voice in this field of economic research. Zaccagnini in the 1940s moved on a different path using the mathematical insights of De Finetti to amend Pareto's theory.

The analysis of this debate can help us understand the reasons why the Cournot model became the dominant approach of oligopoly theory rather late and with some difficulties. Weak from the interpretative point of view, the equilibrium of the best response approach became dominant only when it was included in the new paradigm of game theory. In this new theoretical setting, the model obtained centrality that had been long questioned. It should be noted, however, that the supremacy of the Cournot–Nash approach is not complete, as an alternative path of research is always present. Even the most advanced textbooks (Martin 2002) take into account other behavioral hypotheses, such as those incorporated in Bertrand's model, that are completely different and closer to reality. Ultimately, there is always doubt that the search for certain analytic properties, such as that of the uniqueness of equilibrium, can only be obtained by sacrificing the necessary realism of the theory. There are properties of the formal model that may be of interest to the mathematician, but certainly not to the economist. This epistemological contention may perhaps explain why Nash's equilibrium only slowly developed in the postwar period in the community of economists, mainly because of its fragility in terms of economic rationality, and only when the scientific climate profoundly changed (Hurwicz 1953).

References

Amoroso, L. (1909). La teoria dell'equilibrio economico secondo il prof. Vilfredo Pareto. *Giornale degli Economisti, 19*, 353–367.

Amoroso, L. (1921). *Lezioni di Economia Matematica*. Zanichelli: Bologna.

Amoroso, L. (1930). La curva statica di offerta. *Il Giornale degli Economisti e Rivista di Statistica, 1*, 1–24.

Amoroso, L. (1935). La produzione in regime di concentrazione industriale. *Rivista Italiana di Scienze Economiche, 8*, 15–32.

Amoroso, L. (1942). *Meccanica Economica*. Città di Castello: Macrì.

Bordin, A. (1934). *Lezioni di economia politica. La statica: parte prima*. Padova: Cedam.

Bordin, A. (1936). *Lezioni di economia politica. La statica: parte seconda*. Padova: Cedam.

Bordin, A. (1948). Di taluni massimi di utilità collettiva. *Il Giornale degli Economisti e Annali di Economia, 9*, 174–189.

Bowley, A. (1924). *The Mathematical Groundwork of Economics*. Londra: Macmillan.

Chamberlin, E. (1929). Value Where Sellers are Few. *Quarterly Journal of Economics, 44*, 63–100.

De Finetti, B. (1935a). Il tragico sofisma. *Rivista italiana di scienze economiche, 7*, 362–382.

De Finetti, B. (1935b). Vilfredo Pareto di fronte ai suoi critici odierni. *Nuovi Studi di Diritto, Economia, Politica, 8*, 225–244.

De Finetti, B. (1937a). Problemi di *optimum*, *Giornale dell'Istituto Italiano degli Attuari*, 8, pp. 48–67. English transl. Problems of Constrained Optimum.

In L. Pasinetti (Ed.), *Italian Economic Papers*, vol. III, London: Oxford University Press.
De Finetti, B. (1937b). Problemi di "optimum" vincolato. *Giornale dell'Istituto Italiano degli Attuari, 8*, 112–126.
De Finetti, B. (1943). La crisi dei principi e l'economia matematica. *Acta Seminarii, II*, 33–68.
Edgeworth, F. (1897). La teoria pura del monopolio, *Il Giornale degli Economisti*, 15, pp. 17–31, 307–320, 405–414.
Edgeworth, F. (1922). The Mathematical Economics of Professor Amoroso. *The Economic Journal, 32*, 400–407.
Edgeworth, F. (1925). *Papers Relating to Political Economy*. Londra: Macmillan.
Gaeta, A. (1967). Concorrenza e monopolio nel pensiero di Amoroso. *Il Giornale degli Economisti, 26*, 942–956.
Giocoli, N. (2012). Who Invented the Lerner Index? Luigi Amoroso, the Dominant Firm Model, and the Measurement of Market Power. *Review of Industrial Organization, 41*, 181–191.
Guccione, A., & Minelli, E. (1999). Consumer Theory and Axiomatics: A Note on the Early Contribution by Luigi Amoroso. *History of Politic Economy, 31*, 587–589.
Hotelling, H. (1929). Stability in Competition. *The Economic Journal, 39*, 41–57.
Hurwicz, L. (1953). What Happened to the Game Theory? *The American Economic Review, 43*, 398–405.
Keppler, J. H. (1994). Luigi Amoroso (1866–1965): Mathematical Economist, Italian Corporatist. *History of Political Economy, 26*, 589–611.
Leontief, W. (1935). Stackelberg on Monopolistic Competition. *Journal of Political Economy, 44*, 554–559.
Martin, S. (2002). *Advanced Industrial Economics*. Cambridge: Cambridge University Press.
Mistri, M. (1970). Su due formule amorosiane di concentrazione della concorrenza. *Il Giornale degli Economisti e Annali di Economia, 29*, 257–270.
Pareto, V. (1909). *Manuel d'économie politique*. Paris: Giarde et Briere.
Pareto, V. (2014) [1909]. *Manual of Political* Economy. *A Critical and Variorum Edition*, edited by A. Montesano, A. Zanni, L. Bruni, J.S. Chipman and M. McLure. New York: Oxford University Press.
Pigou, A. C. (1924). *Economics of Welfare*. London: Macmillan.
Pomini, M., & Tusset, G. (2009). Habits and Expectations: Dynamic General Equilibrium in the Italian Paretian School. *History of Political Economy, 41*, 311–342.

Schumpeter J. (1982) [1908]. *L'essenza e i principi dell'economia teorica*. Roma: Laterza.

Shackle, G. (1967). *The Years of High Theory*. Cambridge: Cambridge University Press.

Vinci, F. (1944). *Gli ordinamenti economici*, Milano, Giuffrè. English trans. Economic Institutional System. The Particular Case of Free Competition. In L. Pasinetti (Ed.), *Italian Economic Papers*. London: Oxford University Press.

Von Neumann J. e O. Morgenstern. (1944). *Theory of Games and Economic Behavior*. Princeton: Princeton University Press.

Von Stackelberg, H. (2011) [1934]. *Market Structure and Equilibrium*. Berlino: Springer.

Wicksell, A. K. (1926). *Lectures on Political Economy*. Londra: Routledge.

Zaccagnini, E. (1942). Legami tra curve di indifferenza, di baratto e di domanda. *Il Giornale degli Economisti e Annali di Economia, 4*, 546–562.

Zaccagnini, E. (1947). Massimi simultanei in economia pura, *Il Giornale degli Economisti e Annali di Economia*, 6, 1947, pp. 258–292. English trasl. Simultaneous Maxima in Pure Economics. In A. Peacock, H. Houtakker, R. Turvey, F. Lutz, E. Henderson (Eds.), *International Economic Papers*. London: Macmillan, 1951.

Zaccagnini E. (1953). Scienza economica e postulato *edonistico*, in *Studi in onore di Gino Borgatta*. Bologna: Arti Grafiche.

Zaccagnini, E. (1958). Sulle condizioni di massimo simultaneo. *Il Giornale degli Economisti e Annali di Economia, 16*, 565–594.

10

Dispersion of Power as an Economic Goal of Antitrust Policy

Stephen Martin

10.1 Introduction

The Sherman Antitrust Act became part of US law in 1890. It remains the basis of US antitrust policy and has influenced the development of competition policies around the world.

During the 20 years before passage of the Sherman Act, there was broad public debate in the United States about the rise of large business and the appropriate policy reaction to that rise. A wide range of views were expressed, and this range of views was reflected during Senate debate about the Sherman Act.

At first, the new law was ineffective, and public discussion of the trust issue continued. In 1914, the United States adopted two additional pieces of legislation, the Clayton Antitrust Act and the Federal Trade Commission Act, to complement the Sherman Act.

S. Martin (✉)
Purdue University, West Lafayette, IN, USA
e-mail: smartin@purdue.edu

M. Mosca (ed.), *Power in Economic Thought*, Palgrave Studies in the History of Economic Thought, https://doi.org/10.1007/978-3-319-94039-7_10

By the mid-1940s, a mainstream consensus had emerged that US antitrust policy aimed to pursue both economic and social goals. Economic goals included competitive market performance, high rates of innovation, and productivity growth. Social goals included the dispersion of economic and other kinds of power and fairness in market processes. It was thought that these goals were mutually consistent and that policies adopted to promote one of them would promote the others as well.

In its formative phase, US antitrust pursued these goals by promoting competition. Section 1 of the Sherman Act promoted competition among active firms by prohibiting agreements not to compete. Section 2 of the Sherman Act promoted potential competition by prohibiting monopolization, which today an economist would describe as the erection of strategic barriers to entry to achieve or maintain monopoly[1] power. The antitrust laws did not object to monopoly that resulted from competition on the merits.[2]

The original Section 7 of the Clayton Act prohibited mergers carried out by acquisition of shares of stock, "where in any line of commerce … the effect of such acquisition may be substantially to lessen competition, or to tend to create a monopoly". The legislation was aimed at "the development of holding companies and at the secret acquisition of competitors through the purchase of all or parts of such competitors' stock".[3] The Congress that passed the Clayton Act in 1914 intentionally excluded mergers carried out by acquisition of the assets of one company by another company from the coverage of Section 7. Such mergers would be public knowledge. As long as the fact of a merger was known, if it created profit opportunities for existing or potential rivals, competition from those rivals would get the best market performance possible. This passive publicity approach avoided any direct government control of market structure.

[1] Here and throughout the chapter I use the word "monopoly" in the antitrust sense of having the power "to raise price and exclude competition" (American Tobacco Co. et al. *v.* U.S. 328 U.S. 781 (1946), at 811), not in the economic sense of "a single firm supplying a market into which entry is costly (limited monopoly) or impossible (complete monopoly)".

[2] For present purposes, we can define "competition on the merits" as profitable firm conduct that does not involve agreements with other firms (so it does not violate Section 1 of the Sherman Act) and does not depend for its profitability on denying actual or potential rivals the opportunity to compete (so it does not violate Section 2 of the Sherman Act).

[3] Brown Shoe Co. *v.* U.S. 370 U.S. 294 (1962) at 313.

In 1950, the Celler-Kefauver amendment to Section 7 of the Clayton Act abandoned the passive approach and prohibited mergers carried out by asset acquisition, where "the effect of such acquisition may be substantially to lessen competition". The extension of Section 7 to asset acquisitions and the requirement to assess the future impact of a merger on competition made economics central to the application of merger policy. With time the enhanced role of economics spread to other areas of antitrust.

In the interwar period, University of Chicago economists, like economists generally, supported antitrust policy as a bulwark against regulation. The 1950 transition from passive to active merger policy accelerated a change, underway since the late 1940s, in the views of Chicago economists toward antitrust policy. From the mid-1950s onward, lawyers and economists working in the Chicago tradition were harshly critical of received antitrust policy.

One element of this criticism was Robert Bork's rereading and reinterpretation of congressional intent toward the Sherman Act. Bork's conclusion (1966, p. 11) was that "since the legislative history of the Sherman Act shows consumer welfare to be the decisive value it should be treated by a court as the only value". It is now understood that when Bork wrote of "consumer welfare", what he meant was what economists call net surplus, the sum of consumer surplus and producer surplus.

Bork's analysis of congressional intent is associated with the rise of the so-called "economic approach" to antitrust, which holds that antitrust policy should concern itself with and only with practices that reduce surplus in one or the other of the two meanings given to the term "consumer welfare" and that other alleged purposes of antitrust policy are ruled out, on the ground that they are not "economic".[4]

But if aggregate welfare depends on market outcomes for which there are no markets, then an antitrust policy that maximizes consumer surplus or minimizes deadweight loss is inefficient *in an economic sense*, because it ignores the economic consequences of missing markets. I show that social preferences about aspects of market performance not captured by consumer surplus or net surplus can be included in standard economic

[4] "Economic approach" is a misnomer. Hovenkamp (1985, p. 218) notes that US antitrust policy from the 1950s to the mid-1970s was fully informed by contemporary mainstream economics.

models. I use preferences about market structure as an example, but the point is general and applies, for example, to preferences about net neutrality, about political contributions by businesses, about genetically modified organisms, about carbon emissions, and other externalities resulting from market activities.

I further argue that the role of economics in analyzing market performance is limited to characterizing the costs and benefits of pursuing alternative policy objectives and that economics as a science is agnostic concerning what policy goals should be.

10.2 Related Literature

This chapter is related to a large body of work by legal and economic scholars. References to parts of that literature are given at appropriate points throughout the chapter. Here I mention three papers that make contributions particularly related to the conclusions I draw.

Adams et al. (1991) examine the efficiency of equilibrium outcomes in a two-good general equilibrium framework. If both sectors are perfectly competitive, the equilibrium outcome is Pareto optimal, and efficient in the Pareto sense.[5] Pareto optimality fails if one or both markets is imperfectly competitive or in the presence of joint production by a firm with market power. Whether or not a merger that supports market power improves welfare depends on whether gains in production efficiency, if any, outweigh reductions in consumer welfare.[6] They also make the point that a firm with market power may profitably choose not to produce some products that consumers would pay for, if the goods were available at competitive prices. This is a missing-market issue of the kind I take up in Sect. 10.8.

[5] As Arrow (1969, fn. 1) explains, "An allocation of resources through the workings of the economic system is said to be Pareto efficient if there is no other allocation which would make every individual in the economy better off". He later remarks that (1969, pp. 49–50) "Of course, as Pareto already emphasized, the proposition provides no basis for accepting the results of the market in the absence of accepted levels of income equality".

[6] Williamson (1968) famously makes this point in a partial-equilibrium framework.

Brock and Obst (2009) incorporate preferences about market concentration in a general equilibrium model. I incorporate preferences about market concentration in a partial-equilibrium model (Sect. 10.8). A partial equilibrium version of their result, that a full welfare optimum requires equality between the marginal loss of utility due to reduced output and the marginal gain of utility from decreased concentration, holds in my model.

Hovenkamp (1982) examines the argument that antitrust policy should have the maximization of efficiency as its unique goal, using three alternative efficiency standards (maximization of consumer welfare, Pareto optimality, and wealth maximization). His conclusion (1982, p. 30) that "Antitrust policy must come to grips with the fact that people may sometimes be willing to pay higher consumer prices to realize certain values, and that these values cannot always be determined in the voluntary market" is an implication of the model I develop in Sect. 10.8. His view (1982, pp. 28–29) that economics can inform the law by determining the costs of alternative policies is much the same as the position I take in Sect. 10.9.

10.3 The Formative Era

Economic Changes

The US economy was fundamentally transformed over the 25 years following the end of the American Civil War. Railroads, themselves the first firms to operate at national scale (Chandler 1965), spanned the continent and made possible a single national market. In sectors of the economy that involved economies of large-scale production, markets came to be dominated by large firms that achieved low unit cost and used railroad transportation to supply vast geographic areas.[7] Farmers, small firms that

[7] Chandler (1977) emphasizes three factors that combined to support enduring positions of market leadership by large firms: economies of continuous operation, as in distilling, flour milling, oil refining, sugar, and steel; backward and forward vertical integration; and effective management. See also Lamoreaux (1985).

found themselves competing with large firms, and employees of railroads and other large firms all took exception to the changes that followed.

Agricultural regions depended heavily on railroads, which were often local monopolists or duopolists, to ship grain and livestock to industrial food processors. Railroad rates were high in local monopoly markets, low in local oligopoly markets. Railroad collusion during economic downturns, imperfect though it may have been (Ellison 1994), was bitterly resented by farmers. Farmers were hostile to railroad rate discrimination and supported state legislation to regulate railroad rates (Farmer 1924; Miller 1954).

Local businesses similarly resented competition from distant, lower-cost large-scale firms that could profitably undersell them in their home markets. They lobbied state governments for protection against out-of-state rivals, sometimes with success (Hollander 1964; McCurdy 1978). Had such laws not been invalidated by the US Supreme Court, under the Commerce Clause of the US constitution, there would have been no national US economy, but rather a crazy-quilt of state markets. Local businesses that faced competition from large firms remained unhappy after protective legislation was struck down.

In industries supplied by large firms, workers found themselves on the supply side of monopsonistic markets for labor services. The post-Civil War period saw the rise of organized labor in the United States, a rise sometimes marked by civil unrest.

Thus the creation of a national US market brought forth interest groups-agriculture, small business, and organized labor-that criticized "the trusts". Segments of the general public looked askance at the development of private firms that were larger, in terms of employees or income, than some state governments. When state antitrust legislation proved ineffective, aggrieved parties turned to the national government for relief.

The topic of the rise of large business was never far from the public eye. Economists, political scientists, sociologists,[8] lawyers, businessmen,[9] and reformers all contributed to the ongoing public dialogue about the rise of

[8] The boundaries between these disciplines were less distinct than is now the case.

[9] On business sector intervention in this broad public debate, see Destler (1953).

trusts.[10] Discontent with the ramifications of large firms was widespread.[11] It cannot be said that US antitrust, in its formative period, pursued specifically economic goals.

The Progressive Movement

Enforcement of the Sherman Act ramped up slowly and was hobbled by restrictive court interpretations. The national debate on trusts and their consequences went on, unabated.

Economists were active in this debate both before and after passage of the Sherman Act. They were not enthusiastic about *laissez-faire*. Nor were they enthusiastic about the prospect of widespread government intervention in the economy, preferring to rely on competition for industries of decreasing or constant returns to scale and inclined toward what would now be called public utility regulation for industries of increasing returns to scale.[12]

A recurring element in the debate about trusts was the speed of entry. If the response to incumbents' economic profits was swift, large-scale entry, incumbent firms would not be able to exercise market power, and no antitrust policy would be needed.[13] John Bates Clark, one of the founders of the American Economic Association, came to view predatory price discrimination and restrictive manufacturer-distributor contracts as entry-deterring strategies that could allow incumbent firms to exercise persistent monopoly power.[14] Clark was one of four members of a public service committee that prepared a first draft of the 1914 Clayton Act (Fiorito 2013).

---

[10] See U.S. Library of Congress (1907) for a bibliography of publications on the trust issue.

[11] In the 1911 *Standard Oil* decision (221 U.S. 1, at 83–84), Justice Harlan portrayed the rise of trusts as threatening a kind of economic slavery.

[12] The classification of industries according to the nature of returns to scale is due to Adams (1887, p. 55) and emerged during the national debate over trusts. Williams (1990, pp. 94–96) notes that Adams elaborated on John Stuart Mill's concept of natural monopoly.

[13] Adams (1897), Giddings (1887), and Gunton (1888). Seventy-five years later, rapid entry was the economic mechanism underlying the theory of contestable markets.

[14] Clark (1900, p. 407, two paragraphs in the original): "[I]t is potential competition, that is, the power that holds trusts in check. The competition that is now latent, but is ready to spring into activity if very high prices are exacted, is even now efficient in preventing high prices. It is to be the permanent policy of wise and successful peoples to utilize this natural economic force for all that it is worth. At present, it is not an adequate regulator. The potential competitor encounters unnecessary obstacles when he tries to become an active competitor".

Section 2 of the Clayton Act prohibits price discrimination, and Section 3 prohibits restrictive manufacturer-distributor contracts (in both cases, where the effect may be substantially to lessen competition or tend to create a monopoly). Both provisions followed Clark's views.

The provisions of the Clayton Act are highly specific. The Federal Trade Commission Act is general: it establishes the Federal Trade Commission as an independent agency within the executive branch, and its operative provision, Section 5, prohibits unfair methods of competition.

The Sherman Act, the Clayton Act, and the Federal Trade Commission Act are the pillars upon which the superstructure of US antitrust rests. There have been amendments to these "big three" laws, one of which is discussed later, and specialized supplementary legislation. Some legislation exempts specific sectors (agricultural cooperatives, insurance) from the coverage of antitrust.[15] Regulatory legislation sometimes assigns responsibility for matters usually thought of as falling in the antitrust sphere to regulatory commissions (such as the Federal Communications Commission). The Webb-Pomerene Act of 1918 and the Export Trading Act of 1982 allow firms to form joint-sales agencies-that is, to collude-for sales on foreign markets, provided there are no repercussions for competition on the US market.

For present purposes, namely examination of the range of goals ascribed to the antitrust laws, the Robinson-Patman Act of 1936 must be mentioned. It amended the Section 2 Clayton Act prohibition against price discrimination with the aim of protecting small grocery stores from the competition of national chains. The legislation was drafted by a lawyer for the United States Wholesale Grocers' Association (Kintner 1978, p. 2895).

In its 1951 *Standard Oil of Indiana* decision, the Supreme Court wrote (340 U.S. 231 at 248–249, internal citations omitted, emphasis added)

> The heart of our national economic policy long has been faith in the value of competition. In the Sherman and Clayton Acts, as well as in the Robinson-Patman Act, "Congress was dealing with competition, which it

[15] Tradition, idiosyncratically, exempts organized baseball from antitrust rules.

> sought to protect, and monopoly, which it sought to prevent". ... We need not now reconcile, in its entirety, the economic theory which underlies the Robinson-Patman Act with that of the Sherman and Clayton Acts. It is enough to say that *Congress did not seek by the Robinson-Patman Act either to abolish competition or so radically to curtail it that a seller would have no substantial right of self-defense against a price raid by a competitor.*

In an accompanying footnote, the Supreme Court noted that "It has been suggested that, in theory, the Robinson-Patman Act as a whole is inconsistent with the Sherman and Clayton Acts". The footnote is more to the point than the text of the opinion, and the frankly protectionist intent with which the Robinson-Patman Act was adopted cannot be reconciled with an efficiency-oriented antitrust policy.

10.4 From Adoption to Mid-Century

The Sherman Act and the Federal Trade Commission Act are written in terms of broad generality. The operative provisions of the Clayton Act are more specific, but still leave substantial margin for interpretation. Congress delegated to courts the task of fleshing out the framework it had established in adopting the three basic antitrust laws. In the words of Senator Sherman during Senate debate (21 Cong. Rec. 2460 (1890)):

> I admit that it is difficult to define in legal language the precise line between lawful and unlawful combinations. This must be left for the courts to determine in each particular case. All that we, as lawmakers, can do is to declare general principles, and we can be assured that the courts will apply them so as to carry out the meaning of the law, as the courts of England and the United States have done for centuries.

Courts have accepted this mandate, and in rendering decisions, have expressed a range of views on the goals of the antitrust laws.[16]

[16] Crane (2015) points out that these objectives were all manifest during debates on the Sherman Act and the Clayton/FTC Acts. I am indebted to Nicola Giocoli for this reference.

Promote Fairness of Market Processes

In its 1897 decision finding the *Trans-Missouri Freight Association* in violation of Section 1 of the Sherman Act, the Supreme Court recognized that market processes could disrupt established economic relationships, creating winners and losers and severe hardship for the latter (166 U.S. 290 (1897) at 323):

> In any great and extended change in the manner or method of doing business it seems to be an inevitable necessity that distress and, perhaps, ruin shall be its accompaniment in regard to some of those who were engaged in the old methods. A change from stage coaches and canal boats to railroads threw at once a large number of men out of employment; changes from hand labor to that of machinery, and from operating machinery by hand to the application of steam for such purpose, leave behind them for the time a number of men who must seek other avenues of livelihood. These are misfortunes which seem to be the necessary accompaniment of all great industrial changes. It takes time to effect a readjustment of industrial life so that those who are thrown out of their old employment, by reason of such changes ...may find opportunities for labor in other departments than those to which they have been accustomed. It is a misfortune, but yet in such cases it seems to be the inevitable accompaniment of change and improvement.

The social decision to use free markets to allocate resources dictates that such disruptions be accepted, *when they result from competition in free markets*. There is no such presumption if disruption is the result of artificial aggregations of economic power (166 U.S. 290 (1897) at 323–324):

> It is wholly different, however, when such changes are effected by combinations of capital, whose purpose in combining is to control the production or manufacture of any particular article in the market, and by such control dictate the price at which the article shall be sold, the effect being to drive out of business all the small dealers in the commodity and to render the public subject to the decision of the combination as to what price shall be paid for the article.

In this view, the Sherman Act seeks to maintain fairness in market processes in order to maintain public support for a market system of resource allocation.

Maintain Competition

In 1927, in its opinion involving a challenge to a trade-association-mentored cartel, the Supreme Court wrote that the purpose of the Sherman Act was to maintain competition (U.S. v. Trenton Potteries 273 U.S. 392 at 397):

> Whether this type of restraint is reasonable or not must be judged in part at least in the light of its effect on competition, for whatever difference of opinion there may be among economists as to the social and economic desirability of an unrestrained competitive system, it cannot be doubted that the Sherman Law and the judicial decisions interpreting it are based upon the assumption that the public interest is best protected from the evils of monopoly and price control by the maintenance of competition.

Prohibit Unreasonable Restraint of Trade

In the 1933 *Appalachian Coals* decision concerning a proposed joint sales agreement, the Supreme Court ruled that the Sherman Act prohibited only undue restraints of trade (288 U.S. 344 at 359–360, emphasis added):

> The purpose of the Sherman Anti-Trust Act is to prevent undue restraints of interstate commerce, to maintain its appropriate freedom in the public interest, to afford protection from the subversive or coercive influences of monopolistic endeavor. …
>
> In applying this test, a close and objective scrutiny of particular conditions and purposes is necessary in each case. Realities must dominate the judgment. *The mere fact that the parties to an agreement eliminate competition between themselves is not enough to condemn it.*

It is often said that this decision was an aberration, reflecting the severe economic conditions of the Great Depression. Yet, the decision is cited by subsequent Courts, when they find it convenient to do so.

Prohibit All Restraints on Trade

The 1940 *Socony-Vacuum* case involved collusion in the US oil refining industry. The force of the resulting Supreme Court decision is that the Sherman Act rules out *any* agreement on prices (310 U.S. 150 at 221):

> But the thrust of the [*per se*] rule is deeper and reaches more than monopoly power. Any combination which tampers with price structures is engaged in an unlawful activity. Even though the members of the price-fixing group were in no position to control the market, to the extent that they raised, lowered, or stabilized prices they would be directly interfering with the free play of market forces. The Act places all such schemes beyond the pale and protects that vital part of our economy against any degree of interference.

Promote Dispersal of Power

For Justice Douglas, dissenting in the 1948 *Columbia Steel* merger case, the Sherman Act aimed to disperse power (334 U.S. 495 at 536)[17]:

> In final analysis, size in steel is the measure of the power of a handful of men over our economy. That power can be utilized with lightning speed. It can be benign or it can be dangerous. The philosophy of the Sherman Act is that it should not exist. For all power tends to develop into a government in itself. Power that controls the economy should be in the hands of elected representatives of the people, not in the hands of an industrial oligarchy. Industrial power should be decentralized. It should be scattered into many hands so that the fortunes of the people will not be dependent on the whim or caprice, the political prejudices, the emotional stability of a few self-appointed men. The fact that they are not vicious men but respectable and social-minded is irrelevant. That is the philosophy and the command of the

[17] See Fox (1981, fn. 72) for references.

Sherman Act. It is founded on a theory of hostility to the concentration in private hands of power so great that only a government of the people should have it.

Monopolization

Two opinions by Judge Learned Hand, issued almost 30 years apart, bracket the range of interpretations given to the Sherman Act Section 2 prohibition of monopolization.

Corn Products Refining

The Corn Products Refining Co. was a dominant firm, formed by merger, that used deferred loyalty rebates, bogus independents, and below-cost pricing to maintain its market position.[18] Judge Learned Hand's 1916 opinion in a US government monopolization case made clear that the Sherman Act had no objection to monopoly obtained by competition on the merits (U.S. *v.* Corn Products Refining Co. et al. 234 F. 964 at 1015)[19]:

> The national will has not declared against elimination of competitors when they fail from their inherent industrial weakness. On the contrary, it has declared with great emphasis against any methods by which such weaknesses might be concealed; in so doing it has assumed a positive purpose toward industry, has established a norm to which competition must conform. This purpose the Corn Products Refining Company has persistently and ingeniously endeavored to thwart from the outset. Its constant effort has been to prevent competitors from that test which would in the long run discover whether they could manufacture as well and as cheaply as itself.

---

[18] For a contrary view, see Peckham (1983).

[19] This interpretation closely tracks a well-known portion of Senate debate before passage of the Sherman Act, in which Senator Kenna asked if Section 2 would condemn a firm that had a monopoly because it was able to undersell all rivals, and Senator Edmunds replied that Section 2 would not apply to such a case (21 Cong. Rec. 3151).

Alcoa

Judge Hand's 1945 opinion in the *Alcoa* monopolization case found both economic and social goals behind the antitrust laws.[20] The economic goals related to the good market performance expected to result from the stimulus of actual competition or the threat of potential competition (148 F.2d 416 at 427):

> Many people believe that possession of unchallenged economic power deadens initiative, discourages thrift and depresses energy; that immunity from competition is a narcotic, and rivalry is a stimulant, to industrial progress; that the spur of constant stress is necessary to counteract an inevitable disposition to let well enough alone. Such people believe that competitors, versed in the craft as no consumer can be, will be quick to detect opportunities for saving and new shifts in production, and be eager to profit by them. In any event the mere fact that a producer, having command of the domestic market, has not been able to make more than a 'fair' profit, is no evidence that a 'fair' profit could not have been made at lower prices.

Judge Hand also found broader social purposes in the Sherman Act (148 F.2d 416 at 428–429; footnote omitted; not set off as a list in the original):

- We have been speaking only of the economic reasons which forbid Monopoly, but, as we have already implied, there are others, based upon the belief that great industrial consolidations are inherently undesirable, regardless of their economic results. In the debates in Congress Senator Sherman himself …showed that among the purposes of Congress in 1890 was a desire to put an end to great aggregations of capital because of the helplessness of the individual before them.
- That Congress is still of the same mind appears in the Surplus Property Act of 1944… and the Small Business Mobilization Act… Not only

[20] Judge Hand's opinion was later endorsed by the Supreme Court (American Tobacco Co. et al. *v.* U.S. 328 at U.S. 781 (1946) at 812–815).

does § 2(d) of the first declare it to be one aim of that statute to 'preserve the competitive position of small business concerns,' but § 18 is given over to directions designed to 'preserve and strengthen' their position. …

- Throughout the history of these statutes, it has been constantly assumed that one of their purposes was to perpetuate and preserve, for its own sake and in spite of possible cost, an organization of industry in small units which can effectively compete with each other.

Regarding the first bullet point, the remarks of Senator Sherman to which Judge Hand refers deal among other matters with public concern about inequality in the distribution of wealth that was thought to follow on the heels of trusts.[21] In the second bullet point, Judge Hand notes that the Congress of 1944 was concerned to promote small business.[22] In the third bullet point, he recognizes the implication of similar sentiments expressed in the Sherman Act debate in 1890. Those legislative sentiments are inconsistent with the view expressed in *Corn Products Refining* (and in Senate debate before passage of the Sherman Act) that US antitrust does not object to dominant market positions based on competition on the merits. They cannot be reconciled with the hypothesis that Congress conceived of the goals of antitrust policy exclusively in terms of the maximization of consumer surplus or the minimization of deadweight loss.

Résumé

Courts, following the congressional mandate to "carry out the law", have imputed a variety of purposes to the Sherman Act and companion legislation. Writing after this period, Areeda described the possible goals of antitrust policy (1983, p. 534):

[21] See 21 Cong. Rec. 2460.

[22] *Alcoa* charged the Aluminum Company of America with monopolization in violation of the Sherman Act. The Surplus Property Act of 1944 set conditions for the federal government to dispose of aluminum plants it had constructed as part of the war effort.

Let me begin by stating summarily the other possible goals of antitrust beyond maximizing consumer welfare. They include the political and social values of dispersed control over economic resources, multiple choices for producers and consumers free of the arbitrary dictates of monopolies or cartels, equal opportunity, equitable income distribution, and "fairness" in economic dealings. As a general proposition, such goals are attractive to many citizens and perhaps most of them.

It should also be obvious, however, that these very goals are widely served by that effective competition which maximizes consumer welfare.

10.5 Celler-Kefauver[23]

The shift from the passive, publicity approach to merger control of the original Section 7 of the Clayton Act to the active antimerger policy of the 1950 Celler-Kefauver Act was motivated by concern about the social and political consequences of the rise of large firms, not its economic causes or effects[24]:

> The control of American business is steadily being transferred … from local communities to a few large cities in which central managers decide the policies and the fate of the far-flung enterprises they control. … Through monopolistic mergers the people are losing power to direct their own economic welfare. When they lose the power to direct their economic welfare they also lose the means to direct their political future.

In his next remarks, Senator Kefauver invoked the lessons of recent history, that the concentration of economic power in the hands of the few led to either Fascism or Socialism. In the words of Bok (1960, pp. 236–237):

> To anyone used to the preoccupation of professors and administrators with the economic consequences of monopoly power, the curious aspect of the debates is the paucity of remarks having to do with the effects of concentration on prices, innovation, distribution, and efficiency. To be sure, there

[23] Martin (1959) and Bok (1960) discuss the legislative history of the Celler-Kefauver Act.

[24] Senator Kefauver, 96 Cong. Rec. 16452, 1950.

were allusions to the need for preserving competition. But competition appeared to possess a strong socio-political connotation which centered on the virtues of the small entrepreneur to an extent seldom duplicated in economic literature.

In its first opinion applying the amended Section 7, the Supreme Court summarized as follows congressional intent in amending Section 7 (370 U.S. 294 (1962) at 315, footnotes omitted):

> The dominant theme pervading congressional consideration of the 1950 amendments was a fear of what was considered to be a rising tide of economic concentration in the American economy. …Other considerations cited in support of the bill were the desirability of retaining "local control" over industry and the protection of small businesses. Throughout the recorded discussion may be found examples of Congress' fear not only of accelerated concentration of economic power on economic grounds, but also of the threat to other values a trend toward concentration was thought to pose.

The Supreme Court noted the explicit statement in a Senate Report that the amendment aimed to give antitrust a tool to stop a trend to increased concentration before it became irreversible (370 U.S. 294 (1962) at 317–318, emphasis added): "The intent here . . . is to cope with monopolistic tendencies *in their incipiency* and well before they have attained such effects as would justify a Sherman Act proceeding". If a merger would not worsen market performance, but could be expected to be the first of a series of mergers that would, in total, worsen market performance, congressional intent was to block the merger.

10.6 Bork on Legislative Intent

From the early post-World War II period, University of Chicago economists developed views inimical to what they sometimes referred to as "collectivism" (Brown et al. 1955).[25] This included a reversal of Chicago

[25] Curiously, speakers in congressional debate before passage of the Celler-Kefauver Act explicitly referred to the amendment as a device to avoid collectivism. See Bok (1960, fn. 51) for references.

economists' interwar support for antitrust policy.[26,27] One element of this program was Bork's analysis (1966, 1967, 1978) of congressional intent behind the Sherman Act, based on the debates reported in the Congressional Record. Bork quotes extensively from congressional debates. He gives 21 instances in which senators or representatives referred to the trust problem as one of raising price to the consumer, advancing cost to the consumer, and the like, which suggests speakers' concern with the impact of monopoly pricing on purchasers. He gives eight instances in which speakers referred to restraint of trade or the like, which to a modern economist might suggest an interest in minimizing deadweight loss.

Much of Bork's discussion makes sense only if "consumer welfare" is taken to mean "the welfare of purchasers". To give one example of what could be many, writing of an antitrust rule against mergers leading to monopoly, Bork makes a clear distinction between consumer welfare and producer welfare and argued that Congress gave priority to consumer welfare over producer welfare (1966, p. 11, emphasis added):

> The argument for this rule in Congress, however, shows that it derived in large measure from a desire *to protect consumers from monopoly extortion.* Insofar as other classes, such as small producers who sold to or bought from monopolists, were to be benefitted, that benefit was not seen as conflicting with the consumer-welfare rationale but rather as reinforcing it. Where producer and consumer welfare might come into conflict … Congress chose consumer welfare as decisive.

---

[26] Fetter (1932) published a statement of support signed by 127 economists that saw the antitrust laws as an alternative to more invasive approaches, "preserving the policy of free markets for industrial products whereby individual and small corporate enterprise may be assured unhindered opportunity to demonstrate through efficiency, service and low prices to the public, its right to survival in business" and opposing "widening and extension of the realm of public price fixing in industry and commerce [which] must impose an impossible burden upon governmental agencies of control and irreparable injury to the political and social, as well as economic, interests of the whole people". Seven of the signatories (Paul H. Douglas, S.E. Leland, H.A. Millis, S.H. Nerlove, Henry Schultz, Jacob Viner, and Chester W. Wright) were affiliated with the University of Chicago.

[27] On the change in attitude of Chicago economists toward antitrust, see Martin (2008, 39, 43–49). On the central role of Aaron Director, see Bork (1993, p. 12). On the Second Chicago School generally, see Reder (1982), Kitch (1983), and Van Horn et al. (2011).

If "consumer welfare" means "protecting purchasers from monopoly extortion", it does not include the welfare of the owners of firms that exact monopoly prices.

The only hint that what Bork intends by the term "consumer welfare" is the combined welfare of consumers and producers is an oblique turn of phrase in his introduction (Bork 1966, p. 7, emphasis added):

> My conclusion, drawn from the evidence in the Congressional Record, is that Congress intended the courts to implement (i.e., to take into account in the decision of cases) only that value we would today call consumer welfare. To put it another way, the policy the courts were intended to apply is the *maximization of wealth* or consumer want satisfaction.

Bork (1967, p. 242) is more explicit: "My thesis is that existing statutes can be legitimately interpreted only according to the canons of consumer welfare, defined as minimizing restrictions of output and permitting efficiency, however gained, to have its way". In *The Antitrust Paradox*, after defending a consumer welfare goal for antitrust for 110 pages, Bork explains that the surplus that purchasers lose by paying high prices is not a loss of consumer welfare, but an income transfer (1978, p. 110):

> Those who continue to buy after a monopoly is formed pay more for the same output, and that shifts income from them to the monopoly and its owners, who are also consumers.

Bork's turn of phrase has hopelessly muddled these waters, with courts citing Bork in support of the position that antitrust policy aims to maximize consumer welfare, then making arguments that conceive of harm to market performance in terms of the welfare of purchasers, not net surplus.

Nor have legal scholars found Bork's argument convincing; law journals are strewn with alternative interpretations of the goals of US antitrust policy.

Fox writes (1981, p. 1154) that "[T]he claim that efficiency has been the goal and the fulcrum of antitrust is weak at best. The values other than efficiency that underlie the commitment to power dispersion, economic opportunity, and competition as market governor demand equal attention". For Lande (1982, p. 150) "Each antitrust law grew in part out of a desire to define and protect consumers' property rights, an antipathy toward corporate aggregations of economic, social, and political power, and a concern for small entrepreneurs". Rowe (1984, p. 1560, in footnote 295) observes that "Not unexpectedly, the 1890 debates reveal a mix of social, economic, and political concerns".

Brodley regards the economic and noneconomic goals of antitrust as mutually compatible (1987, p. 1022, footnote omitted):

> [T]here is a unity between the pragmatic substance of antitrust-its economic goals-and the law's animating spirit-its social and political foundations. Thus, the pursuit of the correctly defined economic goals of antitrust will generally advance the social and political objectives of the law as well.

Posner (1987, pp. 209–210, footnotes omitted, emphasis added) denies Bork's principal conclusion:

> The legislative history makes clear that the [Sherman] Act was aimed at the great trusts (cartels and monopolies) of the time, but is not single-minded concerning what aspect of the trusts was reprobated. Some members of Congress wanted to punish the trusts because the trusts restricted output and raised price, and thus hurt consumers. Others believed that the trusts, whether through economies of scale or other efficiencies, produced a greater output at lower price, thus helping consumers (in both the short and long run) but hurting inefficient competitors. Still other members of Congress relied on both reasons for supporting the Act, believing that it would both help consumers and help the trust's competitors. The modern economic analysis of monopoly has made the inconsistency of these two reasons transparent. *But no one in 1890 understood the economic concept of efficiency; it hadn't been developed yet.*

Adams and Brock regard the economic goals of antitrust as subsidiary to its political goal, maintenance of a free society (1987, p. 1116)[28]:

---

[28] The same position was taken by the German Ordoliberal School.

> The primary purpose of antitrust is to perpetuate and preserve a system of governance for a competitive, free enterprise economy. Efficiency and consumer welfare constitute ancillary benefits that are expected to flow from a system of economic freedom. ...Antitrust calls for a dispersion of power, buttressed by built-in checks and balances, to guard against the abuse of power and to preserve not only individual freedom, but also more importantly, a free system. Antitrust is founded on a theory of hostility toward private concentration of power....

Hovenkamp writes of Bork's work (1989, p. 22, footnotes omitted)

> [Bork] concluded all too quickly that because some members of Congress knew that demand curves slope downward (i.e., that output is reduced as prices rise), that they also had a modern conception of allocative efficiency and the social cost of monopoly. Not a single statement in the legislative history comes close to stating the conclusions that Bork drew.

In sum, we can agree with Ginsburg (2014, p. 947) that Bork's analysis of the legislative intent underlying the Sherman Act has been rejected by the Academy.

10.7 Kaldor, Hicks, and Potential Compensation

It is in the nine pages of Chapter 5 of Bork (1978) that Bork explains his expansive use of the term "consumer welfare". The issues involved in that usage are the subject of a large economics literature, to which Bork does not refer, and can be presented with reference to Fig. 10.1.

It depicts a market supplied by a single firm, a monopolist in the antitrust sense, that can set a price p_E that is greater than its marginal cost c without inducing entry by higher-cost potential competitors.

If the market were perfectly competitive, price would equal marginal cost c. Output would be Q_c. The area of the triangle cDF is *consumer surplus* under perfect competition. Like Hicks (1942, p. 126), Bork follows Marshall (1920, p. 125) definition of consumers' surplus as "The

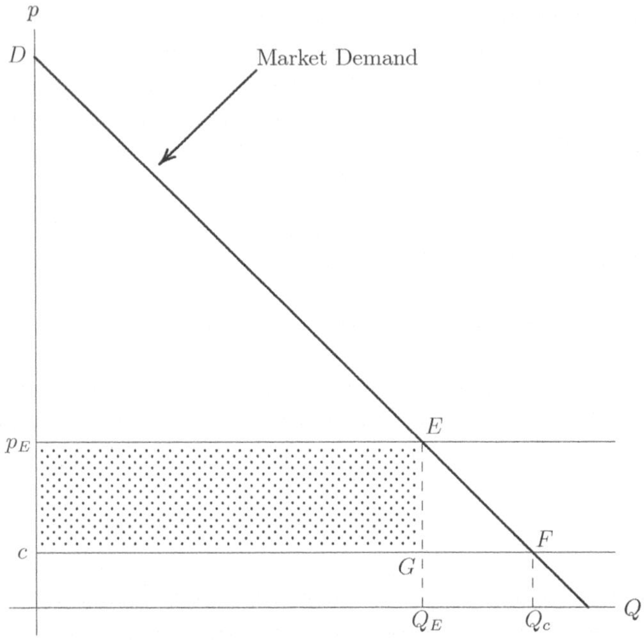

Fig. 10.1 Consumer surplus vs. net surplus (constant marginal cost c, entry-inducing price p_E)

excess of the price which [consumers] would be willing to pay rather than go without the thing". Thus consumers' surplus is a monetary amount, not a measure of utility. $\Delta\pi$ is not a measure of the utility the owners of the firm gain when they spend their additional income in other markets. ΔCS is not a measure of the utility consumers lose when they reduce spending in other industries.

If the market is supplied by a single firm that sells Q_E units of output at price p_E, the firm earns an economic profit in the amount of the shaded rectangle cP_EEG. Relative to perfect competition, this economic profit is a transfer of purchasing power from the consumers who purchase the good at the price p_E to the owners of the firm. It is also a monetary amount.

Consumers' surplus at price p_E is the area of the triangle p_EDE. Consumer surplus under monopoly is reduced by an amount equal to the area cp_EEF. If the increase in owners' income is set against the lost consumers' surplus, what is left, the area of the triangle *EFG*, is the deadweight loss due to monopoly power.

Consumers who remain in the market under monopoly reduce spending in other markets by an amount equal to the area of the rectangle cP_EEG. The owners of the firm increase spending in all markets in which they buy by an identical amount. That the changes in income of the two groups are of the same monetary amounts does not imply that the changes in satisfaction of the two groups are the same. What one can say from Fig. 10.1 is that consumers would spend less for the privilege of being able to continue to buy Q_E units than they would be willing to spend to buy Q_C units of output, and that the owners of firms have economic profit $(p_E - c)Q_E$ to spend under monopoly that they would not have under competition. The figure tells us nothing about the implied changes in satisfaction.

We are thus led to the issue of interpersonal welfare comparisons, as were Robbins (1938), Kaldor (1939), and Hicks (1939). Robbins entered into a discussion of the welfare consequences of relaxing nineteenth-century restrictions on the importation of corn into England. The resulting lower price of corn would make consumers better off and farmers worse off, just as the price increase shown in Fig. 10.1 would make consumers worse off and the owners of the firm better off. Robbins' view was that it was not possible to measure the net welfare impact of the change without making the assumption that consumers and farmers had "equal capacity for satisfaction". He argued that there was no basis in economic science for making such an assumption.

In the analysis of the welfare impact of monopoly power, if lost consumers' surplus and increased economic profit represent comparable units of satisfaction, then deadweight loss represents the net welfare loss due to monopoly power. But, Robbins' position implies, there is nothing in economics as a science that allows us to say that changes in identical monetary amounts of income represent identical changes in satisfaction.

Kaldor (1939), seconded by Hicks (1939),[29] responded with what is now called the Kaldor-Hicks *potential Pareto improvement* welfare criterion. A reallocation of income is a Pareto improvement if it makes some

[29] In a lecture that was probably delivered in 1954, Hicks expressed the view that he and Kaldor "had gopne wrong" in 1939. See Kanari (2006).

individuals better off and no individuals worse off. A reduction in the tariff on corn is not a Pareto-improving policy change: it makes consumers better off and farmers worse off. If, however, the government were to levy lump-sum taxes on consumers and make lump-sum distributions to farmers in an amount just sufficient to compensate farmers for lost income, and consumers were still better off with a lower price of food, there would be a Pareto improvement.[30]

Kaldor proposes to look at what the net welfare impact of a policy change would be *if* these kinds of lump-sum transfers from winners to losers were made, whether or not the transfers actually are made; whether compensation should be given or not (1939, p. 550) "is a political question on which the economist, *qua* economist, could hardly pronounce an opinion".

With this approach, Kaldor sought to avoid interpersonal comparisons of satisfaction (1939, p. 551, footnote 1). The consensus of the literature is that this does not work (Winch 1965, p. 406)[31]:

> The original version of the compensation principle, now generally referred to as the Kaldor-Hicks criterion ..., under the assumption that full compensation will in fact be made, is uniquely free from either interpersonal comparison or value judgment. ...Under the assumption that all changes will be offset, the only question is whether the amount of money collected from gainers will be enough to compensate losers; all comparisons are in hard, homogeneous dollars. It is only when the possibility, or desirability, of compensation is questioned that problems arise. Then some people might be worse off, and it becomes necessary to compare changes in satisfaction.

In the context of the income transfer impact of monopoly power, we can write a weighted sum of economic profit and lost consumer surplus as

$$\theta_1 \Delta\pi + \theta_2 \Delta CS. \tag{10.1}$$

[30] "Lump sum" means that taxes are levied and subsidies granted in ways that do not alter individual behavior other than through the implied change in income. As a practical matter, it is impossible to implement lump-sum transfers.

[31] Winch comments on welfare measurement using the compensating variation, an alternative to consumer surplus due to Hicks.

In a move from competition to monopoly, the change in profit $\Delta\pi$ is positive, and the change in consumer surplus ΔCS is negative. If $\theta_1 = \theta_2 = 1$, (10.1) becomes deadweight loss, the statistic is implied by the Kaldor-Hicks potential Pareto improvement criterion and championed by Bork under another name. If $\theta_1 = 0$, $\theta_2 = 1$, (10.1) becomes lost consumer surplus, which is what is relevant under a consumer welfare standard. But there are no theorems in economics that tells us what the weights should be. Weighting changes in income equally, $\theta_1 = \theta_2 = 1$, does not avoid interpersonal comparisons: it is simply one of many possible choices about the way the income changes of the two groups might be summarized in a single statistic.

Stigler's reaction to the potential Pareto improvement principle was that whatever weightings are used should be indicated up front (1943, p. 359): "There is grave danger in leaving the value judgments unspecified except by implication…".[32] After a careful review of the economics literature on the topic, Chipman and Moore agree (1978, p. 581):

> After 35 years of technical discussions, we are forced to come back to Robbins' 1932 position. We cannot make policy recommendations except on the basis of value judgments, and these value judgments should be made explicit.

10.8 Missing Markets and the Goals of Antitrust

Under stringent assumptions that include existence of a complete set of competitive markets, the First Theorem of Welfare Economics tells us that equilibrium is Pareto optimal (Koopmans 1957, Essay 1). This result fails if some markets are not competitive. It fails if some goods are public goods. And it fails if there are missing markets (Newbery 1989).

[32] See similarly Slesnick (1998).

There are many consequences of market activities for which there are no markets. In some such cases, as, for example, carbon emissions, governments may attempt to create a market that would not otherwise exist. But there may be preferences about other consequences of economic activity for which this is impossible. Individuals may prefer net neutrality over differential pricing for internet service/product suppliers. Individuals may prefer that there be information sources expressing a range of viewpoints, even though they disagree with some of those viewpoints. Individuals may prefer that the corporations should not be able to make unlimited political contributions, or have preferences about absolute firm size. Individuals may prefer that markets be less concentrated rather than more concentrated, even markets for products they do not buy, because they object to the consequences of the rent-seeking expenditures they expect to occur in concentrated markets. It is straightforward to include preferences about the outcomes of market activity for which there are no markets in standard economic models. I illustrate this by comparing two models of a market with linear demand, one in which there are no preferences about market structure and one in which there are preferences about market structure. In the second model, welfare is reduced if market concentration, an indicator of market and other dimensions of power, exceeds a threshold level.

Demand

No Preferences About Market Structure

As is well known, a linear demand curve can be derived from a micro-level model of N individuals, each purchasing 1 or 0 units of the homogeneous good and each with a reservation price that is uniformly distributed on the interval $\left[0,a\right]$. With such a specification, individual utility in the market for the homogeneous good is

$$u_i = \begin{cases} x_i - p & x_i \geq p \\ 0 & x_i < p \end{cases}, \tag{10.2}$$

where the individual reservation price x_i is uniformly distributed on the interval $[0,a]$. The implied inverse demand equation is[33]

$$p = a - bQ. \tag{10.3}$$

As is also well known, the inverse demand equation (10.3) can also be derived from a quadratic aggregate welfare function for the good in question,

$$U(Q) = aQ - \frac{1}{2}bQ^2. \tag{10.4}$$

Preferences About Market Structure

A specification of individual utility in the market for the homogeneous good if individuals have preferences about market structure is

$$u_i = h_i(y_i - p) + \begin{cases} x_i - p & x_i \geq p \\ 0 & x_i < p \end{cases} - \begin{cases} \frac{1}{2}\beta(m_D - m)^2 & m < m_D \\ 0 & m \geq m_D \end{cases}, \tag{10.5}$$

where m is the number of firms in the market, m_D is the individual's preferred number of firms, and $\beta > 0$ is a parameter that determines the strength of preferences about market structure.

The assumptions made in the following section about the supply side of the market imply that firms produce identical amounts in equilibrium. The number of firms m is then a complete description of equilibrium market structure: the smaller is m, the more concentrated is the market.[34] Preferences of the form (10.5) imply that if the market is more concentrated than an individual prefers, $m < m_D$, individual utility is reduced.

---

[33] In (10.3), $b = a/N$.

[34] m is the inverse of the Herfindahl index, perhaps the most common measure of supply-side concentration.

If the market is less concentrated than the individual prefers, $m \geq m_D$, individual utility is determined as in (10.2).

For simplicity, I suppose all individuals have the same preferred number of firms.[35] This specification implies that individual welfare falls as the number of firms falls short of the preferred number of firms.

The implied aggregate welfare function is

$$U(Q, m_D, m) = aQ - \frac{1}{2}bQ^2 - N\begin{cases}\frac{1}{2}\beta(m_D - m)^2 & m < m_D \\ 0 & m \geq m_D\end{cases}. \tag{10.6}$$

In this specification, individuals have preferences over market structure, but there is no market for market structure. Inverse demand in the market for Q is again given by (10.3).

Supply and Cournot Equilibrium

Since the alternative specifications of individual utility yield the same aggregate demand, Cournot equilibrium values are the same for preferences of both types.

There are m firms. Let constant marginal cost c and fixed cost F be the same for all firms, so the firm cost function is

$$C(q_i) = cq_i + F. \tag{10.7}$$

In this linear inverse demand constant marginal cost model, firm i's objective function is

$$\pi_i = (a - c - bQ)q_i - F. \tag{10.8}$$

[35] This is not essential for the results that follow. It is straightforward to modify the model so some individuals' preferences do not involve market structure, or to allow the preference parameter β to differ across individuals. An Appendix giving details is available on request from the author.

Cournot equilibrium output per firm is

$$q(m)=\frac{1}{m+1}\frac{a-c}{b}. \tag{10.9}$$

Equilibrium price is

$$p(m)=c+\frac{a-c}{m+1}, \tag{10.10}$$

and equilibrium profit per firm is

$$\pi(m)=\frac{1}{b}\left(\frac{a-c}{m+1}\right)^{2}-F. \tag{10.11}$$

We follow common practice and treat the number of firms as a continuous variable. Then the equilibrium number of firms m_{LR} makes profit per firm equal to 0:

$$m_{LR}=\frac{a-c}{\sqrt{bF}}-1. \tag{10.12}$$

If we substitute (10.12) into (10.9) and (10.10), we get the corresponding long-run expressions:

$$q_{LR}=\sqrt{\frac{F}{b}} \tag{10.13}$$

$$p_{LR}=c+\sqrt{bF}. \tag{10.14}$$

Minimum Number of Firms

Suppose the government specifies a minimum price,[36]

$$p_\mu = c + \frac{1}{2}(a-c) - \frac{1}{2}\sqrt{(a-c)^2 - 4\mu bF}, \tag{10.15}$$

where

$$\mu > m_{LR}$$

is a target number of firms.

Profit per firm is

$$\pi_i = \frac{1}{2}\left[a - c - \sqrt{(a-c)^2 - 4\mu bF}\right]q_i - F.$$

If there is free entry, the number of firms adjusts until $\pi_i = 0$. Then output per firm is

$$q_\mu = \frac{2F}{(a-c) - \sqrt{(a-c)^2 - 4\mu bF}} = \frac{1}{2}\frac{1}{\mu b}\left[a - c + \sqrt{(a-c)^2 - 4\mu bF}\right].$$

Total output is μq_μ, the market-clearing price for which is

$$a - b\mu q_\mu = p_\mu.$$

Thus with free entry, the market is supplied by $\mu > m_{LR}$ firms at a price $p_\mu > p_{LR}$.

[36] A consistency condition is that the discriminant on the right be nonnegative. This implies an upper bound on μ, $\mu \le \dfrac{(a-c)^2}{4bF}$.

p_μ is below the monopoly price. It rises as μ rises. The difference

$$p_\mu - p_{LR}$$

is the cost to purchasers, per unit of output, of having a less concentrated market structure.

Welfare

In this section, I use a numerical example to illustrate the welfare consequences of a minimum-number-of-firms policy.[37]

Let $a = 10,000$, $b = 1$, and $c = 0$. Then the inverse demand equation is

$$p = 10{,}000 - Q.$$

If $F = 4,000,000$, the long-run Cournot number of firms m_{LR} is 4, each producing output $q_{LR} = 2000$. The market-clearing price is $p_{LR} = 2000$.

If there is a minimum price $p_\mu = 4000$, then with free entry the market is supplied by $\mu = 6$ firms, each producing $q_\mu = 1000$ units of output.

The welfare consequences of a minimum-number-of-firms policy depend on the structure of preferences.

Preferences Independent of Market Structure

If preferences are independent of market structure, the subaggregate welfare function is

$$\hat{U}(Q) = 10{,}000Q - \frac{1}{2}Q^2. \tag{10.16}$$

[37] It may be that the comparison between long-run Cournot equilibrium and minimum number of firms equilibrium is not the relevant comparison. It might be that with m_{LR} firms, tacit collusion is an equilibrium, either in a repeated game or as in Selten's (1973) static collusion model. If a deconcentration policy destabilizes tacit collusion, it can increase welfare even if the population is indifferent toward market structure. See footnote 38.

In Cournot equilibrium, firms break even. Since profit per firm is zero, aggregate welfare is simply consumer surplus,

$$CS_{LR} = \frac{1}{2} Q_{LR}^2 = 32{,}000{,}000. \tag{10.17}$$

If government sets price $p_\mu = 4000$ and there is free entry, consumer surplus is reduced:

$$CS_\mu = 18{,}000{,}000. \tag{10.18}$$

Increasing the number of firms in the market reduces welfare if the population is indifferent toward the number of firms that supply the market.[38]

Preferences Dependent on Market Structure

Alternatively, let preferences depend on the number of firms in the market,

$$\hat{U}(Q, m_D, m) = 10{,}000Q - \frac{1}{2}Q^2 - N \begin{cases} \frac{1}{2}\beta(m_D - m)^2 & m < m_D \\ 0 & m \geq m_D \end{cases}, \tag{10.19}$$

and let $\beta = 700$.

For the example, consider the case that $m < m_D$. Then

$$\hat{U}(Q, m_D, m) = 10{,}000Q - \frac{1}{2}Q^2 - 3{,}500{,}000(m_D - m)^2. \tag{10.20}$$

using $a/N = b = 1$ to get $N = 10, 000$.

[38] If tacit collusion on monopoly output is sustainable with four firms, consumer surplus (per period) is 12,500,000. If tacit collusion on monopoly output is not sustainable with six firms, a minimum-number-of-firms policy improves market performance even if there are no preferences about market structure.

The long-run Cournot equilibrium values are as before, $m = m_{LR} = 4$, $p_{LR} = 2000$, $q_{LR} = 2000$.

If $m_D = 6$, Cournot equilibrium aggregate welfare is

$$\hat{U}(Q, 6, 4) = 18{,}000{,}000.$$

If the government sets price $p_\mu = 2763.9$, then $\mu = 5$ with free entry. Each firm produces $q_\mu = 1447.2$ units of output, and aggregate welfare is

$$\hat{U}(Q, 6, 5) = 22{,}680{,}340.$$

This is greater than net social welfare in long-run Cournot equilibrium. If preferences extend to market structure, then some reduction in concentration increases welfare.

10.9 Conclusion

From its inception, the mainstream view of US antitrust was that it pursued a range of mutually consistent goals. Closer-to-competitive market performance, for example, promotes economic efficiency in the sense of minimizing cost and effectively allocates resources across markets. It also sustains public belief in the fairness of market processes and so maintains support for a market system of resource allocation, despite the fact that a dynamic market system creates winners and losers.

From the post-World War II period onward, legal and economic scholars associated with the Chicago School of antitrust analysis[39] have sought, with much success, to narrow the focus of antitrust, arguing that it should promote allocative and productive efficiency, and that other possible goals are inadmissible because they are not "economic".

My argument in this chapter is that what is called an "economic" approach is no such thing, and by its nature, could not be. Economics does not teach that antitrust policy should seek to minimize deadweight

[39] I borrow the term from Posner (1979).

loss due to monopoly power, or to maximize consumer surplus, or to protect small firms, or to reduce market or aggregate concentration, to the exclusion of other goals. Economics provides tools to measure the costs and benefits of such policies; the choice among them, if choice there must be, is outside the realm of economics (Robbins 1932, p. 129, footnote omitted)[40]:

> [T]here are no economic ends. There are only economical and uneconomical ways of achieving given ends. We cannot say that the pursuit of given ends is uneconomical because the ends are uneconomical; we can only say it is uneconomical if the ends are pursued with an unnecessary expenditure of means.

Bork, as Ginsburg (2014) says and as noted earlier, has been rejected by the Academy. But as he also notes (Ginsburg 2014, p. 949), the Academy has failed to persuade the judiciary: landmark antitrust decisions often cite Bork in support of an "economic approach" that sees antitrust as maximizing net surplus.[41] The continued adherence of US courts to policy prescriptions for imperfectly competitive markets generated by a school of thought that insists most markets can be treated, most of the time, as if they were perfectly competitive (Reder 1982) presents a challenge to mainstream economists. The adherence of the Supreme Court,[42] if in a unclear way, to a reading of legislative intent that antitrust

---

[40] See similarly Arrow (1974, p. 17): "Rationality, after all, has to do with means and ends and their relation. It does not specify what the ends are".

[41] There is more than circumstantial evidence that parts of the judiciary have not grasped the meaning Bork gives to the phrase "consumer welfare". Ginsburg (2014, p. 945) hails the Supreme Court's *Reiter v. Sonotone* decision for its embrace of the consumer welfare standard. Yet, in that decision, the court views the antitrust treble damage provision as (442 U.S. 330 at 343) "a means of protecting consumers from overcharges resulting from price fixing", which is a remark about the welfare of purchasers. In *Jefferson Parish Hospital*, the Supreme Court refers to increased monopoly profit due to price discrimination as a social cost of market power (466 U.S. 2 (1984) at 14–15). But under Bork's net surplus standard, price discrimination which tends to increase output improves market performance (Bork 1978, pp. 394–398); increased monopoly profit is merely a transfer from purchasers to the producer.

[42] See Ginsburg (2014, fn. 50) for citations to lower-court opinions that admit the possibility of a range of goals for the antitrust laws.

scholars reject as indefensibly narrow creates a quandary for those scholars when they seek to formulate antitrust policy advice.[43]

Bork himself, however, explained why it is worthwhile to put forward mainstream economic results (Bork 1967, pp. 242–243):

> Antitrust policy is determined, far more than most people realize, by the Supreme Court. Reform is as likely to come through change in the intellectual world which ultimately reaches the Court as by any other means.

Acknowledgements I thank the University of Bologna for its hospitality during the sabbatical visit when this chapter was written. I am grateful for comments received during seminar presentations at the University of Bologna, at the 14th annual meeting of the Italian Association for the History of Economic Thought, "Power in the History of Economic Thought", at the University of Salento, at the Centre for Competition Policy, University of East Anglia, from Nicola Giocoli and Herbert Hovenkamp. Responsibility for errors is my own.

References

Adams, C. F. (1897). The Pace of Corporate Action in Our Civilization. In N. S. Shaler (Ed.), *The United States of America* (Vol. II, pp. 191–213). New York: D. Appleton and Company.

[43]The divergence between antitrust economics and the retreat of antitrust that is justified in the name of antitrust economics has itself become a topic of scholarly research. Among the factors that Giocoli (2015) identifies as possible explanations for the enduring charm that Chicago antitrust economics holds for the judiciary are ideology, ease of administrability, and an awkward fit between courts' requirements for scientific rigor and the approach of modern industrial economics to tailor theoretical and empirical models to specific markets. As noted earlier, the late-1940s shift from the First Chicago School to the Second Chicago School was motivated in part, and perhaps a large part, by antipathy toward "collectivism". Ideology certainly has had some role in the Second Chicago School. (The accounts of Manne (2005) and Priest (2005) of the early development of law and economics are instructive in this regard.) Links to the judiciary may have been forged by law and economics "summer camps" for judges, the sources of funding for which had libertarian leanings (Meyer 2016). Certainly a world-view that treats most markets as competitive, most of the time, will support easily administrable interpretations of the antitrust laws. This leads to the kind of policy that Simons (1936, p. 72) called an "open season on consumers". But it is easy to administer. It is true that modern industrial economics is largely a library of industry-specific models. If it is the generality of Second Chicago School antitrust economics that explains its allure for US courts, then it becomes difficult to explain the disenchantment of those courts with the Structure-Conduct-Performance framework, which itself offered a general framework. There are also instances in which private plaintiffs have suffered in US courts because they did not provide sufficiently specific evidence; see Virgin Atlantic *v.* British Airways plc 69 F. Supp. 2d 571 (1999).

Adams, H. C. (1887). Relation of the State to Industrial Action. *Publications of the American Economic Association, 1*, 471–549.
Adams, W., & Brock, J. W. (1987). Antitrust and Efficiency: A Comment. *New York University Law Review, 61*, 1116–1124.
Adams, W., Brock, J. W., & Obst, N. P. (1991). Pareto Optimality and Antitrust Policy: The Old Chicago and the New Learning. *Southern Economic Journal, 58*, 1–14.
Areeda, P. (1983). Introduction to Antitrust Economics. *Antitrust Law Journal, 52*, 523–537.
Arrow, K. J. (1969). The Organization of Economic Activity: Issues Pertinent to the Choice of Market Versus Non-market Allocation. In *The Analysis of Public Expenditure: The PBB System* (Vol. I, pp. 59–73). U.S. Joint Economic Committee, 91st Congress, 1st Session, U.S. GPO, Washington, DC.
Arrow, K. J. (1974). *The Limits of Organization*. New York: W. W. Norton & Company, Inc.
Bok, D. C. (1960). Section 7 of the Clayton Act and the Merging of Law and Economics. *Harvard Law Review, 74*, 226–355.
Bork, R. H. (1966). Legislative Intent and the Policy of the Sherman Act. *Journal of Law and Economics, 9*, 7–48.
Bork, R. H. (1967). The Goals of Antitrust Policy. *American Economic Review, 57*, 242–253.
Bork, R. H. (1978). *The Antitrust Paradox: A Policy at War With Itself.* New York: Basic Books. Second edition, 1993, with a new Introduction and Epilogue.
Brock, J. W., & Obst, N. P. (2009). Market Concentration, Economic Welfare, and Antitrust Policy. *Journal of Industry, Competition, and Trade, 9*, 65–75.
Brodley, J. F. (1987). The Economic Goals of Antitrust: Efficiency, Consumer Welfare, and Economic Progress. *NYU Law Review, 62*, 1020–1053.
Brown, S. G., Director, A., & Weaver, R. M. (27 February 1955). Who are Today's Conservatives? *University of Chicago Roundtable*, Number 881.
Chandler, A. D. Jr. (1965). *The Railroads: The Nation's First Big Business.* New York: Harcourt, Brace & World, Inc.
Chandler, A. D. Jr. (1977). *The Visible Hand: The Managerial Revolution in American Business.* Cambridge: Harvard University Press.
Chipman, J. S., & Moore, J. C. (1978). The New Welfare Economics. 1939–1974. *International Economic Review, 19*, 547–584.

Clark, J. B. (1900). The Necessity of Suppressing Monopolies while Retaining Trusts. In *Chicago Conference on Trusts* (pp. 404–409). Chicago Conference on Trusts. Chicago: Civic Federation of Chicago. Reprinted 1973 by Arno Press, Inc.

Crane, D. A. (2015). All I Really Needed to Know About Antitrust I Learned in 1912. *Iowa Law Review, 100*, 2015–2038.

Destler, C. M. (1953). The Opposition of American Businessmen to Social Control During the Gilded Age. *Mississippi Valley Historical Review, 39*, 641–672.

Ellison, G. (1994). Theories of Cartel Stability and the Joint Executive Committee. *Rand Journal of Economics, 25*, 37–57.

Farmer, H. (1924). The Economic Background of Frontier Populism. *Mississippi Valley Historical Review, 10*, 406–427.

Fetter, F. A. (1932). The Economists' Committee on Anti-Trust Law Policy. *American Economic Review, 22*, 465–469.

Fiorito, L. (2013). When Economics Faces the Economy: John Bates Clark and the 1914 Antitrust Legislation. *Review of Political Economy, 25*, 139–163.

Fox, E. M. (1981). Modernization of Antitrust: A New Equilibrium. *Cornell Law Review, 66*, 1140–1192.

Giddings, F. H. (1887). The Persistence of Competition. *Political Science Quarterly, 2*, 62–78.

Ginsburg, D. H. (2014). Bork's 'Legislative Intent' and the Courts. *Antitrust Law Journal, 79*, 941–951.

Giocoli, N. (2015). Old Lady Charm: Explaining the Persistent Appeal of Chicago Antitrust. *Journal of Economic Methodology, 22*, 96–122.

Gunton, G. (1888). The Economic and Social Aspect of Trusts. *Political Science Quarterly, 3*, 385–408.

Hicks, J. R. (1939). The Foundations of Welfare Economics. *Economic Journal, 49*, 696–712.

Hicks, J. R. (1942). Consumers' Surplus and Index-Numbers. *Review of Economic Studies, 9*, 126–137.

Hollander, S. C. (1964). Nineteenth Century Anti-Drummer Legislation in the United States. *Business History Review, 38*, 479–500.

Hovenkamp, H. (1982). Distributive Justice and the Antitrust Laws. *George Washington Law Review, 51*, 1–31.

Hovenkamp, H. (1985). Antitrust Policy after Chicago. *Michigan Law Review, 84*, 213–284.

Hovenkamp, H. (1989). Antitrust's Protected Classes. *Michigan Law Review, 88*, 1–48.
Kaldor, N. (1939). Welfare Propositions of Economics and Interpersonal Comparisons of Utility. *Economic Journal, 49*, 549–552.
Kanari, T. (2006). J. R. Hicks' Unpublished Lecture Notes: Another Shot at Welfare Economics, Lecture I. *The History of Economic Thought, 48*, 84–97.
Kintner, E. W. (1978). *The Legislative History of the Federal Antitrust Laws and Related Statutes.* New York and London: Chelsea House Publishers.
Kitch, E. W. (1983). The Fire of Truth: A Remembrance of Law and Economics at Chicago, 1932–1970. *Journal of Law and Economics, 26*, 163–234.
Koopmans, T. C. (1957). *Three Essays on the State of Economic Science.* New York and elsewhere: McGraw-Hill.
Lamoreaux, N. R. (1985). *The Great Merger Movement in American Business, 1895–1904.* Cambridge and elsewhere: Cambridge University Press.
Lande, R. H. (1982). Wealth Transfers as the Original and Primary Concern of Antitrust: The Efficiency Interpretation Challenged. *Hastings Law Journal, 34*, 65–151.
Manne, H. G. (2005). How Law and Economics was Marketed in a Hostile World: A Very Personal History. In F. Parisi & K. Rowley (Eds.), *The Origins of Law and Economics* (pp. 309–327). Cheltenham, UK and Northampton, Massachusetts, USA: Edward Elgar.
Marshall, A. (1920). *Principles of Economics* (8th ed.). London: The Macmillan Press Ltd. http://www.econlib.org/library/Marshall/marP.html.
Martin, D. D. (1959). *Mergers and the Clayton Act.* Berkeley and Los Angeles: University of California Press.
Martin, S. (2008). The Goals of Antitrust and Competition Policy. In W. D. Collins (Ed.), *Issues in Competition Law and Economics* (pp. 19–84). Chicago: American Bar Association.
McCurdy, C. W. (1978). American Law and the Marketing Structure of the Large Corporation, 1875–1890. *Journal of Economic History, 38*, 631–649.
McCurdy, C. W. (1979). The *Knight Sugar* Decision of 1895 and the Modernization of American Corporation Law, 1869–1903. *Business History Review, 53*, 304–342.
Meyer, J. (2016). *Dark Money.* New York: Random House.
Miller, G. H. (1954). Origins of the Iowa Granger Law. *Mississippi Valley Historical Review, 40*, 657–680.

Newbery, D. M. (1989). Missing Markets: Consequences and Remedies. In F. Hahn (Ed.), *The Economics of Missing Markets, Information, and Games* (pp. 211–242). Oxford University Press, Oxford.

Peckham, B. W. (1983). Trust Busting Reconsidered: United States v. Corn Products Refining Co. *Utah Law Review, 1983*, 737–824.

Posner, R. (1979). The Chicago School of Antitrust Analysis. *University of Pennsylvania Law Review, 127*, 925–948.

Posner, R. (1987). Legal Formalism, Legal Realism, and the Interpretation of Statutes and the Constitution. *Case Western Reserve Law Review, 37*, 179–217.

Priest, G. L. (2005). The Rise of Law and Economics: A Memoir of the Early Years. In F. Parisi & C. K. Rowley (Eds.), *The Origins of Law and Economics* (pp. 350–382). Cheltenham, UK and Northampton, MA, USA: Edward Elgar.

Reder, M. W. (1982). Chicago Economics: Permanence and Change. *Journal of Economic Literature, 20*, 1–38.

Robbins, L. (1932). *An Essay on the Nature and Significance of Economic Science*. London: Macmillan.

Robbins, L. (1938). Interpersonal Comparisons of Utility: a Comment. *Economic Journal, 48*, 635–641.

Rowe, F. M. (1984). The Decline of Antitrust and the Delusions of Models: The Faustian Pact of Law and Economics. *Georgetown Law Journal, 72*, 1511–1570.

Selten, R. (1973). A Simple Model of Imperfect Competition, Where 4 are Few and 6 are Many. *International Journal of Game Theory, 2*, 141–201.

Simons, H. C. (1936). The Requisites of Free Competition. *American Economic Review, 26*, 68–76.

Slesnick, D. T. (1998). Empirical Approaches to the Measurement of Welfare. *Journal of Economic Literature, 36*, 2108–2165.

Stigler, G. J. (1943). The New Welfare Economics. *American Economic Review, 33*, 355–359.

U.S. Library of Congress (1907). *List of Books Relating to Trusts. With References to Periodicals* (3rd ed.). Washington: Government Printing Office.

Van Horn, R., Mirowski, P., & Stapleford, T. A. (Eds.) (2011). *Building Chicago Economics*. Cambridge: Cambridge University Press.

Williams, P. L. (1990). The Attitudes of the Economics Professions in Britain and the United States to the Trust Movement, 1890–1914. In J. D. Hey & D. Winch (Eds.), *A Century of Economics* (pp. 92–108). Oxford: Basil Blackwell.

Williamson, O. E. (1968). Economies as an Antitrust Defense: the Welfare Tradeoffs. *American Economic Review, 58*, 18–36.
Winch, D. M. (1965). Consumer's Surplus and the Compensation Principle. *American Economic Review, 55*, 395–423.

Part IV

Managing Power: Economists as Policy Makers

11

Jean-Baptiste Say on Political Power (1793–1832)

Emmanuel Blanc and André Tiran

11.1 Introduction

The French Restoration saw intense political debate with the fall of Napoleon Bonaparte and the reinstatement of Louis XVIII as well as the advent of Louis-Philippe's July Monarchy. J.-B. Say was one of the founding fathers of French liberalism in terms of political theory, and his influence on the French liberal group under the Restoration was far greater than is generally thought. This liberal group emerged from the constitutional monarchists, the Girondins; during the initial stages of the 1789–93 French Revolution, they formed the 'liberal opposition' which was to be in conflict with policies under Napoleon and the Restoration throughout the first three decades of the nineteenth century.

Liberalism featured such traditional themes as the limitation of the state, a written constitution, a representative government with accountable ministers, the protection of civil rights, freedom of speech and the

E. Blanc • A. Tiran (✉)
Centre de recherche Triangle UMR CNRS, University of Lyon, Lyon, France
e-mail: andre.tiran@univ-lyon2.fr

M. Mosca (ed.), *Power in Economic Thought*, Palgrave Studies in the History of Economic Thought, https://doi.org/10.1007/978-3-319-94039-7_11

control of budget expenditure. Some other key issues were the king's power and his relationship with the Charter, individual freedom and constitutionalism, the analysis of the origins of political power, the nature of freedom, the relationship between the individual and the state and the role of religion and the Church. It was a novel analysis of the relationship between man and state, and J.-B. Say played a key role in this tradition. The whole of the liberal group engaged in a consistent political struggle about all these issues. J.-B. Say conducted his struggle through his teaching at the *Athénée,* the publication of articles and above all his influence on Charles Comte and Charles Dunoyer. His obsession was the stabilization of the Republican political order.

J.-B. Say appears as a man of transition on several counts. It is to be noted that his life (1767–1832) straddled two eras, the classical period and the beginning of romanticism. On the one hand, he still belonged to the second generation of the Enlightenment, not to the physiocrats and enlightened despotism but to the generation of revolutionaries such as Honoré de Mirabeau (not his father Victor), Turgot, Necker, Condorcet, Isnard, Cabanis, Destutt de Tracy, in short to the 'Ideologues', the Girondins and the Liberal Republicans. On the other hand, he was a contemporary of Chateaubriand (*Travels in America* 1827), Stendhal (*Racine and Shakespeare* 1823, *The Red and the Black* 1830), who was one of his sharp-eyed readers, Victor Hugo (*Hernani* 1830), Lamartine (*Poetical Meditations* 1820) and even Balzac (*The Physiology of Marriage* 1829), Musset (*Tales from Spain and Italy* 1830, *The Whims of Marianne* 1833) and Vigny (*Stello* 1832).

The opinion on J.-B. Say has often been grievously warped by Marx's and Walras' readings. For reasons which we do not develop here, they seriously distorted and even mutilated Say's thinking.[1] However, Marx is not accountable for the short-sightedness of many uninformed readers, who view Say as the representative of bourgeois conservatism or social reaction. Quite the opposite is true; one will have a much more accurate view if one considers that J.-B. Say's school of thought and political stance are on the far left of the political spectrum. This is why Saint Simonians,

[1] See E. Blanc et A. Tiran "introduction" in *J.-B. Say. Œuvres Morales et Politiques*, vol. V, directed by E. Blanc et A. Tiran, pp. 10–42. *Œuvres complètes complètes de Jean-Baptiste Say,* coordinated by André Tiran, Economica, Paris, 2003; J.-B. Say, *Olbie ou Essai sur les moyens de réformer les mœurs d'une nation,* introduction et notes de J. P. Frick, Presses universitaires de Nancy, Nancy, 1990.

Proudhonians and all the younger generations referred to Say between 1814 and 1832. Charles Comte and Charles Dunoyer took their inspiration directly from him, as did Benjamin Constant. Say is on the far left because, as we shall see, he was opposed to the Bonapartists, as well as to the monarchists and Jacobins. He was a staunch Republican and never caved in, nor did he accept honours in exchange for submission, paying a high price in terms of his career in France.[2] J.-B. Say is also viewed as concerned solely with economic matters such as free trade, value, the law of markets (Say's law), and so on. He is said to have been responsible, more than anyone else, for the divide between economics and politics.

We know that J.-B. Say intended to write a book on the principle of utility. In his handwritten notes he wrote: "I use my Athénée course on the principle of utility for my Practical Politics".[3] As a matter of fact, the only published text we have is a 50-page *Essay on the Principle of Utility.* Published for the first time just one year after his death by his son-in-law Charles Comte in the 1833 *Mélange et correspondance d'économie politique*, it was also included later in the editions of his *Complete Course.* In this chapter, we use these documents to verify if it is possible to extend J.-B. Say's principle of utility to morality and to politics. It comprises three parts. The first one focuses on documenting specific and little-known aspects of J.-B. Say's political struggle (1793–1803). The second one is concerned with the period of the theorization of politics from his moral utility perspective (1814–1832). The third one deals with the exercise of power.

11.2 J.-B. Say's Political Struggle Until 1814

Scant knowledge about J.-B. Say's life has led to significant errors,[4] which is why we would like to point out some biographical facts. J.-B. Say was 22 years old when the Revolution broke out and he supported it enthusiastically.

[2] See E. Blanc et A. Tiran, "introduction" in *J.-B. Say. Œuvres Morales et Politiques*, vol. V, directed by E. Blanc et A. Tiran, pp. 10–42. *Œuvres complètes de Jean-Baptiste Say,* coordinated by André Tiran, Economica, Paris, 2003.

[3] *J.-B Say. Œuvres Morales et Politiques*, vol. V, directed by E. Blanc et A. Tiran, pp. 289–727. *Œuvres complètes de Jean-Baptiste Say,* coordinated by André Tiran, Economica, Paris, 2003.

[4] E. Blanc et A. Tiran, "Introduction", in *J.-B. Say. Œuvres Morales et Politiques*, vol. V, directed by E. Blanc et A. Tiran, pp. 10–42. *Œuvres complètes de Jean-Baptiste Say,* coordinated by André Tiran, Economica, Paris, 2003.

He was a Republican all his life. During that period he was employed at *Courrier de Provence*, Mirabeau's magazine, managing subscriptions. He was therefore deeply immersed in political action albeit at a very humble level. Testifying to his commitment to the Revolution is the brochure he wrote on the freedom of the press,[5] as well as his enrolment as a volunteer in the company of arts of the Year II Campaign.[6]

J.-B. Say's Role in the 1793–1800 Decade

Contrary to the notion spread by the first biographical notes in the nineteenth century,[7] J.-B. Say's initial role in the review *La Decade*[8] focussed on subjects unrelated to political economy proper. One may thus safely infer that he did not have a clear vision of what he would do later, at least during the first years of the *Decade*. He was 26 years old when the philosophical and literary *Decade* came into existence.[9]

All the authors who appear extensively in his unpublished works (Voltaire, Montesquieu, Rousseau, Diderot, Helvétius, d'Holbach, Condorcet) were mentioned in the *Decade*. J.-B. Say's brother, Horace Say, wrote that "philosophy brought about the Revolution, that is, the

[5] J.-B. Say, "De la liberté de la Presse", in *J.-B Say. Œuvres Morales et Politiques* vol. V, réalisé par E. Blanc et A. Tiran, pp. 147–160. *Œuvres complètes de Jean-Baptiste Say,* coordinated by André Tiran, Economica, Paris, 2003.

[6] See E. Blanc et A. Tiran "introduction", *Ibidem*, pp. 10–42.

[7] « Jean-Baptiste Say », *Nouveau Dictionnaire de l'Économie Politique*, de Léon Say et Joseph Chailley, Guillaumin, Paris, 1892. A. Thoisnier Desplaces, « SAY (Jean-Baptiste) », *Biographie universelle ancienne et moderne* 1843 (Tome 38, pp. 176–182). Verger F.J., « Notice sur M. Say », *Annales de la société royale académique de Nantes et de la Loire Inférieure*, 1832.

[8] Jean-Baptiste Say (J.-B. Say), at the beginning of the Revue *La Decade*, served as general secretary of editorial staff and director of the printing company that prints the journal. Until the end of the 1790s, his contributions to the journal will focus in particular on the theatre, reviews of literary works, certain political issues, but not on any political economy issues. Régaldo Marc, *Un milieu intellectuel : la Décade Philosophique (1794–1807),* Lille III-Paris, Champion, 1976.

[9] J.-B. Say is one of the founders of the Revue *La Décade*. See André Tiran, "Notes biographiques sur Jean-Baptiste Say", De Boeck Supérieur | « *Innovations* », 2014/3 n° 45 | pg. 171–215 and Evert Schoorl, *Jean–Baptiste Say: Revolutionary, Entrepreneur,* Economist, Routledge, 21 nov. 2012; Régaldo Marc, *Un milieu intellectuel: la Décade Philosophique (1794–1807),* Lille III-Paris, Champion, 1976, p. 703

shift from monarchic institutions to republican institutions".[10] The *Decade*'s landmark authors were Condillac for ideology, Rousseau for education, Diderot for literature and drama but also religion, Condorcet for social mathematics, Beccaria and lastly Adam Smith, whose translations the *Decade* draws attention to.

Two of the century's great philosophers, Montesquieu and Rousseau, were the butt of criticism and disagreement from some members of the *Decade*, including Say. He and his brother Horace spoke out vigorously against the separation of powers between the legislative and the executive advocated by Montesquieu and also against the idea of general sovereignty put forward by Rousseau. Say went as far as opposing the inclusion of the Declaration of Human Rights in the preamble to the Constitution. In a report, J.-B. Say chided Montesquieu for his "imaginary principles of honour, virtue and awe"[11] and his systematic spirit. J.-B. Say's position against Rousseau stemmed from the same practical stance but also involved a more fundamental opposition in the case of political views. He considered the concept of 'general will' vacuous and dismissed writers who talked about "the state of nature: a figment of the mind which is of little import to us".[12] There is no direct reference to Condorcet by Say in the *Decade*.

The Decade: J.-B. Say and the 'Ideologues'

The *Decade* was first published at a time when the struggle was waged through the implementation of new institutions and legal and legislative measures which were to shape the future. The *Decade*'s political action consisted in commentaries, reports on articles and in political statements.

---

[10] See André Tiran, "Notes biographiques sur Jean-Baptiste Say", De Boeck Supérieur | «*Innovations*», 2014/3 n° 45 | pp. 171–215.

[11] J.-B. Say, "Olbie" in *Œuvres Morales et Politiques*, vol. V, directed by E. Blanc et A. Tiran, pp. 185–238. *Œuvres complètes de Jean-Baptiste Say*, coordinated by André Tiran, Paris, Economica, 2003.

[12] *ibidem*

The *Decade* was formed during the height of the Reign of Terror, of which the editors approved, though not in all its aspects. Even after the Reign of Terror, the *Decade*, namely J.-B. Say's brother Horace, justified this political era as follows: "It was the government's very activity, vigour and cruelty that helped it to find unsuspected resources in France. It was able to put them to good use and drive back our enemies' shrewd and cold armies".[13]

The advent of Thermidor was hailed as a return to justice and humanity, albeit tentatively. The editors of the *Decade* successfully campaigned for the complete rehabilitation of the Girondins, with Condorcet and Marie-Joseph Chénier being granted articles on the subject in the magazine.[14]

The Prairial and Germinal events harshly brought to light the *Decade*'s editors' place in society. Alarmed by the impending social turmoil, the editors condemned the 1793 Democratic Constitution. They also supported the Thermidorians' action to repeal the rules which had been imposed to remedy the shortage of food and the economic crisis. Thus they defended economic liberalism while also exposing the authoritarian measures' ineffectiveness. Regarding morality, the *Decade* rejected the behaviour of the 'nouveaux riches', which went against their Republican ethos. Above all, they condemned the return of the Catholic religion and the priests. Hostility towards religion and the Church was the *Decade*'s editors' most deeply seated attitude. In his essay *Olbie,* J.-B. Say maintained that the Catholic faith had made man sad, glum and numb.[15] He wrote a comedy featuring an adulterous priest. Nevertheless, the members of the *Decade* opposed religious persecutions as they believed that all churches should be under the orders of civil authority, but freedom of conscience and worship should be respected. J.-B. Say was actively anticlerical. It must be said, however, that although he remained

[13] See E. Blanc et A. Tiran, "introduction" in *Œuvres Morales et Politiques,* vol. V, directed by E. Blanc et A. Tiran, pp. 10–42. *Œuvres complètes complètes de Jean-Baptiste Say,* coordinated by André Tiran, Paris, Economica, 2003.

[14] Condorcet committed suicide in prison at the time of terror and André Chénier was guillotined. André Tiran, "Notes biographiques sur Jean-Baptiste Say", De Boeck Supérieur | « *Innovations* », 2014/3 n° 45 | pp. 171–215.

[15] J.-B. Say "Olbie" in *J.-B. Say. Œuvres Morales et Politiques,* vol. V, directed byE. Blanc et A. Tiran, pp. 185–238. *Œuvres complètes de Jean-Baptiste Say,* coordinated by André Tiran, Paris, Economica, 2003.

an atheist through and through, hostile to religion and priests to the last, he did not take the same stance to his family's Calvinism, which he viewed with great sympathy.

The Year III Constitution and J.-B. Say's Criticisms

The Year III Constitution established the two-degree voting system based on the poll tax whereby there were at most 30,000 voters, and legislative authority was vested in the 'Council of Five Hundred' and the 'Council of Elders'. Executive authority was entrusted to a five-member *Directoire*. The *Directoire* was not entitled to inititate legislation.[16]

During the debate preceding the implementation of the Constitution, the editors of the *Decade*, through Amaury Duval and J.-B. Say, took the floor to guide the debate in the direction they deemed favourable. J.-B. Say spoke out in an article entitled *A few thoughts on the project for a constitution of the 'Commission of Eleven'*[17] criticizing the organization of executive authority because he believed it might restore the power of high-ranking civil servants, that is, all the former Versailles bureaucrats. As the number of ministries was too small, the latter would be in control.

He opposed the separation of powers since he saw it as a source of conflict and inefficiency: "Instead of providing them (the different authorities) with means to fight each other, we should identify the two authorities' strengths".[18] According to the editors of the *Decade*, for the

[16] The *Directoire* is a French political regime which was in place during the First Republic, from 26 October 1795 (4 brumaire year IV) to 9 November 1799 (18 brumaire year VIII). It takes its name from the board of *Directoire*, that is, all five directors, heads of government between whom the executive power and ministers are divided, in order to avoid tyranny. Put in place at the end of the Reign of Terror by the moderate Republicans of the Thermidorian Convention, the regime re-establishes the censal suffrage, which serves to elect the two legislative chambers, the *Conseils des Cinq cents* and the *Conseil des Anciens.*

[17] André Tiran, "Notes biographiques sur Jean-Baptiste Say", De Boeck Supérieur | « *Innovations* », 2014/3 n° 45 | pp. 171–215. And, introduction in *Œuvres Morales et Politiques,* vol. V, réalisé par E. Blanc et A. Tiran, pp. 43–142. *Œuvres complètes de Jean-Baptiste Say,* coordinated by André Tiran, Paris Economica, 2003.

[18] André Tiran. « J.-B. Say, Essai de biographie sur J.-B. Say » *in* « Manuscrits inédits sur la monnaie, la banque et la finance précédé d'un Essai de biographique sur J.-B. Say. » : *Numéro spécial hors série des Cahiers monnaie et finance*. Centre de recherche monnaie Finance et banque, p. 247, 1995, Jean-Michel Servet and https://halshs.archives-ouvertes.fr/halshs-00117641.

Constitution to be valid, it had to reach three main objectives: to bring the nation's elite to power, not to inflate people's emotions, flaring passions and votes of enthusiasm and to avoid conflict between the different powers.

But what is most striking in J.-B. Say's criticism is his refusal to include the Declaration of Human Rights in the preamble to the Constitution. For him, a constitution is a "contract based on the interests of the parties revokable at their will".[19] With this refusal, he rejected the whole set of Republican beliefs, stating that the political system is merely a form of practical organization between individuals. Not only is this declaration of rights superfluous, it can also lead to disorder as he said very clearly:

> The Declaration states that the law is the expression of the general will, and the Constitution provides that it is simply the will of the Council of Five Hundred and the Council of Elders [...] Therefore it is quite safe to say that a declaration of human rights, which was very useful at the time of the Revolution when the intent was to establish principles which would overthrow the former government in people's opinion, was at least superfluous now that most of these rights have been recognised and that laying down the others is pointless.[20]

This remarkable quotation testifies to J.-B. Say's fundamentally bourgeois and moderate stance. In this respect, he was not different from the *Decade*'s other editors. In his view, there was no such thing as general will; it was merely a meaningless abstraction. Only individual wills existed and those that could express themselves were those with a fortune or an education.

J.-B. Say proposed the following preamble to the Constitution:

> The people of France, desirous to guarantee each individual that makes it up tranquility, the security of his person and property and the freedom compatible with a large association has decided to organize its government as follows.[21]

---

[19] André Tiran, "Notes biographiques sur Jean-Baptiste Say", De Boeck Supérieur | « *Innovations* », 2014/3 n° 45 | pp. 171–215.

[20] *Ibidem*.

[21] *Ibidem, op.cit.* pp. 171–215.

But J.-B. Say's opinion about what a constitution was and its role is more complex, as he himself wrote:

> We know from experience that it does not suffice to decree, accept, swear to a constitution for it to endure. It must be so appropriate to the people and the circumstances that it was made for that the need to change it does not even arise. All that it commands must seem so easy, so natural that one gets used to it without effort; for through habit alone are most men attached to institutions.[22]

In fact, ever since the beginning of the *Directoire*, the *Decade*'s editors had been campaigning for peace and domestic stability. Their opinion was to have no bearing on the adoption of the Year III Constitution, which disregarded all their criticism.

The *Directoire*

The *Decade*'s direct political involvement is most obvious during the years 1795–1800. This is when Horace Say took charge of the domestic policy column. Unlike previously, he did not confine himself to comments and information; he also defended stances on current political issues. Throughout this period the *Decade* supported the *Directoire*'s policies, including Baboeuf's condemnation.[23] After the Fructidor crisis under the second *Directoire*, J.-B. Say went on the front line to support the measures taken by the regime in power.[24] He condoned the purge decided by the *Directoire* in an article, asking "whether there are cases when it is permissible to violate principles".[25] His answer to the question was yes, supported by examples from the previous political period:

---

[22] André Tiran, "Notes biographiques sur Jean-Baptiste Say", De Boeck Supérieur | « *Innovations* », 2014/3 n° 45, p. 198.

[23] Babeuf, who is blamed for the conspiracy of the *Conjuration des Égaux*, is condemned to death. He is guillotined on the 8th Prairial year V.

[24] André Tiran, "Notes biographiques sur Jean-Baptiste Say", De Boeck Supérieur | « *Innovations* », 2014/3 n° 45, p. 199. J.-B. Say writes various articles in the *Decade* to defend the new government's policy.

[25] André Tiran, "Notes Biographiques Sur Jean-Baptiste Say", De Boeck Supérieur | « *Innovations* », 2014/3 n° 45, p. 199.

> It was respect for the principle of the judiciary's independence that led the Commission of the Twelve to acquit Marat and his accomplices. If, following Cicero's example in a similar circumstance it had had the conspirators shot the next day, 200,000 unfortunate victims of the Terror, from hapless Bailly to Roucher, would still be alive.[26]

The policy of stabilization of the Republic and law and order embodied by J.-B. Say and his brother Horace prevailed over the revolutionary order represented by Guinguené and Amaury Duval.[27] Historians have highlighted the pivotal role played by the Institute's 'ideologues', Sieyès, Cabanis and Volney in Bonaparte's coup.[28] It was the *Decade* that relayed the Brumairians' rallying cry:

> Yes, you must unite but it must be a union of all the talents, all the knowledge, all the virtues that the Nation holds. Ignore all party lines, call on all patriots; let the feeling of impending danger unite all those who rallied in 1789 under the banner of human rights and have never forsaken it since.[29]

This article was part of a series whose sole purpose was to bring back order in the country and restore public trust. Immediately after its announcement, the *Decade* supported the 18 Brumaire Coup. This string of events pointed strongly to the direct involvement of the *Decade*'s editors, including J.-B. Say, in the preparation of the coup. Several arguments bolster this theory. The opinions expressed in previous months were in full agreement with the coup's proclaimed political objectives. Sieyès and Cabanis had long-standing personal connections with the *Decade*'s editors; they moved in the same salons; they referred to the same values. With its position as a magazine, its relations in the political and literary spheres and in the salons, the *Decade* was the ideal tool for centralizing information on the preparation of the coup and influencing

---

[26] *Ibidem op. cit.* pp. 199–202. J.-B. Say means that strict compliance with the law in extraordinary circumstances can lead to disasters.

[27] There was a debate in the board if J.-B. Say and his brother will be on the side of Bonaparte and the Brumairiens.

[28] Sergio Moravia : *Il pensiero degli idéologues. Scienza e filosofia in Francia (1780–1815).* Firenze, La Nuova Italia Editrice, 1974; Schlieben-Lange Brigitte, Knapstein Franz. « Les Idéologues avant et après Thermidor. » In *: Annales historiques de la Révolution, française*, n°271, 1988. pp. 35–59.

[29] André Tiran, "Notes biographiques sur Jean-Baptiste Say", De Boeck Supérieur | « *Innovations* », 2014/3 n° 45, p. 202.

what we would now call the 'political class' of the period. Horace Say, the *Decade*'s chief editor, had connections with Bonaparte. He had taken part in the expedition to Egypt and had been appointed battalion commander by Bonaparte on this occasion. In the run-up to the coup, Bonaparte had diligently courted ideology circles. Madame d'Helvetius had received him in her salon in Auteuil. He had dined with members of the Institute.[30] Before leaving for Egypt he had asked J.-B. Say to make a list of the books he should take with him on the expedition. Bonaparte had spared no effort to garner the support of those he would later call the 'ideologues'. In the new political organization brought about by the 18 Brumaire Coup, J.-B. Say saw a return to the principles of 1789. He conveyed the hopes he vested in the new regime ten days later in an article:

> Let us hope that the organization of our new government, which opens a constitutional door for all improvements, will bring a new order that is more favourable to morality and humanity into this part of the administration as into many others.[31]

To conclude on this point, another argument may be considered to support the thesis of the *Decade*'s involvement in the Brumaire coup: the appointment of four of its founding members—Andrieux, Guinguené, Lebreton et J.-B. Say—to the *Tribunat*.[32]

The *Consulat* and the *Tribunat*: Final Political Struggles (1799–1804)

For the editors of the *Decade*, the establishment of the *Consulat* marked their access to high political office.[33] Four of them, Andrieux, Guinguené, Lebreton et J.-B. Say were appointed tribunes and represented Sieyès'

[30] The members of the Institute included a large number of scientists and a majority of 'ideologues'.

[31] André Tiran, "Notes biographiques sur Jean-Baptiste Say", De Boeck Supérieur | « *Innovations* », 2014/3 n° 45, p. 203.

[32] Lebreton, Guinguené, Andrieux are members of the journal *La Décade*, which is the organ of ideologues. They are appointed by Bonaparte as members of the *Tribunat, a* new institution of the Republic.

[33] Until then, ideologues only had the status of journalists, they were directly appointed to the highest political positions.

group in the new regime's political authorities. The *Tribunat* comprised 100 speakers elected by the Senate. It was divided into several sections representing the various sectors of political action. The orators discussed the draft bills proposed by the Council of State, which was appointed by the First Consul. J.-B. Say was a member of the finance commission and was to present several reports. From his essay *Olbie,* we know that he intended to write a treatise on political economy—which he indeed did during his three-year stint on the *Tribunat.* He wrote in *Olbie*'s summary: "A good treatise on political economy must be the first moral do book".[34]

It was Guinguené's intervention[35] in the *Tribunat's* internal affairs section calling on his colleagues to oppose Bonaparte's special court project that triggered the conflict between them. Bonaparte reacted to his opposition by having a violent charge against the group of 'ideologues' published in the *Mercure de France* of 16 Pluviose Year IX under the title *Observations.* The article denounced:

> these bewildered minds which, randomly applying the absolute principles of abstract metaphysics, establish the most conflicting systems according to their passions. There are a dozen or fifteen of them and they think they are a party.[36]

What is remarkable about Bonaparte's attack was the discrepancy between its vehemence and the supposed insignificance of the group it targeted. The truth is that Bonaparte felt compelled to vilify the group of 'ideologues' because he viewed them as a genuine threat, that is, as an active political force. In the face of Bonaparte's attack, the *Decade*'s editors gave up the struggle. On 16 Pluviose Year IX, J.-B. Say wrote to Amaury Duval:

> Andrieux thinks that we should discontinue the Decade's political column altogether, perhaps resume it when we are free to do so. It is my opinion too. In the meantime, we both think that you should not write either positively or negatively, directly or indirectly, about the speeches delivered at

[34] See "Olbie" in *J.-B. Say Œuvres Morales et Politiques,* vol. V, by E. Blanc et A. Tiran, pp. 191–194. *Œuvres complètes de Jean-Baptiste Say,* coordinated by André Tiran, Paris, Economica, 2003.

[35] This is the first public demonstration of an opposition to Bonaparte.

[36] *Mercure de France*, 16 Pluviôse, an IX, p. 319.

> the Tribunat, nor should you comment on the infamous rant that the government has published against us under the title *Observations*.[37]

This precautionary advice was tantamount to giving up the political struggle altogether. For over a month the *Decade* refrained from political comment. In 1801, J.-B. Say renewed his public adhesion to the 18 Brumaire regime, though in unenthusiastic terms. But Bonaparte pursued his onslaught and decided to purge the *Tribunat*. Andrieux, Lebreton and Guinguené were evicted. J.-B. Say, who was not very vocal, was only evicted in 1804.[38]

This is what he later wrote about this period: "Too weak to oppose usurpation and unwilling to serve it I had to give up the platform, and cloaking my ideas in general terms I wrote some truths which could be of use in all times and places".[39] Hence the enduring hostility J.-B. Say nurtured against Bonaparte. The following are a few telling remarks. Relating a conversation he had with Bonaparte, he wrote:

> I once ventured to reproach Napoleon with corrupting the nation. I could not possibly convey the subtle disdain with which he responded: 'Don't you know yet that one governs men better by pandering to their vices than to their virtues?'[40]

In an answer to a student in one of his *Athénée* classes on 17 January 1816, J.-B. Say wrote:

> I must admit that I do not know of any crime equal to his (Bonaparte's). He is guilty, not only of the evil he has done, but also of spurning the good that was available to him and that has never been as easy for anybody.[41]

---

37 Aulard, *Paris sous le Consulat*, Tome II, pp. 160–161.

38 The cleansing of the *Tribunat* was almost exclusively at the expense of ideologues. Out of the 20 members or allies of the *Decade*, in his monumental thesis, Marc Regaldo quotes the names of Guinguené, Andrieux, Say, Marie-Joseph Chénier, Daunou, Dupuis, Saint Aubin, Ganilh, Desrenaudes, Mailla-Garat, Jacquement, Laromiguiere and Benjamin Constant, p. 470.

39 ASSE E. « Jean-Baptiste Say, *Nouvelle biographie générale*, Tome 81, p. 232.

40 André Tiran, "Notes biographiques sur Jean-Baptiste Say", De Boeck Supérieur | « *Innovations* », 2014/3 n° 45, p. 207.

41 *Ibidem, op. cit.*, p. 208.

He also wrote under the title *Bonaparte's financial infamy*: "The sacred funds of the *Monts de Piété* (charity pawnshops) meant as loans to the poor were taken and replaced by treasury bonds to the amount of 4,400,000 pounds".[42] To conclude on the bitterness he must have felt about his contribution to the establishment of Bonaparte's regime, one can quote this comment: "What is understood as a strong government is no more than a more powerful felony than the others".[43]

11.3 The Extension of the Principle of Utility to Morality and Politics

Was Say a utilitarian? From the viewpoint that concerns us here, we consider two issues simultaneously. The first one is fairly general and addresses the question whether Say can be seen as a man of transition in terms of analysis or whether he definitely belonged to what Michel Foucault called 'the classical age',[44] not in its physiocratic aspect but from that of Condillac, Galiani, Graslin and Destutt de Tracy. The latter chose as a starting point value, what is received, the good seen from the angle of the person who needs it, asks for it and is willing to give up what he owns in order to acquire this other thing which he deems more useful and which he values more. The second issue, the body of this study, dealt with the analysis of the principle of utility and whether extending it to morality and to politics indeed led J.-B. Say to utilitarian philosophy.

These two questions are related in that, using J.-B. Say's manuscripts on *The Principle of Utility*, we eventually demonstrate that although Say

---

[42] *ibidem*

[43] *ibidem*

[44] Foucault Michel, *Les mots et les choses,* éd. Gallimard, Paris 1966, p. 209. Referring to the two currents of value, he writes: "Some ask themselves under what condition - and at what cost - a good can become a value in a trading system, others under what condition an appreciation judgment can be transformed into a price in the same trading system. One can understand why the analyses of the Physiocrats and those of the utilitarians are often so close and sometimes complementary; why Cantillon could be claimed by some - for his theory of the three land incomes and the importance he gives to the earth - and by others - for his analysis of the circuits and the role he makes play to the money; why Turgot could be faithful to Physiocracy in the Formation and distribution of wealth, and very close to Galiani in Value and Money".

belonged to the classical age, he may be seen as one of its last representatives, since his attempt to root morality in enlightened utility may appear with hindsight as an almost desperate construct to contain (in both senses) the forces of self-interest and individual utility by these same forces of self-interest and individual utility but in an enlightened form.

This however is not a neutralization of these forces in a kind of Hobbesian war of all against all nor is it the result of a providential composition of the invisible hand type (Adam Smith). Much less still a 'rational utilitarianism' resulting from a Darwinian selection process, which appeared later in H. Spencer's evolution theories signalling the advent of modernity. It happened simply because judicious (i.e., enlightened) utility was its own limit and thus a strong enough shield, together with justice, against rampant individual interests, permitting society's effective if not harmonious functioning. It appears then that reason and knowledge contain the principle of utility, in the dual sense of including it and reining it in. This is what we aim to show using manuscripts, some of them unpublished, by J.-B. Say.

Utility as the Principle of Individual Morality

In his *Principle of Utility*, Say attempted to extend the reach of economic utility in order to become the foundation of morality. Thus he presented a general theory of judgement based on the useful versus the harmful. This of course was not a pioneering idea and he was probably influenced by J. Bentham, whom he met on 14 December 1814 in Ford Abbey on his journey to England. He visited Brider Will prison and he had obviously read the *Theory of Punishment and Rewards*, published in 1811 (with further editions in 1823 and 1827), which he mentioned several times, together with the 1820 edition of his *Treatise on Civil and Penal Legislation* in *Practical Political Economy*. He also mentioned Chastellux's *On Public Happiness*. Like Bentham, Say attempted to extend the economic model of utility to all of society but he did so as a French disciple of the Enlightenment, hence the question whether he belongs to the utilitarian current. As Say did not define the notion of utility very clearly, he was able to use it extensively in his analysis of morality and politics. It must be noted first that Say did not move away completely from a work as sacrifice theory; indeed, any good for which a person is willing to sacrifice another good or productive service (labour) is useful. "The value of a thing", he wrote "is equal to the sacrifice required to obtain it, provided however that it is sufficiently useful to determine men to make such a sacrifice".[45] For him, utility was everywhere and was always a reward for effort. Utility could thus extend to the entire social field within a vast *Theory of Punishment and Rewards*, an illustration of economic calculations in terms of costs and benefits present in J. Bentham's utilitarianism as well as in all of neo-utilitarian trend from Irving Fisher to Gary Becker.[46]

But does the analysis of J.-B. Say's moral utility allow us to link him to this trend? Several passages in the manuscripts allow us to state that the principle of utility is the foundation of individual morality. If a morality of duty is imposed from outside, it always tends to be re-evaluated in terms of its utility by those concerned. Say quickly shifts from economic to moral and political utility, economics being a moral and political science.

> We have seen that the principle we have named the principle of utility far from contravening the principles of the most stringent morals strictly conforms to them, and that applied to the relations of governments to peoples, or to peoples among themselves, is worthy of the mature human being, of advanced man. If some thought that this was outside the field of Political Economy […], I would like to draw their attention to the fact that the main pursuit of political economy is to examine phenomena related to values, which are mainly based on our tastes, our opinions, our needs as members of family and society—it is in this regard a moral and political science.[47]

[45] *J.-B. Say. Notes et pièces diverses*, vol. VII, T. I : *Manuscrits*, directed by E. Blanc, G. Jacoud, J.-P. Potier, p. 493. *Œuvres complètes de J.-B. Say*, Economica 2018, coordinated by par A. Tiran.

[46] Amartya Sen, Bernard Williams, *Utilitarianism and Beyond*, Cambridge university Press and Maison des sciences de l'homme, Paris, 1982. Becker, Gary S., *A Treatise on the Family*. Cambridge, MA: Harvard University Press, 1981.

[47] *J.-B. Say. Leçons d'économie politique*, vol. IV, directed by G. Jacoud, P. Steiner, pp. 123–124. *Œuvres complètes de J.-B. Say*, Paris, Economica, 2003, edition coordinated by par A. Tiran.

It seems that political science, the science of the useful, is to become the foundation of all science of society. Say's economic notion of utility is very vast. Indeed the 'science of wealth' can extend to anything useful and if utility is not confined to rare goods, then all forms of human action can be viewed from this standpoint. Indeed, Say plainly announces his project in his handwritten notes:

> Write a little work entitled "The Principle of Utility" or simply "On Utility". I would first define utility in its greatest extent, the ability to serve man [...] I would show that in the efforts men expand, all that does not aim for utility is sheer ignorance, unsound interest, lunacy; that bringing men back to the principle of utility means bringing them back to the healthy use of their reason and to their greater happiness. Apply this to Politics, to Political Economy, to all the sciences. Publish this only after my other works. This will be the key, the last word.
>
> In *Political Economy* I look at utility as a fact, the foundation of which I do not examine. In this work I examine the use, the real benefit we get from the goods we use. In *Political Economy,* I examine the value we place on a good. Here I examine whether we are right in placing value on it.[48]

This is very clear and the reference to Bentham quite explicit:

> The principle of utility. The greatest happiness of the greatest number. With the nature of man and things, as it is, the greatest good of the greatest number. All that aims for it complies with the principle of utility.[49]

He points out, however, that "on close scrutiny Bentham calls all the reasons that are not based on the principle of utility sophisms. Try to find out for several different cases if Bentham is indeed right".[50] Yet Say's main pursuit is not exactly Bentham's. He seeks to build a morality on the nature of man and the nature of things as experience and observation discover them.

---

[48] *J.-B. Say. Notes et pièces diverses,* vol VII, T. I : *Manuscrits,* réalisé par E. Blanc, G. Jacoud, J.-P. Potier, p. 172. *Œuvres complètes de J.-B. Say,* edition coordinated by A. Tiran, Paris, Economica, 2018.

[49] *Ibidem,* p. 170. In the manuscript, the second sentence is crossed out.

[50] *Ibidem,* p. 171.

As a matter of fact, he seeks an alternative to the morality of duty based mainly on religious superstitions. Utility is his materialistic tool in the fight against morality stemming from religions, whose foundations often seem random and fanciful to him. This is reminiscent of the Girondin's liberal anticlericalism and the Protestant's iconoclasm. In this connection, he quoted passages from Madame de Stäel's *Corinne, or Italy* on several occasions,[51] wondering at her apology of useless religious pomp:

> I love – she says – the lavish tribute men pay to what promises them neither wealth nor might; I can see selflessness in it and were we to repeat such religious splendours to excess, I love how these extravagant earthly riches are expended for another life; time for eternity; enough care is taken for the economy of human affairs. Oh how I love the useless! the useless, if life is but toil for a paltry gain; but if we are on this earth on our way to heaven, what better thing to do than to elevate our soul so that it will sense the infinite?[52]

His comment is a stark reminder of economic reality:

> However valuable the useless is to reach the infinite, it is no use for living and yet we have to live while we are on our way to heaven; but we can only live thanks to goods that sustain our existence and these goods can only be acquired through the intelligent labour we call industry. If Madame de Staël had not taken care over human affairs or if Mr Necker had not taken care of them with thirty years' diligent work on her behalf, she would have been in a very sorry plight here below, and the whole nation would soon become no less destitute in this life were it to look mainly after the other [life].[53]

Say tried to demonstrate that there is no opposition between honesty and utility, between duty and utility. For him, utility, as long as its effects are considered in time and space (society), contained its own morality in

[51] *Ibidem*, p. 169. See also vol. V, *Œuvres morales et politiques*, directed by E. Blanc, A. Tiran, p. 357, and vol. IV, *Leçons d'économie politique*, directed by G. Jacoud, P. Steiner, pp. 143–144 and 145–146, *Œuvres complètes de J.-B. Say*, edition coordinated by A. Tiran, Paris, Economica, 2003.

[52] *J.-B. Say. Notes et pièces diverses*, vol. VII, T. I : Manuscrits, par E. Blanc, G. Jacoud, J.-P. Potier, p. 169. *Œuvres complètes de J.-B. Say*, edition coordinated by A. Tiran, Paris, Economica, 2018.

[53] *Ibidem*, p. 169.

both senses of the word. It was the only rule according to which we know what we should allow or forbid to our tastes. Freely interpreting a passage from Malthus, he wrote:

> When we say that passions should be subjected to reason, all we really mean is that one has to follow one's passions when they are not harmful and suppress them once they do become harmful. We have no other way of telling good from bad than looking for what is useful and what is harmful.[54]

From Individual Utility to General Utility or from Morality of Utility to Morality of Duty

One can understand that the individual is capable of recognizing what is useful or harmful for himself but how to shift from the notion of individual pursuit of happiness to the imperative of general and social utility? Utilitarianism ensures this compatibility through a system of civil or religious sanctions. But the issue remains unsolved since the obligation for all to strive for the common good through legislation must be derived from individual biases towards personal utility. The principle of *the greatest good for the greatest number* cannot be demonstrated unless one admits, as Sidgwick was to point out, that a 'benevolent spectator' wants general utility. Once again Say worked his way out of this dilemma by showing that it is *useful* to conform to custom and the law and that these are to some extent the residual expression of the collective interests of society's members.

His utilitarianism did not attempt to do away with a prevalent moral code that was not utilitarian as long as its effects were useful to society. The passage from the individual to the collective was not achieved through the war of the interests of all against all, nor through their providential spontaneous convergence, but indeed through the voluntary adherence to a morality of duty. Clearly not any morality of duty, as for Say the principle of duty in itself did not conflict with the principle of utility.

[54] T. R. Malthus, *An Essay on the Principle of Population in two vol., from the third London*, Washington city, Weightman, 1809, vol. II, book IV, chap. IX, pp. 420–425.

Firstly, because the latter had to be used to evaluate the former, any duty that was not deemed useful after its collective evaluation in terms of its useful and harmful effects by enlightened individuals did not endure long. Secondly, because it was informed (i.e., enlightened) utility; thus it compelled us (duty) into consistency over time (not giving up future utility for present utility) and space (ability to evaluate the implications of choices made).

Let us examine these three points.

Utility evaluates the morality of duty. In a state of freedom, what succeeds and endures is that which is useful. The principle of duty is violated when it is arbitrary, which for Say meant that it contravened common sense. Resorting to common sense sounds like a poor argument unless one points out that for Say it meant in agreement with the nature of things. In some respects, Say appears quite close to Hayek's philosophy of law[55]: good institutions were those that in the cultural selection were best adapted and survived as a consequence. However, the morality of duty, quite an important notion in Say's work, could not arise from a spontaneous order. The 'benevolent spectator' who wanted general utility was the enlightened class, and at a deeper level even the reason for science itself, with Political Economy at the forefront.

Indeed economy in the everyday sense of the word is already a collective and individual virtue, which Say was intent on proving with the example of savings. The principle of utility compelled the enlightened mind into foresight through 'temporal consistency'.

> I would like to point out that the more advanced man is, the more capable he is of resisting the lure of the moment and of adjusting his actions according to distant motives. [...] On close scrutiny, one realizes that moral and virtue almost always consist in knowing how to give up a present or forthcoming satisfaction for a greater but distant benefit; which implies the fortitude, the *strength* to resist present temptation, hence the name *virtue*, which, as you know, means *strength*. The same goes for the quality named *economy*. Private economy [...] consists in preserving useful goods.[56]

---

[55] F. Hayek, *Law Legislation and Liberty : Rules and Order* (1973); *The Mirage of Social Justice* (1976); *The Political Order of a Free People* (1979).

[56] *Op. cit.*, Vol. IV, *Leçons d'économie politique*, pp. 123–124.

Utility also forced the enlightened mind into 'spatial' consistency. In a free society, the moral and social order was generated by a more or less conscious construct of *enlightened* people, those who, like men of science, were more far-sighted and could thus gauge the full consequences of a decision. "More or less conscious" because it was ultimately the logic of enlightenment, that is, science, that expressed itself through them. Albeit a liberal, Say had inherited the French Enlightenment's kind of constructivism, a product of the development of science, which obviously did not agree with Hayek's philosophy of spontaneous order. Let us take a closer look at Say's handwritten notes.

Regarding the fact that there is no opposition between a morality of duty and the principle of utility, his stance was clear. He wrote:

> Most of the philosophers who have attacked utility as the best motive (that can be given) for human actions, have set against it the principle of duty, which they deem preferable. But I do not think that those who have supported the principle of utility have ever claimed that man should infringe his duties; but they have maintained that the question is to determine what characterizes the duty of man.[57]

As for the nature of duty, he said:

> Some intend to make duty the principle of our actions; but what does duty consist in? For a devout priest it means remaining chaste. [...] The principle of utility teaches us what the duty of doing that which is useful consists in. Useful to whom? [...] Useful to the one who acts? Yes; but further elaboration is required here.[58]

About the shift from individual to general utility, he adds:

> Does it consist in acting at others' expense? Surely not, for this would entail that which is harmful to somebody. As such it would not be the principle of utility any more since it would, for some of us at least, be the principle of harmfulness.[59]

---

[57] *Op. cit.*, vol. VII, *Notes et pièces diverses*, T. 1 : *Manuscrits*, p. 173.

[58] *Ibidem*, p. 173.

[59] *Ibidem*, p. 173.

In Say's view law and custom, although they did not necessarily uphold everyone's interest, were useful to all and should they have ceased to be, they would not have been followed any longer.

> Here law, or custom, which often lays down the law, steps in and does not allow that which is harmful to others. Other considerations show that it is useful to submit to law and custom. Can I do that which the law permits and is very necessary to me but harmful to others? Here further considerations are required in our reflection. One has to be liked by the other men among whom one is to live [...] In truth, the principle of utility is usually applied because it is based on common sense and on the true interest of society. The principle of duties is often infringed because it is arbitrary, with one demanding duties which are not recognized by another. The principle of utility alone can provide rules to establish what constitutes duty.[60]

It remains for us to show in what way enlightened men were also virtuous in Say's view and how political economy led to virtue. First of all, what is an enlightened man?

> In a few words, by enlightened man I mean a man with enlightened judgment; the more enlightened one is, the better one behaves, for then one has a better grasp of consequences.[61]

> You can see the analogy between economy and virtue, or, rather that economy is a virtue, an effort, the sacrifice of a present well-being with all its allure, for a future, superior and more desirable well-being but which one does not feel as acutely because it is not within reach yet and one has to await it.[62]

> But to resist the lure of the moment, to perceive and to appreciate this remote well-being, this future benefit, one requires self-control, knowledge and judgment; one has to be used to exercising this remarkable tool of human reason. In one word, one has to be an advanced man, rising above the brute inherent in the nature of our being. And please note that this

[60] *Ibidem*, p. 173.

[61] *Op. cit.*, vol. IV, *Leçons d'économie politique*, p. 125.

[62] *Ibidem*, p. 124.

leads us to a result quite opposed to J.J. Rousseau's paradox. This result is that enlightenment fosters virtue.[63]

Say's conclusion regarding Rousseau's posture is clear enough not to require any comment.

11.4 J.-B. Say and the Exercise of Power

At the end of this analysis on Say and the question of power, what conclusion can we draw? The elements of his biography prove that during the ten years of the French Revolution, he pursued political action both as a volunteer in the revolutionary armies and as a political journalist and was elected in the institutions of the consulate. This first phase can be seen as militancy in the traditional sense of the word. His experience allowed him to observe closely the mechanisms associated with the exercise of power, as well as the men who occupy positions of power. The actions and thought of Say are entirely focused on the realization of the Republic. It is the specific framework of the French conception of the Republic and its link with the role of education that are decisive. J.-B. Say was aware[64] of the problems that Republicans faced concerning the question of trade and personal property corrupting the purity of morals and threatening freedom by weakening the love of the public good. He conceived his treatise on political economy as a Republican manual for the formation of mores and the learning of institutions.

Say's *Olbie* (1800) and the first edition of the *Treaty of Political Economy* (1803) were major attempts to provide a modified version of commercial republicanism. Commercial republicanism was conceived as a form of republicanism that gives an important place to market mechanisms. In his view, the development of a competitive market is something that can effectively combat arbitrariness. The market is understood as a mechanism capable of freeing the individual from the arbitrariness of the powerful, that is, the owners.

[63] *Ibidem*, p. 124.
[64] *Ibidem*, p. 124.

When Say separates political economy from politics, the fundamental point is no longer to establish a constitutional republicanism but to transform the nation by introducing Republican ways such as frugality and industry and enlightened self-interest; these had to be coupled with a more egalitarian distribution of wealth in order to fight poverty and create a larger middle class.

The market is understood by the authors of this current as a mechanism capable of freeing the individual from the arbitrariness of the powerful, or the owners. As Say separated political economy from politics, he revealed his loss of faith in Clavière's approach: the basic point was no longer to establish a constitutional republicanism, but rather, to transform the nation by introducing such Republican manners as frugality, industry and enlightened self-interest; these were to be coupled with a more egalitarian distribution of wealth in order to fight poverty and to create a larger middle class.

His deep involvement in the teaching of political economy was directly related to the importance he gave to manners and to the role that political economy could play in order to ameliorate French society from top (the legislators and the administration) to bottom.[65] Far more important was the creation of a Republican political culture based on a blend of commercial ventures with traditionally conceived virtuous manners. Without a cultural transformation, any projected political innovation would be doomed to failure. Implicit in this passage are the other goals of moderate wealth and education for all.

From 1815 onwards, Say significantly changed his position, with the end of the Napoleonic Empire. Without calling into question what he had previously written, he began writing a manuscript entitled *Practical Policy*. In this manuscript, the question is focused on the effectiveness of the action of the various institutions of the state apparatus from the point of view of the general interest. This work is therefore a recognition that the political economy treaty is insufficient to build a republic. The citizens must therefore not only have the Treaty on political economy but also a Treaty on practical policy. Unlike what many commentators may

---

[65] Philippe Steiner, « Republicanism French Revolution: An Intellectual History of Jean-Baptiste Say's Political Economy (review) », *History of Political Economy* 34.4 (2002) pp. 820–821.

have thought, then, there is no radical disconnection between economics and politics. The citizen of the French Republic must have both works in his hands. In the second part of his life, Say argued that it is the action on representations that individuals themselves form and their actions in society that are decisive. To act on representations is to direct the action of men. This is based on scientific knowledge and disseminated through instruction. For J.-B. Say, power must not be handed over to experts or scholars but, instead, must remain in the hands of citizens. These citizens are those of the middle class, that is to say, those who live solely on their talent and their work.

The freedom of the individual is thus inscribed in the political order, but it is not entirely there, which is why Say challenges the conception of Rousseau's general will. The field of action of freedom is also that of economic activity because it is there that man can achieve his happiness. Responsibility is based on the refusal to believe in the mechanical and absolute laws of social life. The topic is at the centre of his vision, thus explaining the importance attached to the entrepreneur's initiative. His faith in the development of reason does not rest on technical and positivist rationality. For Say, the realization of social bonding requires that individuals partially submit to a totality. Yet this totality is beyond the state, and its position does not imply in any way that the constraints of action, structures and institutions are unknown. It is the conception of a structural or institutional individualism. The implementation of the individualistic principle and its consequences in the economic order are in some cases so destructive that they require recourse to the state. This also explains why, at the end of his life, Say sought to define the rules that should govern this state action in society.

Say's analysis leads to the definition of responsible individualism versus irresponsible individualism. He does not believe in the invisible hand, of which there is no reference in the six editions of the Treaty. Nor does he believe in the laws of history as they were stated at the time. He sought greater clarity among his fellow citizens, even if it is not without blindness, about the role that education can play. Every citizen must be aware of the objective constraints to which he will be confronted in his quest for happiness. The development of democracy, of the Republic, cannot be a matter for experts, and if there are scientists, their knowledge must be widely disseminated to all citizens. It is therefore a concept opposed to that of self-sufficient individualism without rules. For Say, what we need is not an exhortation to pure virtue but responsible intelligence and applied humanism. This, of course, is the doctrine of interest.

11.5 Conclusion

From a theoretical point of view, what makes people move, and how are passions and interests regulated? We know the economic response: individuals pursue, independently of one another, their selfish interests, understood as a maximization of their advantage (utility) under the constraint of scarce resources, with the market arbitrating their disputes. We also know Hobbes' answer: men are driven by their selfish interests and only the monopoly of violence of a *Leviathan* state can prevent them from killing each other. The question then is: how is a harmonious and peaceful society possible if men are selfish and more concerned with their private interests than with the public good? Two types of opposing doctrines have developed in response. The first, of a political nature, is that of the Social Contract theorists (from Hobbes to Rousseau). The Hobbesian theory is based on the impossible conciliation of *law* and *freedom*, an antinomy to which liberal political economy would bring another solution, of an economic nature, and whose principal thinker in the eighteenth century would be A. Smith.

J.-B. Say inherited and distinguished himself from these two currents. He inherited the conceptions of an organizing and prescriptive state linked to the French Revolution, of which he was an ardent defender; however, against the Jacobins and against Napoleon, he turned to the political economy inherited from Smith, the only one capable of reconciling law and freedom, under the express condition that the people be enlightened, explaining thus the fundamental role of the state in education, an idea he shared with Condorcet. Say remains a man of Enlightenment, a classic in the sense of Michel Foucault.

References

Amartya, S., & Bernard, W. (1982). *Utilitarianism and Beyond*. Paris: Cambridge university Press and Maison des sciences de l'homme.

Asse, E. « Jean-Baptiste Say », *Nouvelle biographie générale*, Tome 81.

Aulard, Paris sous le Consulat, Tome II, pp. 160–161.

Becker, G. S. (1981). *A Treatise on the Family*. Cambridge, MA: Harvard University Press.

Blanc, E., & Tiran, A. (2003). Introduction, *J.-B. Say. Œuvres Morales et Politiques*, Vol. V, r directed by E. Blanc et A. Tiran, Paris, Economica, pp. 10–42.

Evert, S. (2012, November 21). *Jean–Baptiste Say : Revolutionary, Entrepreneur, Economist*. London: Routledge.

Foucault, M. (1966). *Les mots et les choses*. Paris: Gallimard.

Hayek, F. (1973). *Law, Legislation and Liberty: A New Statement of the Liberal Principles of Justice and Political Economy, Vol. 1. Rules and Order*, 1982. London: Routledge & Kegan Paul Ltd., Reprinted 1993, 1998 by Routledge.

Hayek, F. (1976). *The Mirage of Social Justice*. Chicago: University of Chicago Press.

Hayek, F. (1979). *The Political Order of a Free People*. Chicago: University of Chicago Press.

Malthus, T. R. (1809). *An Essay on the Principle of Population in Two Vol., from the Third London* (Vol. II, Book IV, Chap. IX, pp. 420–425). Washington City: Weightman.

Mercure de France, 16 Pluviôse, an IX (p. 319).

Moravia, S. (1974). *Il pensiero degli idéologues. Scienza e filosofia inFrancia (1780–1815)*. Firenze: La Nuova Italia Editrice, 865 p.

Régaldo, M. (1976). *Un milieu intellectuel : la Décade Philosophique* (1794–1807). Lille III-Paris, Champion, p. 703.

Say, L. (1892). « Jean-Baptiste Say », *Nouveau Dictionnaire de l'Économie Politique*, de Léon Say et Joseph Chailley. Paris: Guillaumin.

Say, J.-B. (1990). *Olbie ou Essai sur les moyens de réformer les mœurs d'une nation*, introduction et notes de J. P. Frick. Nancy: Presses universitaires de Nancy.

Say, J.-B. (2003a). Vol. IV, *Leçons d'économie politique*, réalisé par G. Jacoud, P. Steiner. Paris: Economica.

Say, J.-B. (2003b). Vol. V, *Œuvres morales et politiques*, réalisé par E. Blanc et A. Tiran. Paris: Economica.

Say, J.-B. (2018). Vol. VII : *Notes et pièces diverses,* T. I : *Manuscrits*, réalisé par E. Blanc, G. Jacoud, J.-P. Potier. Paris: Economica.

Say, J.-B., *Œuvres complètes de Jean-Baptiste Say,* coordinated by André Tiran. Paris: Economica.

Schlieben-Lange Brigitte, Knapstein Franz. (1988). « Les Idéologues avant et après Thermidor. » In *: Annales historiques de la Révolution française*, n° 271.

Steiner, P. (2002). Republicanism French Revolution: An Intellectual History of Jean-Baptiste Say's Political Economy (Review). *History of Political Economy, 34*(4), 820–821.

Steiner, P.-H. « Intérêts, Intérêts sinistres et intérêts éclairés : problèmes du libéralisme chez J.-B. Say ». *Cahiers D'économie Politique*, N° 17, pp. 21–40.

Thoisnier Desplaces, A. (1843). « SAY (Jean-Baptiste) » *Biographie universelle ancienne et moderne* (Tome 38, pp. 176–182).

Tiran, A. (1995). « Essai de biographie sur J.B. Say » *in* « Manuscrits inédits sur la monnaie, la banque et la finance précédé d'un Essai de biographie sur J.-B. Say. » : Numéro spécial hors série des *Cahiers monnaie et finance*. Centre de recherche monnaie finance et banque. Now in https://halshs.archives-ouvertes.fr/halshs-00117641

Tiran, A. (2014/3). « Notes biographiques sur Jean-Baptiste Say », De Boeck Supérieur | «*Innovations* », n° 45 | pp. 171–215.

Tiran, A., & Blanc, E. (2003). Introduction. *J.-B. Say. Œuvres Morales et Politiques*, vol. V, réalisé par E. Blanc et A. Tiran, Paris, Economica. *Œuvres complètes de Jean-Baptiste Say,* coordonnées par André Tiran. Paris: Economica.

Verger, F. J. (1832). « Notice sur M. Say », *Annales de la société royale académique de Nantes et de la Loire Inférieure.*

12

Keynes and Eucken on Capitalism and Power

Raphaël Fèvre

This chapter offers a comparison of John M. Keynes (1883–1946) and Walter Eucken (1891–1950) from what can be broadly described as a political economy viewpoint. Apart from a few comments (Karsten 1997, p. 653; Meijer 1994, p. 31; Kolev 2010, p. 15), this comparison appears fairly unexplored. While they never met, nor effectively had occasion to converse, their *rivalry* eventually extended beyond the individual level to embody two post-war economic programmes: namely Keynesianism in Great Britain (and the USA) versus ordoliberalism in West Germany (and later the European Union). Why did their two supposedly "new" liberal ways point at so different—albeit influential—post-World War II programmes? My contention is that elements of the response can be found by considering together theoretical conceptions and national and international contextual points related to the question of power in modern capitalist society.

R. Fèvre (✉)
Centre Walras-Pareto, University of Lausanne, Lausanne, Switzerland

M. Mosca (ed.), *Power in Economic Thought*, Palgrave Studies in the History of Economic Thought, https://doi.org/10.1007/978-3-319-94039-7_12

Keynes probably never knew anything of Eucken's person and works.[1] By contrast, Eucken made several stimulating references to Keynes, although never in a systematic way. This initial viewpoint suggests to some extent a *David* versus *Goliath* comparison, Keynes being, as Bradley Bateman and Roger Backhouse (2013, p. 68) noted, probably the most celebrated and influential economist of the twentieth century, in both the academic and the public sphere. This chapter openly tilts the balance in the direction of Eucken's ideas, these being far less familiar to the general audience.

Walter Eucken was a German economist, head of the Fribourg School of Law and Economics. In spite of his early death, Eucken had a decisive impact on the post-war reconstruction of West Germany, in practical as well as in intellectual terms.[2] Together with Wilhelm Röpke (1899–1960), he is recognized as one of the founding fathers of German ordoliberalism. In the same post-World War II years that saw the Keynesian programme gaining so much ground in the Anglo-Saxon World, at least according to the "stylised history" (Bateman 2006, p. 272), West Germany was forging its own path: the so-called Social Market Economy, grounded on ordoliberal principles (Muresan 2014; Sally 1996; Tribe 2007; Watrin 1979). The chapter investigates to what extent contradictions between *rule-oriented* ordoliberal policies and *discretionary* Keynesian demand management, and more precisely between Eucken and Keynes, can be explained through a common concern they actually shared: a keen attention to the issue of power and its consequences in the modern capitalist society.

The aim of this chapter is twofold. First, to compare John M. Keynes' and Walter Eucken's respective ideas on the issue of economic power. Second, to analyse the consequences this entails on both Keynes' and Eucken's visions of how to manage a market economy. In a nutshell, the chapter shows that if Keynes put his faith in the complementary nature of private and public bodies as a way to reach a balance of interests,

[1] I have found not a single reference to Eucken—who published his first English-language article after Keynes' death—in the *JMK Collected Writings*, or in one of the major biographies on Keynes by Roy Harrod (1951), Donald E. Moggridge (1992) and the tree volumes, later merged in one, by Robert Skidelsky (2005).

[2] For presentations of Eucken's work and his place in ordoliberal thought, see, among others, Heinz Rieter and Matthias Schmolz (1993) and Viktor Vanberg (1998, 2001, pp. 37–52).

Eucken favoured the existence of an independent office in charge of monitoring competitive market structures, disempowering private agents.

12.1 Laissez-Faire Versus State Socialism: A Dead End

Before going on to the substantive differences shown respectively by Keynes' and Eucken's programme or to what extent does Keynes' "middle course" (1944, p. 386) connect and contrast with Eucken's "third way" (1946a, p. 140), I first address their common rejection of both laissez-faire Liberalism and State Socialism.

Actually, to qualify as an exponent of an alternative road—whether "middle" or "third"—it is necessary to identify the two opposite paths departed from, thereby uncovering, beyond their evident contradictions, the deep common ground they had not perceived, and which was indeed the source of their errors. By taking them as the two sides of the same medal, it is then possible to arrive at the *real* alternative, overriding the opposition now shown to have been barren. Thus goes the "third road" rhetoric that ironically enough is possibly the busiest of all roads.

The Bolshevik revolution of October 1917 set a new wind blowing across the countries of Europe: "the world embarked on the competition of economic and political systems" (Klaes 2006, p. 257). The successive hyperinflation of the German economy (1923) and collapse of modern capitalist economies, from the stock exchange to the real economy (1929), left liberal ideals discredited, to say the least. The State gradually started to encroach on market relationships. The rise of authoritarian *régimes* in Italy, Russia or Germany, and then the spread of wartime planning economies in the Western countries brought this trend to its culmination. Capitalism was bound to fail and disappear: Socialism was the *inexorable* new way, Liberalism was obsolete.

Neither Keynes nor Eucken followed this current, later to be retraced from various points of view, most lucidly in Josef A. Schumpeter (1942), Karl Polanyi (1944) or Gunnar Myrdal (1951). Capitalism was indeed facing a sorry end, but it needed to be overhauled rather than simply left behind. Or in Keynes' own words: it needed "improvements in the technique of modern capitalism by the agency of collective action" (Keynes 1926b, pp. 292–293).

Of course, Keynes and Eucken were far from being the only proponents of alternative roads for the post-war period. Important contributions made their way throughout the Western countries, opening out a wide spectrum of "middle" ways, which in fact gained much ground as soon as the political and economic hardships of the 1930s hit home. The book by the British Conservative politician (future prime minister) Harold Macmillan—*The middle way: a study of the problem of economic and social progress in a free and democratic society* (1938)—is a paradigmatic example of discussions arising in Britain about domestic policy, while the political climate of Germany did not leave so much room to expound alternative ways.

In the post-war context, the main issue lay in how best to move on from war to peacetime economies. To cite but a few examples, proposals ranged from what can be termed "planning for competition" solutions (Allais 1948; Jewkes 1948; Rueff 1948; Simons 1948), through the adherents of Keynesian mixed economy (Hansen 1947; Harrod 1947; Meade 1948; Robbins 1947), to the various market socialism solutions (Lange 1949; Lerner 1944; Tinbergen 1947). However, Keynes and Eucken remained outstanding on the strength of their sound historical and philosophical perspectives, with programmes inspired entirely by the need to supersede the barren opposition between laissez-faire and State Socialism.

Tenacious in the "considerable continuity in his attitude toward the role of the state" (Backhouse and Bateman 2009, p. 649), Keynes showed no sympathy towards State Socialism and certainly never saw it as a viable alternative. He would have no truck with the brand of Socialism that "offers no middle course, because it also is sprung from the presuppositions of the era of abundance, just as much as *laissez-faire* individualism and the free play of economic forces (…)" (Keynes 1925, p. 304).[3] For

[3] From Keynes' point of view, State Socialism already looked like an antique relic unable to face contemporary challenges: "it misses—he wrote—the significance of what is actually happening" (1926b, pp. 290–291), a statement reaffirmed much later by underlining that "the Communist doctrine—as he put it to Hayek—is so desperately out-of-date, at least in its application to U.S.A. and Western Europe" (1944, p. 385).

Keynes, the base that both laissez-faire Liberalism and State Socialism shared, consisted in an outmoded interpretation of twentieth-century Capitalism, which failed to perceive what John R. Commons qualified as a new era, a "period of stabilisation" (ibid.). But even if Keynes' criticism of laissez-faire in his celebrated essay (1926b) is more systematic and damaging,[4] it also reflects his closeness to the liberal tradition, his will to improve it from the inside.

In a similar spirit, Eucken endorsed the equivalent equation while considering that "*Capitalism* and *Socialism* are fighting on a doctrinal level; but *de facto* they merge together" (1946b, p. 17, my translation). A remark that he made clear not for an academic audience but in one of the three reports drawn up for the Scientific Advisory Committee of the French zone. Even though somewhat in agreement with Keynes' stance on laissez-faire, Eucken saw himself as a harsher critic. He attributed a twofold importance to the task, because the critique of the economic policies that he held to have been, with laissez-faire rampant, the source of all the present problems, also offered the opportunity to work on a great deal of interesting historical material:

> Keynes' criticism is global and oversimplifies the task. More incisive criticism is possible, and is necessary. It is necessary because it is particularly the economic policy of *laissez-faire*—that formed the basis for the further development of economic policy—which offers an abundance of detailed economic experience. (Eucken 1949, p. 222)

[4] Firstly, Keynes sets apart pure utilitarianism à la Bentham, from the authentic liberal tradition. Secondly, he argued that laissez-faire is more a political ideology spread by publicist or expansionists agents (Keynes scorned Frédéric Bastiat), than a founding component of the discipline, consecrated by its leading exponents (Adam Smith for instance). Thirdly, laissez-faire principles did in fact constitute an efficient doctrine for the ninetieth century, but "have ceased to be applicable to modern conditions" (1925, pp. 300–301).On the one hand, Keynes reduces laissez-faire to two postulates: (1) the Spencerian view of evolution and progress and (2) the money motive as sufficient driving force—or "incentive"—to maximum efficiency (1926b, p. 283). On the other hand, his criticism of the "metaphysical principles" of laissez-faire revolves around three major points: (1) the conception of liberty, (2) the articulation between individual and social levels and (3) the idea that, in some domains, confidence in collective action is more appropriate than individual action.

Like Keynes, Eucken saw the critique of Liberalism as a starting point for re-foundation.[5] He was nevertheless deeply averse to all kind of socialism.

At the conceptual level, he focused on the place of individual *plans* under different kinds of economic systems and offered a penetrating analysis of *Third Reich* economic planning formulas, and of the early post-war period (Eucken 1948d; Eucken and Meyer 1948). Eucken also pointed out a common factor between the centrally administrated economy (*Zentralverwaltungswirtschaft*) and laissez-faire: they both failed to perceive the difference between the "rules of the game" (the economic framework) and the "playing of the game" (the ongoing economic process). In both cases, consumers lost their freedom of choice, and, with it, their ability to direct production towards maximum efficiency:

> "*Less*," say the advocates of laissez-faire; "*more*," cry the central planners. Friends of compromise solution seek a middle way. They would like the state to plan and, at the same time, to give scope for private planning and initiative. But the problem needs to be stated differently if it is to be solved. (1951, p. 95)

In the case of laissez-faire (Eucken 1949, p. 223), the price and quantity of certain commodities are the results of corporate firms, monopolies, trusts or cartels planning,[6] whereas in the case of a centrally administrated economy, price and quantity are the result of a year(s)' plan made by a governmental department. In conclusion, "what experience of *laissez-faire* goes to prove is that the economic *system* cannot be left to organize itself" (Eucken 1951, p. 93). In a sense, Keynes,[7] like Eucken,

---

[5] As from the 1920s, the liberals turned to self-criticism. *Le colloque* Walter-Lippman held in Paris in 1938 is a good example of what is labelled now as the beginnings of the neoliberal stream. If invited, Eucken was unable to obtain authorization to travel abroad (Burgin 2012, pp. 65–67, 70–78). Together with Eucken and the ordo-movement, Wilhelm Röpke offers a detailed reading of the historical liberalism (*historische Liberalismus*) weaknesses (see Fèvre 2015).

[6] While mainly focusing on firms, Eucken warned against all kinds of "interest (or pressure) groups" (*Gruppeninteresse*), which included also "employer associations, trade unions". The "instability of money" facilitated the emergence and exercise of these groups (see Eucken 1949, p. 223).

[7] "[T]he result of filling in the gaps in the classical theory is not to dispose of the 'Manchester System', but to indicate the nature of the environment which the free play of economic forces requires if it is to realise the full potentialities of production" (Keynes 1936a, pp. 378–380).

did not flatly reject laissez-faire as complete nonsense but rather sought to identify the weaknesses that put it out of touch with the contemporary state of affairs. Like Eucken, Keynes too attempted to undermine some of the cornerstones on which Marxist or Socialist criticism was based. In this respect, they fell in line with Overton H. Taylor's—a Harvard economist—pungent observation that "the real economist's utopia is now and forever laissez faire" (1934, p. 187). And they both sought to identify those very specific tasks which fell on the State, "those functions which fall outside the sphere of the individual, those decisions which are made by *no one* if the State does not make them" (Keynes 1926b, p. 291). As the reader might expect, they do not agree at all on the contents of such "functions" and "decisions".

12.2 Keynes' Economic Problem Versus Eucken's Social Question

So far, the international context has served for a better understanding of the major issues which Keynes and Eucken, among others, were faced with. However, the conditioning of the political, economic and social history of the twentieth century, in the UK, on the one hand, and in Germany on the other hand, is decisive in lighting their—often widely divergent—ways. To clarify the crux of the Keynes/Eucken disagreement, we then focus on the final goal each was pursuing: solving the "economic problem" for Keynes, settling the "social question" for Eucken.

In the *General Theory (GT)*, Keynes targeted the "failure to provide full employment" and the "arbitrary and inequitable distribution of wealth and incomes", as the two main economic shortcomings of contemporary societies (1936a, p. 372). It might reasonably be argued that Keynes provided a much more convincing response to the former consideration than to the latter. True, the Liberal Party had long been taking an interest in the distributive problem, most significantly with Lloyd George's path-breaking *people's budget* of 1909–1910 (with unprecedented taxes on the wealthiest), but also thanks to Winston Churchill's influence through the Board of Trade (1906), "Social welfare in Britain was a Liberal innovation" (Tribe 2009, p. 76).

Settling these "economic problem(s)", as Keynes' called it (1930, p. 325, 1936a, p. 378), thus means putting an end to mass unemployment, or, more pragmatically, "securing a rate of employment that was as high and as stable as possible" (Backhouse and Bateman 2012, p. 13).[8] This full employment objective is a crucial key to conciliating social justice with economic efficiency and individual liberty, a balance that Keynes (1926a, p. 311) saw as "the political problem of mankind".

In the USA and UK cases, wartime price control had proved an efficient mechanism for allocation of both goods and jobs (Paesani and Rosselli 2017). Keynes, writing to Hayek, expressed confidence in "the very fact of the economic problem being more on its way to solution than it was a generation ago" (1944, p. 385).

Eucken's view on this matter is drastically different. In order to secure the satisfaction of the needs of the many through the markets, economic power, not unemployment, is at the heart of Eucken's definition of the (new) *Social Question*. One major feature of the "new" *Social Question* is that *all* workers are equally affected: those employed in industry of course, but also the "farmers, craftsmen, merchants and the learned professions" (1948b, p. 269): individuals being affected not just as workers, but—possibly even more damagingly—in the common function they all share in a market economy, as consumers.

German experience since the 1930s convinced Eucken that the absence of unemployment could be compatible with massive shortages of commodities on the markets, and so compatible with "a profoundly antisocial economic order" (1951, p. 66). He concluded that if "full employment can exist together with economic distress", then "full employment should not, in any circumstances, become the only objective of economic policy" (Eucken 1948a, p. 43, see also 1951, p. 65). As early as 1940, Eucken had laid the basis for this position: "[w]hen the

[8] Backhouse and Bateman noted elsewhere (2009, p. 659) that it had not been Keynes' purpose from the outset: it arose in the 1930s when his "emphasis switched from the dangers posed by inflation, international debts, or prolonged expansion, to the threat posed by high unemployment". Earlier works on the *Social Consequences* of inflation (or deflation) provide good examples of the younger Keynes' concerns (1972a, p. 75), still without the rule automatism that gives too much power to the banks, which should not be "vitally concerned" with "modest fluctuations in the value of money" (1972b, p. 152). Nevertheless, Skidelsky (2005, pp. 567–568) also observed that Keynes—even after the *General Theory*—continued to be highly concerned with inflationary pressure.

economy is dominated by a central administration fluctuations take the form of shifts in consumption, not in employment" (1940, p. 261).

The ordoliberal—and thus Eucken's—allergy to Keynesian medicine probably has to do with the unhappy, if not frankly negative (see Hudson 1985, p. 49), reception of the German version of the *GT*, published in the same year as the original text.[9] Prior to the publication of Keynes' *GT* (1936b), Germany had already had its own "anticipators" (Klausinger 1999) or "proto-Keynesians" (Backhaus 1985, 1997), such as Werner Sombart, Wilhelm Lautenbach or the young Wilhelm Röpke and Hans Neisser, which accounts for the similarities between the German economic policies of the 1930s and the general spirit of the Keynesian programme. By the beginning of 1932, the Brüning government was considering to fight recession, deflation and unemployment by means of creating jobs, based on experts' recommendations from the *Braunskommission* Röpke participated in (Fèvre 2018). But this programme did not come under way until Hitler finally reoriented it towards "massive rearmament" on coming to power (Garvy 1975, p. 403; Tooze 2001, p. 170), concurring with Joan Robinson's subsequent observation that "Hitler had already found how to cure unemployment before Keynes had finished explaining why it occurred" (1972, p. 8). Overhasty as it may seem, the connection of Keynesian policies with authoritarian-like tendencies appeared to German liberals all too plausible.[10]

Eucken's concern with the *Social Question* permeates his entire work. Here, he followed the German path, which, from Friedrich List to Karl Marx or the Historical Schools and *Kathedersozialismus*, showed a keen interest in this type of inquiry.[11] Otto *von* Bismarck is credited with having established the first assistance model of a Welfare State,[12] and

[9] In particular, on account of a brief (so-called ambiguous) passage in the German preface, see the article by Schefold (1980) and Hagemann (2014).

[10] Within a broader perspective, the study directed by Peter E. Hall (1989) on *The Political Power of Economic Ideas: Keynesianism across Nations* showed how Western countries' counter cyclical fiscal policies against unemployment came about primarily without any reference to Keynes. Franklin D. Roosevelt's New Deal is an obvious example, but other examples can also be seen in Sweden, France or Italy (see also Bateman 2006, pp. 283–286).

[11] See the works by Erik Grimmer-Solem (2014, p. 89), Heino H. Nau (2000, pp. 508–510) and especially Birger P. Priddat (2004, p. 53).

[12] Notably the establishment of the social security system as from the early 1880s. This was followed by laws on insurance for accidents in the workplace (1884), subsequently addressing invalidity and old age (1889).

economists—first and foremost Gustav *von* Schmoller—as well as social scientists played leading roles in the elaboration of labour legislation (Schefold 2008; Schmidt 2006). Following Carl Menger's path ([1891] 2013), Eucken had once again to demonstrate that liberal principles can favour social progress and welfare better than socialist ones and in what sense.

Eucken explicitly addressed the issue in two articles published in the same year (1948a, 1948b), one actually entitled *Die Soziale Frage*. Two years later, at the invitation of Lionel Robbins and Hayek, Eucken came to London for a series of lectures at the London School of Economics and Political Science (LSE; Vanberg 2001, p. 38). Parts of these LSE lectures, posthumously published as *This Unsuccessful Age* (1951, p. 56–68), also provide noteworthy insights on this issue.

If we bring together Eucken's texts on the *Social Question*, a particular combination between economic freedom and social justice emerges: the notion of power is the key to understand how Eucken tried to resolve their antagonism.[13] Eucken's thesis can be summed up with a quasi-syllogism: in an industrialized economy, the problem of (the concentration of) economic power is "the obverse aspect" of the lack of freedom (1951, p. 40). However, "the problem of freedom in the modern world is very closely connected with control of the economic process" (1948a, p. 37). Consequently, to find a way to settle the *Social Question*, it is necessary to address "the vast problem of regulating economic and social power" (1948b, p. 272). This is the only way to restore freedom,[14] and thus justice, that is, "a functioning and humane order" (1949, p. 219).

[13] Growth or economic efficiency is not a vital concern for Eucken because he saw it as a natural result of this "well-functioning economic and social order" (Eucken and Böhm 1948, p. viii, my translation).

[14] On Eucken's definition of economic liberties: "The development of the framework in which businesses and households can plan and act freely is governed by the economic policy under which the framework is supervised. Businesses are free to choose what they produce, what technology they use, what raw materials they purchase and what markets they wish to sell on. Labourers are not obliged to serve in a particular form of employment either. They enjoy freedom of movement and the right to a free contract of employment. Freedom of the consumer exists, but not the freedom to choose how to define the rules of the game or the forms which the economic process takes" (1949, p. 227).

> Here our analysis of German experience penetrates to the heart of the social problem—freedom. It was lack of freedom that gave rise to frustration. The hegemony of private or public concentrations of power endangered the rule of justice, and lack of security arose from lack of freedom. (Eucken, 1951, p. 64)

The fundamental consequence here is that order takes precedence over freedom, the latter being a result: economic freedom is a conquest that derives from governmental action.[15] The solution to the problem of economic power lies in the social regulation of private powers and the obvious self-restraint on the part of public bodies. From Eucken's standpoint, failure to recognize this issue means, for liberals, failure to achieve the goal of freedom:

> The structure designed to accommodate the sequence of economic events requires continuous governmental supervision and possibly organization in an age of industrialization. But within these commodity and labour markets—in other words, in everyday economic life—there must be freedom. That is the real goal. Without freedom, there can be no solution of the social question. That creates a basic assumption underlying the social organization of working regulations—a precondition which is lacking if the workers on the labour markets are confronted by monopolistic employers or public authorities. (Eucken 1948b, p. 275)

To Eucken's way of thinking, the Keynesian approach had got it all wrong by confusing causes and consequences. Full employment cannot be a primary objective of economic policy, because it is the result—not the cause—of a well-functioning economic order. In Eucken's words: "[s] atisfactory control of the whole process and through this 'full employment'—yes. Full employment alone, by ignoring or mashing the problem of control of the economic system—no" (1948a, p. 45).

As we saw, the approach of Keynes and Eucken calls for active government; their blueprint for the State is *interventionist*. By targeting the issue of unemployment or the question of economic concentration, Keynes and Eucken unsurprisingly led State action on conflicting paths with their new approaches.

---

[15] For comparable readings, see Keith Tribe (1995, p. 212) or Werner Bonefeld (2012, p. 4).

12.3 Interventionist Solutions: "Middle" Versus "Third" Way

In his essay *The End of* laissez-faire, Keynes (1926b, p. 291–292) saw monetary policy, information transparency, population control and, in particular, guidance of investments and savings (*intaglio* of consumption) as belonging to the State *agenda*. Ten years later, his *GT* would provide the theoretical foundations for and a more explicit set of economic policies on the matter of investment/saving orientation to secure full employment. In fact, Keynes praised "a middle course between allowing the free play of market forces and public intervention to prevent waste and distress to consumers and producers" (Fantacci et al. 2012, p. 457). Of particular interest for this study are Keynes'—repeatedly mentioned—"euthanasia of the cumulative oppressive power of the capitalist to exploit the scarcity-value of capital" through cheap money (low interest rate) and "somewhat comprehensive socialisation of investment" (Keynes 1936a, p. 375–376, 379). These two structural policies came to play a prominent role with regard to the issue of "economic power". Coherent with this theme, another major concern of Keynes lay in the impact of the financial sector, with the contemporary tendency that "the speculative ability or power will dominate over business ability in modern capitalism" (Arena 2010, p. 875).

By contrast, Eucken held that the State should secure the appropriate framework to create the conditions for competition, a situation in which agents are price takers, at least at a subjective level. This was the founding principle of the order-based policy (*Ordnungspolitik*) that Eucken was advocating, for "the achievement of general equilibrium requires the establishment of certain market forms and monetary systems; and this is the primary task of economic policy" (1951, p. 68). Spontaneously formed economic orders do not necessarily lead to *complete* competition (*vollständige Konkurrenz*). Thus, a functioning order is by no means a passive task for the State, which must—consistently—intervene on a wide-ranging scale (once again building on concrete experimentation):

> The problem will not solve itself simply by our letting economic systems grow up spontaneously. The history of the last century has shown this

> plainly enough. The economic system has to be consciously shaped. The detailed problems of economic policy, whether of agricultural policy, trade policy, credit, monopoly, or tax policy, or of how the whole economy, national and international, and its rules, are to be shaped. (1940, p. 314)

Critical of the spontaneous conception of modern capitalist development, both Keynes' and Eucken's conceptions of interventionism have to be understood in relation to their conceptions of human behaviour.

For Eucken, the problem lies in the fact that the individual "lust for power" (*Machtstreben*) cannot completely vanish but can at best be minimized through constitutional principles.[16] Eucken's thought reflects a conception of economic agents, on both the demand and the supply side, as a permanent threat hovering over the competitive order, because agents are driven by a rent-seeking behaviour:

> The supplier and the customer always—wherever possible—seek to avoid competition and to acquire or assert monopolistic positions. There is an omnipresent, strong and irrepressible urge to eliminate competition and to acquire a monopolistic position. Everyone espies possibilities of becoming a monopolist. (Eucken, 1949, p. 222)

Eucken remarked that "economists are always in danger of missing the significance of struggles for power (*Machtkampfe*), their fury and brutality" (1940, p. 263). Having witnessed, from the 1920s on, the proliferation of cartels and the merging of economic interests of large companies or trade unions with those of the Reich, Eucken became convinced (see, for instance, 1951, pp. 29–40) of the absolute necessity to address this issue. He devoted his work mainly to this end, seeking to grasp the implications of the issue of power in economic and political terms.

From Keynes' viewpoint, if the driving forces of Capitalism are the "intense appeal to the money-making and money-loving instincts"

[16] This framework, based on fundamental articles of the "economic constitution" (*Wirtschaftsverfassung*), is composed of the criteria of (1) price consistent with complete competition, (2) stability in the value of money, (3) open markets, (4) private property, (5) freedom of contract (with limitations), liability and (6) consistency of economic policy. On Eucken's (1952, pp. 254–303) constitutive and regulative principles, see Grossekettler 1989, 1994 for discussion.

(1926b, p. 293),[17] that failed to satisfy his elitist conception of humankind on—broadly speaking—ethical grounds, the technical problem lay elsewhere:

> [M]any of the greatest economic evils of our time are the fruits of risk, uncertainty, and ignorance. It is because particular individuals, fortunate in situations or in abilities, are able to take advantage of uncertainty and ignorance, and also because for the same reason big business is often a lottery, that great inequalities of wealth come about; and these same factors are also the cause of the unemployment of labour, or the disappointment of reasonable business expectations, and of the impairment of efficiency and production. (Keynes 1926b, p. 291)

Despite Keynes' "realistic and pessimistic view of human nature" (Lagueux 1998, p. 262), the main issue lay in these psychological flaws,[18] of which underinvestments (and so underemployment equilibrium or disequilibrium[19]) are the results. This combination of greed and blindness at the individual level leads to error or conventionality (rational from the agent's point of view), resulting in irrationality on the social scale. This is one of the major justifications for unilateral government intervention in the market process. These views are consistent with Keynes' will to overcome individuals' limitations through collective wisdom, a possibility he did express in *The End of* Laissez-faire.

Clearly, the philosophical conceptions of human nature favoured by Keynes and Eucken do not result in the same stream of ideas. On this specific issue, David R. Andrews showed that "the later Keynes accepted Hume's sceptical conclusion that custom and not reason is the 'guide to life'" (1999, p. 21). It would be necessary to examine to what extent Eucken's conception of the individual "will to power", for instance,

[17] For another illustration, see Keynes (1936a, p. 374). Gilles Dostaler (2007, pp. 163–166), both on his own account and together with Bernard Maris (2009), insisted on the Freudian flavour of Keynes' interpretation of the *auri sacra fames* as a primitive instinct persisting in the age of Capitalism, with all the problems that lead, for example to excessive savings or clinging to the gold standard with more passion than good sense.

[18] Or "socio-psychological attitude" as Anna M. Carabelli and Mario A. Cedrini (2015, p. 14) recently coined it.

[19] On this controversial issue among Keynesians, see Michel de Vroey (2004).

remained along the same lines as thinkers like Karl Marx, Arthur Schopenhauer or Friedrich Nietzsche. However, the influence of past thinkers should, once again, not be attributed with so much weight as the international context: Keynes, like Eucken, facing the rise of big-business Capitalism, was driven to speak out about the spread and impact of economic power in modern society.

For these two doctors at the bedside of Capitalism, one of the challenges was, on the one hand, to reduce power to the minimum possible presence (Eucken 1951, p. 38) and, on the other, to aim at a balance amongst the powers, resting on equal shares of power for the various groups (Keynes 1927, p. 643, 645). To address these scenarios, Keynes and Eucken envisaged "planning" practices to achieve ends that lay beyond the reach of private agents alone (and in particular firms). As the following section explains, they favoured two different solutions. Keynes asked for a planning of investments by middle-range organizations or corporations, that is, collective wisdom working for a better ongoing market economy. While Eucken sought planning the forms of the economic systems, and the existence of a Monopoly office as referee, that is, wisdom of the market enabled by limitation of rent-seeking behaviours under the watchful eyes of a State regulator.

12.4 Managing Power in the Capitalist Society

Keynes saw the rising power of corporations and "joint stock institutions", but this "tendency of big enterprise to socialise itself" entails a possibility to reach a balance (1926b, p. 289). The alternative to struggling with this trend, which "would be useless as well as foolish", was to embrace and direct it: "[o]ur task is to take advantage of it, to turn it into the right channels" (1927, p. 643). Keynes advocated control of power, but without involving the central State, as discussed above.[20] Rather, he

[20] It must be noted that Keynes was never a strong supporter of growth in the size of the State (Backhouse and Bateman 2012, p. 13), and "the creation of intermediate institutions was an assault on laissez faire, but not an endorsement of a state directed economy" (Atkinson and Oleson 1998, p. 1025), not a plea for State Socialism (see Davis 1992).

gave pride of place to intermediate, decentralized and semi-independent institutions, such as the unions (1925, p. 305). So his macroeconomic programme should be implemented alongside structural *meso*-economic encouragement. Keynes' praise of "the socialization of investment" relies on collective wisdom, but within the scope of a liberal government, that is, the level of centralization of decision should be minimal, under the constraint of the adequate regulation of liberal society (1927, p. 643). For instance, playing a part in a corporation helps public authorities to impose social standards for workers' conditions (ibid., p. 646). Keynes saw public/private complementariness as a vital strength (Brittan 2006, p. 185; de Carvalho 2008, p. 209), but within the limits of the classical functioning of competitive markets. Indeed, on microeconomic grounds, Keynes did not seem to offer any serious objections to the classical analysis. In the *GT*, the assumed perfect competition refers to "price-takers'" positions or "zero degree of monopoly", which constitute(s) "the benchmark assumption of Marshallian economics" (Hayes 2008, p. 283). In that respect, Keynes "remained committed to the idea of competitive decentralisation decision-making as the principle of economic organisation" (Witztum 2013, p. 315).

Neither individuals, nor the central State, Keynes was in favour of a corporatist solution (Crotty 1999)—within the boundaries of parliamentary democracy structures (1926b, pp. 288–289, 1927, p. 645). Keynes trusted the capacity of the Parliament to rise above narrow vested interest. Like Pigou (1935, p. 126), he was convinced that "the British Civil Service" and "politicians", while "subject to great pressure", remained staunch in an "unquestionable public spirit" and "are never in this country personally corrupt". The German case is altogether different. In early post-World War I Germany, distrust of parliamentary government in modern mass democracy was widespread, going far beyond Carl Schmidt's influential work (see Kennedy 1988). Eucken progressively changed his mind on this issue, from conservative rejection in the 1920s and 1930s to a more democratic position after World War II. But he remained in any case convinced that the rise of private powers was the most direct threat to democracy, eventually leading to the "surrender" of parliament in favour of "the preponderance of the central administration in economic decisions" (Eucken 1948a, p. 32).

For his part, Eucken understood the problem of "economic power" as a three-way alternative level of control: "control by state central bodies, control by groups, or control by competition" (Eucken 1949, p. 225). The first level corresponded to the State Socialist solution, the second to Keynes' (and possibly parliament democracy), while the last was a solution promoted by Eucken (ordoliberal). To Eucken's mind, "the crucial advantage of a competition-based order, namely that power is so fragmented (*zersplittert*) that it no longer has a harmful effect" (1946a, p. 142) ruled out any other solution. From this viewpoint, the succinct conclusion Irene Oswald-Eucken (Walter Eucken's daughter) came to, that "the order of competition transfers one of the most important political achievements of the European political tradition to the economy: the balance of power" (1994, pp. 40–41), is in some respects misleading, for it is not so much about finding a balance as, rather, about disempowering.

But for Eucken, the competitive solution had nothing in common with a *law of the jungle* state of affairs, at least after the regulation Eucken advocated, constituting an order-based policy (*Ordnungspolitik*). Next to the constitutive principles (defined above), which should minimize the risk of undue acquisition of power, a Monopoly office (*Monopolamt*) was to keep watch over competition, to prevent any "battle for monopoly" by "impediment or injurious competition" and encourage "performance competition" (*Leistungswettbewerb*) in markets (1949, p. 259). This independent organization—"a central figure in the modern, industrialized state [...], just as indispensable as the Supreme Court" (ibid., p. 241)—does so by watching that costs are playing their role of "regulative factor(s)" (ibid., p. 228): "a monopoly office has the task of dissolving avoidable monopolies and supervising unavoidable ones" (ibid., p. 241).[21]

Once Eucken's position is clarified, the line of criticism he took on Keynes' views becomes fairly evident. Encouraging group coordination is tantamount to encouraging the formation of pressure groups, which can

[21] If this particular function will find its way through West German (and later European) politics, it should be noted with Keith Tribe that in 1949, "a Labour government (...) created the Monopolies (and Restrictive Practices) Commission to report on private-sector cartels and monopolistic firms, making it the first government in Europe to introduce legislation directed to the ending of restrictive practices and the promotion of competitive markets" (2009, pp. 76–77).

support monopoly positions, but also bias the legislative framework towards private interests, as opposed to the common good. So in Eucken "anarchy and exploitation"—as John K. Galbraith (1954, p. 1) later outlined the competitive solution—arise not from competition but rather when "the direction of the processes of the economy by 'professions' is not capable of reconciling own interests and common interests, it means group anarchy" (1949, p. 223, 226).

Eucken did not believe that a central administration would contain its own market power (1948a, p. 32), nor had he any confidence in Keynes' corporatist balance of power. Paradoxically, an independent Monopoly office, or a Central Bank, established on the strength of economic power, did not disturb Eucken because "economic power should only exist in a competitive order to the extent necessary to maintain the competitive order" (1949, p. 238). More than a merely technical question (of the marginal cost equalizing market price), the problem of power concerns different kinds of institutional dynamics: like all forms of market structures, market openness—in modern terms "contestability"—*intra* and *extra* business sector interactions, the influence of the unions and associations and the influence of great corporations on the democratic (parliamentary) decision-making process (see Fèvre 2017). Additionally, independent or semi-independent institutions like Central Banks and, of course, the monetary systems themselves are of vital significance when it comes to power relationships.

In his 1949 article on *The Competitive Order and Its Implementation*, Eucken specifically reacted to Keynes' recommendations in *The End of* Laissez-faire:

> [I]t is surprising that Keynes even dared suggest such forms of order [autonomous associations, professions and similar mandatory corporations], which science has long recognized as only achieving a fragile equilibrium of the economy, tending towards disequilibrium. Experience has confirmed this on numerous occasions. If in the coal the mining, the iron, the cement or the potash industries, the trade or the workforce are combined in autonomous groups, group anarchy arises (…). (Eucken 1949, p. 225)

It was in fact far from "surprising" on the part of Keynes, who never believed in the intrinsic stability of the private sector (see Bridel 1987, p. 187) and found the application to it of the concept of "equilibrium" rather puzzling.[22] Eucken's disenchanted experience of German history impeded proper theoretical discussion, even if his conception of "science" here is most likely based on Heinrich *von* Stackelberg's work (1934, p. 26), which demonstrated the vulnerability to shocks or "instability" of partial monopoly and oligopoly market forms.[23]

Eucken's observation quoted above nonetheless remains sound in its own terms, defending a particular framework on the structural level. Indeed, Keynes' solution defined by Eucken as group direction of the economic process, in his words an "anarchical co-existence of groups of monopolists" (1948b, p. 274), did not constitute a stable condition. Ultimately, it would arrive at one of the two *equilibria*: direction by the State or by competition (1949, pp. 225–226).

12.5 Concluding Remarks

On his return from Bretton Woods after so much intensive discussion, Keynes died as the result of a series of heart attacks on April 21, 1946: he was sixty-two years old. While in London for his LSE conferences, Walter Eucken suddenly died of the same disorder on March 20, 1950, at the age of fifty-nine. Neither Keynes nor Eucken were to make it to

[22] Keynes, like Marshall, is "analysing systems in motion: equilibrium was but a point attractor in such a process" (Backhouse and Bateman 2006, p. 12). Eucken proved to be more in line with the Walrasian viewpoint, against the Cambridge tradition. The concept of equilibrium is one of the conflicting (and controversial) issues between our protagonists that are beyond the scope of this chapter.

[23] In his obituary to Stackelberg, Eucken reported that even if initially (1930s) the former "had shown certain sympathies for the [Italian] corporative state", he eventually (1940s) "had come to the conclusion that the competitive order is the only principle by which the economic problems of our time can be solved, but he drew a sharp distinction between the competitive order and a system of laisser-faire, and he was fully aware of the importance of the task of elaborating a suitable legal framework for such a competitive order" (Eucken 1948c, pp. 133–134). Eucken stressed this change as he is credited with having played a key role in his turn away from Nazi (early and) full commitment to a more liberal position (Keppler 1994, p. 25, 172–173). Further evidence for this reading is to be seen in Stackelberg's place as a propagator of ordoliberals' ideas in Spain during his Madrid period from 1944 to 1946 (see Ban 2012; Fuertes 1996).

the second half of the twentieth century, but they were nevertheless destined to play key roles in shaping post-war conceptions of State responsibilities vis-à-vis a (decentralized) market economy for their respective countries, and beyond.

Just like Keynes, Eucken saw the role of the economist as that of a keen observer of the genuine economic situation, anxious about the limited time-frame contingencies. To their rejection of laissez-faire, both economists added, with the same logic, the dismissal of the methods of State Socialism, marking a decidedly forward-looking departure from the ideas then in vogue in Europe. Fundamentally, Eucken and Keynes focused on their own times, casting off from the old philosophies of "defunct economists" (Keynes 1936a, p. 383), who left in their wake in the stream of ideas: "the waves often lap banks long after it has passed from sight" (Eucken 1948b, p. 271). They both claimed to bring new answers in line with current issues.

In a quest to overcome the scarcity of capital and depriving money of its store of value function—which means "the euthanasia of the rentier"—or to neutralize the exercise of power on the formation of market prices, Keynes and Eucken revealed their aspirations to adjust the internal dynamics of Capitalism. Current economic and political institutions were indeed the source of a deleterious power. While Keynes insisted in the unequal access to capital investments, Eucken associated power to monopolistic and oligopolistic positions held by some firms in the market. Liberal interventionism was then required by both Keynes and Eucken. If the former put his faith in complementariness between private and public bodies as a way to reach a balance among interests, the latter favoured the existence of an independent office in charge of monitoring competitive market structures, disempowering private agents.

References

Allais, M. (1948). Le problème de la planification dans une économie collectiviste (2). *Kyklos, 2*(1), 48–71.

Andrews, D. R. (1999). Continuity and Change in Keynes's Thought: The Importance of Hume. *The European Journal of the History of Economic Thought, 6*(1), 1–21.

Arena, R. (2010). Corporate Limited Liability and Cambridge Economics in the Inter-War Period: Robertson, Keynes and Sraffa. *Cambridge Journal of Economics, 34*(5), 869–883.

Atkinson, G., & Oleson, T. (1998). Commons and Keynes: Their Assault on Laissez Faire. *Journal of Economic Issues, 32*(4), 1019–1030.

Backhaus, J. G. (1985 [2009]). Keynesianism in Germany. In T. Lawson & H. Pesaran (Eds.), *Keynes' Economics, Methodological Issues* (pp. 209–253). London/Sydney: Routledge.

Backhaus, J. G. (1997). Keynes' German Contenders 1932–1944: On the Sociology of Multiple Discoveries in Economics. *History of Economic Ideas, 5*(2), 69–84.

Backhouse, R. E., & Bateman, B. W. (2006). A Cunning Purchase: The Life and Work of Mayard Keynes. In R. E. Backhouse & B. W. Bateman (Eds.), *The Cambridge Companion to Keynes* (pp. 1–18). Oxford: Cambridge University Press.

Backhouse, R. E., & Bateman, B. W. (2009). Keynes and Capitalism. *History of Political Economy, 41*(4), 645–671.

Backhouse, R. E., & Bateman, B. W. (2012). Keynes and the Welfare State. *History of Economic Thought and Policy, 1*(1), 7–20.

Backhouse, R. E., & Bateman, B. W. (2013). Inside Out: Keynes's Use of the Public Sphere. *History of Political Economy, 45*(suppl 1), 68–91.

Ban, C. (2012). Heinrich von Stackelberg and the Diffusion of Ordoliberal Economics in Franco's Spain. *History of Economic Ideas, XX*(3), 137–157.

Bateman, B. W. (2006). Keynes and Keynesianism. In R. E. Backhouse & B. W. Bateman (Eds.), *The Cambridge Companion to Keynes* (pp. 271–290). Cambridge: Cambridge University Press.

Bonefeld, W. (2012). Freedom and the Strong State: On German Ordoliberalism. *New Political Economy, 17*(5), 1–24.

Bridel, P. (1987). *Cambridge Monetary Thought: The Development of Saving-Investment Analysis from Marshall to Keynes*. London: Macmillan.

Brittan, S. (2006). Keynes's Political Philosophy. In R. Backhouse & B. W. Bateman (Eds.), *The Cambridge Companion to Keynes* (pp. 180–198). Oxford: Cambridge University Press.

Burgin, A. (2012). *The Great Persuasion: Reinventing Free Markets Since the Depression*. Cambridge, MA: Harvard University Press.

Carabelli, A. M., & Cedrini, M. A. (2015). On "Fear of Goods" in Keynes's Thought. *The European Journal of the History of Economic Thought*, (Published online), 1–34.

Crotty, J. (1999). Was Keynes a Corporatist? Keynes's Radical Views on Industrial Policy and Macro Policy in the 1920s. *Journal of Economic Issues, 33*(3), 555–577.

Davis, J. B. (1992). Keynes on the Socialization of Investment. *International Journal of Social Economics, 19*(10/11/12), 150–163.

de Carvalho, F. J. C. (2008). Keynes and the Reform of the Capitalist Social Order. *Journal of Post Keynesian Economics, 31*(2), 191–211.

De Vroey, M. (2004). *Involuntary Unemployment: The Elusive Quest for a Theory.* London: Routledge.

Dostaler, G. (2007). *Keynes and His Battles.* Cheltenham/Northampton: Edward Elgar Publishing.

Dostaler, G., & Maris, B. (2009). *Capitalisme et pulsion de mort.* Paris: Albin Michel.

Eucken, W. (1940). *Die Grundlagen der Nationalökonomie / The Foundations of Economics.* (T. W. Hutchison, Trans.). London-Edinburgh-Glasgow: W. Hodge, 1950.

Eucken, W. (1946a). Letter to Professor F. A. Hayek, March 12 - HIA FAH Papers, Box 18, Fo. 40. (reproduced and translated from original German). In R. Leeson (Ed.), S. Saou (Trans.), *Hayek: A Collaborative Biography: Part 1 Influences from Mises to Bartley* (pp. 138–143). Hampshire: Palgrave Macmillan, 2013.

Eucken, W. (1946b [1999]). Über die Gesamtrichtung der Wirtschaftspolitik / Propos sur l'orientation générale de la politique économique. In W. Oswalt (Ed.), *Ordnungspolitik* (pp. 1–24). Münster, Allemagne: LIT Verlag.

Eucken, W. (1948a). Das ordnungspolitische Problem / What Kind of Economic and Social System? In A. Peacock & H. Willgerodt (Eds.), *Germany's Social Market Economy: Origins and Evolution [1989]* (pp. 27–45). London: Macmillan for the Trade Policy Research Centre.

Eucken, W. (1948b). Die Soziale Frage / The Social Question. In H. F. Wünsche (Ed.), D. Rutter (Trans.), *Standard Texts on the Social Market Economy: Two Centuries of Discussion* (pp. 267–276). Stuttgart: Gustav Fischer Verlag, 1982.

Eucken, W. (1948c). Obituary: Heinrich von Stackelberg (1905–1946). *The Economic Journal, 58*(229), 132–136.

Eucken, W. (1948d). On the Theory of the Centrally Administered Economy: An Analysis of the German Experiment. (Part I & II). *Economica, 15*(58, 59), 79–100, 173–193.

Eucken, W. (1949). The Competitive Order and Its Implementation. *Reprinted in Competition Policy International [2006], 2*(2), 219–245.

Eucken, W. (1951). *This Unsuccessful Age: or the Pains of Economic Progress.* London-Edinburgh-Glasgow: W. Hodge.
Eucken, W. (1952 [2004]). *Grundsätze der Wirtschaftspolitik / Principes de politique économique.* (E. Eucken & K. P. Hensel, Eds.) (7th ed.). Tübingen: Mohr Siebeck.
Eucken, W., & Böhm, F. (Eds.). (1948). Vorwort - Die Aufgabe des Jahrbuchs. *ORDO: Jahrbuch Für Die Ordnung von Wirtschaft Und Gesellschaft, 1,* VII–VXI.
Eucken, W., & Meyer, F. W. (1948). The Economic Situation in Germany. *Annals of the American Academy of Political and Social Science, 260,* 53–62.
Fantacci, L., Marcuzzo, M. C., Rosselli, A., & Sanfilippo, E. (2012). Speculation and Buffer Stocks: The Legacy of Keynes and Kahn. *The European Journal of the History of Economic Thought, 19*(3), 453–473.
Fèvre, R. (2015). Du libéralisme historique à la crise sociale du XXe siècle: la lecture de Wilhelm Röpke. *Revue économique, 66*(5), 901–932.
Fèvre, R. (2017). Le marché sans pouvoir: au cœur du discours ordolibéral. *Revue d'économie politique, 127*(1), 119–151.
Fèvre, R. (2018). Was Röpke really a *proto*-Keynesian? In P. Commun & S. Kolev (Eds.), *Wilhelm Röpke: A Liberal Political Economist and Conservative Social Philosopher* (pp. 109–120). Springer.
Fuertes, J. V. (1996). Stackelberg and His Role in the Change in Spanish Economic Policy. *Journal of Economic Studies, 23*(5/6), 128–140.
Galbraith, J. K. (1954). Countervailing Power. *The American Economic Review, 44*(2), 1–6.
Garvy, G. (1975). Keynes and the Economic Activists of Pre-Hitler Germany. *Journal of Political Economy, 83*(2), 391–405.
Grimmer-Solem, E. (2014). From Sciences of State to Modern Economics. In V. Barnett (Ed.), *Routledge Handbook of the History of Global Economic Thought* (pp. 86–94). London/New York: Routledge.
Grossekettler, H. G. (1989). On Designing an Economic Order. The Contributions of the Freiburg School. In D. A. Walker (Ed.), *Twentieth-Century Economic Thought* (Vol. II, pp. 38–84). Aldershot Brookfield (Vt.): Elgar.
Grossekettler, H. G. (1994). On Designing an Institutional Infrastructure for Economies: The Freiburg Legacy After 50 Years. *Journal of Economic Studies, 21*(4), 9–24.
Hagemann, H. (2014). The German Edition of Keynes's General Theory: Controversies on the Preface. *Research in the History of Economic Thought and Methodology, 32,* 159–166.

Hall, P. A. (Ed.). (1989). *The Political Power of Economic Ideas: Keynesianism Across Nations*. Princeton: Princeton University Press.
Hansen, A. H. (1947). *Economic Policy and Full Employment*. New York: McGraw-Hill Book Company.
Harrod, R. F. (1947). *Are These Hardships Necessary?* London: R. Hart-Davis.
Harrod, R. F. (1951). *The Life of John Maynard Keynes*. London: Macmillan.
Hayes, M. G. (2008). Keynes's Degree of Competition. *European Journal of the History of Economic Thought, 15*(2), 275–291.
Hudson, M. (1985). German Economists and the Depression of 1929–1933. *History of Political Economy, 17*(1), 35–50.
Jewkes, J. (1948). *Ordeal by Planning*. London: Macmillan.
Karsten, S. G. (1997). A Perspective on US and German Socioeconomic Policies. *International Journal of Social Economics, 24*(6), 652–665.
Kennedy, E. L. (1988). Introduction: Carl Schmitt's Parlamentarismus in Its Historical Context. In C. Schmitt, E. L. Kennedy (Trans.), *The Crisis of Parliamentary Democracy* (pp. xiii–xlix). Cambridge, MA: MIT Press.
Keppler, J. H. (1994). *Monopolistic Competition Theory: Origins, Results, and Implications*. Baltimore/London: The Johns Hopkins University Press.
Keynes, J. M. (1925 [1972]). Am I a liberal? In D. E. Moggridge (Ed.), *Essays in Persuasion [The Collected Writings of John Maynard Keynes-IX]* (pp. 295–306). London/Basingstoke: Macmillan.
Keynes, J. M. (1926a [1972]). Liberalism and Labour. In D. E. Moggridge (Ed.), *Essays in Persuasion [The Collected Writings of John Maynard Keynes-IX]* (pp. 307–311). London/Basingstoke: Macmillan.
Keynes, J. M. (1926b [1972]). The End of Laissez-Faire. In D. E. Moggridge (Ed.), *Essays in Persuasion [The Collected Writings of John Maynard Keynes-IX]* (pp. 272–294). London/Basingstoke: Macmillan.
Keynes, J. M. (1927 [1981]). Industry, Economy, Currency and Trade. In D. E. Moggridge (Ed.), *Activities 1922–1929 [The Collected Writings of John Maynard Keynes-XIX]* (Vol. 2, pp. 638–760). London/Basingstoke: Macmillan.
Keynes, J. M. (1930 [1972]). Economic Possibilities for our Grandchildren. In D. E. Moggridge (Ed.), *Essays in Persuasion [The Collected Writings of John Maynard Keynes-IX]* (pp. 321–332). London/Basingstoke: Macmillan.
Keynes, J. M. (1936a [1973]). Concluding Notes on the Social Philosophy Towards Which the General Theory Might Lead. In D. E. Moggridge (Ed.), *The General Theory [The Collected Writings of John Maynard Keynes-VII]* (pp. 372–384). London/Basingstoke: Macmillan.

Keynes, J. M. (1936b [1973]). *The General Theory [The Collected Writings of John Maynard Keynes-VII]*. London/Basingstoke: Macmillan.

Keynes, J. M. (1944 [1980]). Letter to Professor F. A. Hayek, June 28. In D. E. Moggridge (Ed.), *Activities 1940–1946 [The Collected Writings of John Maynard Keynes-XXVII]* (pp. 385–388). London/Basingstoke: Macmillan.

Keynes, J. M. (1972a). Social Consequences of Changes in the Value of Money. In D. E. Moggridge (Ed.), *Essays in Persuasion [The Collected Writings of John Maynard Keynes-IX]* (pp. 59–75). London/Basingstoke: Macmillan.

Keynes, J. M. (1972b). The Consequences to the Banks of the Collapse of Money Values. In D. E. Moggridge (Ed.), *Essays in Persuasion [The Collected Writings of John Maynard Keynes-IX]* (pp. 150–158). London/Basingstoke: Macmillan.

Klaes, M. (2006). Keynes Between Modernism and Post-Modernism. In R. Backhouse & B. W. Bateman (Eds.), *The Cambridge Companion to Keynes* (pp. 257–270). Oxford: Cambridge University Press.

Klausinger, H. (1999). German Anticipations of the Keynesian Revolution?: The Case of Lautenbach, Neisser and Röpke. *The European Journal of the History of Economic Thought, 6*(3), 378–403.

Kolev, S. (2010). Hayek as an Ordo-Liberal. *HWWI Research Paper, 5–11*, 1–22.

Lagueux, M. (1998). Was Keynes a Liberal and an Individualist? Or Keynes Reader of Mandeville. *Cahiers D'économie Politique, 30*(1), 255–263.

Lange, O. (1949). The Practice of Economic Planning and The Optimum Allocation of Resources. *Econometrica, 17*, 166–171.

Lerner, A. P. (1944). *The Economics of Control: Principles of Welfare Economics*. New York: Macmillan, 1964.

Macmillan, H. (1938). *The Middle Way: A Study of the Problem of Economic and Social Progress in a Free and Democratic Society*. London: Macmillan.

Meade, J. E. (1948). *Planning and the Price Mechanism: The Liberal-Socialist Solution*. London: G. Allen and Unwin.

Meijer, G. (1994). Walter Eucken's Contribution to Economics in an International Perspective. *Journal of Economic Studies, 21*(4), 25–37.

Menger, C. (2013). Les théories sociales de l'économie nationale classique et la politique économique moderne [1891]. *Cahiers Philosophiques, n° 133*(2), 106–117.

Moggridge, D. E. (1992). *Maynard Keynes: An Economist's Biography*. London/New York: Routledge.

Muresan, S. S. (2014). *Social Market Economy*. Bonn: Springer.

Myrdal, G. (1951). The Trend Towards Economic Planning. *The Manchester School, 19*(1), 1–42.
Nau, H. H. (2000). Gustav Schmoller's Historico-Ethical Political Economy: Ethics, Politics and Economics in the Younger German Historical School, 1860–1917. *European Journal of the History of Economic Thought, 7*(4), 507–531.
Oswalt-Eucken, I. (1994). Freedom and Economic Power: Neglected Aspects of Walter Eucken's Work. *Journal of Economic Studies, 21*(4), 38–45.
Paesani, P., & Rosselli, A. (2017). The wartime economy and the theory of price controls. In Y. Ikeda & A. Rosselli (Eds.), *War in the History of Economic Thought: Economists and the Question of War* (pp. 198–217). London: Routledge.
Pigou, A. C. (1935). State Action and Laisser-faire. In *Economics in Practice* (pp. 107–128). London: Macmillan and co.
Polanyi, K. (1944). *The Great Transformation*. New York/Toronto: Rinehart.
Priddat, B. P. (2004). Gustav Schmoller: l'économie comme moralité institutionnalisée. In H. Bruhns (Ed.), F. Laroche (Trans.), *Histoire et économie politique en Allemagne de Gustav Schmoller à Max Weber: nouvelles perspectives sur l'école historique de l'économie* (pp. 53–74). Paris: Éditions de la Maison des sciences de l'homme.
Rieter, H., & Schmolz, M. (1993). The Ideas of German Ordoliberalism 1938–45: Pointing the Way to a New Economic Order. *European Journal of the History of Economic Thought, 1*(1), 87–114.
Robbins, L. (1947). *The Economic Problem in Peace and War: Some Reflections on Objectives and Mechanisms*. London: Macmillan.
Robinson, J. (1972). The Second Crisis of Economic Theory. *The American Economic Review, 62*(1/2), 1–10.
Rueff, J. (1948). The Case for the Free Market. *Foreign Affairs, 26*(3), 528–541.
Sally, R. (1996). Ordoliberalism and the Social Market: Classical Political Economy from Germany. *New Political Economy, 1*(2), 233–258.
Schefold, B. (1980). The General Theory for a Totalitarian State? A Note on Keynes's Preface to the German Edition of 1936. *Cambridge Journal of Economics, 4*(2), 175–176.
Schefold, B. (2008). Schmoller, Gustav von (1838–1917). In S. N. Durlauf & L. E. Blume (Eds.), *The New Palgrave Dictionary of Economics* (2nd ed., pp. 303–304). Basingstoke: Nature Publishing Group.
Schmidt, K.-H. (2006). Long-term Views of the "Social Question" in Germany During the 19th and 20th Century. *Journal of Economic Studies, 33*(4), 269–283.

Schumpeter, J. A. (1942). *Capitalism, Socialism, and Democracy*. New York/ London: Harper.
Simons, H. C. (1948). *Economic Policy for a Free Society*. Chicago: The University of Chicago Press.
Skidelsky, R. J. A. (2005). *John Maynard Keynes, 1883–1946: Economist, Philosopher, Statesman*. New York: Penguin Books.
Stackelberg, H. F. von. (1934 [2010]). *Marktform und gleichgewicht / Market Structure and Equilibrium*. Heidelberg: Springer.
Taylor, O. H. (1934). Economics Versus Politics. In *Economics of the Recovery Program* (pp. 160–188). York: The McGraw-Hill Book Company.
Tinbergen, J. (1947). Central Planning in the Netherlands. *The Review of Economic Studies, 15*(2), 70–77.
Tooze, J. A. (2001). *Statistics and the German state, 1900–1945: The Making of Modern Economic Knowledge*. Cambridge [etc.]: Cambridge University Press.
Tribe, K. (1995). *Strategies of Economic Order: German Economic Discourse, 1750–1950*. Cambridge/New York [etc.]: Cambridge University Press.
Tribe, K. (2007). Ordoliberalism and the Social Market Economy. *History of Economic Thought, 49*(1), 155–160.
Tribe, K. (2009). Liberalism and Neoliberalism in Britain, 1930–1980. In P. Mirowski & D. Plehwe (Eds.), *The Road from Mont Pèlerin: The Making of the Neoliberal Thought Collective* (pp. 68–97). Cambridge, MA/London: Harvard University Press.
Vanberg, V. (1998). Freiburg School of Law and Economics. In P. Newman (Ed.), *The New Palgrave Dictionary of Economics and the Law* (Vol. 2, pp. 172–179). London: Macmillan.
Vanberg, V. (2001). *The Constitution of Markets: Essays in Political Economy*. London: Routledge.
Watrin, C. (1979). The Principles of the Social Market Economy — Its Origins and Early History. *Zeitschrift Für Die Gesamte Staatswissenschaft / Journal of Institutional and Theoretical Economics, 135*(3), 405–425.
Witztum, A. (2013). Keynes's Misguided Revolution. *OEconomia, 3*(2), 287–318.

13

Power and Economics in Italy: From the Social Conflicts of the 1970s to the Euro-Crisis

Piero Bini

13.1 Introduction

It is generally held that economists leave little room for the analysis of power, apart from the power associated with the dominant firms in the market. However, while power was to remain off-limits for mainstream economists, it has never ceased to continue to attract, and challenge, the "peripheral" economists (Cf. Bartlett 1989, p. 3).

With this research dedicated to the case of Italy, we set out to verify whether a history-of-economic-thought approach, given its tendency to cross historical data with theoretical developments, may offer some useful pointers to exit from this zero-sum confrontation between those who hold that power can be kept out of economic analysis, and those who

I wish to thank Carlo Cristiano, Manuela Mosca, Claudia Rotondi and Luca Sandonà for kindly commenting on a previous version of this text. Any errors or omissions are of course my sole responsibility.

P. Bini (✉)
School of Economics and Management, University of Florence, Florence, Italy
e-mail: piero.bini@unifi.it

M. Mosca (ed.), *Power in Economic Thought*, Palgrave Studies in the History of Economic Thought, https://doi.org/10.1007/978-3-319-94039-7_13

consider power itself an economic phenomenon, albeit appearing under another guise.

Our chapter on this verification affords occasion to observe how manifestations of power generate conflict and change. And we see how the outcome of these dynamics also affects the type and intensity of the economic counterforces that these manifestations of power trigger into action. In short, power in the economy shows not one face but two, as in a dialectical process. This is an issue that has not received very much attention in the history of economic thought. Outstanding among the studies offering some contribution on the subject is the work by E. Böhm-Bawerk (1914), according to which power does not act beyond or against the laws of economics but through them. Any manifestations of power (e.g., high wage claims asserted with prolonged strikes) that lacked the support of the laws of economics would be short-lived. Albeit taking a very different scientific approach, John K. Galbraith (1957) also sees the dynamics of power as tending to come into coordination with the economy. In fact, he argues that when power takes on a particular form—as, for instance, an oligopoly on the supply side—it will endogenously generate countervailing powers—such as a new bloc of buyers, for instance—able to promote the public well-being.[1]

As we see, this optimistic viewpoint taken by the two great economists finds no particular confirmation in our study, which aims to argue out the issue of power in relation to economy and economics as experienced in Italy from 1970 to 2014.

We develop our argument along two different levels of analysis. The first is a matter of ideas, and it concerns the lines of research followed by Italian economists in the period under consideration. Here the questions we seek to answer are: what representations of power emerge from their studies and what social and institutional power management technology did these studies implement? The second level of analysis concerns the realities, and the significant question is: what role have power relations played in determining economic policy decisions and the (frequently

[1] Among the various criticisms to this position, see in particular Stigler (1954).

unsatisfactory) macroeconomic outcomes for the Italian economy in the same period?[2]

In pursuit of some answers to the questions set above, we have divided the period 1970–2014 into three main sub-periods. The first covers the 1970s, which saw considerable social conflict in Italy. Under the influence of a composite scientific programme of political economy to which Sraffian, Keynesian and Marxian theoretical approaches very much contributed, the most significant manifestation of emerging power came from the working class. The next period covers the 1980s, which saw an abnormal increase in Italy's public debt. Meanwhile, in the field of economic studies, the principle of time inconsistency and the theory of rational expectations paved the way for the emerging power of the Central Bank. The third period spans the 1990s and 2000s, when the power of the Maastricht rules made itself felt. The first decade saw Italy joining the Eurozone under the aegis of the rising international influence of freely shifting capital flows. The second decade witnessed the outbreak of the Great Recession and signs of the Euro-Italy crisis. As for the scientific debate, Italian economists embarked upon critical research into the theory of optimal currency areas, the paradigm of varieties of capitalism and the doctrine of economic austerity.

These three broad sub-periods are surveyed in as many corresponding sections. In the conclusion we see how these sub-periods tie together.

13.2 Power and Economics in Italy in the Years of Social Conflict

The 1970s constituted a complex, at times dramatic decade in Italy. Following the collapse of the international payment system based on the dollar (1971) and the sudden rise in international oil prices (1973), the Italian economy was severely shaken, deviating from its growth trend. Negative effects ensued at the level of unemployment, inflation and public finance.

---

[2] That these were the questions we chose to raise and, indeed, the very way we chose to formulate them may be seen as bearing out the increasing influence exerted by the work by Michel Foucault (2008) on the subject of the reciprocal influence between power and the economic sphere.

In political terms, it was a decade of striking electoral success for the Italian Communist Party (PCI) and the proliferation of left-wing ideas. As in many other countries in the West at the time, in Italy, too, generational antagonism and the protests of student movements became alarmingly conflictive. In the field of industrial relations, the 1970s began in Italy with the so-called hot autumn of 1969, heralding the dawn of a long season of strikes, social conflict and wage demands that surged to a peak in 1975.

These new political and social winds were also keenly felt by the Italian economists, many of whom advanced radical criticism of various aspects of neoclassical economics and favoured greater state intervention in the economy, also supporting some forms of planning. At the same time, most of them sympathised with the programme the workers were fighting for and undertook to support it scientifically with studies developing along three theoretical approaches: Sraffian, post-Keynesian and Marxian.[3]

We begin with Sraffa. With reference to his major work (Sraffa 1960), some Italian economists stressed the logical groundlessness of the neoclassical aggregate production function, which was negated by the circular relationship between the measurement of the total capital value and its relative rate of return. As a result, they argued, the theory of distribution based on the marginal productivity of the productive factors was also to be abandoned, and with it—since it was recognised as lacking in consistency—the proposition affirming an inverse relationship between real wage rate and the level of employment.[4] The general implication of this proposition was that no endogenous equilibrating mechanisms of distributive variables exist, and also that this theoretical system has—as they were beginning to say—a degree of freedom that neoclassical theory lacked. For "closure" of the model, resort should have been made to a broad menu of elements drawn from political choices or institutions or,

[3] It is beyond the scope of this relatively concise chapter to provide detailed information on the Italian economists of the period. Those interested in a more exhaustive review of this argument are referred to Bini (2013).

[4] See, for instance, Spaventa (1974). For a broad outline of Sraffa's contribution, see Roncaglia (2005: 435–466).

for instance, the collective bargaining power of the trade unions. As Ezio Tarantelli observed:

> The most widely accepted theory of income distribution, at least in Italy, is without doubt the one advanced by Sraffa. (…) This theory has represented a "liberating bath" for all those economists who believe, and to my mind rightly so, that the distribution of income between wages and profits is a question of relative power between the two (or more) income classes, and not a variable that can be determined solely on technological grounds (Tarantelli 1988 [1979]: 863).

In this quotation a power-based approach to wage theory clearly emerges.

In the same period, other Italian economists, taking a post-Keynesian approach, distanced themselves from the neoclassical synthesis. First of all, they needed to extend the principle of effective demand to the analysis of accumulation and growth. Their representation of the investment function was characterised by highly volatile entrepreneurial expectations capable of preventing the attainment of full employment both in the short and in the long term.[5] In order to counteract the instability of the investments, they suggested many types of public intervention in the economy to sustain the aggregate demand and achieve a process of authentic socialisation of investments.[6] Furthermore, they rejected the income policy based on the criterion of proportionality between labour productivity and wages, seeing it as a sort of pseudo-scientific legitimisation of a *conservative* type of long-term income distribution. In short, they traced out a dynamic picture of the economy which highlighted the macroeconomic failures of the market and the need for them to be remedied by delegating strong powers to the public authorities, all the better if implemented on a basis of systematic planning.

Finally, we must consider Marxian economic thought, upheld at the time by numerous authors in Italy who were, however, divided when it came to Sraffian economics. Some pointed out the non-historical nature

---

[5] See, for instance, Izzo et al. (1973).

[6] In particular, the need to involve the public enterprise system was vigorously argued by Graziani (1969).

of the latter and the departure from Marx lying in failing to deal with the issues of labour exploitation and the supersedence of capitalism.[7] Conversely, there were other Marxist-oriented economists[8] who expressed appreciation of, on the one hand, Sraffa's demonstration of logical inconsistency of the marginalist theory of distribution and, on the other hand, his positive approach accrediting once again the classical notion of surplus and the conflicting relationship between wages and profits.

In short: between the late 1960s and early 1970s, a sort of spurious doctrinaire alliance among various scholars was formed that extended from the strictly Sraffian to the post-Keynesian economists who did not subscribe to the neoclassical synthesis, as well as including a fair number of Marxian economists. This alliance was fostered by the idea that, first, by bringing together the above-mentioned theoretical streams of thought it was possible to obtain a new paradigm and, second, that this would afford scientific support for an alternative social and institutional system or in any case one that differed from market economy capitalism. We have chosen the term "conflict paradigm" to christen this complex research programme.

With regard to the power issue in particular, the three (heterodox) approaches of economics described above, albeit differing in many respects, show some common features. First of all, for them power is not only a sociological or political phenomenon but may at times constitute an input, or at other times an output, of their theoretical construction. Specifically, in the case of Marx, power is the essential inner core of the theory of value and the driving force within the processes of exploitation. In the case of Sraffa's economics, it emerges as uneliminable residue in the pure theory of distribution. In the case of the post-Keynesians, it appears in the form of a particular top-down regulation of the economy on the part of public authorities, and is deemed above all essential to ensure economic growth. Second, it is surely significant that the Italian economists contributing to the three research approaches supported patterns of

---

[7] We refer here to economists such as Domenico Mario Nuti, Claudio Napoleoni, Guido Carandini and indeed many more. For various internal developments in the Marxist debate in Italy at the time, see Gattei (1981).

[8] Among these scholars we may mention Pierangelo Garegnani, Andrea Ginzburg, Ferdinando Vianello and Sebastiano Brusco.

power relations more favourable to the workers and, at the same time, able to bring about a mixed economy or even supersede market economy capitalism. It was undoubtedly a leftward leaning school of economic thought. As a third consideration, the three lines of research entailed challenges to various aspects of the mainstream theoretical models, such as the IS/LM model or the above-mentioned relation between wage rate and labour productivity. The need was to shake off their intellectual influence, considered a form of social power, or even to abandon equilibrium analysis itself, suspected of resting on an authoritarian assumption.[9] Thus these economists sought to propose alternative regulatory tools and strategies, such as protectionist policies and import substitution, in order to achieve a greater degree of compatibility between wage rises and external constraints.[10]

As for the balance of power in the Italian labour market of the 1970s, the following data refer to the average annual percentage increases in productivity and the nominal and real wages per capita in the years 1968–1975.

	Nominal wages	Real wages[a]	Productivity[b]
1968–69	6.8	4.8	5.9
1970	19.9	15.0	6.2
1971–72	10.9	5.6	3.8
1973–75	22.7	7.1	2.4

[a]Deflated by the real changes in consumer prices
[b]Value added per employee
Table contained in Rossi (2007): 9. Source: Prometeia and Istat

These data illustrate a "reverse income policy". As the workers' power increased, the link between rises in wages and productivity was shattered. In the system of scientific synergies that came to form around what we have called the "conflict paradigm", a special role was played by debate on the wage rate as an "independent variable". This concept took on the significance of an instrumental magnitude for accelerating the change of the ruling class of the country and heightening contradictions in the market economy. The result was a meta-theoretical concept of wage as a price

[9] Cf. Graziani (1981).
[10] On this issue, see, for instance, Pivetti (1974) and (1976).

governed prevalently by social forces and power relations. According to some observers, this point of view ended up by validating the idea of a guiding mission of the trade unions, also within the sphere of the political projects.

As Takata pointed out with more general reference,[11] in the Italian historical context at the time the workers were demanding not only higher wages but also: (1) the creation of a modern welfare system; (2) enhancement of their political representation; and (3) a stronger social standing. In short, on the basis of this complex of motivations the Italian workers were calling for a different distribution of power in companies, in society and in the political sphere.

The fact is that the equilibrium of power in Italy in the 1970s effectively tilted in favour of the workers, not only in absolute and relative increase in real wages, but also in other respects: the "Statuto dei Lavoratori" (Workers' Statute) was enacted in 1970 to defend their rights in the factories. An indexing mechanism was applied in 1975 for 100% protection of wages against inflation. The bargaining power of the unions was also to be seen in the increasing safeguards regarding firing, decent workplace conditions and less harsh working methods and paces. Fundamental reforms were being devised to create an advanced welfare state covering the fields of education, health and pensions.

In terms of the aims of civilised society and moral progress, it was a period that saw particularly interesting and innovative developments. On the other hand, the repercussions that this season of conflicts had on the economic and institutional order were not equally positive. First of all, the antagonistic culture that developed in the firms and in society significantly lowered the already poor credit enjoyed by market institutions and culture in Italy. It also weakened some traditional elements of the process of accumulation in Italy, such as the low-unit costs of labour, the ample supply of savings, the financial engineering operations, the agreements between companies and the synergies with the public powers. Further, we also need to consider the fact that some of the leading actors found themselves negatively involved in the social conflict at that time. Here we are referring, for instance, to big private and public companies, banks and

[11] See Takata (1995), p. 157.

the civil service. These actors failed to achieve the higher competitive levels that might have balanced out the greater power gained by the workers. A sort of potential counterbalance might have come about from the increase in the system of small companies enjoying the chance to apply more flexible management to the labour force. However, as Zamagni (1994) noted, given their dimensions and culture, the small firms had neither the power to condition public authorities, nor the motivation to change their own management criteria. Italy's stagflation, too, can be interpreted in the light of an unbalanced clash of powers. In some circumstances, in the attempt to curb price dynamics, a restrictive monetary policy was adopted which, while on the one hand producing the expected recessive effects, on the other hand failed to restrain wage claims and cost-push inflation.

Actually, one of the aims pursued by the workers, or at least a part of them, was to shake up the old system of social relations. The fact that some of the manifestations of the workers' emerging power were incompatible with market economy capitalism did not always lead the social and political actors of the time (including the trade unions) to exclude them from the practicable solutions, but rather to pursue them with even more determination. Between the Marxist and liberal approach to social conflict, it was often the former that guided social behaviours.

As it turned out, the historical phase of worker's power in Italy was characterised by high inflation rates, growing public debt and a more dramatic increase in the unit costs of labour than seen in the other major European countries or the USA.[12] It emerges clearly from specific analyses as well as the data that the soaring deficits and prices in the 1970s were not so much to be attributed to oil shocks as to the sharp increase in public spending (unaccompanied by corresponding increase in taxes) and wages.

Within the research perspective followed in this chapter, the above observations bear out the interpretation according to which some of the manifestations of power occurring in the 1970s exceeded the point beyond which, instead of generating competition able to stimulate new efforts and superior quality on the part of other collective actors, they

[12] Cf. for example, the analysis carried out by Ciocca (2007).

actually obstructed them. That is to say, they exceeded what we call here the critical point of power.

In the second half of the 1970s the Italian economy plunged into a state of emergency. Prolonged economic crisis began to freeze off the sympathy of a growing share of public opinion—and also of some economists who had previously endorsed it—towards this "conflict paradigm". The hegemony of left-wing economic thought and the social conflict in industrial relations began to decline.

13.3 The Schizophrenia of Powers in Italy in the 1980s

In Italy the 1980s saw a new zeitgeist emerging. Political ideologies and the vitality of the collective actors involved with the working class began to decline, although their influence over the real processes of politics and the economy was not yet completely exhausted (cf. Gervasoni 2010). On entering into the age of mass consumption, the Italians began to perceive the values of individualism in terms of dominant ethic. In the political sphere, legislation on public spending tended to respond to the bottom-up pressures from the lower levels of political representation rather than being bound by top-down, centralised government decisions. In particular, an anomalous situation of keen competition emerged within the coalition governments between the Socialist Party, playing an increasingly important role, and the Christian Democratic Party. A protagonist in the events of that period observed that

> (e)ach party (in the coalition) … saw participation in the government as a way to enhance its own electoral consensus, to play it on a different board pursuing a strategy alternative to that of the ally. The duel between Craxi [Italian Socialist Party] and De Mita [Christian Democrat Party] was emblematic. (Scotti 2005, pp. 165–166)

Of the two leaders cited here, Bettino Craxi was the leading political protagonist of the 1980s. As Prime Minister from 1983 to 1986, he challenged the Communist Party (and to some extent also the Christian

Democrat Party), cutting the wage escalator in 1984. From the economic point of view, this helped cool down inflation. However, after this trial of strength, despite his victory the leader of the Italian Socialist Party (PSI) showed scant inclination to advance further along the road of reforms or, in particular, to clean up public finances.[13] In this connection, a point to bear in mind is that, given the disinflationary policy stance the Italian monetary authorities adopted in the 1980s (unlike that of the 1970s), monetisation of the public deficit had become a practice finding ever less implementation. Consequently, progress to a balanced budget would have required, in terms of ideal political action, reduction of public expenditure and/or an increase in taxation. At the same time, however, the implementation of fiscal restrictions was seen as particularly problematic as it would leave either party scant scope to utilise public resources to maintain electoral consensus. The confrontation between these two parties increasingly took the form of a theoretical match played out at the level of public choice based on logrolling. In short, this approach meant largely refraining from cuts in public spending, raising taxes, applying capital levy on property or fiscal deflation, to say nothing of decisions to default on the public debt. Each of these measures would have provoked opposition from significant sections of the Italian social classes and, as far as the last-mentioned decision is concerned, the many holders of the public debt. So under the influence of a zeitgeist encouraging short-term rather than long-term objectives, and of convulsive competition between the parties participating in the government, an increase in the public debt offered an obligatory residual solution, disguising a problem of power and leadership as a matter of economy.

Thus, as ratio to Gross Domestic Product (GDP), the Italian public debt soared from the 60% of 1979 to 105% in 1992.

Some economists interpreted this situation as a non-cooperative game in the income distribution arena between actors who were at the same time strong enough to prevent the cost of fiscal adjustment being blamed on them but too weak to succeed in placing this cost on the shoulders of other social actors.[14] Once the politically costly decisions to balance the

[13] This assessment is also confirmed by a close collaborator of Craxi in that period, Gianni De Michelis (2005), p. 175.

[14] Cf. Alesina (1988).

budget had been put off to some indefinite time in the future, public expenditure was employed as "manna from heaven".[15]

Going on, now, to some specific considerations on the state of economic thought at the time, the major innovations at the international level came from a series of studies that subjected the rational, enlightened view of public intervention in the economy to critical reappraisal.[16] In the 1980s Italy, no few economic studies were still under the influence of the theoretical currents looking back to Sraffa, Keynes and Marx. However, a growing number of scientific papers also began to address such issues as the principle of time-inconsistency, consumers' rational expectations, the theorem of Ricardian equivalence and the crowding out doctrine. In general, all these studies gradually contributed to undermining the conviction that there is a trade-off between unemployment and inflation, stressing by contrast the counter-productiveness of broadly discretionary economic policy by the public authorities, deemed a source of inflation and inefficiency.[17] In short, in the light of the main interpretative lines characterising these studies, individual choices were deemed able to anticipate and neutralise the traditional fine-tuning of economic policies, with a new perspective opening on an economy as a system of diffused powers, no longer concentrated. As we see in the next section, where we address the emerging power of international finance, this intriguing representation of power did not have an easy life.

In any case, it was also in the period under consideration that the analyses of a group of Italian scholars who would subsequently go under the name of "Bocconian economists" began to make headway. With regard to exchange-rate policy, Giavazzi and Pagano (1988) pointed out that if a country is unable to acquire an effective monetary and economic policy discipline autonomously due to its historical or institutional peculiarities, it can nevertheless achieve as much hooking on to some external authority.

In Italy's economic and monetary policies, this new way of thinking was in fact already making headway by the end of the 1970s with the

---

[15] See De Cecco (1989), p. 229.

[16] For the Italian debate on this issue, see, for instance, Cesarano (1980).

[17] For instance, see Arcelli, Di Giorgio (1991). A general overview on this topic is in Asso (2004).

choice to join the exchange-rate mechanism of the European Monetary System (EMS), followed in turn by ratification of the "divorce" between the Treasury[18] and the Bank of Italy in 1981. In consequence of this decision the latter was no longer obliged to purchase the bonds that found no placement on the market. This decision, like the successive ones of a similar stamp, entered into one general design, namely to implement the principle that the power to create money should be entrusted to persons other than those who have the power to spend it. It added up to the assertion of a new monetary constitution and a new map of power. In particular, it established that the optimal management of money implied that the Central Banking could enjoy considerable autonomy and anti-inflationary credibility. The main consequence of all this was that the Italian Central Bank's commitment to fighting inflation and sustaining the exchange rate of the Italian lira dissolved the link between fiscal deficit and the creation of money.

In Italy many experts turned their attention to the subject of Central Bank autonomy.[19] As pointed out above, we must not lose sight of the fact that Keynesian theory still enjoyed a certain credit in the debate of the 1980s in Italy. A number of Italian economists continued not to rule out deficit spending a priori, admitting the possibility of monetary financing for it.[20] Moreover, a number of experts including Giangiacomo Nardozzi warned against the risk of falling into the rhetoric of the "myth" of the German Central Bank[21] and its uncompromising anti-inflationary stance. Others, like Giacomo Vaciago, stressed the non-neutrality of money, which meant that while accepting the principle of Central Bank autonomy, the latter would in any case need legitimation on the part of the political system.[22] In short, for the majority of Italian economists a generally positive endorsement of the autonomy of the central banker

[18] The Treasury Minister who promoted the "divorce" was Beniamino Andreatta, an economist by profession. He was an outstanding figure in Italy's economic policy in the 1980s. On Andreatta, see Sandonà (2017).

[19] See, for instance, Jossa, Panico (1988), Masciandaro, Ristuccia (1988), Arcelli (1992), Nardozzi (1993).

[20] See Graziani (2001), pp. 190–192.

[21] Cf. Nardozzi (1992).

[22] Cf. Vaciago (1992).

was usually qualified to rule out total independence from the executive powers or any excessively rigid interpretation of the aim of price stability.

However, Carlo Azeglio Ciampi, the Italian central banker at the time, took a rather more clear-cut view of the matter. Control of money was to be separated from the needs of the Treasury once and for all. And the model to follow was precisely that of the Bundesbank, having monetary stability as the sole objective, with the possibility to assert this objective even in opposition to the government. Furthermore, in the actual experience of the 1980s, a policy of high interest rates was to be pursued in support of the exchange rate of the lira, which was in turn expected to put a brake on inflation and instigate Italy's productive system with a view to restructure and generate more significant increases in productivity.[23]

Confirming this aptitude to play the part of a leading actor in Italy's economic policy was also the interest Ciampi showed in the link between monetary policy and fiscal policy. On the one hand, he deemed it illusory to expect rigorous control of money to lead to mechanical rebalancing of the public finances.[24] On the other hand, however, he also held that if the real interest rates were high, they would constitute a positive stimulus for the parliament and government to reintroduce the budget constraint principle at all the levels of the public finances.[25]

In the field of economic studies, support for the central banker's point of view came from Mario Monti. He took a positive view of the prospect that Italy's monetary policy could pursue a number of aims: not only to achieve price stability but also to oppose expansion on the part of the government and its discretionary measures, as well as the excesses of the welfare state.[26]

---

[23] There was no lack of criticism of, or indeed of different points of view towards, this plan to reorient the Italian economy. Cf. for example, De Cecco (1992), Kregel (1993), Fratianni and Spinelli (2001), Sartor (2005).

[24] Cf. in this connection Banca d'Italia 1983 Annual Report, Final Considerations, p. 15.

[25] Cf. for example, Banca d'Italia 1982 Annual Report, Final Considerations, p. 35.

[26] See the contributions published in journals by Monti (1981a, b) and the comment on them made by Paolazzi (1993).

The reasoning behind this approach was conducted in terms of rational expectations and games theory, and was structured on the following considerations.[27] An autonomous monetary policy able to generate high interest rates would raise the political cost of a given public deficit.[28] Given this greater cost and assuming invariance in the marginal social utility the government expects to obtain from the public expenditure, the new optimal (for the government) position is obtained in relation to a deficit smaller than the previous one. In this case the monetary policy of high interest rates would achieve its disciplinary purpose. However, the fragmentary conditions and conflicts within the coalition governments of the period described above all point to a certain weakness in these coalitions.[29] In such a state of affairs, the case may arise that as the political cost of the deficit increases, the need for the members of the government to resort to it increases even more. In these circumstances, the braking mechanism of a high rate of interest will not suffice to block the primary public expenditure.

Actually, this situation reflects a paradox that came about in the Italian scenario of the time. We have parties that might also be seen as "devouring" and making a voracious abuse of power,[30] having an abundant supply of public resources to play with but at the same time fragile, being unable to secure the consensus of public opinion for decisions that lacked the backing of public spending.

In contrast with this type of policy groping for votes in the electoral market, the Central Bank stressed the restrictive aspect of monetary policy. The real interest rates, which had been negative as from 1972 sinking

---

[27] A summary can be found in Bruni, Monti (1992). However, the authors themselves were not entirely convinced of the effectiveness of this approach, recommending that the budget constraint be stated in the Constitution.

[28] In this approach the greater political cost of the deficit corresponds to the current value of the taxes which the policymaker will have to levy in the future to pay off the public debt thus generated. Discount of future taxes is achieved employing a discount rate equal to the intertemporal preference rate of the policymaker. The value assumed by this rate reflects the extent and promptness attributed by the latter to the capacity of public expenditure to satisfy his need for political consensus in the electoral competition.

[29] The same weaknesses emerge from the broader analysis conducted by Grilli et al. (1991). On the issue of Italy as a "weak state" from 1960s onward see also Della Sala (1997), p. 19.

[30] This expression is by Guarino (1988), p. 272.

to the low point of −7% in 1980, rose to +3% in the period 1981–3,[31] climbing as high as +6% in the second half of the 1980s, proving, moreover, two percentage points higher than the average real interest rates of the G7 countries.[32] This was an extraordinarily heavy burden for the Italian economy.

On the growth of public debt in the 1980s a range of different opinions is still in play. Those placing the stress on the increase in public primary expenditure in those years tend to see in it the true cause of the original increase in public financial needs.[33] This, they deem, was the source of high interest rates and heavier costs in managing the public debt. Others, by contrast, see the contrary causal link predominating. It was, they argue, the increase in interest rates brought about autonomously by the Bank of Italy's stabilisation policy that lay behind the increase in public financial needs, and hence the growth of the public debt.[34]

In reality, on the evidence of the data on the Italian economy, neither of these interpretations can be ruled out. The approach taken here, based on analysis of the powers in conflict, leaves room for both of these readings. On the one hand, with the conditions of confrontation arising within the government coalitions of the time, public expenditure eventually became the arena in which conflict generated the most significant macroeconomic effects.[35] At the same time, however, the institutional prerogatives acquired by the Central Bank subsequent to the "divorce" were so far-reaching as to transform the relationship of dependence on the government to something very like the opposite.

In short, the 1980s were marked by an awkward combination of restrictive monetary policy and expansive fiscal policy—a combination in turn deriving from a situation of imbalance between the powers. On the one hand, there was the enfeebled (by some deemed even irresponsible) power of the political side and on the other hand a Central Bank waxing

[31] Cf. Rossi (2007), p. 57.

[32] Cf. Ciocca (2007), p. 307.

[33] According to Bank of Italy data—cited by Somogyi (2005)—public primary expenditure rose from 37% of the GDP in 1980 to 43% in 1989.

[34] Cf. Giannola and Marani (1990).

[35] Cf. In this connection the observations by De Felice F. (1996), p. 86 ff.

increasingly strong and, indeed, so intent on its mission of promoting a new monetary constitution as to seek to discipline the political institutions, too. However, in its disciplinary endeavours aided by the rate of interest, it surpassed the point beyond which the assertion of its role would produce purely positive effects. Again—as in the 1970s, although in a different context and for completely different reasons—things took a turn beyond the critical point of power.

In conclusion, what with budget policies that were not merely expansive but actually extravagantly munificent and at the same time the first signs of monetary domination, the Italian economy of the 1980s saw a sort of schizophrenia in ruling powers. This schizophrenia was accompanied by reasonably satisfactory income growth, but marked the entry of the Italian economy into a period of financial vulnerability characterised by a huge public debt, which remains even now its basic characteristic.

13.4 The Power of Maastricht

The Emerging Role of International Finance

As we saw in the previous section, a number of serious contradictions emerged in the Italian economy in the course of the 1980s and the early 1990s. The high interest rates and strong exchange rate of the lira, both fruit of the Bank of Italy's anti-inflationary policy, were no longer sustainable in the face of high budget deficits and wage dynamics well above those of the countries participating together with Italy in the exchange-rate mechanisms of the EMS. In consequence of this structural misalignment, September 1992 saw the lira hit by a serious currency crisis. Italy had no choice but to exit from the EMS exchange agreements and fall back on a flexible exchange-rate system. Two options lay open before Italy's public decision-makers in response to this traumatic event. The first was to postpone Italy's participation in the European Monetary Union (EMU) until further notice, while the second meant adopting extremely severe monetary and fiscal policies to get back on the road for Maastricht without delay. After a period of wavering the choice fell on the latter option (cf. in this connection Dyson and Featherstone 1999).

At the same time, on the horizon of the world economy, the beginning of globalisation and the technical revolution in information and communication brought out the formidable role of international finance. Thanks to the control over liquidity it enjoyed and the flexibility and reversibility of its decisions, its scope for manoeuvre was growing at the expense of the real economy and indeed of the states' public finance and monetary policy (Boyer 2013). The growth of international finance to the extent of becoming a leading power rapidly demonstrated that the idea of returning to representation of the economy as a system of diffused small powers was over-optimistic.

No few observers pointed out that in this way a perverse reversal of power between politics and finance was coming about. Nevertheless, the trend to liberalisation of capital movements had taken on global dimensions. In Italy, the decision to move in this direction had been made in 1990. This had entailed the need for the authorities involved in economic policy to respect more binding constraints, as the so-called impossible trilemma already indicated.[36] In the analysis Italy's central banker performed at the time, we find these concerns reflected (see Fazio 1996a, b, 1997). In the case of Italy the trilemma was interpreted in the sense of having to take Germany's monetary policy as the benchmark and flatten out the inflation differential between the Italian lira and German mark. To this end, from 1994 to 1996, the Central Bank adopted a rigorous "anticipatory" monetary policy. To ward off the expected inflation once and for all, it needed to apply restrictive real rates of interest: in 1994–5 to curb the speculative pressures (profit-push inflation) that were making themselves felt in those years; in 1996 to disincentivise wage settlements deemed excessive vis-à-vis productivity; and, as a fixed goal in that three-year period, to motivate the politicians to curb budget deficits (Bini 1998).

The other fundamental objective that needed to be achieved in a great hurry was to restore public finances, a problem still awaiting a solution. Unlike in the 1980s, this time fiscal policy was aligned with monetary policy—in actual fact, all too closely. In the three-year period 1995–7,

[36] According to this principle, in the presence of free international movements of capital flows, monetary autonomy or, alternatively, exchange-rate management is precluded for the economic policy authorities.

subsequent to the containment of public expenditure and a sharp rise in fiscal pressure, the Italian public budget registered primary surpluses, respectively, of 4.4%, 4.1% and 6.7%. The effects of those fiscal policies, it has been observed:

> proved unaccustomedly tough for the Italians [...] The way recovery had been achieved, centred on increased fiscal pressure, politically necessary as it was, had ended up by weighing on a productive structure that was already reeling (Rossi 2007, pp. 101 and 128).

For a broader picture of the Italian economy at the time we must also consider that the total productivity of the factors, already declining in the 1970s and 1980s, showed a further significant drop precisely in the mid-1990s, falling into a state of utter stagnation. A great many more or less incontestable analyses impute the causes of this state of affairs to a series of shortcomings on the supply side of the Italian economy.[37] However, the fact that the rate of productivity growth stalled precisely in those years suggests that some part at least was also played by the marked monetary and fiscal deflation that proceeded in parallel, as we have seen[38] (in this respect, see, for instance, Bagnai 2013. For a different assessment, Ciocca 2007).

The final outcome, summing up the reasons for the two different currents into which interpretations diverge (the one based on supply side, the other on the demand side), was that a perfect storm broke out on the subject of productivity and economic growth in Italy as from the mid-1990s.

Therefore, we can conclude this first subsection relative to the power of Maastricht with the consideration that the Italian euro story began with some economic fundamentals—first of all, productivity—seriously jeopardised, also as an effect of the political will to rush into monetary and fiscal recovery and so join the first group of countries introducing the euro as from 1999.

---

[37] Such as the weakness of Italy's productive specialisation model, or the small average size of the firms or again Italy's difficulty in exploiting the advantages of the technological revolution. The list could go on.

[38] In this line of discussion reference is often made to the law of Kaldor-Verdoorn, according to which growth in productivity is driven by aggregate demand.

Was Italy's decision to join the EMU at this early stage far-sighted or simply wrong? Might not the radiant prospect of Maastricht have so dazzled the Italian decision-makers as to befuddle their powers of judgement? Lacking counter-evidence, there can be no certain answer to questions of this kind. However, an emblematic aspect of the issue remains that over 20 years since then, the question (far-sighted or wrong decision?) still comes up in debate in Italy. This hardly adds up to evidence in favour of the former assessment.

The Power of Maastricht and the Great Recession

The issue of relations between power and the economy clearly became more complicated with the launch of the EMU from 1999. Indeed, after an initial period of confident expectation and especially following the outbreak of the Great Recession in 2008, various criticisms of the EMU were raised by Italy's economists. In particular, they pointed out: (1) the presence of some flaws intrinsic to a currency area lacking political unity and (2) the co-presence of highly diversified institutions, cultures, psychological attitudes and economic behaviours within the Eurozone.

With regard to the first point, renewed attention was paid to the conditions characterising an optimal currency area. In this respect, it was widely held among the experts that the Eurozone fell somewhat short of being optimal. The countries belonging to it had different productive specialisations, insufficient mobility of factors of production, and varying flexibility of prices. As a consequence of these shortcomings, if the area is affected by shocks, a cumulative process of increasing economic distance between the single parts of this area occurs. In such a situation, it happens that the losses borne by some countries are greater than the gains derived from the unification of currency.

According to the theoretical point of view of Kenen (1969), balancing this divergent situation calls for ad hoc institutions and compensatory (financial and fiscal) measures among the countries belonging to the same area. Obviously, this convergent coordination could only be achieved if political unity linked the EMU countries together, which is precisely what has so far been missing in the European project, so that any request a country may advance for financial support in coping with the unbalancing effects of an asymmetric shock comes up against the suspicions of the surplus countries called upon to provide some sort of "mutual assistance" which does not concern them (cf. Bini Smaghi 2013).

The second issue mentioned above concerns the fact that the Treaty of Maastricht adopted an institutional configuration deriving from the one already existing in some Northern European countries, but at the same time significantly different from the one characterising the countries of Mediterranean Europe. The topic under discussion brings us back to the great issue of the varieties of capitalism. Particularly notable among the rules behind this pattern are those regarding far more market-oriented arrangements than are typical of the capitalism of the Southern European countries. Thus the latter, having to embark upon the adaptation of their original institutional structure to the one represented by the rules of Brussels, found themselves handicapped, starting from a competitive disadvantage.

In Italy this process of adaptation began in the 1990s, not without serious difficulties. The proposals for institutional reform were wide ranging, including the need not only to reverse the public debt dynamic and further reduce inflation, but also to contain pay increases and liberalise and privatise many sectors of the economy still under state management. Further, a new legislation introduced various forms of flexibility in the labour market to increase company productivity.[39] In turn, a reform to improve efficiency in the public administration's procedures (christened "devolution") was launched in 1997. However, due to reasons we cannot begin to explain here for lack of space, these manifold reforms to make the Italian economy more competitive failed to produce all the positive effects expected, and thus did not succeed in counterbalancing the social and economic stress Italian companies and citizens had to face in the process of adaptation to the Maastricht rules.[40]

The idea, widespread in the 1990s, that application of (Maastricht's) optimal rules to the Italian sclerotic situation would certainly product positive effects was not entirely borne out by the facts. Actually, Italy's

[39] For a review of this issue cf. Pacella et al. (2013).

[40] On the issue of public administration reform, see the critical comments by Schlitzer (2015).

experience showed that, first, altering institutions is no easy matter and, second, changing the rules is not enough to guarantee improvements (cf. Boettke et al. 2013). In general, the dependence a country has on its own past experience may stand in the way of institutional solutions successfully tried and tested in other countries, depriving them in part or even entirely of their full potential. While institutions can be defined good insofar as they allow for increased efficiency and well-being where they are applied, the form taken by the good institutions is not uniform everywhere because they also depend upon the (moral, anthropological, cultural and customary) specificities that define an actual economic system.

Reflecting on this institutional divide, one may well come to the conclusion that, without political unity and stabilisation mechanisms supplied with common financial funds, the renunciation of sovereignty over the currency and exchange rate by the countries belonging to the European Monetary Union (EMU) does not lead to a sharing of power but to a shift of certain prerogatives of power to the benefit of the "strong" countries at the expense of the "weak" ones, including Italy.[41] This asymmetry also emerged, then, in the increasing imbalances within the euro area, and in the plunging confidence of the member countries, each of which ended up asserting the advantageousness only of those policies that were tailored to their national interests.

Often united in this sort of criticism, the Italian economists were not so united when it came to making more specific proposals. Schematically, we may group these economists in four categories (a more detailed analysis is in Bini 2014):

1. We begin with the economists of Keynesian persuasion, still playing a part in Italian debate.[42] They see the budget discipline prescribed by Brussels as a stupid austerity policy in that it triggers the vicious circle of cumulative deflation. They endorse the argument based on the fallacy of composition where every kind of intrinsically virtuous microeconomic action eventually leads to a self-destructive macroeconomic

[41] The argument regarding the shift of power from the European institutions to Berlin has recently been analysed by Brunnermeier et al. (ed.) (2016).

[42] As is well known, there are many orientations in the field of Keynesianism, from the mainstream neo-Keynesians to the heterodox post-Keynesians. Many discussions of a Keynesian nature are hosted in Keynesblog.

outcome. They believe in the effectiveness of the Keynesian multipliers and that, by virtue of them, increased public deficit spending logically creates the economic-financial scope necessary to guarantee the sustainability of the public debt.

2. The second group of economists adopt a critical approach leaning politically to the left.[43] They agree with certain aspects of the Keynesian approach mentioned in point (1), but add a further critical note of their own, seeing in the economic austerity of Brussels not the simple outcome of wrong thinking but the manifestation of a rationale seeking to weaken the workers and shift power relations in favour of capital. In this interpretation, therefore, the euro crisis was deliberately provoked, and indeed necessary. Taking this line, they asserted against Brussels the power of the working class organised along the lines of direct state intervention, public enterprises, nationalisation and planning.
3. The third group includes authors of various backgrounds, but united in rejecting, from non-Keynesian positions, the austerity of Brussels, defined by Paolo Savona (2012, 2013) as "theoretical folly" or by Quadrio Curzio (2012) as basically recessive. To curb the power of Maastricht, Savona suggested a "plan B" consisting of a programme for Italy to exit from the Eurozone, to be implemented should the EMU persevere in its unreasonable austerity prescriptions. In turn, Quadrio Curzio proposed Europe-wide infrastructure investments, with the Eurozone itself taking on a share of the public debts of the individual member countries. The instrument for this project is the Eurobond. It is hardly surprising if Germany views this proposal with diffidence, seeing in it the risk of discretionary criteria infiltrating the Maastricht rules. By contrast, in the perspective of this chapter, taking the positive view that power can provoke appropriate counter-powers, the Eurobond proposal (or other types of mechanisms able to smooth the economic cycles among the various parts of Eurozone) is well worth considering, having the potential advantage of balancing out the asymmetric policies of Brussels.

[43] See, as a general reference, Cesaratto and Pivetti (2012).

4. The fourth group consists of scholars who have attracted attention with the formulation of the principle of "expansionary austerity" (see for instance Alesina and Giavazzi 2012). The basic idea is that a radical operation of public deficit reduction, if carried out with cuts in public spending and accompanied by appropriate measures (liberalisation of the goods and labour markets, permissive monetary policy and suchlike), will lead to a positive reversal of the expectations of individuals, resulting in an increase in private investment and consumption such as to balance out the initial restrictive measures of the state.

On the basis of the simplified reconstruction of the four main currents of thought in Italian economic debate, we can now go on briefly to see the positions they respectively took vis-à-vis the present power of Maastricht. The Keynesian economists depart from the spirit of the Treaty with a broader conception of the role of the state in the economy, and above all more discretionary than the Brussels rules would admit. In turn, the economists taking a critical position from a left-wing viewpoint totally reject certain aspects of the Maastricht political and social philosophy. Economists belonging to group 3 show a particular sympathy with the ideals of European integration, but at the same time are strongly committed to changing from within some of the rules that guide the decisions of Brussels. The group 4 economists appear to be much more attuned to the Maastricht rules. However, as from 2010 they have begun to show reservations on some of the Maastricht rules deemed too rigid to allow for a relatively smooth exit from the crisis (see, for instance, Alesina and Giavazzi 2014a, b). Some have also pointed out that the EMU regulations—of largely Franco-German inspiration—disregard certain specificities of the Italian economy, based on small and medium-sized firms, creating in practice an element of permanent competitive disadvantage for them (see Zingales 2014).

Clearly, decidedly stronger criticism emerges in the assessments made by the first three of our four groups. In general, they maintain that a significant part of the blame for the imbalances within the EMU is to be imputed to the cumulative process through which the countries characterised by greater efficiency at the outset have seen the advantage over the less efficient countries progressively increasing. Thus the incapacity or slowness shown by the "weak" Eurozone countries in reducing unit costs and getting onto a more competitive footing is not entirely imputable to their own shortcomings. For instance, through the rules imposed by the Maastricht Treaty, Italy has seen unemployment hysteresis sapping its growth potential. Further, the increase in its public debt/GDP ratio and unit costs of labour is not completely due to insufficient political will on the part of Italy's governments, but also to the fall in income, aggregate demand and productivity brought about precisely by the deflationary policies imposed by Brussels (for a different interpretation see, for instance, Schefold 2014).

In conclusion, for all the reasons set out above, there also emerged in the Maastricht policy a "critical point of power" beyond which its rules discouraged the very economic dynamics and decisions that could enhance efficiency. The battle for power on the field of Maastricht is under way. Whichever way you look at it, the combined forces of the "strong" countries still dominate on the hill.

13.5 Conclusions

Power means conflict. Conflict generates change. And change contains within itself the potential for both regressive and the progressive outcomes. On the whole, alas, the results of our research conducted on the case of Italy from 1970 to 2014 suggest that here the process of change was not sufficiently positive.

In the 1970s, the power relations generated by social conflict frustrated the potential of the market economy. While, on the one hand, these power relations led to a somewhat more equitable distributive pattern, on the other hand, they thwarted growth in productivity and implementation of more efficient forms of enterprise organisation.

The following period, the 1980s, saw formulation of a new approach to the role of Central Banks, characterised by independence from the governments and a sound anti-inflationary reputation. This new approach was applied in Italy, too. With governments showing weakness and irresponsibility in more or less equal measure in their failure to contain public spending, the result was the prevailing hard line of the Italian Central

Bank, which took upon itself monetary decisions constituting an aggravating factor in the public debt dynamic.

With the euro entering into its role as a protagonist, the power of the Maastricht rules came into full play. On the one hand, they implicitly granted an institutional advantage to the "strong" countries in the Eurozone, while on the other hand, they explicitly prescribed austerity policies for the "weak" countries to put their accounts in order. Prevalent among Italian economists was the point of view that, with no real political unity or stabilisation mechanisms fuelled with common financial funds, for the Eurozone countries forgoing sovereignty over the currency and exchange rate has led to an effective shift in power towards the strong countries at the expense of the weaker ones.

In the field of economic thought, too, significant changes came about over the span of time considered here. In the 1970s many Italian economists saw the market as being in need of high-security surveillance, to be kept under control with powers external to it. By contrast, as between the 1980s and 1990s, the market and the individual choices gradually found their way back to the core of the economy. In another respect, the 1970s had seen the issue of power emerging as a constitutive part or spillover effect of certain—Sraffian, post-Keynesian, Marxian—theoretical constructions. The relevance of this to our discussion here lies in the way these currents of thought with their heterodox stances identified links between significant manifestations of power, on the one hand, and corresponding economic relations on the other. An emblematic case is to be seen in the concept of wage as an independent variable.

As from the 1980s, however, and increasingly in the course of time, the issue of power found its way into general economic discourse through heterogeneous currents of economic analysis (such as public choice and game theories) examining the rational behaviour of decision-makers as players using power relations to maximise their own utility. Here we are also referring to the neo-institutional approaches which offered new insights into the influence institutions have on the economic performance of a country and its dependence on the past.

In general, the issue of power can be seen to have loomed increasingly large in the studies of the Italian economists both in the 1970s and in the 1980s, continuing in the following years. Returning to the question raised in the first page of this chapter, namely whether or not power has acquired a rightful place in economics studies, we can now answer affirmatively. What is, however, very different is the meaning that the element of power took on in the above various phases of Italian economic thought. In the theoretical formulations of the 1970s, power came out, as it were, from the underground world of heterodoxy. It was an unveiling that at times seemed even to be affecting the very foundations of the entire economic edifice. In the studies of the 1980s and then on, by contrast, power relations were analysed mainly with a view to need-to-know objectives relating to governability. For example, they highlighted the autocratic, conservative character of the Central Bank in relation to its anti-inflationary credibility, or focused on the features of some political act found to be in pursuit opportunistic ends or, again, analysed the inevitable sources of controversy and imbalances of power for countries in transition from national to supranational rules, as in the case of Maastricht. Ultimately, the studies in question amount to hybrid analyses of power, based on interaction between the economic and political spheres. In a sense, we might even speak of a return to the classical way of doing economics, with its manifold references to the institutional context. "Early classical 'political economy' right up to the days of J. S. Mill", Rothschild observed (1971, p. 8), "was fully aware of the sociological and power background of economic events".

Briefly, in Italy we witness transition from an approach (in the 1970s) that saw power as the bugbear of the economy, to another which—applying in particular the methods of the *new political economy*—took power as an object to analyse with the tools of orthodox economics.[44] Clearly, neither the former nor the latter approach covers more than a limited part of the complex map of power. One point common to all the studies on the topic is the recognition of its slippery ubiquity. Nevertheless, our empirical case study of Italy has, we believe, shown that there are manifold links between power, economics and economic realities. It has helped us understand their reciprocal influences, and explore the ways economists have cast light on certain significant aspects.

[44] On certain limits to this approach, cf. Bowles et al. (1999).

As a more general conclusion, the present research has ascertained that the dynamics of power in Italy has been as asymmetric as it has been intense. In practice this means that the powers emerging in various areas and/or historical situations have often exceeded the critical point beyond which, instead of generating competition able to stimulate new efforts and superior qualities on the part of the other counter-powers, they effectively obstructed its functioning. Briefly, in Italy, they generated neither sufficient equilibrium counter-powers (à la Galbraith) nor significant adjustments of power relations to the so-called economic laws (à la Böhm-Bawerk).

In such cases of imbalance between the powers, the need would be for a "third person" with the function of intervening in the play or regulating it to modify the course it is taking (cf. Vatiero 2009). Ultimately, this is the essential role of politics. Nevertheless, in the three phases of recent history examined here, Italy's political class can be seen to have fallen short in performing this maieutic function. In the first phase, no effective arbitration between the various Italian social classes was accomplished. In the second, the challenge of serious reforms in the areas of public finance and welfare was not met, while in the third the institutional changes needed to make the Italian economy more competitive found insufficient implementation.

In the particular case of this third phase, it emerges clearly enough that on the one hand the Maastricht rules bear the responsibility for having exceeded the critical point of power, as we have seen. On the other hand, the protagonists on Italy's political and economic scene have also shown shortcomings, essentially consisting of their incapacity to get over their own historical vices (Berend 2013). The sooner we face up to the fact that this crisis has not one but two major components—the asymmetric power of Maastricht in the face of Italy's weak position on the necessary reforms—the sooner we will find the way out from the Euro-Italy crisis.

References

Alesina, A. (1988). The End of Large Public Debts. In F. Giavazzi & L. Spaventa (Eds.), *High Public Debt: Thè Italian Experience* (pp. 34–79). Cambridge: Cambridge University Press.

Alesina, A., & Giavazzi, F. (2012). The Austerity Question: 'How?' Is as Important as 'How Much'? In G. Corsetti (Ed.), *Austerity: Too Much of a Good Thing?, A VoxEU.org eCollection of Views by Leading Economists*. London: Centre for Economic Policy Research.

Alesina, A., & Giavazzi, F. (2014a, January 5). La soluzione tre per cento. In *Il Corriere della Sera*.

Alesina, A., & Giavazzi, F. (2014b, April 6). Sforare il 3% si può, ma a patti chiari. Tre scelte dure, avete coraggio? In *Il Corriere della Sera*.

Arcelli, M. (Ed.). (1992). *Il ruolo della banca centrale nella politica economica*. Bologna: il Mulino

Arcelli, M., & Di Giorgio, G. (1991). Regole, credibilità della politica economica e discrezionalità. *Rivista di Politica Economica*, July–August, p. 17 and ss.

Asso, P. F. (2004). Dibattiti teorici, integrazione europea ed economia italiana 1970–2000. In P. Bini (Ed.), *I Novant'anni della Rivista di Politica Economica (1911–2000). Teorie economiche, scelte politiche e cultura d'impresa nell'Italia del Novecento*. Special Issue of "Rivista di Politica Economica", pp. 179–255.

Bagnai, A. (2013). *Il tramonto dell'Euro. Come e perché la fine della moneta unica salverebbe democrazia e benessere in Europa*. Reggio Emilia: Imprimatur editore.

Banca d'Italia, *Relazione annuale per 1982. Considerazioni finali*.

Banca d'Italia, *Relazione annuale per il 1983. Considerazioni finali*.

Bartlett, R. (1989). *Economics and Power. An Inquiry into Human Relations and Markets*. Cambridge: Cambridge University Press.

Berend, I. T. (2013). *Case Studies on Modern European Economy. Entrepreneurs, Interventions, Institutions*. London/New York: Routledge.

Bini, P. (1998, December). The Art of Central Banking in Italy: 1993–1997. An Institutional Way to Monetary Stability. *Rivista Internazionale di Scienze Economiche e Commerciali*, n. 4, 647–665.

Bini, P. (2013). The Italian Economists and the Crisis of the Nineteen-Seventies. The Rise and Fall of the "Conflict Paradigm". *History of Economic Thought and Policy, 1*, 73–102.

Bini, P. (2014). How to Escape from the Crisis. The Divergent Opinions of Italian Economists. In A. Varsori & M. Poettinger (Eds.), *Economic Crisis and New Nationalisms* (pp. 115–152). Bruxelles: P.I.E. Peter Lang.

Bini Smaghi, L. (2013). *Morire di austerità. Democrazie con le spalle al muro*. Bologna: il Mulino.

Boettke, P. J., Coyne, C. J., & Leeson, P. (2013). Comparative Historical Political Economy. *Journal of Institutional Economics, 9*(3), 285–301.

Böhm-Bawerk, E. (1914). Macht oder ökonomisches Gesetz? In *Zeitschrift für Volkswirschaft, Sözialpolitik und Verwaltung* (Vol. XXIII, pp. 205–271).
Bowles, S., Franzini, M., & Pagano, U. (Eds.). (1999). *The Politics and Economics of Power*. London/New York: Routledge.
Boyer, R. (2013). The Present Crisis. A Trump for a Renewed Political Economy, *Review of Political Economy, 25*(1), 1–38.
Bruni, F., & Monti, M. (1992). Autonomia della banca centrale, inflazione e disavanzo pubblico: osservazioni sulla teoria e sul caso italiano. In Arcelli M. (Ed.), pp. 31–59.
Brunnermeier, M. K., James, H., & Landau, J.-P. (Eds.). (2016). *The Euro and the Battle of Ideas*. Princeton/Oxford: Princeton University Press.
Cesarano, F. (1980, July). L'efficacia della politica fiscale: una rassegna critica. *Rivista di Politica Economica*, 745–770.
Cesaratto, S., & Pivetti, M. (Eds.). (2012). *Oltre l'austerità*, Roma, "Gli eBook di Micro-Mega", n. 1, www.micromega.net
Ciocca, P. (2007). *Ricchi per sempre? Una storia economica d'Italia (1796–2005)*. Torino: Bollati Boringhieri.
De Cecco, M. (1989). Keynes and Italian Economics. In P. A. Hall (Ed.), *The Political Power of Economic Ideas: Keynesianism Across Nations* (pp. 195–229). Princeton: Princeton University Press.
De Cecco, M. (1992). Note su alcuni problemi relativi al sistema europeo delle banche centrali. In M. Arcelli (Ed.), pp. 21–29.
De Felice, F. (1996). Nazione e crisi. Le linee di frattura. In *Storia dell'Italia Repubblicana. Volume terzo. L'Italia nella crisi mondiale. L'ultimo ventennio. I. Economia e Società* (pp. 5–127). Torino: Giulio Einaudi Editore.
De Michelis, G. (2005). Speech. In G. Acquaviva (Ed.), *La politica economica negli anni ottanta, Preface by Piero Craveri* (pp. 169–176). Venezia: Marsilio editore.
Della Sala, V. (1997). Hollowing Out and Hardening the State: European Integration and the Italian Economy. In M. Bull & M. Rhodes (Eds.), *West European Politics*, Vol. 20, N. 1, January, Special Issue on *Crisis and Transition in Italian Politics*, pp. 14–33.
Dyson, K., & Featherstone, K. (1999). *The Road to Maastricht. Negotiating Economic and Monetary Union*. Oxford: Oxford University Press.
Fazio, A. (1996a). *Razionalità economica e solidarietà*. Bari: Laterza.
Fazio, A. (1996b, October). The Art of Central Banking. In Bank of Italy, "Serie Documenti".
Fazio, A. (1997, June). Economic Growth and Global Markets. In Bank of Italy, "Serie Documenti".

Foucault, M. (2008). *The Birth of Biopolitics: Lectures at the College de France, 1978–1979*, (M. Sennelart, Ed., B. Graham, Trans.). Basingstoke: Palgrave Macmillan.

Fratianni, M., & Spinelli, F. (2001). *Storia monetaria d'Italia. Lira e politica monetaria dall'Unità all'Unione Europea*. Milano: Etas edizioni.

Galbraith, J. K. (1957). *American Capitalism*. London: Hamish Hamilton (First edition: 1952).

Gattei, G. (1981). Sovrappiù e plusvalore in Italia (1960–1980). In G. Guizzardi, & S. Sterpi (Eds.), *La società italiana. Crisi di un sistema*, Introduction by A. Papisca. Milano: Franco Angeli.

Gervasoni, M. (2010). *Storia d'Italia degli anni ottanta. Quando eravamo moderni*. Venezia: Marsilio Editori.

Giannola, A., & Marani, U. (Ed.). (1990). *Tassi di interesse e debito pubblico. Un'analisi del caso italiano*. Napoli: ESI.

Giavazzi, F., & Pagano, M. (1988). The Advantage of 'Tying One's Hands. *European Economic Review, 32*, 303–330.

Graziani, A. (1969). I problemi della politica a breve termine in Italia. In CNR – Consiglio Nazionale delle Ricerche (1969), *La politica economica a breve termine in Italia* (pp. 29–38). Napoli: Liguori Editore.

Graziani, A. (1981). La teoria della distribuzione del reddito. In G. Lunghini (Ed.), *Scelte politiche e teorie economiche in Italia 1945–1978* (pp. 285–340). Torino: Einaudi.

Graziani, A. (2001). *Lo sviluppo dell'economia italiana. Dalla ricostruzione alla moneta europea, Nuova edizione aggiornata*. Torino: Bollati Boringhieri.

Grilli, V., Masciandaro, D., & Tabellini, G. (1991). Political and Monetary Institutions and Public Financial Policies in the Industrial Countries. *Economic Policy, 6*(13), 341–392.

Guarino, G. (1988). Il ruolo della Banca d'Italia. In D. Masciandaro & S. Ristuccia (Eds.), pp. 264–274.

Izzo, L., Pedone, A., Spaventa, L., & Volpi, F. (1973 [1970]). *Il controllo dell'economia nel breve periodo*. Milano: Franco Angeli.

Jossa, B., & Panico, C. (Eds.). (1988). *Teorie monetarie e banche centrali*. Napoli: Liguori Editore.

Kenen, P. B. (1969). The Theory of Optimum Currency Areas: An Eclectic View. In R. A. Mundell & A. K. Swodoba (Eds.), *Monetary Problems of the International Economy* (pp. 41–60). Chicago: Chicago University Press.

Kregel, J. A. (1993). La politica del cambio della Banca d'Italia e la ristrutturazione dell'industria italiana 1980–1985. In G. Nardozzi (Ed.), pp. 59–98.

Masciandaro, D., & Ristuccia, S. (Eds.). (1988). *L'autonomia delle banche centrali*. Milano: Edizioni di Comunità.
Monti, M. (1981a). L'inflazione si combatte ricostruendo lo Stato. In *Il Corriere della Sera*, 27 agosto 1981.
Monti, M. (1981b). Ricetta in tre punti contro l'inflazione. In *Il Corriere della Sera*, 28 agosto 1981.
Nardozzi, G. (1992). Sul mito dell'autonomia della banca centrale. In M. Arcelli (Ed.), pp. 91–96.
Nardozzi, G. (Ed.). (1993). *Il ruolo della banca centrale nella recente evoluzione dell'economia italiana*. Milano: Franco Angeli.
Pacella, A., Realfonzo, R. & Tortorella Esposito, G. (2013). Flessibilità e crescita. Il dibattito in Italia negli anni delle riforme del mercato del lavoro (1990–2010), mimeo.
Paolazzi, P. L. (1993). Strategia e autonomia della Banca d'Italia nel dibattito sulla stampa (1980–86). In G. Nardozzi (Ed.), pp. 157–204.
Pivetti, M. (1974). Esportazioni di capitali e salari reali. In Autori Vari, *Marxismo ed economia. Un dibattito di "Rinascita"* (pp. 27–36). Venezia: Marsilio Editori.
Pivetti, M. (1976). Speech. In CESPE – Centro studi di politica economica del Pci, *Crisi economica e condizionamenti internazionali dell'Italia*, Proceedings of the Conference held in Rome, March 15–17, 1976, Roma, Editori Riuniti, 1° vol., pp. 69–78.
Quadrio Curzio, A. (2012). *Economia oltre la crisi. Riflessioni sul liberalismo sociale* (S. Natoli, Ed.). Brescia: La Scuola.
Roncaglia, A. (2005). *The Wealth of Ideas. A History of Economic Thought*. Cambridge: Cambridge University Press.
Rossi, S. (2007). *La politica economica italiana 1968–2007*. Roma-Bari: Laterza.
Rothschild, K. W. (Ed.). (1971). *Power in Economics*. Harmondsworth: Penguin Books Ltd.
Sandonà, L. (2017). *Nino Andreatta's Economic Thought*, Foreword by Enrico Letta. Bologna: il Mulino - Arel.
Sartor, N. (2005). Speech. In G. Acquaviva (Ed.), *La politica economica negli anni ottanta*, Preface by Piero Craveri, (pp. 83–87). Venezia: Marsilio editore.
Savona, P. (2012). *Eresie, esorcismi e scelte giuste per uscire dalla crisi. Il caso Italia*. Soveria Mannelli: Rubbettino.
Savona, P. (2013, June 3). Follie teoriche di Bruxelles. *Il Sole 24 Ore*.

Schefold, B. (2014). The Economic Crisis and the Euro. Theoretical and Political Reactions to a Singular Historical Experiment. In A. Varsori & M. Poettinger (Eds.), *Economic Crisis and New Nationalisms* (pp. 67–97). Bruxelles: P.I.E. Peter Lang.

Schlitzer, G. (2015, June). L'economia italiana e il paradosso della produttività. In *Liuc Papers*, n. 285.

Scotti, E. (2005). Speech. In G. Acquaviva (Ed.), *La politica economica negli anni ottanta, Preface by Piero Craveri* (pp. 161–168). Venezia: Marsilio editore.

Somogyi, G. (2005). Speech. In G. Acquaviva (Ed.), *La politica economica negli anni ottanta, Preface by Piero Craveri* (pp. 119–121). Venezia: Marsilio editore.

Spaventa, L. (1974). Significato e portata della critica alla teoria marginalista della distribuzione. In Società Italiana degli Economisti, *Essenza e limiti del marginalismo nelle teorie economiche* (pp. 101–130). Milano: Giuffré editore.

Sraffa, P. (1960). *Production of Commodities by Means of Commodities. Prelude to a Critique of Economic Theory*. Cambridge: Cambridge University Press.

Stigler, G. J. (1954, May). The Economist Plays with Blocs. *American Economic Review, 44*, 7–14.

Takata, Y. (1995). *Power Theory of Economics* (D. W. Anthony, Trans., Foreword by Michio Morishima). New York: St. Martin's Press.

Tarantelli, E. (1988 [1979]). La funzione del consumo e le "teorie alternative" della distribuzione del reddito. In E. Tarantelli, *L'utopia dei deboli è la paura dei forti. Saggi, relazioni e altri scritti accademici* (pp. 863–879). Milano: Franco Angeli

Vaciago, G. (1992). Banca centrale tra Governo e mercato. In M. Arcelli (Ed.), pp. 61–70.

Vatiero, M. (2009). *Understanding Power. A "Law and Economics" Approach*. Saarbrücken: VDM Verlag Dr. Müller.

Zamagni, V. (1994). Alcune tesi sull'intervento dello Stato in una prospettiva di lungo periodo. In P. Ciocca (Ed.), *Il progresso economico dell'Italia. Permanenze, discontinuità, limiti* (pp. 151–160). Bologna: il Mulino.

Zingales, L. (2014, January 21). Processo liberista all'euro e all'Italia che non sa crescere. In *Il Foglio*.

Index of Authors[1]

[1] Note: Page numbers followed by 'n' refer to notes.

M. Mosca (ed.), *Power in Economic Thought*, Palgrave Studies in the History of Economic Thought, https://doi.org/10.1007/978-3-319-94039-7

C

The manufacturer's authorised representative in the EU is Springer Nature Customer Service Centre GmbH, Europaplatz 3, 69115 Heidelberg, Germany. If you have any concerns regarding our products, please contact ProductSafety@springernature.com

Printed and bound by CPI Group (UK) Ltd, Croydon, CR0 4YY

05/10/2026

02228128-0015